About the author

Dorothea König was born in Budapest in 1948 and has been living in Switzerland for over 40 years. She has two adult daughters.

She works as a spiritual healer and teacher. She is a qualified and recognized member of the Swiss Natural Healers Association (SVNH). She holds courses in both Germany and Switzerland. She taught in Hungary for several years, led spiritual camps and meditation evenings. She has led and directed meditation groups for many years and does so until her students are able to follow the spiritual way unaccompanied but at the same time they are stronger and more resolute in their everyday lives.

Dorothea's life began totally "normally" and remained this way until she was age 33 when the VOICE spoke to her and began to lead her. It soon transpired that the VOICE had already made vital decisions before she was even born and, albeit quietly, had been directing her life up until that point. It was now that the teaching began. At first she was taught in dreams from the spiritual world and later on while completely conscious in the day.

About the book

Why had the VOICE chosen her as a pupil as had the other enlightened Masters living in the spiritual world?

Who were her Teachers and Masters?

Had she done something in her life to deserve this?

Or perhaps in her previous life or former lives?

Perhaps this teaching was a consequence of all these?

Did she know about this task before her birth?

Or perhaps she had chosen to take it on. But why?

Is there a "fee" for attending such a spiritual school?

How does a person like this change?

And most of all how does her life change?

Where exactly does this path lead to?

Dorothea König's book provides answers to these and many more fantastically interesting and vital questions. She strives to present these experiences to her Readers in a way that allows them to virtually live through them, and so her stories and teachings merge into the consciousness of the Reader: exactly as if the same had happened to him or her.

The author would like the Reader to carry on learning from where her book leaves off.

Does this mean that the next book is already on its way?! ...

Dorothea König

*I Wasn't Just a Housewife
and a Mother ...*

For my daughters
Claudia Ildikó and
Antonia Emőke
and all the members
of my family

Title of the original version:
"Én nem csak feleség és anya voltam ..."
Published by the author
Copyright © 2004 by Dorothea König. All rights reserved

Translated from Hungarian by: Ralph Berkin
Editing: Suzanne Kirkbright

English version
First edition Christmas 2017
All rights reserved
Copyright © 2017 by Dorothea König
dorotheagkoenig@gmail.com

Picture credits:
Cover: © Private ownership of Dorothea König.
Photo of the author by Giovanna Silvani Weidmann (1997).
Pages 8–9: © Dorothea König. Aura photographs of the author.

Prologue quote from
Johann Wolfgang von Goethe, "Torquato Tasso."
Plays. Ed. Frank G. Ryder. New York: Continuum, 2006, p. 192.

Typefont: Filo Pro; GT Sectra Book, Book Italic
Printing and binding: Books on Demand GmbH, Norderstedt
Papier: Creme white, 80 g/m²

ISBN 978-3-9524766-4-2

As I read the text of *Dorothea König's* book, the following words spring to mind: "Man's fate is his own mirror. Exactly the same on the outside as on the inside. We have to live through what has been marked out for us by Higher Powers."

I would say exactly the same about my own life. I had no choice and neither did she. She does what she was called to do. She has to experience the great and the shocking because the world needs her as God blessed her with extraordinary gifts. She has just the same need to do what no one else can do in her place, as the world has of her, and all those who have the joy of meeting her. She is fully aware of the fact that there is no such thing as chance and that she should never give up striving to help those in need.

Her consciousness is continually being refined by her knowledge drawing from the Inexhaustible. The world has never needed a light like this so much as it does today.

Her tales had a deep effect on me. They contain so much wisdom that if these were all acted upon then people would grow wings and fly away.

Mária Szepes
Budapest, 11.02.2005

Mária Szepes is the doyenne of esoterics in Hungary. She is the author of *"The Red Lion" (A vörös oroszlán)*, first published in 1946, Hungary. First available in German translation in 1947, and now also in English, Spanish and Portuguese translations.

Contents

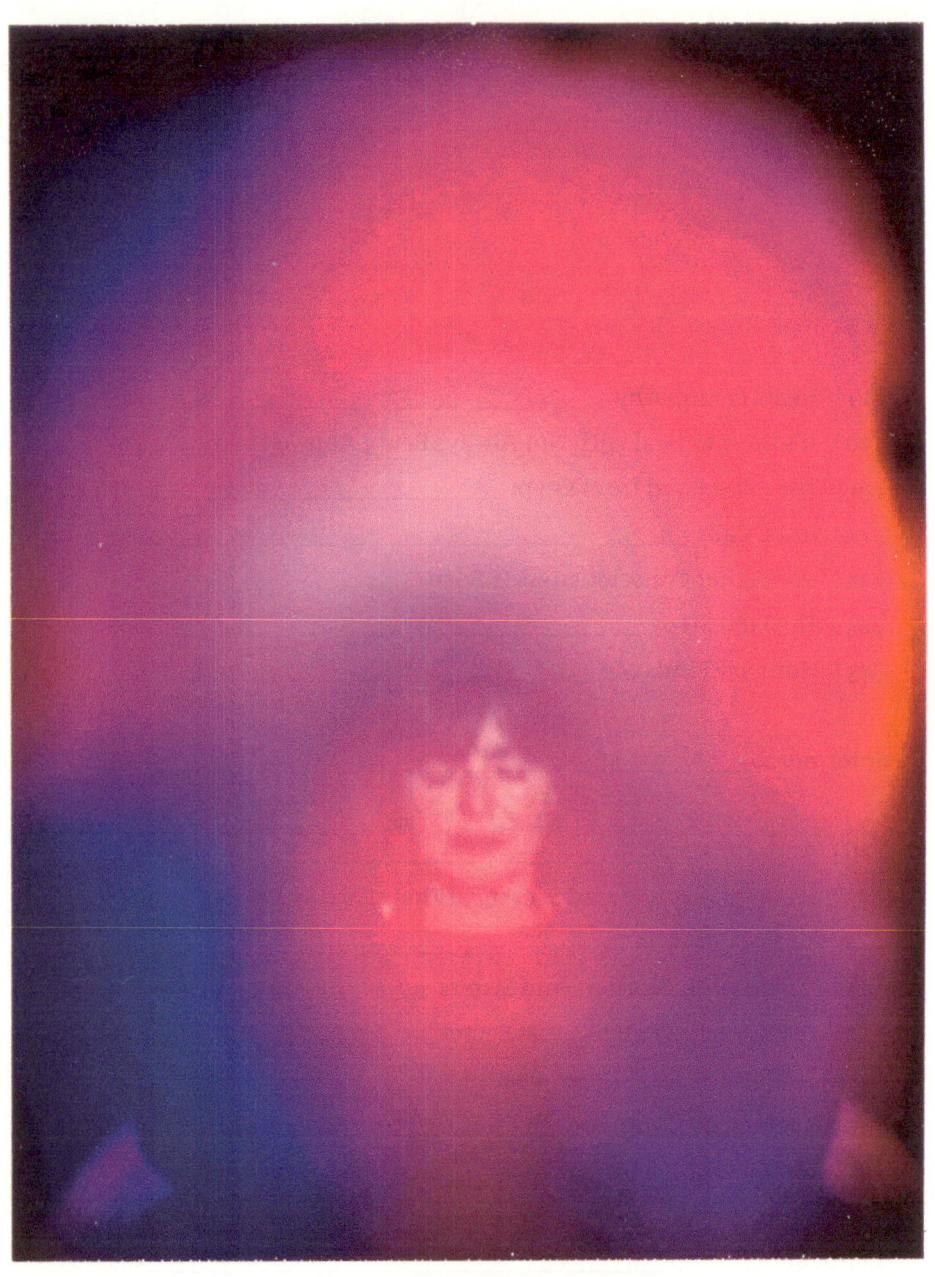

Aura photography of the author, 1994

Aura photography of the author, 2004

"A god speaks very softly in our bosoms,
Softly and very audibly, and shows us
What to accept and what we should avoid."
Johann Wolfgang von Goethe

Prologue

"Write your epilogue when you have finished your book and then write the prologue last of all!" is what I was told by an old friend who knows a lot about writing books. He is the one who offered to put my work in written form or type it into a computer if I dictated the story to him. He thought that it was impossible that I sit down and start to write my book by hand. Our joint project became repeatedly postponed over the years. There were occasions when he had the time and the energy but I thought that the moment had still not arrived for me to be able to publish everything. This would have meant me sharing all too personal experiences with "strangers".

Both of us were able to dedicate time to our joint project in 2001. I had, by now, arrived at a point where I was able to turn the key in the lock that held my secrets and to lovingly offer the events that had occurred to me to those who discovered my book. I got about halfway through the book with my friend when, during a discussion, he said that he "no longer could nor wanted to help in the writing and publishing of my book". The dream that I had the previous night had warned me of what was about to happen. I recalled ancient times in my dream and I lived at the time of the Greek philosophers. I was also a philosopher, as was my friend with whom I was working. We were friends despite our contrasting views and theories. I respected everyone else's thoughts but I believed, lived and taught my own. Then he attacked anyway and couldn't accept my theses or rather was unable to accept that thoughts could exist other than his own.

In the dream, my thesis and my teachings cost me my life. Back in the future, in 2001, right in the middle of our discussion, I couldn't catch my breath and a fiery pain shot through my heart. It was as if I had been poisoned and I thought that my heart was about to take its last beat—thinking back to the dream of the night before and the 1,000s of years of pain that it held. I couldn't do a thing. I needed help and I needed it quickly. My friend, recognizing the danger that I was in, ran frightened straight to the kitchen to get a strong drink of some kind. I tried to stand up but I passed out. I heard a voice as I was falling to the floor: **"Don't be frightened, you are going to collapse but everything is going to be OK."** That is how it happened. Not only did I come around within a couple of minutes but I had regained full consciousness and all my strength.

I said goodbye to my friend and thanked him for his help up until that point. I knew then that no one was going to be able to help me with the writing of my book. This had happened to me and it was me who was going to write about it. "I literally need to write it out of myself; I need to give birth to my baby."

Yes, "birth", that meant the end to a long pregnancy, is the best word to describe the writing of my book. I don't want to give away the secrets of my book beforehand only to say that I was simply the mother of my book; the child that I had carried to full term. The seed was planted in me by other spiritual forces and I promised, despite not remembering anything of this at the beginning, that I would carry, look after, protect and care for it. Then, when the time came, I would bring it into the world and would finally present our joint child; "our book".

The place of birth was no coincidence either. This was despite the fact that I thought that I had consciously chosen Greece. It was only here that I realized that this was the place to explore and relate experiences and truths.

It was while writing my book that I realized that, over the last 22 years, I had sought refuge and protection on one or other island of the ancient Greek motherland just before any great change in my life and, at the same time, drawn energy into myself for the task that I was about to undertake. This is how I had found my way to the islands of Samos, Lesbos, Crete, Pathmos, Naxos, and now to the beautiful Peloponnese Peninsula. This place had been the home to Greek history and philosophy in ancient times.

I can feel the soft breath of my loyal companion, my dog, Naxa, gently stroking my feet. He joined up with me on the island of Naxos and it was impossible to say "no" to the loyal way that he followed me around.

We have walked the streets together ever since, we travel together and he is by my side day and night. He even sits by my side at my practice and I wouldn't be able to imagine my meditation group evenings without him.

The small place that I took myself away to write my book, Ancient Assini, was chosen by chance. One of my oldest friends in Switzerland, Jeanette, whom I have known for nearly 25 years, married a Greek. She spent every summer with her children in Nafplio. Her marriage failed and a year ago she decided to stay there with them and not go back to Athens to her husband. I went to visit her last summer and hoped that I would find a calm and quiet place to write my book the following spring.

I definitely found it. Not only was the apartment on the coast and close to a historically important castle in Ancient Assini, but helpers also arrived here. Yes, in this little out-of-the-way place in Greece. It was as if the ancient Greek gods had prepared everything for my presence here. Not long before I arrived, in April, Jeanette befriended a Hungarian couple who moved here in January to run the new riding school. She soon introduced me to them. Meeting Gergő and his wife Judit proved to be a turning point for writing my book. In fact, I started to rewrite my book again from the beginning and this time not in German but in Hungarian, my mother tongue, and by hand. On hearing this, Judit offered to type it into a computer and she even corrected it. Judit did a massive amount of work. She and her husband were my first readers and I was very curious to hear their opinion.

I held meditation sessions for them and their friends in our free time to deal with the problems arising as a result of the differing views and temperaments that had cropped up during the course of their new work in Greece. None of them had ever experienced anything like meditation before.

It looked for a while as if not only their work here was coming to an end but that the riding school didn't have enough strength to stay open either. They asked for help and I recommended meditation. I asked them to concentrate on their hearts and to ask all their helpers (luckily the Greeks are very devout people) for a way out of what appeared to be an unsolvable situation. Everyone went back to work after the meditation. Later in the evening, when those involved met up again, they shook each other by the hand and they all said, without exception: "Come on, let's give it another go and start the whole thing over again but differently this time."

I knew that this would "now" be a great success. I was happy that I could be here and that I was able to help them.

While writing my book, I also realized why it was that I had wanted to study to become a teacher back in Budapest. I wanted to teach ethics and philosophy to young people but I also wanted to live according to these teachings. There wasn't such a great demand for this kind of teacher under the communist regime and so it was impossible to get into university.

In time, I became attracted to religious science and parapsychology. I read day and night and, in so doing, tried to stifle my hunger for these subjects.

My first yoga book found its way into my hands when I was still quite young. It was Selva Raja Yesudian's book, the Indian doctor and yoga teacher who lived and taught in Hungary before the Second World War. I practised from this book for years; at the time, there was no such thing as yoga teaching.

Today, I am the proud owner of the Yoga Siromani diploma that I received in an Indian ashram. This qualification not only allows me to teach yoga positions—*asanas*—but also to teach ancient Vedanta philosophy.

Life, fate and the spiritual world still led to my becoming a house-wife and a mother, although I acquired a different college qualification, but I was still able to realize my old desire which was to teach.

"Your work is for the future of your children's children; for free thought and life!" said my leader's VOICE.

My gratitude is endless to both my visible and invisible helpers. But also to those who stood in my way and who tried at all costs and with everything at their disposal to talk me out of it. They helped me to persevere and to stand resolute despite everything.

I knew and suspected something. I was searching for something and my motto was, "Just you wait, I'll show you!"

The contents of my book, all that I have gone through—from the first letter to the last—all happened to me and this is how I experienced them. I had to experience all of this for a reason but it could have happened to anyone at all. Why did the Great Spirit choose me? Why did he entrust me with this huge task? I don't know. Perhaps my faith, my perseverance and my purposeful exploration is what did it but perhaps there was another reason that I cannot now know. There were certain events and things happening that I have not been able to write about here. Perhaps this is because I still haven't understood them or because they would seem so unbelievable that my readers would question the truth of what happened. Reading the book still provides a great lesson!

I am happy that I can now hand you my "spiritual child". I hope that it will also help you in your search, in understanding things and strengthen your persistence and belief. But perhaps you will now not have to go through what it is that I have been through! You can carry on where I have left off with this book.

May the Lord of the Skies bless you as he blessed me with his love, trust and protection! May God guide your life too!

With love, *Dorothea*   Ancient Assini, Easter 2003

1

Just You Wait, I'll Show You ...

It was almost the end of 1981. As we had been doing for several years, a group of us agreed to celebrate the end of the year together and to clink our glasses in a toast on New Year's Eve. We had made many good friends and acquaintances since leaving St Gallen to move to the small village just outside Zurich. There were a number of young families living in our street and we started to make friends through our kids. They really enjoyed being together. We mothers cooked in turns. As each family had no more than a couple of children, this meant that the children could spend more time with their friends while the mums got some free time. We spent a great deal of time with the neighbours from our and the next-door building. We trimmed the laundry up at New Year for the children and we made a lot of new toys for them. This left us, the adults, to chat and celebrate in our apartment without being disturbed by them. Every year a different family invited the others. We had four families at our place the previous year, which meant eight adults and eight children. We had been invited to someone else's place this year. I always liked to surprise my guests with all manner of delicacies but this year I was happy not to have to worry about it.

I was feeling strangely tired the day before New Year's Eve. My husband had an idea that filled me with joy and strength. He could see that I wasn't in the best of moods. So, he suggested that the two of us hold a pre-New Year's Eve celebration and go to a Spanish restaurant that we had both been talking about for a long time. I was pleased by the idea as we seemed to get out less and less. My partner often came home from work so tired that I didn't have the heart to bring such things up. He frequently carried on working after dinner on something that he hadn't been able to finish in the office. They expected a lot of him and he wanted to do everything to the best of his ability.

I like beautiful clothes and I had a dress that I had never worn before. I knew that my husband would also really like it. And indeed, he did. I was glad that I had been able to make it to the hairdresser's the day before. On my partner's arm, I could step into the Spanish restaurant that we had been eying, and with a completely new hairdo. The waiters' eyes twinkled as the dress looked fabulous with my high-heeled shoes and my good posture. They hustled and bustled around us especially as it was the day before New Year's Eve and the restaurant was virtually empty.

I had never been in a Spanish restaurant before and so it took a while for us to decide what it was that we wanted to eat. I like shellfish and so I ordered that, while my husband had the famous paella. I hardly ever drink alcohol but we ordered aperitifs in honour of the occasion and fine Spanish wine to accompany the meal.

I felt that something wasn't quite right. I was delighted by the surprise of celebrating New Year with my husband before time and to have supper in such a posh restaurant. Nevertheless, all I wanted to do was to go home when they brought the food to our table. I started to feel quite unwell. I didn't want to ruin the evening and nor did I want to leave the expensive food, so I started eating. Every morsel made me feel sicker and after a while I had to realize it could not go on like that. I went to the bathroom and I could see that I was deadly pale despite all the rouge and powder. I felt a sudden pain as I made my way back to the table. I asked my husband to take me home straight away because I was feeling really ill. He had hardly eaten any of the food we had ordered but he asked for the bill the minute that he saw my pale face and my teeth clenched together from the pain. We paid and set off for the car. I could hardly walk from the pain and I felt very dizzy. I couldn't begin to imagine what was happening to me this suddenly. I thought that it might be appendicitis. Apparently, it can be extremely painful. My husband was very scared as I had been right as rain only half an hour before. He wanted to take me into casualty at the hospital. I wanted to go home as perhaps this sick feeling and pain would go just as quickly as it had appeared.

That's not what happened. I could neither stand nor lie down when we got home. I tried my best to control the pain as I could see how helpless my husband was. It was hard for him to bear—me being in so much pain, and him not being able to do a thing to help.

I lay down on the couch at home in the living room and told him to try and get some sleep because he had to get up early in the morning to go to work. I would also have liked to sleep but it was impossible. There was a searing pain in my whole stomach and the pain radiated in all directions. I wasn't used to being in pain. I was hardly ever ill. My throat had hurt a lot some years before but that had virtually disappeared now. "I live very healthily; I do a lot of exercise and do as much as I can to ensure that my body feels good. But why is this happening now? I hope that if I fall asleep, I am going to wake up with no pain and I'll recall everything as if it were just a bad dream." The opposite happened. I felt the pain even more than before but my thoughts came back to life. I searched for the "why" behind everything that had happened.

I was sad that this was how the lovely evening had ended. We had set off so happily and had been so much looking forward to celebrating together!

I thought about why it was that my husband and I loved New Year's Eve so much. My pen pal came to Budapest for New Year on my invitation and asked for my hand in marriage three days later. That was Christian, my present husband.

We had met two years before, in 1970. I was then working as a receptionist in a hotel and attending evening classes at the Trade and Catering College at the same time. It was around this time that part of the Malév Air Tours group began working with the Swiss Imholz office. Groups came to us twice a week via this office. The groups were led by university students. This wasn't only good for the office but it meant that the groups also learned a lot as they were entrusted to intelligent people. The students also liked the work, since they had the chance to travel to a lot of foreign countries and it provided them with a little bit of financial support for their studies. The trip to Budapest made the office famous and the owner rich. 100 travellers, twice a week, wasn't bad business for Malév either.

We had grown used to the groups in the hotel and we were always happy to see a tour guide we knew stepping through the door. They were young just like us. We talked to them a lot and they were curious to learn about our lives.

New guides came on the odd occasion and Christian was one of them. He was a tall and handsome young man. He hadn't stayed with us before. I started to chat to him as he was very kind and likeable. He asked me for my address before the group left. He said that he took a lot of groups to other countries and he would be happy to send me postcards from wherever he went. I gave him my address, although I knew that they didn't like us corresponding with the guests in the hotel. I simply thought that he was a student too and I was intrigued to know what he would make of this back home. Our correspondence lasted for more than two years. A deep, intimate friendship formed between us. We told each other everything. I had been terribly disappointed in a relationship that I was in at the time and my Swiss friend did all he could to comfort me. We wrote a lot to one another about our pasts and about our previous relationships. After a while, he became my best friend after my two girlfriends. Perhaps it was because he was so far away that I told him all my deepest secrets. I wrote about my childhood and my family. And he told me everything about his. It was completely the opposite of mine. Whereas I practically grew up on the street as my parents divorced when I was very young—and my mother not only worked but also studied—he enjoyed the loving, protective closeness of his parents. He grew up with his sibling in a small village in the mountains. However, he liked the idea of the freedom of my "city kid" world. He was also amazed by the fact that I worked and went to evening school. He also went to a college of economics and found it hard to imagine how it was possible to work at the same time. It wasn't easy but it was possible. I worked five days a week and spent Saturday morning and two evenings sitting behind a desk at college. My head felt heavy enough by 10 pm when I came out of college and I had to be in the hotel by 6 am the following morning. I had been doing this now for three years!

Being as I didn't get a place at university where I had so wanted to study after completing my high school leaving exam, I started to attend catering trade school though I didn't think that I wanted a career in this trade. Albeit with some resentment, I accepted my father's suggestion: the daughter of a friend of my father studied at a cookery school and he was of the opinion that it couldn't hurt for a woman to be able to cook well. The idea was pretty insulting but I didn't have a better idea of my own. "I'll only stay for a year!" I thought to myself.

The course lasted a year and a half but I still wanted to finish it, since I had started now. My first placement was in the kitchens of a famous hotel, the Grand Hotel Margitsziget (Margaret Island). I only worked there for a couple of weeks. I was already to prepare for the university entrance exam again when I was called to see the manager who asked me whether I would like to study hotel and catering. I liked languages and I also liked to travel. I thought that the hospitality industry would not only mean that I would meet lots of interesting people, but this would help me develop my languages and also open up the opportunity for work placements in foreign hotels. The university had been massively oversubscribed for the previous year and so, as there wasn't much chance of success, I said yes.

The college didn't start until the autumn, so I was asked to take up a student placement at another hotel. This is how I ended up at the Szabadság (Liberty) Hotel, where I met Christian a couple of years later. By then, I had finished trade school and I was attending evening classes at the Hotel and Catering College. Christian had just finished university the same semester as me, but he had gone to Paris to study as part of his course. I wrote to him there and then, in December, and I sent him the invitation that I had sent to all my best friends, which was an invitation to a New Year's Eve party at our home. I also wrote that I would invite him too if he happened to be in Budapest. I received a telegram by return of post that read: "I'm on my way!" I hadn't counted on that! I had told my girlfriends a long time ago that the Swiss boy had become my best friend. His thinking, his ideals and his way with people was so similar to mine! After two years of correspondence, I knew him better than anyone else. I told my girlfriend, Zsóka: "If the boy was in Budapest, I could really trust him!" Zsóka was my witness when, after a great disappointment age 21–22, I announced that I didn't trust men anymore and I was never going to get married. I had been doubtful of marriage and relationships from childhood onwards. I had been let down by my boyfriends at high school as they were liars and unfaithful. "But I can really trust this Swiss boy!" I had thought this for a good while. Perhaps it was because he was so far away; perhaps it was because he had such a secure upbringing in that delightful snow-covered, little village depicted in the many photos which he had sent me.

And so Christian arrived from Paris on 30 December 1972 at Ferihegy Airport in Budapest. The door opened and there stood a beautiful young man. I became very hot and I was sure that my face must have been red. Interestingly, Christian's was also red! He also remembered that I was a very pretty girl two years before, but he hadn't bargained on such a change. The young, 22-year-old student had become a mature 24-year-old woman! It really was true that the difficulties of the previous two years, my relationship as well as my work and studies, had changed me a great deal. I had grown up.

Paris had also done Christian a lot of good. It was the air and the people in this cosmopolitan city. The boy who had grown up in a village nestled in the mountains had become an open "man of the world". This second meeting was a turning point in both our lives. Christian spent New Year's Eve at our home and he celebrated with my Budapest friends and mates from college. Everyone liked him from the very beginning, including my mother. I didn't get a day off from the hotel because of all the work and so I worked while he went around the city on his own. When I got off work, I wanted to show him everything that I liked and that had been important in my life up until that point. He already knew my friends but he didn't know my havens, the museums, where I used to hide out! I sought refuge there even when I was still at school. I had sought comfort there as well as direction in my life. I searched for values that were lasting and those goals and heroes that deserved my love and respect. I had not only been let down by my parents as a child but also by the society that I was forced to live in. I only believed in the future. I always stood in front of the statues of heroes, of true people at the National Museum and with deep conviction I would always say, "Just you wait, I'll show you! I am following your example!"

I had been repeating the same thought since I was a little child if I had ever suffered injustice or dishonesty. "Just you wait, I'll show you! You can do this another way!" That is why good examples and something to follow were so important to me.

First of all, I lived in the land of fairy tales where even the smallest were capable of overcoming evil. I wanted to be like that. I knew and I believed that it was possible even in the deceitful and alien world that was Communism, which I had been born into. I wasn't willing to support the system and I began an inner fight against it. I wanted to be good and true and to remain that way despite everything.

I was about four or five years old when I said this for the first time. In fact, I said more than that. We sat down to Sunday lunch and my mother had invited her hateful boyfriend and my grandmother. The man detested me and quite possibly all children. He especially hated me and often said that I was "impossible to handle"! Yet he tried everything that he could to break a child's will. Even on that day, at lunch. I didn't like meat but they forced me. I ate the chicken because it didn't have such a meaty taste but then I only ate a leg. My mother cooked well and liked to cook. That day she prepared fried chicken. As a chicken only has two legs, I immediately announced: "The leg is mine! Well at least one." There were four of us, and I wanted to make sure that I got one for myself.

"You'll eat what you are given," said the stranger. He put a wing on my plate and took a leg for himself. I waited for my mother to say something but she didn't.

"No, I'm not eating that because I don't like it!" I, the dwarf, answered the giant.

"Well you are going to! You can't get down from the table until you have!" said the horrible man again.

"Then I'll stay here forever because I'm not eating the wing!"

So that is what happened. They ate their lunch and I sat at the table with a chicken wing on my plate and I knew that I would rather die but that there was no way that I was going to eat that. Not because of the chicken wing but because of what had happened to me. My mother didn't dare defend me; she betrayed me! I decided there and then that I didn't want a mother who was going to be like this and I never believed in her love again. My poor grandmother suffered along with me—as she told me many times afterwards—but my mother wouldn't have listened to her either as she was fighting so desperately for this man's love.

This was just one incident of many when someone tried to "break" me to "raise" me. It really was true that I was impossible to handle. Although I was suffering inside, even as a small child I decided: "I can't count on anyone and so I have to raise myself to be a hero, to be incorruptible. This is the only way I can become a fearless fighter for truth!"

I told my Swiss friend all about this while we were in the National Museum: that it was impossible to fight on the outside and so I tried to topple evil and injustice with inner strength.

Christian had also sensed this in my letters and he said that he was amazed that I was a young emancipated woman who was fighting within against the whole world for a better future.

I felt that he was a kindred spirit. He had been studying for his major in diplomacy, so he was trying to influence the world through politics. He had clear, true thoughts and it was pleasant to listen to him.

Our ideals and our images of the future were exactly the same. We felt this unity when we were together, when we walked for miles and miles on the avenue or in Buda or in the nearby hills covered in freshly fallen snow. Christian had to go back to Paris on 3 January.

On 2 January, we were on János Hill. We had wobbled our way to the top of the ski lift and we drank mulled wine in a restaurant at the top to warm ourselves up. We were sipping our wine when Christian's face became really quite serious. "I would like to ask you something but I would like you to be completely honest in your answer."

"That's the most natural thing in the world!" I said.

"What would you say if I were to ask you to be my wife?", he said, starting to blush.

"If you were to ask me that, then I'd say yes!" I answered feeling just as nervous.

"Good, then, I've asked."

"Good then, I've answered."

That is how he proposed and I said yes. My mother didn't know whether to laugh or to cry. She was happy that I had found my partner at last despite the fact that she also felt that she was losing her only child. She never realized, or she wasn't willing to realize, that she had lost me long ago.

Christian called Paris to say that he would only be able to go back a couple of days later. Instead of Paris, he flew to Zurich and then took the long train journey to his village of Brienz, high up in the mountains, to see his parents.

"I have found my future wife, and we'd like to have the wedding just as soon as we can."

I suppose his parents must have thought that they were dreaming. Their son broke up with his high-school girlfriend who was waiting to hear him say something reassuring before he left for university, 100s of miles away. Christian was honest and he told the girl: "I don't know whether I'll ever get married or not! I'd like to live for the future and all the opportunities that it holds (and by this he meant his profession). But the first thing is that I'm definitely going to finish university and I want to get to know the world. You can't count on me before I'm at least 30!" That is what the boy, age 20, said.

After a long relationship, he had split up with his new girl-friend for exactly the same reason only several weeks before. The girl had travelled to Paris to visit Christian and she had wanted to spend Christmas and New Year with him. Christian wasn't pleased to see her as she questioned him constantly about their future. So, age 24, he said exactly what he had done age 20. He didn't know if he was getting married at all; he wanted to live for his profession and he wasn't sure he would find it before he turned 30. On hearing this, the girl sulkily split with him, and she went back to Switzerland. At this very moment, my invitation to spend New Year's Eve in Budapest reached him in Paris.

Despite his parents' surprise, they realized that their son had decided. They didn't even ask him what we were going to live on. They respected each other's feelings and that is why my future father-in-law simply asked the groom to be: "Have you thought this through son? Are you clear what it means to remove someone from the surroundings that they're used to?"

Christian replied with a definite yes. The next day they went to the county council offices to request the paperwork needed for the wedding. The process was slowed down, as the bride was a foreigner.

It was slightly more difficult for me to get hold of the papers as I wanted to keep my job as well as continue my university studies. I only let two other people in on my secret besides my girlfriends: my boss at the hotel and my favourite teacher from college. I asked for their advice and their help. My boss at the hotel didn't know how he could be of any assistance as his hands were tied. I was marrying the citizen of a capitalist country; he didn't know how long he could go on employing me in such a position of trust as a hotel receptionist. I needed permission from the Ministry of the Interior and it would soon turn out whether or not my plan would succeed. Success! I managed to stay in the hotel up until the last day, 26 April, because my boss undertook to be my guarantor.

A similar thing happened at college. With the help of my teacher, the director was willing to give his agreement to me completing my final year if it were authorized "from above". At that time, this meant the Ministry of Education. No one thought that I would get permission. I asked for a personal interview. Following my request, they informed me that they would send the decision to the school. The decision was, "yes". I got another "yes" as a Swiss wife and, after the wedding, as a Swiss citizen to finish my final year at college by correspondence. No one imagined I would do it, and that I would be able to do it. I had to write my dissertation that year. I would have to write everything with no help at all and in time for the deadline. I would prepare for the state exam alone and entirely from books. I thought deeply about the list of tasks that lay ahead of me. It was an enormous challenge! What I didn't know then was that this was the least of my challenges. Fate had a much greater test lined up for me!

After the third year, first term exams at the beginning of June, I flew happily with my husband to Switzerland on a Malév flight with about 100 other passengers who were travelling with the Imholz Travel Agency. My husband came for me just as he had done when we first met: as a tour guide.

I was curious about his home and his friends. I only knew his parents who had come to our wedding in Budapest. It was their first time there; their first time in a communist country and the first time that they had met their son's chosen one, their daughter-in-law.

Christian's parents were simple, humble people. I liked them from the very first moment: they were the parents of my adored betrothed and had given my darling husband so much love and security in his childhood. They were vegetarians. I only ordered meat-free dishes for the lunch that we had in our apartment after the wedding. There was a cold buffet and dessert that my friends at the hotel had prepared for us. They had made everything with a lot of love and culinary expertise. Hungarian cuisine doesn't have so many vegetarian dishes, but my wedding did.

The official part of the wedding was in the beautiful registry office on Gellért Square. I didn't show my wedding dress to Christian or anyone else before the wedding. It caused a sensation when I appeared in a museum piece: all silver and white with the dress and the headdress embroidered with pearls. I don't know which queen's wedding dress it was a copy of, but I seem to remember that perhaps it was Empress Sissy's. This is what I had been able to hire. I really did become a queen after the wedding as my husband's name was König. Then I flew to Switzerland, my new home. "It is the end of a period of my life and now a new life is beginning that I, we are going to direct."

"Are you feeling better?" I hear and I feel someone gently stroking my face. I open my eyes and I see a troubled man next to me who fate brought into my life when I was 22. Now, age 33, I have known him for 11 years and I have been his wife for 8 years. "How much he's changed! Now I realize. A few minutes ago another man, perhaps another husband, sat next to me on the plane from Budapest to Zurich."

"I think that I'm feeling a bit better," I replied and it would seem that I had managed to fall asleep at some point. I wanted to stand up but the pain ripped through my stomach again.

"No. No, it hasn't gone away! I think I'll still have to go and see a doctor."

"OK. Then I won't go to work today. I would have only gone in for a few hours to finish something off and that can wait."

We asked the telephone operator which doctor was on duty as I couldn't count on my own GP because of the holidays. I made an appointment with the duty doctor and he was able to see me that morning. He examined me and thought that it was a "gynaecological" problem and, as this wasn't his specialist area, he was unable to give an exact diagnosis. He said that it was probably a cyst. He recommended two things: I could go to the hospital where they would be able to do the operation straight away or he could give me painkillers and I would be able to go and see my own gynaecologist on 3 January.

I heard what he said but I wasn't able to take it in. "I was completely healthy the day before yesterday! What could have happened so suddenly? And an operation? And hospital? My condition can't really be that serious!"

I hoped that it would all go away in three days and, if not, that my gynaecologist would say something else, something not so terrible. I went home with this in my mind and I thought that if I rested and I concentrated all my energy on making it go away, then all the trouble would disappear and I wouldn't need to go and see the doctor.

In any case, I took the painkillers that I had been given. The pain soon went but I became terribly sleepy. So I spent the day in the flat with the family waiting on me. It was strange as I was always the one who scurried around after everyone else. I looked after and cared for all of them when they were weak or sick.

Now it was me who was lying listlessly on the sofa and probably with something terrible in my stomach. The doctor assured me that it wasn't my appendix as this would have meant that I would have been sent to hospital immediately. On the other hand, if it was a cyst then perhaps it could be cured without an operation. I didn't think about the fact that it could be something even more serious, like cancer. I was healthy from head to toe and this was some little problem that we would be able to sort out! I sent my husband over to our neighbours' place that night with the children to celebrate. I was neither in the mood nor did I have the strength. A sort of aimlessness; inexplicable hopelessness started to well up within me.

I was happy that I could be on my own and I would have liked to have slept and to sleep on through the New Year's Eve celebrations and to wake up the next morning and start a healthy New Year.

I fell asleep. I fell back into the dream of the night before. But it wasn't a dream: I was going through my life and now, on the second night, it carried on where it had left off, with my arrival in Zurich.

My brother-in-law and his wife were waiting for me at the airport with an enormous bunch of flowers. They welcomed me with love and happiness as a new member of the family. They took us to their home and received us as their guests. My sister-in-law modestly said that she hoped that I liked the food as she said she didn't know how they cook where I come from. I thought that everything was not only especially delicious but also unique, which I have always liked. I have always tried the local cuisine wherever I have travelled.

My sister-in-law knew that I worked in catering and that I had my chef's qualification. She hoped that I was satisfied with everything, despite the fact that I was a professional. All I could feel was happiness and love as she had cooked and baked in honour of my arrival.

They also had two little children; one was only a couple of months old and the other was almost two years old. They were always doing something that meant that my sister-in-law had to stand up from the table every couple of minutes while we were eating. She calmed the little ones down and checked what they were up to. They were used to having their mother's undivided attention and so they attracted it with their little tantrums and arguments.

My husband told me that my sister-in-law was a wonderful housewife and that she had been a teacher in a home economics college before they were married. Then my sister-in-law went on to tell us that every girl in Switzerland—and nowadays every boy as well—had to complete this school, where they learned everything from cooking and baking to how to run a household including looking after their money, nursing the sick but also sewing and knitting. Laughing, I told them that we learned how to handle a lathe during polytechnic class at communist high school as we had something called "5 + 1 education", which meant that we received a qualification as a lathe operator as well as our school leaving certificate. I reflected on the fact that even though I was about the same age as my sister-in-law, we had grown up in such different surroundings. Her mum was at home and only focused on the family, as I discovered during our conversation. My mother looked after me, did the housework at the same time as working full-time and studying on the side. "Such different influences must have been formed in our personalities!", I thought almost automatically. "How different the examples were that we saw and experienced!" Luckily, I was able to lead the life of an emancipated woman and this was completely natural where I came from. "It must be nice to be just a mum and a housewife, but thank God, that isn't what awaits me! I have studied my whole life and I invested all my energy and free time in this. I am happy that I can work here soon and be alongside my husband at the same time as being independent."

The first few days soon passed in Zurich and then in St Gallen, where I moved to with Christian. He also had a year until his graduation. As for money, we thought that it was best that I should look for some temporary work in a hotel somewhere or in a catering business. Christian stayed as a tour guide, which meant no more than a couple of trips a month but a fixed income. Christian had saved the money that he had earned during his year in Paris. He had wanted to travel the world for a couple of months after he got his degree and to see as much as he could. He decided differently in the end; he made a different choice. We counted what he had saved and along with our extra work we would have enough to live on until we got our degrees.

Christian knew that the goal he had set himself of becoming a diplomat had been made impossible by our marriage as his wife came from a communist country.

"You never know," they informed and warned him in Bern where he had been called in for a "talk". He still gave up what he had imagined for himself as he knew that he had found his partner—and many spend their whole lives searching for someone. Yet some of his friends did warn him, asking him whether he knew me well enough and whether I wasn't just using him to put roots down in the West. Even though Christian was angered by these "friendly warnings", he had known me for three years and, better than anyone else, he knew that I had the chance not only of staying and living in the West but also of marrying money.

The day of the Swiss wedding came at last. My in-laws organized it and so everything was a surprise for me. The only thing that I was left to do was to select the dress. I was startled by the prices in Zurich as our budget was very small. Despite this, and thanks to the summer sales, I found the dress that I wanted and was able to afford it. It was all white, full length, pleated and looked like something that Greek goddesses wore—especially the style that adorns statues of Olympia. I wore a white straw hat, which I had bought back in Budapest, and I decorated the front with a red rose. My hat had a red ribbon wrapped around it and I wore red patent leather shoes. I was holding a bouquet of red roses when I stepped out of the car in front of the Interlaken church. It was the first time that I had seen Christian's friends and his more distant relatives.

Standing next to one another in church, we both vowed to remain faithful partners for better or for worse. I knew that our vows came deep from within our hearts, deep from within our souls! After the wedding (I automatically became a Protestant like my husband) there were horse-drawn carriages waiting for the guests. They took us all around the town which is where Christian had attended school. His whole family had moved here years ago so that their sons shouldn't have the long train journey to school.

Interlaken was so beautiful that I felt as if I was in a fairy tale being driven in a carriage. I was sitting next to my husband, "Mr King" (Herr König) and as everyone addressed one another formally here, even youngsters of a similar age, I was known as Mrs König. There were about ten such carriages following on behind us. I couldn't get enough of the surrounding sights. The mountains were still capped with snow even though it was June. Among them, souring high, was the Jungfrau summit which is always covered in snow and ice. Interlaken Lake tinkled and sparkled as did my eyes and spirit at the wondrous beauty of nature. My adored husband sat beside me holding my hand and watched my joy at the sight of my new home. After our carriage ride, all the guests were invited to a very elegant restaurant by Christian's parents. I still can't quite believe the expense that these modest people went to all for our enjoyment.

The surprises weren't over yet. Christian and his brother had been boy scouts. There was a large boat anchored on the lake for scouts with room for about 50 people. We spent the afternoon on the boat and those who wanted to were able to bathe in the lake.

The evening was also for the youngsters. We were invited to the famous Interlaken Casino by Christian's friends. The band even played a waltz and a Hungarian czardas in my honour. I happily took to the dance floor with my darling husband and showed all the others how a Hungarian-Swiss bride can dance and have a good time. I happily slid close up to my dear, gorgeous husband for the tango who virtually melted into me with love. The waltz was next and we danced and we waltzed and then I suddenly felt unwell. It had all been a bit too much. Perhaps it was the burning sun on the boat in the afternoon? Maybe it wasn't possible to constantly add to the endless happiness? It was nearly morning and so we thought it best that we start to make our way home as the celebrations were due to carry on all day. All of Christian's friends came with us and they were our guests for all the events that followed the next day. Everything was new to me; everything was a surprise. I don't know how many people ended up sleeping in Christian's small family house. The next morning, we put our hiking gear on as we had decided to hike up the hill that towered above Christian's home. A little steam train took us to the look-out point at the top of the hill. It let off steam and blew its whistle as it went, drawing the attention of all those who were making their way uphill.

We unpacked the delicacies from our backpacks when we arrived at the top and we ate and drank all that we had prepared. We made our way back downhill on foot—it took us a good few hours. It was a little too much for me, my feet being more used to the paved streets of Budapest, so I travelled the last couple of kilometres sitting on my husband's shoulders. I was slim and very light but I am sure that my husband didn't even notice the weight.

The last guests eventually dispersed and we were at last left on our own. I looked out of the window in the morning and I was there, and I had woken up, in that place that I had stared at on a postcard of his little village nestled in the mountains sent to me by my pen pal.

We still had a couple of days left before our honeymoon which we planned to spend in Paris on the invitation of some of Christian's friends. We got our little apartment in St Gallen that had been freshly painted for us. It had three rooms, a bathroom and a kitchen. This was my first independent apartment; I had married from the flat where we had returned to with my mother from the Midwifery Institute after I was born. Now I shared a wonderful apartment with my husband and the rent was very cheap. Christian and I had agreed to be caretakers and also to measure out the oil cans in the winter. This is how we earned enough money to heat the place. We had to watch every penny and what we spent our money on. But during these delightful days and weeks we didn't think of the future or of savings. But we wanted to enjoy a happy honeymoon and have something to look back on for the rest of our lives.

I had to pop to see the doctor whom Christian knew in St Gallen, before we took the train to Paris. I had been feeling sick and dizzy in the morning ever since the wedding. I couldn't have been pregnant and so I thought it was perhaps the altitude and all the changes that had taken place in my life that had disrupted my usually great health and good temper. The doctor did all the necessary examinations: he took my blood pressure, looked at my eyes, looked at my tongue, took blood and urine and monitored my pulse. He said that everything was fine but we had to wait until the following day for the results of the tests to come back from the lab. The next day he called and told me happily:

"Congratulations, Mrs König, you are expecting a baby!"

"No, that's impossible!" I replied. "The professor of gynaecology in Budapest told me that I couldn't have children and that is why we didn't need to use contraceptives."

The doctor replied in a happy tone: "I don't know what your doctor told you, but the result is positive and that's a fact!"

I put the telephone down and I kept repeating to myself that this was impossible.

It really did seem impossible because I had gone to see a gynaecologist after I said yes to Christian on 3 January—he had been recommended as a specialist on the contraceptive pill. I had taken them in the past for a couple of months but they made me feel constantly ill and I bled so I stopped taking them. One of my girlfriends told me that there were many more hormone treatments available now and that there was a doctor in Budapest who specialized in such things. They tested the level of hormones in your blood and based on that they recommended the best kind of pill. The doctor said something similar when I went back for the results a couple of days later but he asked that I repeat the test about a month later on a day that he determined. So, I went to see him again. They did the test and he asked me to go back again in a month's time just to make absolutely sure. I seem to remember that he told me that there was something wrong with my blood test results or with my hormone level. The doctor repeated the facts again after the third test: "I don't know why, but you are not ovulating. That's why I asked you back over three months so I could be certain. Although you are menstruating, something appears to be wrong and you are not ovulating."

"And what does this mean?" I wanted to know everything straight away.

"Unfortunately, for the time being, it means that you cannot have children." And then he added reassuringly, "But modern medicine is able to help with hormone therapy. Now, for the time being, as a bride-to-be, you can enjoy intimacy without having to take precautionary measures."

The joy still echoes in my ears. "Well, that's great because neither I nor my husband-to-be would like to have children just yet." We had already discussed the fact that we would perhaps like to live without children and to achieve our goals and practise our vocations but also live for one another.

I just sat by the phone and continued to repeat to myself that this was impossible. "Really impossible! How am I, how are we going to do everything that we want to do? Another year until we graduate and we need to study and earn money for another year. And after that? With a child?!"

I couldn't, I wasn't able to cope with what was going on but I didn't want to either! "A new country, everything is alien, I haven't been here for a month yet and now this sudden change clashing with all my dreams and all my desires!" I was still sitting by the telephone, virtually paralysed, in a state of shock when my husband came home from university. He had to organize something to do with the following term and he had registered me for the intensive German course that the school held for foreign language students.

"Good God! What has happened to you?" he asked and he ran over to me. He later told me that I was as pale as a ghost with wide eyes and I had been icy cold when he had put his arms around me.

Eventually, everything came spilling out and I cried as I hugged him. "We're going to have a baby."

"But that's impossible!" he now said what I had been repeating all afternoon. He pushed me away ever so slightly so that he could take a look at my face and now he understood what had shaken me up so much.

"How did it happen?" he asked, a little calmer now.

"Because the doctor in Budapest said ..." and he went on to repeat what I had said to myself just minutes before.

"If only I knew!" I answered but now I couldn't stand up. I slumped back down onto the chair next to the telephone where I had probably been sitting for hours.

Christian sat down next to me on the other chair and now he was lost in a daze. I couldn't stand the pressure within me any longer and I ran to the bedroom shouting and crying and slammed the door behind me. I wanted to be alone with the terrible news. "Because now my whole life is going to change whether I want it to or not!"

Poor Christian stood up and then he sat on the floor outside the door that I had just slammed in his face. I had to tackle the fact on my own that I was going to be a mother with all the accompanying difficulties and responsibilities. The nightmares of my childhood flashed before my eyes. No one had understood me and I always felt alone. There was no one beside me whom I could have depended on whom I could have trusted. "What sort of mother will I be if I have never had an example to follow? No good example." The thought stayed with me all that afternoon as to how I was going to deal with this immense challenge of not only being a mother but a good mother.

The eternal phrase, the one from my childhood, popped up again, "Just you wait, I'll show you!"

I heard Christian's voice again as he tried to console me from outside. "We are going to be able to deal with this despite everything. Don't you worry!"

I wasn't worried anymore. I had decided that I was going to accept this pregnancy! I opened the door and this is what I said in reply: "I know that we are going to be able to deal with it, despite everything and despite everyone!"

My husband told me that he had called his parents with the good/bad news. Grandparents are normally delighted by such news but even they were a little taken aback this time. They were nervous about their son's degree, his future and me completing my studies. Then the next question to come up was: what are we going to live on? My father-in-law had just retired as an employee of the state; his pension was not so high but still he offered to give us half of his pension to help us through for as long as it took Christian to find a job. This would be at least a year and a half.

So this is how the three of us set off on our honeymoon to Paris the following day.

"Come on Mummy and clink glasses with us!" called the voice of Claudi and when I opened my eyes, my little family was standing in front of me. My family had grown a little since then with the addition of Toncsi.

It was midnight and they had run home from the neighbour's place to welcome in the New Year with me. I looked at my daughters with tired eyes but full of love, and especially on the first one whose arrival had completely revolutionized my life and my ambitions.

My love for them was endless. They were children and their life and happiness depended on me and us. I wanted to give them everything and as much as I could possibly manage so that their lives and especially their childhoods should be happier than mine.

Everything went quiet around me again. My family went back to rejoin the celebrations while the painkillers and tranquillizers continued to take their effect on me.

It really began with taking responsibility. A tiny being had arrived and we had to wait for her in the best way possible. That was the next challenge.

"Even though fate has brought unimaginable changes in my life, in our lives, it somehow had to happen this way," I thought as I lay on the sofa now on the threshold of the New Year, 1 January 1982.

As I write these lines, I know that this is how it had to be and this is the only way things could have happened!

Then I was glad that the burden that awaited me was still several months away. "Nature has organized things so perfectly, giving nine months to carry a child!" It is easy enough, so to say, to "make" a child but the preparation for becoming a mother needs those few months—not only physically but also emotionally and spiritually. As the little child grows within the mother's tummy, so grows the acceptance, protection and love in the mother's heart and soul.
I proudly wore my little plastic badge on my dress and on my coat that I changed every month. It had a little coloured number on it that showed those on the street who daren't ask what month I was.

The honeymoon in Paris was wonderful. Our happiness only increased in the knowledge of our new arrival. My husband already started stroking my still flat stomach that was virtually bursting with muscles. I, on the other hand, started to notice the changes in the mirror. First my breasts started to fill out and I was proud of the fact that I would soon be able to feed my little one with them.

We told everyone the news. They no longer looked on Christian as a student in Paris as they had done only half a year before. He was a husband and soon to become a father. They were also jealous of him because he had a beautiful, Hungarian wife and a bright future. You can always see people's emotions so clearly on their faces even if they want to hide them!

My mother was the only one whom we didn't yet tell the surprising news. But she surprised us when she came; or rather they came, to meet us at the railway station in December. Lacika stood next to her, who had been my mother's partner for two years, and he officially asked for my mother's hand in marriage from Christian and me. It was meant to be a joke of course but the wedding was set for the following day. (It was my mother's fourth and, thank God, her last marriage!) My husband and I were the witnesses and also the only guests. I was towards the end of the seventh month and I would soon have to change the little number seven for a number eight on my winter coat although, all dressed up in my coat, it was still hard to see my surprise. I took my coat off at home and when my mother saw me, she cried with joy: "It can't be true; I'm going to be a grandmother!"

Lacika also cried tears of joy. He liked me as much as Christian and he really was very happy to "be a granddad". And that is what he has been from the very beginning until the present day. My children are grown up now but they still always say: "He's the best granddad in the world."

I had to take my half-year exam at college that went without a hitch because I had prepared very well. My old classmates were all really pleased by the news and all of them, even my teachers, stroked my tummy to see if they could feel the baby moving around.

She had been moving around for a good few weeks and that caused me quite a bit of difficulty towards the end. I would have liked to make up our income a little bit as we had to pay for our trip to Budapest. We also wanted to buy presents for everyone and that is why I had decided in August that I would work for as long as I could manage. By then, I was used to studying at night as that was my only freetime when I was still working in the hotel. So I took a waitressing job in a coffee bar in town. The wages weren't so high but we got a bonus based on the amount of trade. We also got a lot of tips and so I was able to do as I had wished and unpack a big bag of gifts at home at the end of December.

They were rather taken aback in the coffee shop when, at the beginning of December, I told them that this was going to be the last month that I could work there as I was going to be entering my eighth month of pregnancy in January. I wanted to rest a little and prepare myself for the birth that we were expecting at the beginning of March. They hadn't realized until then that I was pregnant. My tummy was good and round by then but the frilly apron and the wallet in the pocket didn't really show the full reality. Perhaps they thought that I had put on a bit of weight and my stomach had grown accordingly but no one had thought for a minute that I might be expecting a baby. My boss was not only upset because this was my last month working there, my workmates and especially the guests liked me, but mainly because I hadn't told him that I was pregnant when I had applied for the job in the first place.

I deliberately hadn't said anything as I really needed the work but who would take on a pregnant woman for not only the summer season but also the Christmas rush? He, and anyone in his place, would have been nervous that I would be sick all the time and be off work a lot and the customers would be disturbed by the sight of a pregnant woman working as a waitress.

I didn't tell them and so they didn't know. And, anyway, I didn't miss a single day. I worked those eight hours just as hard as anyone else. They didn't want to believe me when I told them all the facts. I took it on, I did it, I finished. That was my view on everything.

On the train back to Budapest, all I had left was two months of pregnancy and my dissertation in front of me before the beginning of March.

I greatly enjoyed my dissertation and the topic was familiar to me. I examined the work between the Malév Air Tours office and the Imholz Swiss Travel Agency from the very beginning. It was the first such cooperation for both offices. Both companies were delighted with my work as, up until then, they only had their own statistics to work with and they hadn't compared them with those of the other company. They happily provided me with all the information that I required. Accordingly, I wrote my dissertation in two languages. This took a lot more energy but I hoped that the Swiss company would reward me financially for all the statistics and all my hard work. I got a small letter of thanks but my other hopes weren't realized.

I did, however, get a grant from St Gallen University for the last year. I was a Swiss citizen and I was studying abroad and so, with our low income, I was entitled to the highest possible grant of 600 Swiss Francs. I had to provide proof of my parents' income, which was laughable in Swiss terms, leaving the judgment in my grant allocation in no doubt at all. Christian wasn't entitled to a grant because of his father's income and their family home.

The only thing that made writing my dissertation difficult was my ever-growing tummy. I could no longer sit and write for hours on end as my tummy pressed on my lungs, and I found it increasingly hard to catch my breath. My husband built a counter that I could stand at in the study and so I stood and sat in turn. Even though I was able to hand in the final version of my dissertation by the end of March, I wanted it to be finished before the birth as I didn't see how I was going to be able to finish it afterwards.

Unfortunately, I didn't get it done in time even though there was only the tiniest bit left to do.

I was delighted by the birth. This meant that my darling child was coming into the world and I was finally able to greet this little strong person who broke through despite all medical predictions, as well as my own desire and decision, and found her way home to us. My first daughter, Claudia Ildikó, was born on 6 March and weighed 3.65 kg.

What a feeling it is to hold a newborn in your arms and to see and to marvel at the wonder of nature in reality. Only those know this; those who have seen it and experienced it for themselves. You can write, talk, sing and paint about this but nothing comes anywhere close to reality. Likewise, it had taken me several months to become ready for motherhood and to be able to give birth to my child with such joy. That moment is simply indescribable—when a mother sees her child for the very first time, having held and protected him or her like a great secret within her all along. There is also a conscious acceptance in this moment. Boy or girl, beautiful or less so, intelligent or not, this child is mine and for me the most beautiful and the best.

And so I held, we held, little Claudia in our arms on that bright morning in early March. My husband and I—he had been with me throughout the birth and had mopped my sweating brow with a damp cloth, held my hand and provided me with extra strength in these final moments.

Unfortunately, there were a few problems at the birth and afterwards due to a surgical error. I ran a very high temperature in the hospital and days later it turned out that I had blood poisoning. They were forced to give me antibiotics. I was the one who had so carefully watched what I ate for the whole nine months, I never smoked a cigarette, didn't touch a drop of alcohol and now I was being given antibiotics. "What is this going to do to my milk and more precisely what is it going to do to the baby?!" I had no choice, I had to accept.

I was pleased to be able to go home at last and to forget everything. Everything went well for the first week and my sister-in-law came to help in the first couple of days as Christian had his half-year exams right after the birth. My temperature went up again and I had pain but this time in my breasts. I had now got mastitis, possibly as a result of the first infection. I ran a fever of up to 40 and sometimes 41 and my nose started to bleed from my high temperature. My sister-in-law had to go back to her family and poor old Christian had to concentrate on his exams. Sick, with a high temperature and in terrible pain, I was left with no other option than to go back to hospital. I was an infectious patient, which meant that even my little daughter was isolated from the other babies and they put her out on the terrace. I am sure you think that I am exaggerating but unfortunately not. We had chosen the best and the most expensive private hospital and so we also had to pay for the doctor but we wanted to be the best parents that we could wherever possible, although our surroundings made this even more difficult.

As my temperature started to go down, so the infection in my breasts subsided and I asked Christian to bring my nearly complete dissertation into hospital to me. I had to get it finished as I only had days left before the official deadline. I told him to buy a pastry board that I could write on and so I was able to get it finished and I sent it off to Budapest, to the college, one day before the final deadline. No one believed that I would, that I could, do it and still I managed it. I myself didn't believe it at the end. I don't know where my strength, my stamina came from right at the very end.

Unfortunately, the saddest thing happened. I wasn't able to breastfeed. They stopped my milk with hormones and ointments. I simply couldn't believe that this had to happen as well. A week later, when everything was over, and we were at home at last, I was tired and I sadly bottle-fed my daughter whom I wasn't able to nourish with my own milk.

Christian eventually finished his exams but studying soon began for me again. I had my state exam at the end of May. I needed to study a lot and concentrate. We looked after our little daughter in shifts. As we bottle-fed her, my husband was able to take her out into the fresh air and leave me to prepare for the exam. We shared all the household chores and the stormy sea around slowly started to calm.

I got on a Malév plane at the end of May with little Claudi in a Moses basket. I sat the state exam a couple of days later with the tiny one asleep in the basket by my feet. I soon held a freshly printed degree in my hand. "I've finished another task, another challenge!" This is what I thought to myself as I hurried proudly home to Switzerland, to my husband.

He still had another half a year to go before he completed his studies, and so I took on all the extra jobs so he could focus all his energy on getting a good result. Even though he studied at one of the best universities, his exam result was important when choosing a job. He was always an excellent student and we hoped, despite what we had been forced to go through those last couple of months, that he would be able to complete university. And so he finished with "excellent" and I with "good".

We had been married for a year and a half, both with fresh degrees and a six-month-old delightful, darling little girl in our arms. We had finished everything that we had undertaken. We stood again before the great door that represented freedom. It meant independence from school, from parents: freedom. We had a source of income after having our money tightly controlled, and also our self-realization that we were able to work with pleasure in a certain field not only with the help of our talent and dedication but also primarily our college degrees.

I awoke to the light, it was now morning. My family must have returned home quietly. They were still asleep because it was New Year's Day after all. No one had to go to school or to work. This was my second day in bed and I could hardly wait for it to be time for the doctor to diagnose nothing or at most some minor complication. "I can't even feel it now!" I thought, but I knew this was only because of the painkillers.

2

The YES of
Self-Healing!

3 January is here at last. I can go and see my gynaecologist. I have only been to see him once before, to register as a new patient, because the move to Zurich has not only meant the loss of our circle of good friends but also the loss of practical things like our GP, the dentist and my much-loved gynaecologist. He supervised the birth of my second little girl. It was hard to trust a gynaecologist again after the surgical errors that I had suffered with the birth of my first child. In any other profession, if someone makes a mistake, they throw away the broken part and replace it, but if this happens with a doctor in an operation, it can have serious consequences.

The trauma that I went through with the first birth could obviously be attributed to carelessness (the obstetrician left a wad of cotton wool inside me and they only realized a week later). This could only be treated with what was virtually a new birth. Thank God that it went like clockwork. The pregnancy was untroubled and the birth remained a positive experience in my memory despite all the effort and pain. Unfortunately, because of my previous mastitis, my kind gynaecologist told me while I was still pregnant that they would start to dry my milk up straight after the birth to avoid a similar infection. I believed everything as the previous experiences were very still much alive in my mind. There were only two years between both pregnancies. We decided that if the first little intruder had caused such a complete change in our lives then she should have a little sibling as soon as possible. And then when we are done with bringing up children, we would be free once more and have time for one another. This unity still drove our every thought, our every desire. But now we included our children in this unity and we knew that afterwards there would be our love and that we would be able to live once again in our duo.

I must have been the first to call the medical surgery in the morning, the duty doctor gave a diagnosis and I was able to go straight in for an examination. By now I had given up on the doctor not finding anything. The decreasing effectiveness of the painkillers and the recurring pains pointed quite obviously to the fact that some abnormality, some illness had appeared in my body. The medical examination established the very same.

"Yes, I am only able to reinforce the diagnosis of my colleague," said the specialist. "There is a cyst on the right ovary. It looks to be about seven centimetres on the ultrasound. We are going to have to operate as soon as possible!" he concluded, straightaway reaching for his desk diary.

"But why is it absolutely necessary to operate?" I asked, frightened. It was me whom he was talking about, after all, when he spoke in the first-person plural. "Isn't there perhaps another solution?" I tried a little more. He put his diary back down on his desk. He had probably already found a suitable date, and with what appeared to be a condescending gesture, he answered in a similar tone.

"My dear Mrs König! This is a cyst that is filled with liquid and swollen. It seems to have appeared suddenly and we can assume it will grow very quickly indeed. It is already dangerous at its present size, but if it should continue to grow then it could burst and release its unknown contents. This could have catastrophic consequences for your health."

This sentence concluded his "consultation" and then he took his diary in his hand again. I didn't give up as it was still me that we were discussing. An operation would mean hospital and an even longer period of recovery. I wanted some other option or at least to win a little bit of time to mentally prepare for what appeared to be this unavoidable solution. Besides this, I had a thought run through my head that they would cut my stomach and I could forget my tiny bikini with such an obvious scar. I still had the same figure that I had as a girl but I had done a lot to keep it this way both during pregnancy and after giving birth. Exercise and sport wasn't a drag for me but more like a vital part of my life. I also consciously did my yoga exercises and my tummy, which had grown in the last two months of my pregnancy as if I had swallowed a giant watermelon, was smooth and flat again no more than a few weeks later. It was as if nothing at all had happened in the interim. My girlfriends were jealous but they did nothing at all themselves to achieve similar results.

The second painful thought was that perhaps I wouldn't be able to surf again in Corsica in the summer. I had become completely devoted to surfing over the past couple of years. My favourite piece of sporting equipment was tied to my car from spring to autumn and the wind only had to pick up a little on Lake Zurich for those of us who were "bitten by the bug" to show up. We took to the water trying to outdo one another by showing who could make best use of the wind. I had three weeks to do this in Corsica as we had been going there camping for years and you could always count on a lively breeze. I was a good surfer right from the start despite having a very thin figure and being a woman. I was accepted as "one of the boys" by serious surfers and we soared with our translucent sails on the sparkling sea. I told everyone: "I have found my sport!"

I have adored the sun and water since I was a little girl. The first rays of sunshine in Budapest always enticed me into the swimming pool to sunbathe despite the fact that it was March or the beginning of April. I was the brownest girl at the pool by the start of the summer. This really meant something in those days at the Lukács, the Gellért or the Széchény Baths and later on at Margaret Island and the Palatinus when they opened for the summer. I liked my body and I exercised it, hardened it and stroked it and turned it golden brown with the sun's rays. This meant that the operation would not only spell an end to the bikini and unrestricted sunbathing but also to surfing. It seemed like an impossible thought. With the power of this knowledge and painful loss I continued to "harass" the doctor: "And if we were still to try?" I asked politely.

"Dear Mrs König!" he continued, politely, but I could feel a sense of displeasure at my behaviour behind his words. I hadn't immediately accepted his medical opinion; his decision. "I am the doctor and the specialist here. And the responsibility that goes along with this is also mine. If you insist on not accepting my opinion and reject the operation, then I will not be held responsible for the possibly sudden tragic consequences. Are you fully aware of what you are saying?"

"Yes!" I had said the unbelievable that neither he nor I had counted on. It was the tone of his last sentence that forced me to say it. Someone wanted to force his will on me and wanted to awaken fear within me! I was only asking for time to prepare. Perhaps he was right but I found myself completely unable to accept the tone that he used to address me. I rejected him completely as a doctor who would potentially operate on me or as a figure in whom I could place my trust. He also felt this in my "yes"—his whole medical self seemed insulted (though perhaps something else was going on in his head like his loss of fee for the operation!). He shoved a piece of paper in front of me.

"OK, this absolves me of all responsibility in your case. Don't come back here if tragedy should strike! Sign here to say that you take all responsibility and that I have provided you with all the necessary information with the aim of avoiding this." I signed and I began to doubt his character even more! I knew that I would never come back here again. I was happy when I was able to close the door behind me a couple of minutes later.

"I beg your pardon?" I was getting more and more worked up. "I think that we need to clarify who is here to serve whom. Isn't the doctor here for me? I can be questioning, I can be shy; I can also be unsure! I am the patient after all!" What I went through here had already occurred to me at the doctor's but now I started to defend myself for all I was worth. "I am simply not going to let them treat me like this! And right now, when I need understanding, attention and protection with such a large and dangerous decision to make."

Perhaps the doctor was right in everything that he said but the way that he treated me was completely unacceptable. I stood before him as if I were a dwarf standing in front of a giant who made his decision. But I wasn't a "dwarf" any longer; I was a conscious being who wasn't willing to be treated like this and to have decisions made on my behalf. "There must be another gynaecologist who understands the patient's side and, rather than being despotic, can create an atmosphere or some kind of possibility hand in hand with me as the patient, so that I will not only accept the decision but play a part in helping my recovery from my illness. Even if that means an operation!" I thought it all through on my way home. "I accept my illness as much as I accept my health! I have only known the one up until now and the other was nothing more than a frightening shadow."

I needed help and for someone to support me in this new decision and to give me advice. This new force that had arrived within me started to reduce the importance of my illness in my mind.

I called my in-laws as soon as I got home. They were not only vegetarians but they also followed anthroposophy as taught by Rudolf Steiner. They didn't know yet about my illness as I still hadn't been able to accept it. I just spent day after day hoping that tomorrow everything would be gone as if nothing had ever happened.

My father-in-law patiently listened to everything I had to say.

"Yes, it was because of the way that doctors behaved and the 'one truth' of their knowledge and diagnosis that I sought another path," he said at the other end of the telephone line. "I'd recommend you go to the Birchel-Benner Clinic where you'll find 'another sort of doctor'."

I had already learned a great deal from Christian's parents in terms of alternative diet, treatment of illnesses and my opinion of medication in general.

The highlight of Hungarian cuisine—those various delicious and spicy meat dishes—were completely missing from their table.

My father-in-law had never eaten meat in his life. His parents ran the first ever vegetarian restaurant in Zurich and so he grew up on these foods and later consciously chose to live like this. His wife had found meat-eating an alien habit ever since she was a little girl. She too became a vegetarian by her own volition as soon as she left home. They wanted to consciously live their every step, every decision, and that is how they came to discover the philosophy of anthroposophy. They dictated nothing—I mean nothing—to me but simply lived an example that I started to largely follow.

My mother-in-law had spent her whole life running a home and looking after children and so as a young "beginner mum", I was happy to have an example before me. They only believed in homeopathic remedies or anthroposophy preparations. I tried more and more as time went by and started to protest if the doctor prescribed antibiotics for the children for every little sniff and sneeze. My mother-in-law told me that while her boys had still been at home they had never taken any antibiotics and absolutely no other chemicals. They treated everything with homeopathic remedies or natural methods. I learned from her to use a vinegar-water foot poultice for fever that was completely successful in every case. I also treated my frequent throat infections with homeopathic medicine and mud packs or poultices. I not only accepted my father-in-law's recommendation but I saw it as the first sign of the help that I had been waiting for.

The private clinic was in Zurichberg, which was a very exclusive district of Zurich. The minute that I stepped into the building, I was greeted by a completely different atmosphere. There was something inexplicable in the air for me. It was a hospital and a clinic but it didn't have that smell! There was a pleasant fragrance of flowers and the walls were painted in delicate pastel shades. There were colourful pictures of flowers on the walls, which I assume were medicinal herbs, and there were fresh flowers all over the place. They even had flowers in the office where I reported when I arrived. The atmosphere was completely unlike that of a standard doctor's waiting room. The kindness that was shown to me was real and completely natural. "Well, I feel really good here! This is exactly what I was thinking of!"

At the same time, I thought that I had to be 33 years old with a serious illness in order to find my way to such a place where, the moment I stepped through the door, everything was for me, for the patient. Then, after the first step, that fear and defencelessness were replaced by a sense of well-being and openness.

Thank God, there are an increasing number of such clinics and doctors nowadays, and since then (1982), I have only ever followed this path.

I was greeted in the surgery by Dr Jenny who was the chief consultant and the director of the clinic. He was a pleasant man in his late forties. I told him about the two diagnoses that I had already received and the immediate surgery that had been recommended as the only option. He listened all the way through without saying a word and then led me into the adjoining room and examined me.

"Yes, Mrs König, the diagnosis made by my two colleagues is correct and the recommended operation is standard in such cases."

I could sense from his words that there was a "but" or an "on the other hand" that would possibly mean another way. "Is there another potential solution, another option?" I asked straight away.

"It very much depends whether the patient is willing to take responsibility for their health and to cooperate fully."

"This is it! This is it! This is exactly what I would like!" shouted the joy within me. This is what I had been looking for and this is what I had been missing in the previous visit at the same time as not knowing that such therapy existed. "Yes, of course," I answered. "But what can I do?"

"Are you able to imagine that you have all the strength in your body that you need in order to be healthy again?"

"Yes, I had thought about this myself," I answered shyly but I knew that I hadn't succeeded. I had done nothing more for three days and three nights other than willing this thing to go away. I wanted to sleep so that I would wake up the following morning with everything gone as if it had all just been a bad dream. But, for some reason, it didn't work even though I badly wanted it to!

Dr Jenny asked me another question: "Can you imagine that an illness is the outer manifestation of inner anxiety, discontent or unhappiness?"

"I don't completely understand! Are you saying that there might be some inner cause of my illness? For such a thing as an ovarian cyst?" ("What do the two have to do with one another?" I thought to myself.)

"My dear Mrs König, I would like to ask you a few personal questions. You don't have to answer, if you don't want to, but I would still like you to give my questions some thought."

"I'm happy to answer!" It is only natural between a doctor and a patient.

"How happy are you with your husband? Has everything that you agreed on and planned happened? Or have certain things happened, changes that you accepted but didn't or couldn't do anything about? How satisfied are you with your sex life? Have there been significant changes or disappointments in this area?"

He wasn't able to continue. The tears were streaming down my face. It was as if my best, most intimate friend had asked me and as if someone had been able to see right into my soul; into my heart. The last years really had brought a lot of changes into my life. No, not because of the children. I didn't only accept the children but I saw them as the best possible chance for me to realize my potential as a woman and a mother. However, I would have liked to do something more than the kitchen and the flat and to be a little free of the children from time to time, if it was for only one day a week. My husband was not only unwilling to help me with this but he was completely unable to understand my needs.

"I am the one who is responsible for the financial well-being of the family and you are the one who is responsible for its internal harmony. I have to concentrate totally on my own career as that is what provides a secure future for my family. I am not only unable to help you but I don't think that it is a good idea that you should yearn to do something other than look after the children, the family and the house. You live in Switzerland now and it is not the done thing for a wife to look for work. People think that she doesn't consider the home (children, family) as important and that she is dissatisfied. They also look disapprovingly on the husband in a way that suggests he isn't able to earn sufficient money to support the family."

I can exactly recall which part of the apartment this conversation took place in and also the fact that I listened to my husband in a state of virtual paralysis and I couldn't, I didn't, want to believe that he was the same person whom I had corresponded with for all those years and who not only shared all my ideas but also agreed with them. I couldn't even speak. It was as if I had been shot. Something had been destroyed. Maybe it was faith and maybe it was understanding. I was so heavily wounded that I wasn't able to talk about it for years. I was ashamed of myself that this was able to happen and I was also ashamed of my husband for what he had done to me and what he had done to himself.

In my sadness and pain, the old vow spoke up once more. "I don't know how, BUT I will show you, despite everything and despite everyone that I am going to do this!" There was another BUT in there as well. And that was that: "After this, perhaps I won't need you! Because you didn't want to help me now. I am going to deal with this on my own! BUT then maybe I will be happy to stay independent."

At the same time, I loved him infinitely and I simply couldn't imagine my life without him but I still recognized my will and my determination. Something broke through or simply broke. I still didn't know.

The first sign of my inner decision was that my children had been attending private school for a year by this time. I was not only unhappy with the "state" kindergarten but I was also unable to accept the effect that it had. Claudi had attended a Montessori play group in StGallen from age three to four-and-a-half. I looked for something similar here now we had moved to Zurich. Claudi was now five and had to attend "state" kindergarten. I would have liked to put little Toncsi into a similar playgroup than the one that Claudi had gone to. It was impossible to find a suitable place. There wasn't a playgroup and kindergarten in one place. I had to rush right across Zurich to one in rush hour and then do the same two or three hours later, while simultaneously taking my other daughter to a kindergarten about the same distance away. I eventually gave in. Claudi went to the kindergarten on her own with her friends from the same street, while I took Toncsi twice a week for three hours to the Montessori playgroup. The difference between the two styles became very apparent within two years. While one still had an authoritarian management and tried to form the future Swiss mummies and daddies, the other provided total freedom for children to express, nurture and protect their own abilities and interests. A few weeks after Claudi started kindergarten, I asked the teacher if she could give me a list of the names and addresses of the children. We had only been living there for six months and Claudi wanted to play with "Pete" or "Julie" or invite them to lunch but I didn't know their surnames or where they lived and so I couldn't talk to their parents. You should have seen the woman's face and eyes. (Only a foreign woman could ask such a thing!—showed the expression on her face.)

"We cannot give out such personal information!" That was the reality in Switzerland in 1979, a few kilometres outside Zurich. I somehow managed to get hold of the details but I still can't forget that incident. In St Gallen, the kindergarten teacher started off by inviting all the children and parents to come in so that they could meet. And she was the one who recommended that they get to know the parents of their friends and their homes as it was important for them to see the differences between families as soon as possible. I thought that this was wonderful and we became close friends with a lot of families. The parents were also glad to get together and we invited each other over in the evenings with children but sometimes without the kids. I am still in touch with people some 25 years later.

I also felt this need for a direct approach in Toncsi's playgroup. At the same time, Claudi's teacher started to complain that my daughter (age five!) was not willing to do as she was told.

"I send the girls to the dolly room to play on their own and she wants to do woodwork with the boys."

"And why can't she do that?" I asked. Again, I met with a condescending look that I already knew! The answer was predictable.

"Because the girls have to play in the dolly room and the boys have to do woodwork."

"Well I have got another idea!" I thought, and I felt sorry for my poor daughter.

My husband reckoned that I was blowing things out of all proportion and that I was sheltering the children. He thought that I raised the children very well but he also thought that they too had to fit into the community and future society. But what kind of society? What kind of community?! (The mother in me was furious and so was the child that I had once been.)

I wanted to give my children as much freedom and as many possibilities as I could to allow them to become whole people. They really did try to raise future wives and mothers at Claudia's kindergarten who, up until 1971, didn't even have the right to vote—and they allowed it to happen. They also raised the wives here who used to have to ask for written permission from their husbands to be able to work, otherwise there wasn't a single company that would have been willing to employ them. I definitely didn't want this as the future for my children and nor was I able to accept it as a self-respecting woman.

I finally made my decision, when at the end of the second year, Claudia's teacher decided to keep her back for another year under her control. "I am going to take my children out of here while they still have their strength and are able to defend themselves". The teacher's official report to the school said that Claudia was still not mature enough to fit in and accept decisions. Thank God!

I went to visit all the kindergartens and schools all over again to try and find one where the children could attend together and where they would receive the kind of direction and support that I wanted them to.

I was lucky to find a private school nearby that not only had the first six grades but also a kindergarten. The school was run by parents and teachers together. Everyone worked together in the children's interest. We did everything ourselves. The parents rented the building; they selected new teachers together with the children and the teachers; it was also their responsibility to clean the school and be on duty in the afternoons. It was a massive burden but we took it on. And then there were the school fees. My husband announced that we didn't have enough money for such things and that we couldn't afford it.

"But it's the children, our children, that we are talking about!" I said outraged.

"I grew up in state kindergarten and state school and you can accept something if you want to. Why should we pay to send her privately when there is a good state school here? Why isn't this good enough for you?"

I was hearing it again and it was unacceptable! He could see the difference between the two kindergartens himself! He saw and enjoyed the openness and friendly approach that he experienced in Toncsi's kindergarten and among the parents there and saw the other version in Claudia's kindergarten.

"You can't protect the children from everything!" I can still hear him say. "We haven't got the money to cover it!"

And the conversation was closed. But not with me! "I'm going to do this!"

The following week, I took my husband to the school that I had chosen. He saw that I had decided and I wouldn't listen to all his negative comments. Now only the question of money was open.

"Believe me, I'll soon be earning enough money to pay for the school!" I said to him now very upset and terribly sad.

Now, sitting in Dr Jenny's room, I was already earning enough for the monthly fees and I would go on to earn much more.

The thoughts continued to race around my head. We left St Gallen after six years which meant me having to give up my girlfriends, while the children had to give up their friends and we had to start again from scratch in Zurich. My husband also went through something of a change. He wanted to continue his studies after receiving his degree and he wanted to make his way to the highest rank in the army. All men have to do national service in Switzerland. This isn't for one or two years but they have to serve for several weeks a year up until age 30. If they have a higher rank, this means that they have to serve at least one month a year. This goes on for decades. My husband was well aware of the fact that, in Switzerland, a higher military rank would mean better job prospects and a chance to earn higher wages. His doctorate would provide him with a higher social rank. I wasn't allowed to have a say in this as he was doing this all for his family and for our joint future. But what really happened?

As a soldier, my husband was not only away from home for another month every year but, in this way, the mandatory period was stretched over years. Getting his doctorate also meant part-time work and part-time pay which meant that we had to keep watching the little money that we had. While we saved every penny and went on camping holidays, our friends had been going on more substantial holidays for years and were able to allow themselves the odd luxury. Next to those who didn't even have children, we looked a bit like little, grey mice.

I felt very odd with all these thoughts and images coming into my mind. Up until now, I had considered myself to be happy and satisfied and that is how I was known to everyone, to my husband, to our friends. Where had these thoughts, these feelings been up to now? I didn't even know of their existence and I couldn't remember them. Things had happened in the last couple of years, but as they were painful they seemed to have disappeared somewhere. But they still had to exist if they were appearing now and I remembered them! Is it possible that is what Dr Jenny meant when he said: "Such feelings and thoughts sicken the body"? This idea was completely new to me at the time but when I went on to read and study (Thorwald Dethlefsen, Rüdiger Dahlke, Karl Simonton, Luise Hay) it turned out to be all too true.

When Dr Jenny asked about a change in our sex life, I was only able to answer with a sad, tearful yes to myself. The husband, who I had adored, loved and found the most attractive both mentally and physically, had started to neglect me. We were unbelievably happy at the beginning as only a man and woman can be truly happy together. We fit together like two halves of the same apple. We were constantly giving pleasure to one another and we were full of surprises for each other. Our spirits found each other and the love of our hearts for each other was endless and our bodies found completion and happiness in one another. And it was this husband, this lover, who concerned himself less and less with me. He was either tired or in a bad mood, and I was already starting to hear that I had exaggerated expectations. What did I expect, ask for, or allege? His closeness, warmth, love and our physical happiness! I no longer expected it after a while. My feelings also started to cool off. It wasn't long before I was no longer in the mood. Dr Jenny was right. The waters had been still here for years. We hardly ever approached one another.

Sometimes, the tears stopped during these reflections, and sometimes started again. I didn't even notice that Dr Jenny placed tissue after tissue in front of me that I took automatically and wiped my face and blew my nose. "But I have ended up in an impossible situation now!" I thought. From the outside, it looked as if everything was fine and despite everything, I now had a dangerous illness. "How can this be helped? Now what can I do?" I asked myself and then I answered Dr Jenny with: "Sure, now I can see all the problems that I didn't consciously notice and it is as if I have swallowed everything and closed it all inside of me."

"At the minute, the most important thing to do is to restore your health. As I have already said, our body has everything within it to win back complete health. Illness is a warning, a sign of the impossible position that the body is in. 'I can't work like this. It is impossible to do what I have to do in these conditions.' This is where we have to help and provide all the support that we can. Could you imagine yourself fasting?"

"Fasting? My poor body is suffering enough as it is!" I answered half laughing and half in disbelief at what I was hearing.

Dr Jenny also told me all about this: "The body uses up a fantastic amount of energy to process food. So a patient is able to help their body by giving it less to process and this leaves it with more energy and strength to overcome the illness. If we are lucky, and this is what I believe, then we will be completely successful and you will be able to fully recover."

"It is like a fairy tale with a happy ending! If this can be done with the body then I am fully committed because I believe in fairy tales after all!" I told the doctor who laughed at my response.

"Good, so now we can prepare the plan for the next two weeks!"

"The battle plan and we set off to fight evil!" I laughed to myself. "Where is my fear of yesterday and my helplessness? Where is the superior behaviour of that other doctor? And what has happened to the 'only option' operation?"

I was happy and grateful to my father-in-law! I still feel gratitude towards him as I write these words and I thank him with all my heart. He is now enjoying happiness on the other side but I am sure that he can hear me from there and can sense my love, thanks and gratitude.

"Fasting also helps to cleanse the body and to expel all impurities. Having a cyst, this should be of great help to you. If you can manage to eat only raw vegetables and fruit with plenty of liquid and avoid salt and seasoning for a period of two weeks, then you should be able to achieve very positive results in a relatively short period of time. I can strongly recommend Biotta juices that are pure, biologically natural, vegetable and fruit juices.

"Yes, I have never done anything like it before but I can imagine it."

"It would be good if you could buy pineapple and papaya as they help to remove excess moisture."

I was given pineapple and papaya enzymes that would help to strengthen the whole process.

"I'm starting to feel more and more that this is going to work!" Dr Jenny said as we parted. He said that I should come and see him again in another week.

I smiled and thanked him again for his help thus far and for the massive amount of new information. I only wanted to deal with the thoughts that I was having and that were causing so much fear, once I was fully recovered. "I will do absolutely everything that I can!" I decided. The doctor not only helped in identifying the source of the problem but also believed in me and in the possibility of my recovery. I was beginning to think that this wasn't just about clearing up my cyst and restoring my health but that my self-healing had begun.

I hoped. I really hoped! I wanted to succeed again and I had the tools and the help at my disposal to do so!

Back home, I told my husband and his parents, over the phone, about my experience at the clinic and the diet that Dr Jenny had recommended. I only told my husband the most important parts but I hoped that I would soon have the chance to discuss my complaints, problems and thoughts that had come to light at the clinic so we could again begin to tread the same path.

My mother-in-law told me that she had asked an acquaintance of hers, a Mrs Steiner, who worked with sole reflexology, whether or not she would be able to help me in some way or give some ideas on recovery. Mrs Steiner had been practising this type of therapy for years and recommended that I should try to find a reflexologist nearby as soon as possible. None of her patients had ever needed an operation for a cyst. Massage could help on the way to full recovery.

I was happy to take her advice and I wanted very much to believe what she said. I had heard a lot about Mrs Steiner but I still hadn't met her in person. This woman went on to play a very important part in my life and in my personal growth later on.

I couldn't go and see her now as it was a long train trip to her place and she said that I would have to go several times during the first week at the beginning of the massage course. I found an older lady who lived a lot closer with the help of one of my girlfriends and I made an appointment with her. I wanted to make the most of every possibility, and all the help that I could, in the hope of achieving total success.

A diet of a small amount of raw food and liquids that the doctor had recommended didn't cause any major problem. The only exception that I made was that I didn't give up my morning cup of milky coffee. I found it hard to wake up in the morning without it. I enjoyed fasting with only the light diet of raw vegetables and liquids. This regime was more and more enjoyable because I felt healthier and stronger every day. My husband even managed to get hold of papaya somewhere in town. It was very expensive but money wasn't an issue now. I ate one or two of these every day with half a pineapple.

It was about three days after the examination that I went for my very first sole reflexology massage. It was excruciatingly painful. The woman worked according to the old school of reflexology and applied pressure with her thumb bone, a hard cork and even a metal tool. They don't do this any longer but apply slow deep pressure for longer periods instead of this painful and strong pressure. The whole of my foot was throbbing but I could feel stabbing pain in one particular place. She could hardly touch the soft place under my right ankle bone and I had already snatched my foot away from the lady's lap who was working in front of me sitting on a chair. The pain was terrible. It subsided when she released the pressure.

"The pressure hurts everywhere but the pain is virtually unbearable under my right ankle bone. Please be very careful around that area!" I asked the woman. "You are feeling it very well and reacting very well to the massage!" she said. I didn't really understand, didn't really know what she meant when she said this. "Where you feel the shooting pain is your right ovary. Being as there is a problem there then that is where the pain is particularly strong."

I would have liked to say that it was fine and that she should please keep pressing or to press even harder but that would have been impossible. I could hardly wait for the treatment to come to an end because I could hardly stand the pain. Following the first massage, I said to myself that I was definitely not going back there again. It might well have helped but it hurt so much that I was sure that I wouldn't be able to stand it a second time. I still went two days later as we had discussed. It didn't hurt so much the second time and I even had enough strength to ask a couple of questions about how this method worked.

The elderly lady explained that each part of our body and every organ can be found on the soles of our feet as a larger or smaller area or a precise point. The massage and pressure applied initiates a certain reflex in the given organ giving it more energy as well as accelerating excretion and cleansing. This relieves headaches, migraine and sore throats. It is able to cleanse the liver and the kidneys and even dissolve or push out stones. It also provides a lot of help to the accelerated healing of hand, leg and spine injuries. In my case, the self-cleansing and destruction of the cyst could be aided via the activation of certain points.

I was feeling much better after a week and I stopped taking painkillers after the first day. I drank a lot of fruit and vegetable juice and I would munch on the odd cucumber or carrot during the day. I felt neither hungry nor tired. I felt quite invigorated and I perhaps didn't need my milky coffee in the morning but I am afraid I couldn't give up this little "bad habit".

I was full of curiosity as I made my way to Dr Jenny's for the appointed time. He did another ultrasound and asked me how I felt. "Congratulations, everything has gone as I would have hoped!" he said after examining me. "The cyst has shrivelled from 7 cm to 2 cm. Carry on like this and we will have won the battle Mrs König!"

The news made me very happy. Being as he also thought that foot massage was good, I did everything the same again the following week as I had done previously. By the fourth visit the massage caused me hardly any pain at all. The abdominal pains were now no more than a bad memory and had disappeared completely.

My visits to Dr Jenny, the two-week fast, the enzymes and the four reflexology massages had brought great results.

"Mrs König, complete success! There is no sign of the cyst! You have managed to cooperate fantastically with your body! It has done the absolute most. You wanted to be healthy again and that is what you have become! You should continue to pay close attention to yourself because what has just happened to you was very meaningful in your life. You have managed complete self-healing instead of an operation. Your strong will and determination has achieved the desired result and restored you to full health. All I can do is to congratulate you!" and he offered his hand in farewell. "I have won! We have won!" I congratulated myself and I thought lovingly of my body that had warned me that I hadn't been paying enough attention to those events that were happening to me and around me. I accepted the advice and I said "YES" not only to health but also to rediscovering myself.

I had to experience through pain that the help I had given to the others, nurturing and supporting my husband and my family had made me forget to pay attention to myself and my own wishes, desires and plans and to consider these as being equal to those of the others.

"YES, from now on in I am going to try and live by this lesson!" I said to myself.

3

The Gates of Mystery
Begin to Open

I was not the only one delighted by my sudden recovery. My family were also naturally very happy. Instead of an operation, recovering for weeks and months, scars from surgery and stitches, I had been completely cured. And all this in under two weeks!

These experiences initiated a great deal of thought inside me. In the depths of my consciousness, my thoughts were still revolving around the possible causes of my illness. This made me feel very strange at the beginning and called for peace and quiet. I waited for the best time to be able to discuss all of this with my husband. But what occupied me most of all next to this was my body and the secrets and possibilities that it held within.

I had already heard from Dr Jenny that inner tension and hurt shows itself in the body in the form of illness but I wanted to know more about this. The other thing that aroused my interest was the reflexology of the sole. The pain that appeared along with the illness and confusion, passed with its healing. After living through this and experiencing the result, I often wondered how it works and whether it is really possible to achieve such results with anybody. As a modern person, I didn't think about my body but I took it for granted that it worked and that it worked well. But I had no idea at all about how it worked. I had long since forgotten what I had learned in school but what Dr Jenny said was totally new to me and this is what I most wanted to get to know for myself.

I was only interested in the exercises in yoga and not what had an effect on my organs and how. I had practised yoga intensively since I was student. Then I saw a book by Yesudian entitled "Sport and Yoga". It had been published before Communism. The front-cover image of the Indian man wearing a turban mysteriously attracted me, not just because since I was a little child I adored magicians, especially the ones who wear turbans. They appeared in the circus in Budapest, where my poor father had to take me every month on his visits to Budapest. The programme was always the same: zoo, lunch at Gundel and in its garden in the summer (back then everything was affordable to mere mortals), afterwards the circus and the day finished off in the illuminated amusement park.

They said that the Indian magicians were illusionists. Even the word insulted me. They were magicians. I felt sorry for the adults and the critical children for not being able to believe in this.

Yesudian was not a magician but he knew what to do with his body. My friend had the book in his hand and he let me leaf through the pages. I had the feeling that I was browsing through my own memories, times long passed. When I gave the book back I said, "Interesting, I know the exercises!"

My friend said that this was impossible because they were not taught in Budapest.

"Somehow or other, I still know them and I can do them as well."

The boy didn't believe me, "Well show me then!"

We were just about to go somewhere, so I couldn't sit down to show some of the more complicated positions. Instead, I lifted up my pullover and started to move my stomach muscles to the left and right and up and down. Then I started to separate the muscles and I did this with just the left or the right side.

This exercise looks horrific if you have never seen it before. My friend looked similarly horrified: "That's the *nauli,* one of the hardest exercises to learn! How are you able to this if you have never studied it?"

"I don't know either," I responded.

I couldn't have known this then but this was the exercise that I practised a lot. It was one of the reasons that I had such a flat and muscular stomach. I liked to shock the others at school with this in the changing rooms after the PE lesson. The other exercise that no one else could do was to dislocate their shoulders. These exercises were enjoyable for me and the horror on the faces of the others was entertaining. We had to wear a pinafore at school. This also had a belt. I was often bored in lessons so I would sometimes take my belt off and fasten it to about shoulder width then, holding one end in each hand, I'd bring my arms forwards or backwards over my head. This was always greeted with astonishment in the classroom and the teacher couldn't see a thing when she turned back from the blackboard.

No, I didn't really like school at all. I only wanted to be taught history, languages and especially PE. I was also happy to have ended up in a class that was evaluated four times a year by the College of Physical Education and compared to another parallel class. We had four PE lessons a week and they had two. They wanted to know whether more physical exercise led to better results in academic studies. But they monitored us from a sport and health point of view as well. I don't know what the result of the statistical measurement was but I was able to enjoy more exercise and challenges in those four years. I was among the best in almost all of the exercises. The only thing that I didn't like was the long-distance running. But no one beat me at the short distances.

This had made me very curious about the possibilities offered by more conscious cooperation with my body. The idea of being able to offer more and better to my family with this knowledge really sparked my imagination. The children always had some problem or other besides the typical childhood illnesses: sore throats, stomach aches. My husband was also tortured by awful recurring migraines, tiredness and backache. Perhaps I would be able to do something for them with the help of reflexology points or maybe I could even make these recurring weaknesses disappear. Perhaps it would be possible to strengthen their weaker points or discover the reason for these complaints in the same way as I had heard from Dr Jenny and that I had experienced myself.

I knew from my mother-in-law, who reported to Mrs Steiner on my swift recovery, that she was going to be holding classes in the autumn and starting a reflexology group. She had studied with Hanna Marguardt, the most famous teacher of the period, who was responsible for sole reflexology becoming widely known and accepted. I registered immediately and took my old friend, Judit, along with me whom I knew from St Gallen. They had moved to Zurich at about the same time as us, and I was able to keep our relationship going. Judit's children, a boy and a girl, were about the same age as ours. She was my best girlfriend back then, perhaps because she was also Hungarian. She was the first one whom I was able to tell about those frightening memories that emerged from my subconscious and that had come upon me so unexpectedly with Dr Jenny, during the course of my illness. I started to uncover the hidden-away, painful experiences of the last years of my marriage. Judit was also often ill and her marriage had really run aground. With the little knowledge that we had quickly acquired from the books, which we had read, we were looking for the answers to these problems and illnesses. So, when I mentioned Mrs Steiner's course to Judit, she was happy to come along with me.

The figure of Mrs Steiner, despite the fact that I didn't know her, had intrigued me since my arrival in Switzerland. Her name and events connected to her had often been mentioned in my father-in-law's home. I had got to know her two daughters in the first summer who had been in their teens back then. They were holidaying at my father-in-law's as their mother was on a course. My mother-in-law and Mrs Steiner had met in Interlaken. I had known of Interlaken since our wedding and I knew that my husband and his older brother had attended high school there. And that the whole family had moved to this larger town for a couple of years to save the boys from making the long train journey and so that they could spend their free time with their school mates. The Steiners were their neighbours.

Mrs Steiner had trained to be a nurse before she had married when she had worked in a hospital. After she married the local forester, she had done as all other Swiss housewives and stayed at home and raised their four children. Her marriage was not a happy one. Despite the four children, she decided to get a divorce and start to work again. My mother-in-law helped out as best she could from the very beginning. I only heard words of sympathy for "poor Little Mrs Forester". They didn't call her Mrs Steiner in my family but "little Mrs Forester". Not "Mrs Forester" but "little Mrs Forester". Being referred to as 'little' and by the name, which she had been given due to her husband's work, I gathered that they were talking about a poor woman with four children whom they felt terribly sorry for along with her family, and that she was now in need of help. My mother-in-law, who was secure with her husband and family, was able to do this from the heart. Besides, I also heard that this Little Mrs Forester was studying some kind of hocus-pocus, some kind of sole massage, even though she had a good job at the hospital. Later on, I heard that she had given up her job and opened an independent practice. Besides working and bringing up four children, she also studied and was striving to be fully independent.

For years after the divorce, she was still only referred to as Little Mrs Forester while the sole massage was held to be an unbelievable, if not laughable, method of aiding cures from the very beginning. In time, it became obvious that her earlier nickname had been replaced by Mrs Steiner. Her reputation meant that even my parents-in-law asked for her advice in my case. Mrs Steiner appeared very appealing to me based on what I had heard. A determined woman who was not willing for anything to be done to her against her will. She took responsibility for her own life, her own decisions and consciously dealt with their consequences.

As I had only heard about her at my parents-in-law's house, I inadvertently started to compare the two of them: my mother-in-law and Mrs Steiner. Even though Mrs Steiner was a couple of years younger than my mother-in-law, what she took on and went through was not common in Swiss families. I liked my mother-in-law from the start and I looked for opportunities to learn from her. Now, however, I started to look critically at her example as a Swiss housewife. I had held this as an ideal and had wanted to change accordingly.

My mother-in-law lived totally dependent on her husband. At that time (1970–1980) Swiss wives not only didn't have their own money but they had to account for the housekeeping money that they had been given. My father-in-law decided everything. He decided what and what not to buy, where they went on holiday ... As he was the breadwinner, he was the only one with the right to decide, the only one whose word counted in the family. As the years passed, I was able increasingly to gain a better insight into the lives of the family members. What I unknowingly set as my example at the outset slowly became a warning. Be careful not to depend so heavily on your husband and his decisions! I paid an increasing amount of attention to this after my illness and my miraculous recovery.

The opportunity to meet Mrs Steiner in person made me a little curious and I was slightly in awe after all that I had heard about her. She knew, had experienced and now taught those secrets of the body and indicated the emotions that expressed them. It was these self-same emotions that had started to pulsate in my body emerging as a result not only of the illness but mainly because of Dr Jenny's knowledge and questions. So, it was with curiosity and a slight sense of trepidation that Judit and I set off to go on our first course. The course was not in Switzerland but in Germany at a site specially selected by Mrs Steiner, in a social home just outside Heidelberg.

Judit and I had lots to discuss on the way and so we hardly noticed the journey at all. I was interested to see Heidelberg as it is one of the oldest university towns that many famous figures have passed through. I like the atmosphere of such places and I felt that all the energy that had collected over 100s of years could be felt today and breathed in. I not only admire the great heroes, although ever since I was a child I have looked up to them as my examples, but also those with a lot of knowledge: the philosophers, masters of thought and theory. I hoped that I would have enough time to visit the ancient town at the end of the course and to make my way straight to the street where real wise men had once walked.

First of all, we had to find the place where the course was to be held, which was not easy as the home was in open countryside on the edge of the town. We already knew that we were looking for a home that had been founded for the rehabilitation of psychologically damaged women. They used work therapy in their cure. The residents were given various domestic tasks to carry out which meant that they didn't just help clean the house and keep things in order but they were also given jobs to do in the kitchen. They not only tended the garden but they really nurtured it and they produced the vegetables and plants in the garden that were used in the kitchen. The house looked down the valley from a high vantage point. We later found out that a convent had once stood on this spot for many 100s of years. You could still see several ruins of walls in the outer garden. I found the garden especially beautiful and inviting for walks and relaxation.

Everything was new on the course as was the fact that I was going to be together with people that I didn't know for days on end. I was happy about the twin-bed room that I shared with Judit and even more so because there were some who had to sleep in rooms with four or five others. It was now that I realized that, although I had been living in Switzerland for nine years, I had never been alone. There was always someone by my side from the family: either Christian or the children. Of course, I am not talking about the odd couple of hours spent on my own. The other unusual thing was that, during the workshops, we sat on the floor and worked there for hours at a time.

Mrs Steiner greeted me warmly as she had also heard a lot about me. She was especially happy that I had been cured of my dangerous illness in such a short time by virtually miraculous means. She introduced her daughter who would be assisting her on the course. I only remembered her as a kid in her teens and now I saw her as a serious young woman who was also involved with therapy. "Another fine example", I thought but I looked on her more from the point of view of a mother.

The course began in the evening and when everyone had arrived, we all sat down on the floor. Mrs Steiner placed a candle and a crystal at the centre of the circle. I didn't know what to think of the candle but it remained at the centre of the circle at all times of the day. I came to find out from the introduction that the candle was a symbol of eternal light, eternal knowledge. The crystal also served as a symbol: it was a mountain crystal that broke through all darkness with its purity and its strength. These ideas of Mrs Steiner were all new to me. Though I examined everything with my logic, perhaps I understood it with another part of my consciousness or perhaps I sensed it.

The candlelight had a very strong effect on me. Sometimes, when I stared into the flame for a long time, the world began to change. At first my teacher's voice seemed to come from further and further away and then the members of the group moved away from me but if I blinked, they were all back in their places again. I didn't do this consciously as all my attention was centred on learning and observing Mrs Steiner's work. The group of 15 to 20 only included one man. Judit and I, with the exception of the teacher's daughter, were the youngest ones there.

Although Mrs Steiner explained everything, she saw the purpose of learning as the successful application of knowledge. She said that the material that we had to get through, the knowledge of the points on the sole of the foot, was so vast that perhaps it was better for us to learn how to feel for ourselves first. We looked at the soles of everyone's feet one by one. At the beginning, our teacher pointed out obvious, unusual features that we should note but as time went by she asked us to try out our basic knowledge to recognize the various mounds, obvious alterations in colour or perhaps the reasons for the differences between the two soles. I liked this; I liked it more and more!

On the second day, we each treated an individual for various intervals. It was true that we were able to feel something from the very first touch. This might have meant the way that someone offered me their foot, whether they trusted me or whether they were afraid of every touch. It was also very important if the foot was dry or not or drops of sweat started to appear as that also showed the state of the nervous system.

I was happy to hold the foot in my hand that I was working on at the time. It became obvious that I didn't consider its owner as a stranger any longer. The fact that she was willing to show me the sole of her foot, that we had already studied, which hid her past, emotions and illnesses, meant that she was growing closer to me. I started to get to like everyone in the group through the soles of their feet. No one was a stranger any longer. A sort of family feeling started to form inside me when I thought of the group. The beautiful feet were of less interest to me as they show much less. The more deformed someone's foot was, the greater the empathy with which I held it in my hands and stroked it and massaged it.

The days flew by and we took a short house exam on the last day. Since we knew each other's soles quite well by now, Mrs Steiner brought a new woman with her after lunch from among the people living in the house. She told us to examine the soles of her feet and to try and jointly ascertain the illness and the change. We all sat around the woman's feet with excitement and outbid one another with our observations.

We found the woman's soles very interesting; they had something in them, or rather missing from them, that we hadn't come across before. A line appeared. It was a dividing line perhaps that separated one part from another. It was also interesting for me to handle the feet of the woman who was lying down. I felt as if there was only a very small amount of energy in them or that I couldn't feel the energy.

Our teacher was very satisfied with all that we had sensed and noticed. She said that the dividing line was the most important and that we would need to work on that. The woman neither agreed nor resisted. She just lay there with her eyes closed and listened to what we or Mrs Steiner had to say about her or rather the soles of her feet.

Mrs Steiner told us that the dividing line referred to the division between the upper and lower body and that we should first try to solve this using other methods. First of all, we should try to join up the separated parts of the body: the upper with the lower and the left with the right. This can be helped best with polarization. She said that she needed help to do this from more than one point of view. She told us sit around Klára (that was the woman's name) and that we should all try to concentrate on our heart and on our love. She asked me and her daughter to sit opposite one another to the left and the right of Klára. I thought that she had chosen me because she knew my mother-in-law, although I had realized as the days passed that many of the participants had known her for years either as patients or as interested learners.

Mrs Steiner sat above Klára's head and she placed her hands on the right and left sides of Klára's head. She told us that now she was going to work on the possible conscious divisions within her on the two hemispheres of her brain. It was a little bit too much for me to understand and to see quite what it was that consciously divided the brain that we had seen on the sole of her foot but I was all ears just the same. I waited curiously to see what it was that the daughter and I had to do as we weren't sitting by the soles of her feet but by her upper body. Mrs Steiner asked me to place my left hand on Klára's left shoulder and my right hand on her stomach at about hip height. She asked her daughter to do exactly the opposite, doing whatever I had done with the left with the right and vice versa. This meant that Klára's shoulder was linked to her hip and her right side was linked to her left by the cross that our hands had formed. Mrs Steiner now held Klára's head again on both sides. They closed their eyes and I did the same as I thought it might help me to better feel what there was to feel.

4

I Don't Want to Know Anything About This Ever Again!

What I had felt up until now, when I had held Klára's feet, was only strengthened when I touched her shoulders and especially her lower abdomen. There was virtually no energy in her at all. It was as if she was nearly dead. Despite all this, she must have been around 30 years old and there were no external signs indicating this energy deficiency.

Feelings of empathy, sadness and love ran through my body. I would have so much liked to help her, to relieve her condition. I involuntarily uttered something that went on to have unalterable consequences: **"My God, if I were able to, I would do all that I could to help this woman!"**

In response to my call, a gate opened whose existence I had never as much suspected as to say nothing of what lay hidden beyond. My hand, which lay on Klára's stomach next to her hip bone, began to sink. It was a most inexplicable sensation, as if something were pulling at it. I wasn't able to do anything to resist it at the same time as my brain, my educated mind, said, "No, no. This isn't possible; your hand can't simply enter the body of another person!"

My hand continued to sink further and further until it stopped in some sort of black goo. A chill still runs down my spine as I write these words but it is impossible to express the feeling I had that day. A part of me thought that this black goo seemed to have drawn my hand towards itself. The other part of me thought that the whole thing was impossible and decided that there was no such thing.

The first, the awakening, inner sensation took control. Perhaps it was stronger or maybe it knew more. Touching this black energy was a ghastly sensation especially as I wanted to pull my hand out from where it was. I wanted to lift it out of the black mass but it didn't want to release my hand from its grip. I was very frightened. "I have to pull my hand out of here!" I thought, and I put all my energy into releasing my hand. The struggle consumed the most incredible amount of energy. My hands trembled and I could feel that not only my face but my whole body was drenched in perspiration. But my hand, thank God, began to move. But what was it bringing with it? I was taken aback by the sight of the black goo that I saw on the palm of my hand. "What the heck!" I thought. "With it or without it, I have to pull my hand out of here!" The goo came out in long black strands stuck to the palm of my hand. Finally, with one last determined tug my hand was out of Klára's body but it had this disgusting, foul filth on it.

I became aware of being surrounded by silence, the problem of my hand went away and I spontaneously opened my eyes. There was a group sitting around me and Klára was lying in front of me from whose body I had just managed to pull out my hand. "But that's impossible!" shouted another consciousness within me. My eyes were open and I looked at my hand that was shaking. I was shaking; every bone in my body was shaking. The sweat was even dripping from my forehead. On my hand, although I could no longer see it, I could feel the black slime hanging from me in strands. I looked at Mrs Steiner in alarm for assurance that I had fallen asleep and that this had all been a dream or who knows what. What I really wanted was to find out how to get this disgusting black stuff off my hand. The way that Mrs Steiner looked at me said it all. I can still hear her words.

"Go to the tap and wash your hand under the cold running water and wash off everything that is stuck to it."

"Could she have seen it? Had she seen it as well? But how could she have seen it? None of this is important now," I thought, "just that I get this black mess off my hand." I stood up and realized that

I could hardly walk. I was completely exhausted after what I had done.

The group sat in silence looking on in awe. What was it that they had seen? Had their eyes really seen that I had been shaking and perspiring the whole time? No matter, my hand was clean at last.

I sat back in my place to the right of Klára but Mrs Steiner asked that I lie on the floor and that I should call for the Earth's energy to take everything, which wasn't mine, and I had taken to help someone else.

What was she saying? It was impossible to understand precisely. But she went on. "And you, Dori (that is what my family called me), let everything go and give thanks in your mind that all of this was able to happen."

Now, I was slowly starting to have enough of all of this! I should give thanks for the fact that this blackness had drawn me to itself and then stuck to me? Or perhaps I should give thanks for the fact that I had to pull out a good 15 kg of black strands from Klára's stomach? Or maybe because every bone in my body was trembling and my clothes were stuck to me with sweat? I was ready to pass out from the exhaustion.

Still I thought that perhaps Mrs Steiner knew better! I did as she asked. I tried to let go of everything that didn't belong to me and that I had only taken over so that it might disappear from somewhere else. I even gave thanks that I had been able to help! It was then that I realized that I had prayed to be able to help! However, not in my wildest dreams had I ever suspected that my first ever prayer would lead to such unimaginable events.

Meanwhile, I could hear Mrs Steiner as she informed the group as to what had happened, or what could have happened here. She, herself, didn't know the reason, but it would appear that I had been able to solve Klára's problem. It was then that she addressed the reclining woman for the first time and asked her whether or not she felt anything or whether she felt any better. Klára gave a quiet and very faint, "Yes." And with tears in her eyes, all that Mrs Steiner added was: "Something has happened that I could only ever have hoped for. Klára hasn't spoken for more than 16 years."

I didn't know whether or not I had heard well what she had said or whether I should cover my ears with my hands. My mind, my consciousness, split completely in two. One half had experienced, done and accepted everything, while another half saw this all as impossible, unimaginable and a bad dream.

Klára, on the other hand, had spoken for the first time in 16 years! Have I got anything to do with this? This was precisely what I didn't want to know anything about! An elusive part of me protested, "No, no, I don't want to know anything about this!" I wanted more than anything else to run away from it all and to be left with all these terrible things, nightmares. "I have nothing at all to do with any of this!"

I was lying on the floor as I listened to Mrs Steiner, while she told us all Klára's story as she had heard it from the director of the home. Klára had been living there for years in this psychiatric home. No one knew exactly what could have happened to her. She had been a completely healthy and happy girl until age 16. It was after returning home one Saturday night that her parents and those around her realized that she had begun to change and to shut herself off. She spent less and less time with the others and in the end she stopped speaking altogether. Her parents tried everything but they ran up against a wall. Everyone thought that she looked alive on the outside but that she was dying on the inside. All the specialists suspected some kind of attack and most probably rape. Klára closed herself up after this terrible experience and wasn't willing to live on the outside or take part in outside life.

And now she had spoken for the first time in 16 years! This was more, much more than I was able to deal with or handle. Thankfully, no one asked me anything for I would have been unable to and didn't want to answer. Luckily, the course had come to an end. We could go home the following morning! All I could say to Judit when I got back to the room was: "Something terrible has happened, Judit. I can't tell you and it is impossible to talk about it. Please don't discuss this with anyone and I want to forget all about it just as quickly as I can. I don't want to be involved with anything like this ever again! I have decided! I am never going to touch a stranger's body again! I shouldn't touch them because something starts happening!"

Judit saw what sort of state I was in and she didn't ask anything. That's how we went to bed that night.

All that I wanted to do was to sleep and to forget everything. I locked everything that had happened on the Heidelberg course, and especially the events of the last evening in a little cupboard and I threw the key into the ocean, as far as I could. For ever!

I got home the next day and hugged my little family as perhaps never before. I was at home at last in a reality that is understandable, controllable and acceptable.

I didn't say a word to a soul and especially not to my husband and, thank God, with a conscious effort, I started to forget what had happened to me in Heidelberg in the autumn of 1982.

Perhaps I had just imagined it or the whole thing had been a bad dream?!

5

Illuminating
Hands in the Night

Two years later, by 1984, it actually seemed as if I had managed to forget all about the things that had gone on in Heidelberg. I didn't remember anything at all. I had managed to throw the key so far away as never to open up that cupboard again—it contained such unbelievable, terrible and inexplicable things. My mind works just like anyone else's. I tried to push everything out of sight, which I didn't understand, if it was was painful or had caused any disappointment. Psychologists say that a child would not even make his fifth birthday were it not for the subconscious where we are able to bundle everything away that our little selves cannot deal with, otherwise we would die from the pain and disappointment. The dream with which we came to the Earth has become a completely different reality. We would never be able to cope with it, if not for the cave of our subconscious. And then when we get older!

But let's take an honest look at this: do we take pleasure in retrieving the unpleasant, understanding, cleaning and integrating it into our—now conscious—lives? No, and this is yet another conscious, habitual human quality. And still the higher consciousness desires something else; moreover, if we cannot respond to its fine signs, then it calls our attention to the task in hand and the work to be done with more obvious signals. Such warnings come in the form of illness as well as sudden tragedies in our lives. At times like these, we are forced to come to a standstill and we are often completely unable to move from the shock. At times like these, consciousness makes the most of a break in our defences; it puts something in front of us that we have to deal with but often we don't even bother with it. I had been given such a warning in the form of the illness that I had three years before, and my sudden recovery. It was then that I had sworn not to wait for my husband's help whether he thought that this was a good idea or not, and that I would accomplish the things that were necessary for me. I have to deal with things that are of great importance to me, otherwise my spirit—through my body—will confront me with new difficulties. This will force me to stop on the path, which takes me in another direction to the one that I would choose, and that I have to take.

By 1984, I was feeling satisfied. I had already managed to deal with a lot of the things that I had wanted to. The children were now in state school after three years in private education, yet that had been enough for them, similar to me, to gain strength and to be able to defend themselves against what they thought was not right. Even 20 years on, my daughters still recall the school and the years they spent at the school that was run by parents and teachers as some of the happiest days of their lives. Back then, the seven-year-old school girl went to school every morning with her little sister who was still in kindergarten. They were both proud of one another, and I was also terribly proud of my children as they grew more independent by the day. All the other mothers dashed to and fro taking their children to and from the kindergarten. At that time, school lasted for the whole day in all of Switzerland and most large towns. The children were allowed to go home during the lunch break but the classes started at different times, depending on the class that the children were in. There were a lot of children in many of the classes and so half attended school from 8 to 10 am and the other half from 10 am to 12 noon. Then the next week it was the other way around. They all had to go back to school for 2 pm and classes lasted until 4 or 5 pm. The kindergarten kids attended from 9 to 11 am and from 2 to 4 pm. This meant that if a mother had two, three, four or five children then she was constantly standing either at the window or the door. From here, she was able to check and make sure that they had all arrived safely home. Then she was able to give them her undivided attention before making sure that they set off and reached school again in good time and came safely home again. When my older child, who had classes from 8 am to 12 noon, eventually came home at 12.30 pm, I had to start making lunch right away—I had to start the little gang back off in the direction of school at 1.30 pm. They only had Wednesday afternoons free. They even had to go to school on Saturday mornings. It makes you dizzy to imagine the frantic comings and goings to say nothing of making sense of the whole thing. Of course, the mother didn't only have to run the housekeeping at the same time, with endless tidying, washing and ironing, but also had to do the shopping and make sure that lunch was on the table in time. If a mother had to look after her sick child—or more than one if she had a large family—and there was an epidemic, then the burden that she faced was simply unimaginable. (I am only talking about Switzerland here because that is what I was going through at that time. I write about all of this in full knowledge of the fact that it was even harder for some women in other parts of the world and that would fill the pages of a very thick book indeed.)

God forbid that the mother herself should get ill because then the machine came to an abrupt standstill. Suddenly, it became obvious that Swiss mums did everything and with no recognition whatsoever. They did have the right to vote by this time but all this work was seen as natural despite the fact that they received no financial recognition for it. "They are just at home, they don't work!" is what everyone used to say. Only those who earned money were valued.

I would have liked to help other mothers as well as myself as my situation meant that I was more than able to know what they were going through. Plus, a growing number of people who were willing to talk about this.

They consumed the most unbelievable amount of coffee, alcohol, uppers, downers and sleeping tablets. More and more women whom I knew were becoming seriously ill. It started with many of them with their ovaries which were operated on as a matter of fact. Then, when they started to have problems with their uterus, they were sent for that to be "unpacked" as they had no further use for all the "childbirth machinery" or at least that is what they were told by their doctors. I knew mums who were through with the whole series of operations before they had reached their 40th birthday. I guess they must have been relatively happy too as then they were able to hire a nurse from the county and this was all paid for by their national insurance. These were unconscious opportunities for escape, however, they still became entrenched. They all talked about their illnesses as if they were a completely normal part of life. My sudden recovery was regarded as accidental and more of the exception that proves the rule.

I started to organize cooking lunch together with the other mums in our street. This meant that my children ate lunch with another family once or maybe twice a week and then I had a couple of hours to myself. Then the other mothers had a break when I cooked for a group of children. It was all the same for me to cook for four kids instead of two, and I was all too happy to do so as they enjoyed the company and I really looked forward to my next day off.

All the mums used to chat a lot together and we soon formed ourselves into a small group. There were ten of us who met once a week and we really wanted to do something to change the timetabling system at the school and the kindergarten as it was really very difficult for us all. Many of us had college degrees. There was an economist, a lawyer and another had teaching qualifications. So, everyone freely contributed their knowledge and time. "Blockzeit Schule" (modular school) was the name that we gave to our club. We worked out a system whereby all the children could go to school at the same time and where the younger children and those still in kindergarten only had to attend in the mornings. This meant that the mums and the kids would have more free time and the whole family could organize things to do together on free Saturdays as the dads didn't have to work weekends. It seemed like an illusion 20 years ago but thankfully it's a reality today in most Swiss towns and counties. We were the housewives who were the pioneers and we hoped that we would start people thinking differently, even if we didn't manage a complete change in the system. We wanted to lay the foundation of new possibilities for the next generation of young mothers and we especially wanted to prepare something important for our growing daughters.

I also took part in the "Family Club" where I initiated a second-hand shop for children's clothes. The others didn't believe in it because we lived in one of the wealthiest towns in Switzerland. It is true that there were a lot of rich people, even millionaires, living here due to the favourable tax situation that varied from town to town and one county to the next. But we lived here as well along with a lot of other families who whose financial situations weren't all rosy. Skiing holidays were expensive for us as well, especially because the children were growing so quickly and we needed to buy new ski suits and poles every year. We were able to donate the old ones to a charity that sold them on again for a small fee. My idea was to be able to swap the ski suits and sports equipment, that had sometimes been used for no more than a couple of weeks, for larger size. I tried this out once in the "Family Club" to see whether it would work in reality and thejumble sale-style affair was a great success. This led to the county giving me premises where we held a jumble sale once and then twice a week. It worked simply: the mums arrived with outgrown clothes and agreed how much they wanted to sell them for, and then I added on 10 or 20 % to cover the overheads and my meagre wage. The next mum was over the moon to be able to pick up a pair of skis or an item of clothing for half or even a quarter of what she would have paid in the shops. The jumble sale is still going today and is being run by what must be about the fourth mum.

Later I started something else going with another mum and we managed to make it work: we took charge of the traffic control in our street. We lived in a cul-de-sac on the edge of a forest in completely idyllic surroundings. My husband and I did our best to provide somewhere in the country with good air, out of the town for the children. It was much the same with our first apartment that was four or five kilometres out of Zurich. But still the street held hidden dangers. There were tall, modern buildings on either side of the street surrounded by trees and pretty parks with a good few playgrounds. The fact that there was no through traffic in the day meant that the children ran back and forth across the road all day from one playground to another and didn't give a thought to any danger. The real traffic started to appear around 4 pm which is exactly when the little kids started to get home from kindergarten and primary school. This is when the first dads started to get home from work and the single people in the area also started to arrive home in their fast cars. They didn't give a second thought to the children playing in the area. I soon found out about a little boy who lived a few houses down—he was confined to a wheelchair for life after running out in front of a car arriving home on his way back from the playground. All the mums were interested in the best way to reduce the risk. It was just before the county elections. One of the parties soon took up our cause and made slowing down the traffic part of their campaign—they even wanted to establish "play streets". Along with the other mums, we delivered questionnaires to every household and we outlined the advantages of our proposals to every single resident (slower traffic, less noise, less exhaust fumes and mainly the safety of our children). We ran into a lot of difficulty with some of the older residents but we won in the end. All the streets that were selected back then are still enjoying calmer, safer traffic some 20 years later.

I like to find energy and time for such matters and I asked my husband to help me. He wasn't able to support me because he was so involved with his work and with moving onward and upward. An awful lot was expected of him and he liked to achieve absolutely everything that was required of him.

I now had a goal and I had more opportunity to make money. I was proud of the fact that I was able to pay my children's fees for three years as I had said that I would. All this was provided by the opportunities of my surroundings. The husband of one of my girlfriends was a fashion photographer. They asked me to lend them a hand in getting him commissions. I had to go around advertising agencies with his photos and I got to keep a large commission on the work that I brought in. In a short time I was also able to give him work. I had made friends with the owner of an advertising office when she was the president of our private school. She instantly offered my photographer work and even offered me new opportunities. She edited numerous fashion catalogues and they needed lots of child models. Now a good girlfriend of mine, she was primarily thinking of the children and especially the single parents of children who had once attended our little school. This would give the children something to do and something very different to school with a little bit of pocket money, while the mothers were given an hourly fee for their children. She paid me per child and by the hour to organize, transport and sometimes dress the children. As time went on, other agencies started to ask me for children but they also asked me for mums and grannies too. Over the years, I became the owner of one of the most well-known child photo agencies and it brought a very nice income. I ran the whole thing from home with just a desk and a telephone. It was no longer my job to ferry the children around and I only dealt with the organization and the day-to-day running. I was managing to do everything by telephone by the time that my daughters went back to state school from private school.

Alongside this, it still remained very important for me to be completely present in my children's lives. I only worked during the hours that they were either attended school or private classes.

My husband's career was also doing very well. He had moved to a new company and this time as managing director. Before he finally decided, he asked me to join him to have dinner to which he had been invited by the company owners. The impression I got was very unpleasant as were the dreams that I went on to have that night. I said the same to my husband and I asked him not to take the job. I asked him to spend a bit of time and think how he could best make himself independent of the companies, the owners and the bosses. He was very well known and respected in his profession. His vocation wasn't fixed to any one place, so I thought that it would be a good idea if we lived in a larger apartment or house where he would also be able to work from home.

He saw this as an uncertain solution and that is why he took the job in the interest of the future and the security of his family. Years later, unalterable consequences came to the fore within our own family.

We were both very happy and so was the whole family. Everyone was doing what they loved and in a way that they wanted to. We didn't have any problems with the kids. They were bright and hardworking and naturally cheeky just like all kids of their age.

My husband and I were invited to a lot of official dinners and balls as part of his previous job. It was quite natural for me to accompany him on trips abroad and to conferences and this was expected in the "higher ranks of society" to which we now belonged. Everyone appeared with their wife and I, as my husband's companion, had to learn the local customs.

My wardrobe altered accordingly. I had very elegant, expensive frocks that acted as accessories when appearing in such places, since my my appearance not only spoke for the affluence of my husband but also of his company.

I really liked these receptions, conferences and balls at the beginning. It is true that we were among the youngest of those attending such events but in time we grew bored with them along with our peers. I liked fashion but this was all that these women could talk about. It was very important that they show up wearing such and such a brand. This didn't mean a thing to me: just that it should first look beautiful. And I was always interested in the price as well. Neither of us made enough money to squander it on such things, and so I ended up discovering second-hand clothes shops for adults where I was able to buy my "one-night wonders" and at really low prices. We still went camping when we went on holiday but now we went for three weeks at a time. We liked the freedom and the simplicity.

Everyone saw us as happy. Our friends were keen to invite us around because we created a good atmosphere as we were enjoying this way of life. We were by all accounts successful and some were sometimes even jealous of us. They said things like: "Married for ten years and still so happy," and, "the husband is a company director and only just 35, his wife is bringing up two kids and still managing to earn a wage and be successful. But the main thing is that they are happy!" The same couldn't be said for all the couples in our circle of friends.

It was just at that time when we had finally sorted everything out and had more time to dedicate to each other that an unexpected event took place in my life.

It happened in late autumn 1984. I woke in the night to see something lit up in our bedroom. "Did we forget to switch the bedside lamp off or let the roller shutter down?" This is the kind of thing that went through my mind as I struggled to fully open my eyes. But I quickly closed them tight shut again. This time I opened them more cautiously but what had seemed unbelievable was still true—it had remained true. My hands lay on the duvet and were glowing. My first reaction was to shove them under the quilt but they shone through it. I lifted them out again and stared at them transfixed. I had two enormous red hands giving off a red light and they were about twice the size of normal hands. There was blue-white light shining out of the ends of my fingers to a distance of about 20 centimetres. I turned them around and looked at them in detail even though the room was in pitch darkness. "What could this be? Are these the hands that I saw disappearing into Klára's stomach? This means that it could break into material and illuminate it? Just like now with the duvet!" Maybe the light that it was giving off was what brought about the change that allowed the black goo to be pulled out for Klára to be able to speak again after 16 years of silence. Even these thoughts seemed totally unbelievable and I had tried to forget them for two years but they were still true! I had managed to convince myself with time that I had imagined everything that had gone on back then.

My next thought was: "Can other people see it?" I started to gently nudge my husband with my elbow who lay sleeping next to me to get him to wake up. He eventually started to move. I acted quickly.

"Tell me what you can see in the room."

He was half asleep but wasn't really able to think too much about his answer, he opened his eyes a tiny bit and said: "There are two lamps shining on the duvet." And then he turned over onto his other side and went on sleeping as if nothing had happened.

He didn't remember anything about it the next morning. But I sure did! "So he had seen it as well! This means that they can be seen by the naked eye in the dark just like a laser or x-rays. But why is it shining out of my hands or more to the point, why is it shining out of me?"

I had done everything that I could to prevent something like that happening to me ever again! I didn't accept it! Maybe I had just been imagining things! I didn't touch people and I most definitely never prayed to be able to help. But it happened all the same! I would even have been able to convince myself that it was a bad dream, that I had been forced to experience this in Heidelberg and if it had really happened then maybe it was the result of the pity that I felt for Klára and my prayer. I could explain all this with my "fairy tale faith". And now, when I hadn't done a thing: "I am busying myself with so many other things and I haven't given it a thought for ages! And now this happens!"

"OK, then what should I do with you?" I asked the hands that had given off blue light glowing from some strange power. My question somehow was also asking: "Where can I hide you away and lock you out of sight?" But it also had a ring of helplessness to it.

In that instant, I knew perfectly well that there was no point in fighting it, and that this was going to happen again!

The feeling might have been the same when the twins in Erich Kästner's "Lottie and Lisa" met for the first time and realized that there were two of them.

I had two hands like that! It was years afterwards after that I read about this special quality in a book by Bob Monroe called

"Another Body". He could also travel with his second body. I was really surprised that people have told me over the years that they have seen me in a room or here and there where I knew I had never been. The most interesting is what my goddaughter told me about myself 12 years later.

But let's get back to the present "impossibility" that was starting to look like reality but a different kind of reality to the one that we are capable of grasping in our everyday consciousness. We (or at least I) dream that we are flying in our sleep without ever having wings. Here there is no space, no time and no weight and we can be here and there in a matter of seconds.

But my hands were somehow different—they were here, and I could pinch myself. Things hurt but they stayed real.

OK, but what did this all mean? Quite possibly there is something inside me that might be abnormal and not run of the mill. My childhood came to mind when I had suffered so much from the very same thing. I saw things then that others didn't see and I knew things that other people didn't know but happened in time. Then there must be something "not normal" in me after all. "I do what I want to overcome it but it is going to come up again and again!"

"But perhaps it will calm down if I accept it!" I thought. Maybe this is another talent that I was born with like my good hearing and movement. So few people are born who go on to become famous musicians, painters or ballet dancers and perhaps this is a similar kind of talent that not only need to accept but to spend time developing.

But the counter-argument popped up: "I don't know anyone who has had a thing like this happen to them and maybe they will just say that I am lying like they did when I was a child. And maybe I'll end up in the madhouse if I even mention it to a doctor!"

In the meantime—I think—hours could have passed because the morning light started to filter into the room through the chinks in the roller blind. During that time, I was able to accept the ability that I had hidden deep within. The one thing that did help me was the thought that this power was perhaps there to help others.

"Then I really must embrace what it is that I can do with my hands and pass it on to others! It is quite possible that if I die they are going to ask me up there, 'What exactly did you do with your talent?'"

I knew that I not only had to accept but also to develop and therefore to touch people. The thought wasn't so reassuring and made me quite frightened. But I decided nevertheless! I told my husband everything the next morning about what had happened in the night and all about Heidelberg as well. Christian listened with care and love all the way through. No one was ever able to understand me and feel me like he could. (Of course, if he wanted to and he could.)

"I have always felt that there was a special kind of energy within you, but I hoped that it would never show itself," he said.

"What do you mean by that?" I asked surprised.

"I can't explain what I mean. There was something and there is something around you or inside you that I have never felt with anyone else. But what should we do now?" he asked.

6

The Call of
the Spirit World

I told Christian that I'd also been thinking about the same question all night long when one of my dreams suddenly came back to me. "Perhaps this is the reason for everything? Could the explanation be here?" A dream that I hadn't recalled for years suddenly reappeared from the sea where I loved to make everything disappear.

I can still remember the dress that I was wearing at the time. I was wearing a housecoat and it was early morning. It was in summer 1981 around my 33rd birthday. The children had been back at school for a couple of days: they were in kindergarten after the summer holidays. I suddenly felt an interesting, unusual tiredness descend upon me. I had slept well that night and had drunk my morning milky coffee and had a snack to eat with it, so it couldn't be low blood pressure that was causing it. I didn't have to go anywhere and the children only got home from school and kindergarten in the early afternoon (from the wonderful private school that they had now been attending for about half a year). This meant that I was able to allow myself the luxury of having a little lie down on the sofa in the living room. I fell into a deep, deep sleep and I heard these words from a deep, venerable VOICE:

"From now on some very special things are going to happen to you. You are going to have to take notes about these experiences immediately after they occur; you won't even believe the next day that they really happened to you. In time you will have to write a

book about these experiences and the title will be: 'I wasn't only a housewife and mum to two little girls.'

This book will provide help to other people to show them that everything that has happened to you could easily happen to them as well. It will also give them strength to be able to accept everything that happens to them, so they will know that they are not alone either. They are driven in the same way that you are but they don't dare believe and that is why they close themselves off so that we cannot reach them. They need us and your book will show them that cooperation is possible and important."

After I had told my husband about this, it suddenly became clear that there was a job to be done—but how? I told him that I needed him now more than ever before to stand by me as I didn't really know what it was that was happening to me either. Nor did I know how or what to do with this power and responsibility that had suddenly become crystal clear to me. "I am guided, entrusted with a mission and I would like to make this happen."

My husband took me lovingly in his arms and said: "I'll support wherever I can!"

And so this is how I accepted my task even though I didn't really know what it would be. I somehow felt that everything would change in my life and around me as a result of this acceptance.

Throughout the next day, all I could think about was that perhaps my illness with the cyst on New Year's Eve in 1981 had something to do with this as well as my sudden and marvellous recovery. Perhaps the reason that I went on a course in reflexology recommended by Mrs Steiner was to awaken my interest in the possibilities of healing! It was now obvious that all I had gone through on the course was a continuation of this. "But what could Mrs Steiner know? Is it possible that she, too, is in on the secret? Or is it that she only saw talent in me? But how interesting it was that she knew my mother-in-law! Maybe that isn't by chance! Is it possible that there are threads running through this that we have no idea of? Is it possible that nothing is accidental?!"

I had to stop there because I felt as if I had stumbled across a secret that I only had a sense of and I was still a long way off knowing the answer. I was happy that my husband understood and helped. I was happy now, after what had been a difficult two years, that he had more time for me and that he supported me in this serious decision.

I was rather nervous but I registered as soon as I could for Mrs Steiner's next course. For the time being, I didn't know anyone else other than her who dealt with things like this. But nor was I keen to tell anyone about it. Mrs Steiner had not only witnessed everything that had gone on but she also knew about my complete recovery, and so I saw her as already being in on my secrets.

She met me on the first day with a broad smile on her face. "I am so pleased to see you again and just as pleased that you were able to accept the job that you have to do. I know that you were shocked by what you experienced in Heidelberg but I saw your special abilities and dared to hope that you could somehow deal with what had happened with you there. You are the only one who can accept and take this on!"

This is how I started to acquaint myself and learn all about this special world. I took course after course in reflexology. I considered it to be a very effective method that made no use of special preparation or implements. I've always got my hands with me. It was also really practical.

Besides, I got to know about Aura-Soma and I started to use that as well (in 1984!). Then came the healing stones and the Tarot. I read an incredible amount about natural healing and alternative medicine. I was completely absorbed. Everyone in the family was all too happy to offer me their foot to practise on. Soon the kids wouldn't go to sleep at night until I had massaged the soles of their feet. Claudia was given a dental brace and I was happy because I knew where the points were that could ease the first pains but also reduce the time needed for the brace. I was also able to reduce my husband's tiredness in the evenings and I used massage to freshen him up. This meant that now he was happy to go to the movies with me or for me to snuggle up in bed with him.

I was interested in everybody's sole. More and more of my girl-friends came along and my hairdresser now told me all her complaints and I didn't have to pay at the beautician's either as Évike was now coming to me for reflexology.

We didn't have any medicines in our house at all or at least not the usual kind. I followed my father-in-law's example and I tried to find the homeopathic doctor in Zurich. I found her in the person of Dr Elisabeth Huber and she has been helping my every bodily and spiritual problem as well as those of my family ever since.

Certainly a lot a faith is required for natural healing methods but the definite thing is that they have no side effects and they increase a person's responsibility both in healing an illness and maintaining good health.

My new vocation preoccupied and replenished me. I was happy that I was not only able to help my immediate family but that I could help and advise my friends and acquaintances. I was glad to carry on with my paid work alongside all of this. The secret remained hidden inside me and no one else knew about it other than Mrs Steiner and my husband.

In autumn 1985, I spent a two-week holiday alone with my husband and without the children just as we had done in previous years. We picked the Greek island of Samos as a friend had told us that the place was beautifully warm at this time of year and that the wind was excellent for surfing. So we booked everything through a travel agent specializing in surfing holidays. They organized the air tickets, accommodation, surf school—the complete package. All that we had to do was pack and then simply enjoy the holiday.

We cherished these two weeks without the children and it gave us time to rediscover each other and the things that we had sometimes lost through the mad rush of the year. Surfing was our shared passion and we were completely mad about it.

It was still a habit of mine then to take loads of books along with me as you never know and I didn't want to be bored. But this time I knew that all I would have time for besides surfing was to sunbathe and so I took just the one book and that was "Between Lives" by Shirley MacLaine: Everyone I knew was raving about this book, and now on Samos I was not only forced to understand why, but I also got a great number of answers to those questions that were occupying me. The famous Hollywood actress describes her spiritual awakening in this book and her travels to worlds that we only know from fairy tales. I believed her every word. There were a lot of things that seemed foreign to me then: her visits to a medium where spirits were conjured up or where they spoke for themselves. She also wrote about spiritual healing options from Sweden to New Mexico that she had come across on her travels. She learned about beings from other solar systems when she was in the Peruvian hills and she also learned from the knowledge held by shamans. I literally jumped headfirst into the book. This was THE BOOK that I really had to read. It helped me to believe in the things that I was now having to experience but it also showed me experiences and possibilities that might still be waiting for me.

I shared classes and surfing with my husband like sister and brother but now I was even willing to let him have more of his due share so that I could carry on reading in peace. This was really something quite new and my husband was already allergic to my book with the picture of the actress on the cover, and couldn't wait for me to finish it. I thought that this was because he wanted me to spend more time with him. No! It turned out that he was extremely keen to find out what the book was about that had been important enough for me to give up my surfing. I had a good laugh at this and happily handed him the book so that he could read it himself. This left me with a couple of days' undisturbed surfing and I virtually forgot about Christian. He disappeared into the book just like I had. Sometimes I gave him some music to listen to that had been lent to me by our surfing instructor. Christian sat with headphones on, completely immersed in my reality that I had experienced all alone up until that point.

The book was finished and the tape cassette returned and an interesting discussion began between us that was probably also a turning point even though we didn't realize it at the time.

"You know that it is the first time that I have ever read about such things," he began. "I do understand and I can imagine it but it's a completely alien world to the one that I live in. I'm still going to do everything that I can to help. The thing that I am not going to be able to accept is that that we don't direct our lives but they are directed by superior beings. I want to live my own life and I want to create my happiness here on Earth so that no one can make decisions above me!"

I listened to him and asked myself how we were going to go on living together if our attitudes were so completely different?

7

Teaching from
Spiritual Beings

I had so many questions that couldn't be fully answered by my wider reading. The main thing that I wanted to do was to get to know the kind of people who had had similar things happen to them. I still didn't dare tell my friends about all that had happened to me over the last couple of weeks , although the urge to talk about it was getting stronger all the time. I was interested in how others had been able to accept these challenges and how their lives had changed as a result. I was worried for my family and my marriage and my continued life together with my husband.

Opportunity arrived purely by chance. I was hanging out the washing in the laundry with a neighbour. His marriage was a little unusual. His wife was a painter and he mainly worked as a writer. He did have a law degree and worked as an advisor to a couple of companies and he did all this from a home office.

They both lived for their families and the vocations that they had found for themselves. They shared the housework and today it was the husband's turn to do the washing. I'm not quite sure how the subject came up, but while we were hanging out the washing, he started to tell me about an experience that he had during a trip to the UK. He was visiting relatives who lived in a remote area in a little village. He liked staying at the place but the grandmother had died quite recently and they told him about some very curious goings on. Sure enough, he also saw pictures suddenly fall off the wall, the door slamming shut and photos fell over on the sideboard with no earthquakes, storms or other potential natural causes.

The family were not only not surprised by this, or in any way horrified, but instead made kind remarks as if this were the most natural thing in the world.

"Oh, Granny's at it again! She's trying to tell us something but we don't know what it is."

And that was that. People believe in the existence of spirits in England and that individuals return after their death in the form of ghosts to the place they used to live. Sometimes all they want to do is to shock or express their dissatisfaction with certain things that have happened after their death but many of them are unable to accept the fact that they have died.

I stood virtually motionless with a damp towel in my hands that I had been just about to peg to the line, and listened to my neighbour's tale. Everything that the relatives had said was true. Despite being an educated man and thinking that it was all a load of superstitious nonsense, he was himself forced to experience the exact opposite. The spirit of the deceased—perhaps because he had simply laughed at what he had heard—seemed to single him out from the very first moment that he had arrived to prove its existence with various incidents. My neighbour was left in no doubt about the truth of what he had been told.

It was pretty obvious that I was particularly interested in what he had said, and so he added that a Parapsychology Society existed in Zurich that held talks and showed similar films. I called the very same day and asked them to send me a programme of events. At last, I had come across people who were interested in much the same things as I was.

I soon joined the society and so I was invited to attend an annual members meeting. There I was introduced to the various group leaders and their specialist areas. There were those who tried to record the voices of "ghosts", others who were interested in dreams and spiritual healing as well as spiritual development. That was the only group that was closed. It had been formed ten years before and it had exactly ten members. I was interested in how they worked. I figured that this was the group where I would be able to get the most help and understanding. The problem was that I couldn't join that group and they didn't want to start another one.

Not long after the annual meeting there was a leaflet in their monthly brochure. The leaflet carried a piece from the leader of the closed group which said that their spiritual leaders had instructed them that a new group should be started, and that it should be made up of ten members. There must have been over a 100 people who put their names down but I was one of the ten who were accepted to join. The spiritual leaders allowed the formation of a further two groups after ours, and they asked for a new group to be started every year after that. And that is how I became part of the group that I have been actively involved in for the last 16 years.

It really is true that this group, or rather the group of those from above, was the one that I had been longing for. I received the answers to all of my questions through their group leader. But it was even more than that: I was now being guided and protected.

Franz, the leader of the group, is a full transmedium and has been involved with his wife from the outset. Through him, our leaders from above spoke to us. His wife also has talents as a medium and it was her job to protect and care for her husband. She sat with her eyes closed for the whole time in a state of meditation and watched and made sure that everything was going as it should. Her husband first said a prayer and then presented his body, or rather his voice, to be directed by those from above. He was standing or sitting with his eyes open, but I soon sensed a change in his personality and a change in the surrounding force field. Franz's voice got much deeper and his eyes started to twitch. They were around him and the whole room filled up with pleasant, strengthening energy that radiated trust and love towards us.

I was happy when I heard that before Franz had become involved with this rather unusual vocation, his background had been very similar to mine. His daughter had begun with asthma as the result of a rather heavy cold and they had to give her rather powerful drugs to ease her constant coughing. Franz is an expert in rugs and carpets from the East; he worked in a shop that sold them. He started to make enquiries about alternative methods that would help his little girl. He also discovered reflexology and used it to help his daughter and was able to cure her completely. In the meantime, he became aware of his force field and experiences that were a little out of the ordinary. He found a spiritual group where they noticed his abilities as a medium. He developed and strengthened his talent and devotion in a group run by an English medium and eventually became a full transmedium.

Franz's group is run by higher spiritual beings beings—they speak so that speak so that we can also sense their spiritual maturity. They are members of a large group known as the "White Friends" who were either risen, completely cleansed Masters or spirit beings who have never had earthly incarnations. They work on the spiritual development of earthly beings and lifting them out of the material world.

They have taught us so much. Some of these insights concerned everyday things but they taught us through the enlightenment of the masters. This is how they taught us all about healthy eating and how to keep our bodies in the ideal condition. The first thing that they spoke about was keeping the body clean and about movement, yet they also talked about the all-important faithfulness in close personal relationships and how we reach purity of thought and feeling.

As time went on, the topics and the challenges that we faced became harder and harder. We slowly started to build up a new, clean body with higher resonance. We went through weeks and months of teaching and practise on the subject of chakras, the energies within us and their conscious application as well as healing colours.

My spirit was overjoyed and could hardly wait for the next meeting with the other members of the group and their earthly and heavenly leaders but my body was finding the sudden changes hard to cope with. My body opened up during the exercises and enjoyed a freer, lighter existence. The problems started after the meditation and exercises: I was really cold at the beginning and I started to shake like someone with a high fever. I could hardly wait to get home and soak in a long hot bath. As time passed, I learned to control not only the opening up of my body but also to close its energy centres afterwards. Then a new phenomenon appeared. Despite the fact that I had completely returned to my conscious state, I sensed a permanent light within me and mainly around me. It was just as if I were wearing a veil except that this veil was woven from fine strands of pure light. I know that this glowing force offered me protection but also held the sense of my higher consciousness.

I wasn't capable of going home like this. I had the feeling that my loved ones weren't going to understand me or that I wouldn't understand them. This light removed me from the "lowering force" of day-to-day life. I wasn't left with a great deal of choice as to what to do, and so one evening a fortnight after meditation, I went into the restaurant on the corner and really stuffed "my innards", and mainly with meat. It was only then that I was able to go home with enough weight inside me to hold me down. I became a vegetarian later on and started to take a keener interest in what I ate. As I no longer ate meat, I used to find that strong smoke, noise and moving in a jostling crowd of people helped me to regain the weight of my body and not to feel the light and lightness of my spirit. So I used to go to a disco for half an hour or so and set off for home with blocked up ears and stinking of cigarette smoke.

The little "tricks" that I came up with seem a little laughable or stupid but the difference that I felt in the members of my family and especially between my husband and myself began to cause me more and more pain and so this is how I came back down to "their floor."

Back then, my husband only had to step inside the door and I knew what sort of day that he had had. I could sense the energies that he was bringing into the family. Now, I was able to understand why my little children had started to argue all the time or why they got all agitated when daddy eventually came home from the office.

They didn't have enough defence either and so they were able to sense what their daddy was bringing home from the outside world into our peaceful home.

I had more and more trouble sensing this and dealing with it as I was no longer willing to dirty myself, weigh myself down and to dampen my spirit so that I could handle the energies that other people were giving off. I knew that what I had been introduced to and what I had learned was not only true but I sensed that I could be genuinely happy if I followed this path.

I studied and I practised at the same time. I hoped beyond hope that my husband would also manage to find a way of joining me on my path. The path that I was following was by no means simple and there were only a few people left in the medium group that I attended. By the end, only one or two of them were left. I knew that I had found my path and I was willing to do all that I had to.

I made a lot of new friends at the talks and events held at the Parapsychology Society. It was here that I met someone else thanks to my teacher, Franz Lichtenecker. I was connected to him by a very deep friendship and a very old link—it was Rudolf Passián whom I have lovingly called Rudika ever since. He became a great help to me in that period. He turned up time and again in my life and accompanied me on my first ever "official visit" to Hungary. Mr Passián researches paranormal abilities and is acknowledged in the field.

I met him at one of his talks and even though there is a good 30 years between us, we formed an immediate friendship. He recommended a couple of the many books that he had written, saying I most definitely had to read them. Right away he mentioned that a medium was soon to arrive from Finland and I should go to see her talk. He said that he had never come across anyone like her before. He was referring to Aulikki Plaami, the famous singing medium. There was no question about it and I went along to the talk, although I had my doubts about people who performed as mediums before an audience.

Aulikki's performance really was quite unique. Her talent came to her after a serious accident. She had sung a little before the accident but her husband was a professional musician and he noticed a dramatic change after the accident. She started to sing in both deep and high octaves that was a rare talent even in those who sang professionally. She also sang songs and arias, which she not only didn't know, but could never have had the opportunity to learn. Plus, she had never learned to read sheet music. Her husband had been trained in music and he got her to sing; he also noticed that she not only knew the songs but also the voices seemed familiar to him. His wife sang in the voices of Mario Lanza, Edith Piaf, Elvis Presley and Bing Crosby as well as others and after a while she started to adopt their gestures as well.

I sat with my eyes closed and was convinced that I was hearing Lanza, Piaf and Presley. They were somehow there in the room and sang through this fragile, middle-aged woman.

It was my first experience of a performance by a medium, yet I was completely won over by the whole thing. I had no idea how it worked but I knew for a fact that the voices were real as it would have been impossible to learn something like that and there was no way that it could be copied. However, it wasn't this that really took hold of me. I found Aulikki very attractive. I had to go over to her after the performance as if I were being pulled in by a magnet. It was as if she were waiting for me, she gave me a hug and said that she would really like it if I attended the full-day course that she was going to hold with her husband's help.

There was only the one place left on the course that ran the next day I was allocated the place despite the fact that a lot of people had applied after the success of her performance.

The events of the following day provided me with a completely unforgettable experience. Various beings appeared via Aulikki's body from the other world who now lived in their spiritual bodies.

Carmen was the first to appear and she really cheered everyone up as most people were attending a channelling for the first time, much like me, and didn't really know what to expect. Carmen was the spirit of a Spanish girl who had died when she was 16, and she told us about how she lived in the spirit world. She reassured us that there was no need to fear death because there was a much more beautiful world for us "over there" because everything there was imbued with love. She said that she knew we all had to live our lives with responsibility over here but she asked us not to forget to be light and happy. She had been happy her whole life on Earth— she said laughing—and asked us whether we would like to hear a few little songs that she had learned when she had lived "in this world". Of course, we said that we would and she not only sang with the charming voice of a young girl but flew into a Spanish dance. Mrs Plaami was a middle-aged woman, as I have said, but now she suddenly gained new youth and she really danced with the fire of a 16-year-old before our very eyes.

Then a deceased sister superior appeared. She spoke of the importance of the spiritual way here on Earth because there was no chance to continue our development up there. It is here that we are able to lay the foundation of where we will get to and who we will live with in the other world. With this she was referring to the spiritual family and group. She answered questions that the group put to her and shed light on the causes of some of the personal problems suffered by the questioners.

We could feel completely different energies after the break when Mrs Plaami fell back into a trance and Dr Hermann took control. Aulikki's voice grew very deep and she took on the movements of an old man. Dr Hermann first worked on everyone as a chiropractor. The little Mrs Plaami "pummelled" us all one by one even though she was quite a fragile thing herself. She made bones crack, knelt on people's backs and pressed her elbows into frozen muscle tissue. The spine was Dr Hermann's main speciality. After he had done with us, even the older members of the group sat straight up in their seats as if they had just come out of the army. Dr Hermann came across abnormalities and illnesses and gave their names in Latin which Aulikki's husband, Seppo, looked up in dictionaries and medical manuals and translated for us.

Then came the homeopathic recommendations. As Dr Hermann was a spiritual being he could see into and through our bodies and he warned "his patients" to alter their lifestyle or diet. Then Mr Plaami acted as his assistant and told us what homeopathic preparations were required.

I watched the whole thing in total fascination: sometimes in silence and sometimes through my own experience. When everyone was done—there must have been about ten of us—he gave everyone personal advice on the development of their spiritual abilities. He sat on a chair and spoke to us all in turn.

He only stood up from his seat once and that was when it was my turn. I started to feel the same magnetic attraction that I had felt the night before as Mrs Plaami or rather Dr Hermann walked slowly towards me. I started to shake and got into such a state that I thought I was going to faint. Then Dr Hermann spoke to me and said: *"Don't I know you from somewhere?"* and I just burst into tears. I cried like I had as a frightened, desperate young child. I cried like I had when no one had understood me and I felt so terribly alone. Through Mrs Plaami, Dr Hermann's voice now became the voice of an infinitely loving person.

"Oh, my God, how I would like to take you in my arms now and calm you and stroke you but I still cannot tell you why I can feel your pain so strongly and where we know each other from." (Many years later, when I could make contact with the spirit world myself, Dr Hermann told me that I had been his wife in a previous incarnation. He had been a healer and I had been his greatest help and we had loved each other very deeply.)

He related the following about my present life to reassure me: *"The people you are living with or who are close to you are not bad people but they just aren't able to understand you. They live on another spiritual level and are driven by other goals. Try to look on them in this way and their strangeness will be a little easier to deal with. I would like to ask you one thing,"* he went on, *"Will you allow me to take over your protection?"*

A sound managed to leave my lips to indicate yes.

"I promise that I will not rest until you find your true group and your true family where there is only love, music and dance along with the joy of knowledge."

I couldn't stop crying for the longest time, not even when Aulikki returned to being a simple Finnish woman with all of her guests returned home. What I had experienced made my body shake on the outside and my heart-soul on the inside. The spirit of Dr Hermann told me everything that I had been missing since my childhood: the true love and compassion that I had once known!

They recorded everything that had happened that day on tape and I played the conversation with Dr Hermann again and again for comfort and strength to follow the path that I had chosen if I felt particularly depressed or not understood.

I soon had the chance to tell Mr Passián all that had gone on. He was of the opinion that the spiritual connection between us really must be very deep and important as Dr Hermann had never been known to speak to anyone in such personal detail before.

Dr Hermann also appears in Brazil, via a local medium, where he uses his other name of Dr Fritz and performs spiritual operations. He operated on Rudolf Passián when he was in Brazil and was rushed into hospital with gallstones. Rudolf thought it the best option to be operated on my Dr Fritz via a medium. The medium drank a whole bottle of scotch, went into a deep trance and cut Rudolf open with a pocket knife and extracted a stone that completely corresponded to the one shown on the x-ray that he had taken at the hospital. The operation was completely bloodless and there was no scar where he had made the incision; he was left with a red line on his skin for a couple of days as if he had just been scratched but that quickly disappeared. Not only was Rudolf now free of pain but he was back to his old self after no more than a day's rest.

I have had a lot of spiritual experiences that link me with Rudolf Passián and the one with Dr Hermann was one of many.

It was Boxing Day and a couple of months after the séance with Mrs Plaami when I heard a voice tell me to call Mr Passián. I didn't pay much attention at first and just carried on cooking in the kitchen. I seem to recall that my family had gone to the ice rink but I wasn't in the mood, so I had stayed home to make the lunch.

The voice repeated its request and after the third time, I went over to the telephone. It was the second day of Christmas somewhere around noon. I don't really like disturbing people at times like this, though I had sent Mr Passián a Christmas card and he had sent one to me.

I reluctantly told my friend who picked up the phone that a voice had asked me to call him but I really didn't know why. I was ashamed that I had heard a voice and it had given me a task but only it knew why.

Mr Passián had already heard the Dr Hermann cassette and he seemed to think that it must be him, especially as I had not had contact with any other spirit being at that time. He asked me whether or not I could contact him but I answered in disbelief that I had never done anything like that before. He asked me to try my best because perhaps I had called him on the telephone to tell him something really important. He had a health problem and it was quite possible that he was going to need an operation. Maybe Dr Hermann, if that was him, would be able to help. "OK. I'll have a go! If I manage to then I'll call Mr Passián back," I responded. (Our relationship was still quite formal.)

I sat down on the edge of the sofa as my family wouldn't be back for a good hour and I had got the lunch almost ready. I let myself go and released my thoughts which soon worked as I had not only been practising in the Lichtenecker group but at home on my own whenever I could. Then I asked to be connected—if possible—to the spirit who had just spoken to me. Dr Hermann immediately indicated that he had picked up the connection.

I could hardly believe what was going on as I had never had contact with spirits like this before and I had definitely never sought to contact them myself. I immediately asked what was the cause of Mr Passián's illness and Dr Hermann gave a definite answer: *"His illness is caused by the ring that he wears on his finger and that he has forgotten to remove. All he has to do is to take the ring off and his illness will soon disappear without the need for any further intervention.*" Then he added, "*The three of us, including Rudolf, know one another from Mongolia. We were all three of us fighters on horseback. That is where Rudolf's foot problem has its roots in his behaviour with regard to the enemy.*"

I still can't quite believe that I was able to make contact with a spirit. I could hear a man's voice speaking to me but not with my outer ear. Despite all this I was still sceptical.

The speaker could sense this and continued to speak. "*Ask Rudolf Passián whether or not he received a book yesterday that had a book mark in it with flower patterns on it.*" And then he added: "*The bookmark was made in Mongolia.*"

There was a sudden silence as if someone had just put the phone down. I wondered what Mr Passián was going to say about all of this. I called him at once. "I really do have a ring on my finger, it's my wedding ring and I only really keep it on out of habit."

He also said that he completely understood the message as he had been living apart from his wife for more than ten years and the message was telling him to put his personal life in order at last.

The long, drawn-out divorce soon took place and a couple of years later Rudolf happily said yes to "his guardian angel" who had been sent to him from the spiritual world in the form of his young wife.

The foot problem was true as well. Rudolf had been sent to the German front when he was quite young and he was shot in the foot. This led to his capture where they didn't do anything about his injury or his considerable pain. And he bears the consequences of his injury with him to the present day. (Now he understood the reason for the penitence as his behaviour when he was a Mongolian warrior.) He was in unbearable pain as a prisoner of war and saw death as offering the only relief. He constantly asked the Lord to send him his angel of redemption. He did send an angel in the end but some 40 years later. That is why he needed to take the old ring off as Dr Hermann had instructed, so that he could take the new one from the hand of the angel who was standing at his door even then but could only be seen by the spirit of Dr Hermann.

The thing about the book was real as well. On the previous day, Rudolf really had received a book as a Christmas present from a friend with an embroidered bookmark in it.

Rudolf Passián was delighted by the news and congratulated me on my clear and obvious reception of the message. I didn't know what to do with this experience there and then; I was delighted to hear the car parking and my children's laughter as the family returned home for lunch. I hurried back to the kitchen and managed to meet all the expectations placed upon me.

"But let's forget about it just as quickly as we can!" was my subconscious opinion at the time. As time passed I started to doubt whether this had ever really happened at all. I only started to write my experiences down a couple of years later when the VOICE reminded me to do everything that it had asked me to in a dream. I just couldn't say no to the VOICE and so I wrote down everything that had happened to me over the previous years, despite the fact that I didn't want to at all. At least now there was a written record of the "unusual things" that had happened to me. (That the VOICE had told me would happen way back in 1981.)

Even after this, Dr Hermann continued to draw attention to this by his constant reappearance saying that he would keep all the promises that he had made. He mainly helped me to believe in help not only from the spirit world but also in his personal good will.

I went on living family life just as before and didn't tell anyone in the family about my experiences. They weren't particularly interested anymore and they didn't believe any of it anyway. I did try on the odd occasion but the way they looked at me gave it all away and they even said things like: "Won't you just leave me alone with all this stuff! If you believe then that's one thing but don't keep wanting me to believe in it as well." It sounded rather like: "It's your business if you believe in fairy tales and superstitions." So we were all together on the outside but all went our separate ways on the inside.

One winter, my husband and I decided that we didn't really want to go away skiing in the holidays. The girls were at a ski camp with their school and so they were able to enjoy their fill of winter sports. We fancied going off to warmer climes in the dead of winter. Eventually we plumped for Lanzarote, one of the Canary Islands, for the dramatic volcanic landscape, the heat and of course the surf. There was wind here all year round for our all-time favourite sport. We didn't end up surfing in the end because we were so blown away by the beauty of the place that we spent the whole time driving around in a hire car.

One day we set off to get to a little cove surrounded by rocky outcrops that was described in our guidebook as especially beautiful. And it was. Everyone was sunbathing in the nude so we stripped off completely and let the sun caress every part of our bodies after leaving the cold winter behind us at home. The sand here was volcanic and had great swathes of brown, red and black in it. I lay in the sun and I could virtually feel the fire glowing and rumbling deep down in the Earth that sometimes springs up in the form of scalding steam.

I could hear a voice. It was talking about me. It praised me for my progress, growing faith, and cooperation but was mainly satisfied with me as a mother. How I raised my daughters with such freedom at the same time as offering them so much security and so on ..."OK, enough of the self-praise!" I thought and I jumped into the water. Then I lay back down afterwards and stretched out in the sun but now I sunbathed on my tummy. My arms were next to me on the black sand hot from the sun.

I heard the voice again: *"Well, if you have the chance to be lying in the sun then at least turn your palms to face the sun and you can replenish the chakras in your hands."*

I pretended not to have heard a thing though I was surprised to hear that there are chakras in the hands as I didn't know that then. I couldn't carry on with my thoughts as my hands suddenly started to move. It was as if they were attached to invisible strings and were being manipulated by a puppeteer. My hands were lifted up and turned around.

I went back into the sea to cool down and then I suggested to my husband that we start to make our way as I had cooked enough for one day.

Two days later, back in Zurich, I had to make a call to Néné von Muralt who was the president of the Parapsychology Society. We started to chat and she asked me if I would like to come along to a medium meeting that afternoon. Someone had just cancelled before my telephone call and she didn't know who else she would be able to contact in time. I only had an hour before the meeting with the medium. She said that it was to be with Gaye Muir, one of the most well-known mediums from the UK, and all the tickets had been sold for weeks.

Aulikki had been the first and last medium whom I had visited up until that point. It was unexpected but I jumped at the chance.

Gaye Muir was a middle-aged woman with glasses who gave me a rather stern look just as the session began. "There is a spirit in my midst!" she said. She described what it looked like (that agreed completely with a picture that appeared in a book written by Rudolf Passián) and she told me that a Dr Hermann wished to speak to me. "He tells me," she continued, "that you have no idea how difficult it is for a spirit to move matter and especially a human body. He wouldn't have had to move your hands a few days ago if you had believed him in the first place."

Perhaps I should have been ashamed of what had happened but my self-defence was so natural, it came from within. It was just like my development was happening on the outside on this un-known path where unexpected and unbelievable things occurred on a regular basis.

At the same time, I could sense that I was being looked after and I was being watched and directed on my path with a great amount of love.

8

Inner Cleansing

I used to sit down and meditate nearly every day after my girls had gone back to school after lunch. I didn't do any special exercises but just sat and tried to empty my mind of thoughts.

I did exactly the same on the day in question. I could feel my breathing becoming slower and more relaxed and my body starting to let go and calm flowing through me. I was beginning to concentrate on my breathing again when I heard the VOICE. **"You must stop eating meat!"**

This startled me and I completely returned to my standard consciousness. I didn't hear the VOICE so often then and I was overcome by excitement. But I didn't agree with what I was being told. "Why shouldn't I eat meat?"

"Because it isn't good for you."

"Why wouldn't it be good? For one thing, we need it for a healthy balanced diet and the other thing is that I really like it!"

"That's not what I'm talking about! You are going through a spiritual development under our direction. The resonance of your body and your whole being is going to be much higher. Animal protein has a very low resonance. If you go on eating meat then you are going to create an unnecessary potential difference in your body and it will eventually make you ill."

Way back then I didn't even know what resonance was. I could only have been attending Mr Lichtenecker's group for half a year or so and I was still at a very early stage. I was just beginning in meditation and I really didn't know what the VOICE meant when he talked about a potential difference occurring because I was eating meat. I needed to eat meat and especially after group mediation. It earthed me! And anyway, I liked meat and I didn't want to give it up. (Strangely I never liked meat as a child and I had to be forced to eat it.)

The VOICE was silent and I had said what I thought, in the usual way, it was instantly forgotten.

We went on a trip with some friends of my husband's and their families. There must have been ten families, kids and all and we set off on bikes to Lake Greifensee which wasn't too far away. The atmosphere was great with weather to match and the sun shone brightly in the sky. Soon we had the barbecue piled high with mouth-watering treats. Everyone had prepared something special or bought something delicious from the butcher: pork, chicken, mutton delicacies with baked potatoes and corn on the cob. There were even grilled vegetables with tasty sauces that someone had prepared. And this was all washed down with a suitable amount of drink. Then we played games, swam and the day slowly came to an end.

I started to feel unwell on the way home. I thought that it must have been all the sun as it was the beginning of the summer and the sun had been particularly hot, nor was I used to that much alcohol and I'd drunk more as it went so well with the spicy food. Perhaps I'd had a couple of sips too many. (And that was the difference between half a glass and a full glass.) Or perhaps it was the sun combined with the strength of the wine? I only hoped that it wasn't something that I had eaten because that could be dangerous!

Despite a very pleasant day, we were all worn out so we went to bed a bit earlier than usual. I soon fell asleep. I woke up in the middle of the night feeling very ill and I had to make a dash to the bathroom and all the delicious stuff that I had eaten passed back through my mouth but in a much less pleasant form. Brrr! It makes me shiver just to think about quite how sick I was that night! "So it must have been the meat that wasn't fresh after all! Thank heavens I was able to throw it all up!" I thought. The next morning, I was surprised to find that no one else in the family was ill but I was just as pleased. "It looks like it was only me who ate the bad meat."

I was soon forced to change my point of view. The problem wasn't with the meat, it was with me! My metabolism was either not willing or no longer able to accept meat. It didn't matter how often I tried to eat meat after that, I always ended up with a re-run of the bathroom scene. And it wasn't just meat but anything with meat in it. I was a vegetarian pretty soon. It was against my will but to the delight of my health.

16 years have passed since then and I find the thought of eating meat quite unimaginable. Today it is just as important for me for ethical reasons as it is for health and spiritual development. For me, animals are sentient beings and they are willing to give up their lives to feed those of a higher order (humans). It is always the being of lower rank that sacrifices itself for the development of a higher one. That is why plants are eaten by animals and animals by humans. We all now know that it is possible to live a healthy life without eating meat. And our spirit, our soul, can develop much more easily and it is pleased when we accept fewer of those "sacrifices" that we don't necessarily need.

I used to think of animals not only as friends but as siblings when I was a small child. It then took me another 40 years to rediscover this way of thinking.

The warning that I had received showed once again that my development and formation of my spirit was being constantly monitored and protected from potential mistakes and dangers.

And especially if I was able to accept this right away!

9

Leaving My Body
for the First Time

I was really looking forward to the first big meeting with the old Lichtenecker group. Three groups took part in the Christmas meditation: there were the "old ones" who had been together for 12 years, then our group that had been studying and practising together for about a year and finally those who had only started group meditation a month or so before.

I'd already had a lot of great experiences with group meditation and mostly with the help of our spiritual leader. I practised a lot at home but I still wasn't able to achieve that same level of resonance that I did when I was with the group. So I was really curious to see what it would be like with a large group. I thought there would perhaps even be more of our higher leaders' present than with our small group.

Franz and Esther had decorated the room that couldn't otherwise be described as being particularly beautiful or atmospheric. We used to practise in a basement that had pleasant pictures hanging on the wall but it still remained a basement. However, all we had to do was to close our eyes and listen to Franz's spiritual instruction and we were filled with a pleasant sensation and masses of light.

This time the meditation started off with a little music before Franz started to speak. He talked about the spiritual meaning of the Christmas mystery when I started to feel that something was happening to me. I always held my hands with the palms turned upwards resting on my knees. My hands started to rise up as if they were being pulled up by lots of invisible thin threads. I tried to stop this happening with my will and strength but this only resulted in me falling swiftly back to a state of everyday consciousness. I started to let go again and my hands started to rise up again. I gave up and just let it all happen, whatever that was.

The invisible strings lifted my hands to chest height. My palms were still facing upwards and my arms were held outstretched and open to the skies. It was odd because I couldn't just feel that my arms were held out like this but I could see them as well!

I felt a sharp tug—a very small one—and now I was sure that I could see not only my arms but also my body with outstretched arms and eyes closed sitting on a chair. "So, now I'm outside my own body!" This was the part of me speaking that stayed thinking just as long as it possibly could and wanted to explain and understand absolutely everything.

A moment passed and now I could see the whole group followed by a strong but not blinding light. I saw light beings. There were a great number of them and they were standing in a circle. They were standing a long way away from me, yet I still felt that I belonged among them. Then I realized that I had a body of light just like theirs. There were only three very bright figures of light standing close to me. The size and strength of their light was different to the ones who were standing in a circle. These three light beings were transmitting an indescribably pleasant feeling towards me. It was more than love, it was acceptance. It's not something that can be described in words! One of the three was glowing with a greater and more powerful light than the other two. It was this one who spoke to me.

"We greet you, GLORIA. Welcome! We are very relieved to see you again and that you have found your way back to us. We would like to give you a gift. Take this gift with you when you go back down and divide it between the members of your group. Give it to everyone who comes to you for help and for healing!" With this it placed an orb of light in my hand that was almost as large as my upper body. It was completely weightless because it was made from pure light. It was strange to hold and to feel something that had no substance; it still had shape and radiance. It was just like my hands, my arms and my whole body that were all made of light. But this orb had a different radiation to my body. Perhaps I could call it the light of knowledge and the radiation of healing power.

The light being continued to look at me with infinite love after he had given me the orb of light and the feeling stayed with me even when I started to feel that my being was about to be transformed again.

I slid back into my body that was still sitting and now sat holding the orb of light. Then the light slowly dissolved into my body. Then I heard Franz's voice calling me back to everyday consciousness. I didn't return willingly. I would have liked to keep the wondrous feeling for just a little while longer and especially that loving smile that I had experienced—in another consciousness—just moments before.

The others started to chat and Franz asked everyone to describe what they had experienced. I couldn't and I didn't want to tell anyone what had happened to me and where I had been. I knew everything was true but my consciousness still protested. "You haven't got your own group because you're still a beginner yourself! And you are most definitely not called Gloria! They must have thought you were someone else!"

The other, more conscious part of me remained silent—deeply touched by the experience. But the gift and the name were still not clear to that part of me. "Why did they call me Gloria? Maybe I'll have my own group one day that I'll teach and lead myself." I didn't really know the answer but I did know that those who were directing me certainly did know and would help me to achieve it.

Everyone was moving around in the room. Tables were set up and slowly the contents of bags were tipped out onto the table. Our group began their Christmas celebrations in the material world as well.

I just sat at our table but I couldn't swallow a thing. Thankfully they were talking about everybody else's experiences or were taken up with other subjects and so they didn't pay special attention to me at all.

I would have liked to have been there where I had received such a hearty welcome and I wanted to go on feeling those eyes on mine that could look at me with such indescribable love.

10

Meeting People
from My Former Lives

The Parapsychology Society held a lot of very interesting talks. I attended as many as I could manage. This is how I came to meet Harald Wessbecher, a speaker at one of these sessions, who became a very good friend and followed my development for many years.

Harald also had a talent as a medium and he travelled to the United States and studied and experimented under Bob Monroe after reading his book entitled, "Another Body". Bob Monroe developed the Hemisync method which helped in linking the two hemispheres of the brain so that they should not continually operate separately from one another. This can bring out paranormal abilities as well as develop them further. It is not my job to say whether this method is good or bad and whether such things should be forced or rushed. I was interested in all kinds of things back then and I wanted to get to know as much as I could.

Harald had studied to be an architect but when I met him he was only teaching and holding medium sessions. A spiritual being appears through him who calls himself simply Harold II and who claims never to have had an earthly incarnation.

Harald's first talk to our society was on the subject of dreams and the importance of dreams. He was quite a bit younger than me and his talk was really humorous and interesting. He talked about the possibilities that lay within lucid dreams and also the importance of recollecting dreams. Well, even though I had always dreamt a lot, I really wasn't able to recollect so many of them. Though I had

had the odd important dream that I would never again be able to forget. There were also those that I had forgotten for a shorter or greater length of time but was able to recall later. (Generally, these were the ones that I wasn't able to deal with at the time or that I had to forget for a short while.)

Harald also spoke about the different kinds of dreams. There are those that deal with everyday problems and there are teaching or warning dreams and then there are those that we dream and they actually take place sometime later. The spiritual world is also able to easily touch us and teach us in this state of consciousness.

His talk about dreams was so successful that it was held again a couple of days later. I thought I would give it another go myself and see if it interested my husband and so I asked Christian. He surprised me by saying yes and I sat happily by his side and listened to the whole talk all over again.

Christian liked it a lot and the unbelievable happened when he signed up for his first ever workshop that was going to be held the following weekend. There they worked with the Hemisync method. Christian wanted very much to go on his own as I was by then something of a "pro" in these matters. I had to laugh at this as I still only considered myself to be an enthusiastic beginner but I guess that I was a few grades up from beginner when compared to him. The other consideration was that only one of us could be away from the family for a whole weekend at one time. I was happy to take on the work at home for the weekend if it meant that my partner was going to try a little something in the name of self-development!

The weekend workshop was somewhere near Zurich. Come Sunday night and I didn't want to believe my eyes (despite the knowledge of my everyday consciousness!) A completely different man, a completely new man, stepped through the door compared to the one who had left only a couple of days before. I didn't only know this man coming in but I loved and respected him endlessly. The husband who stepped through the door was the one to whom I had said "yes" way back in 1973.

The change in my husband wasn't external but rather internal. He was glowing with happiness and his love embraced my whole being. "I have had an indescribable experience. I would never have believed that such things existed and even less so that I should have experienced them. I really want to get to know more about all of this. Now I not only fully understand what a person feels after such an experience but I also understand that I can't stop here. I want to know everything as well and to live my life based on this knowledge."

"We are saved!" And my heart and spirit rejoiced. The husband whom I had thought lost had returned to me and now we could go on hand in hand. I really couldn't believe this sudden and unexpected change as it was a 180 degree about turn.

He didn't tell me what he had gone through over the weekend and I didn't ask. I know that it was hard to come to terms with these things right at the beginning and even harder to talk about them. The only difference was that I would have been able to believe what it was that he had experienced.

Christian became completely independent. I had my Lichtenecker group and he had his Harald group. They only met Harald once or twice on a couple of weekend courses, but they had a group leader who held meditation sessions once or twice a week and who was able to provide answers to problems that had sprung up while practising at home to a cassette. The woman who led the group had been studying with Harald for several years.

The members of the group also met up with one another individually to practise with the cassette and Christian often got together with this or that member of the group. He often met up with Gerald whom he got on well with and got to really like. Christian also went to see the female leader of the group for individual instruction but also for a massage. I can't recall what method the woman used at the time.

I was pleased to see this development in Christian and the independent path that he was taking. He had been working with the group for a good few months when he rang me from work one day to say that they weren't going to be meditating in the usual place that evening but somewhere else, and that they could take a guest along. So my husband ceremoniously invited me to join him and to come along to the evening meditation with his group.

It is hard to describe how happy and proud I was for him. I could meditate along with my husband's group and more importantly with him. The pure joy that I felt at the thought of this melted away so many years of pain and fear!

The session was in Würenlos in the Emma Kunz Healing Cave. Emma Kunz was not simply a healer but also an extraordinarily rare individual. She worked as an untrained housekeeper but also painted in her free time. "Perhaps the people of the 21st century will understand," as she was so used to saying. She warned people, much in the same way that Einstein had, that we only use a very small percentage of the possibility provided by our brain and our personal will. She had an answer for any question. She knew how to heal any illness that you might care to mention and she sought the answer to almost everything with the use of a pendulum.

We started off by looking at the pictures in the Healing Centre exhibition. The pictures were totally unique. They were more like architectural drawings or drawings of a freemason's temple, hiding immeasurable knowledge within them.

I stood transfixed in front of one of the pictures. I was looking at a picture on the wall that I had seen in a dream the night before. It had coloured lines radiating from a central point like rays of the sun, branching out in a semi-circular form. After having seen Harald's talk and reading a book that he had recommended by Patrizia Garfield called "Creative Dreams", I had started to keep a paper and pencil on my bedside table. Although it was in black and white, there was this picture scribbled on a piece of paper next to my bed that I was now standing and looking at only a couple of hours later. I really hadn't counted on this! Unfortunately, in my excitement, I told my husband all about this and saw a look of sadness run across his face. He didn't have to say a word because I knew exactly what he was thinking: "There's no point me trying to catch up with her, she is always going to outdo me." It was his first major disappointment and it had happened just when he had invited me along to meditate with his group.

I was also very sad and I would have liked to have taken back everything that I had said but there had been some truth in what Christian had felt. And I couldn't do anything to help or prevent this!

Emma Kunz had also discovered the healing cave where she had often visited to, as she said, recharge her batteries. There was group meditation held right there in the cave where I had another extraordinary experience that I couldn't tell my husband after what had just happened.

The experience that I had in the cave touched me so deeply that I took nearly all my friends and acquaintances there afterwards. On the first visit of Péter Müller and his wife we also went there, to that sacred place.

Harald's talk about dreams brought many more dreams out in me. Harald himself appeared in my dream the night after his talk and he said that he would take me on as a student. I had another recurring dream after the talk or rather it was a recurring individual who kept appearing in my dreams. It was a young man but appearing in different clothes and in different periods. Beyond his youth, his hair was also always the same—shoulder-length and almost white. It was so blond. His eyes were a piercing blue and his whole manner was chivalrous. I had learnt for Garfield's book that we can wake up during our dreams and know that we are dreaming (conscious dream, lucid dream) and then we can get involved in the process of the dream. The next time that the blond man appeared in my dream he was in a long black, Pelerine-like coat. I asked him: "Tell me, why are you constantly turning up in my dreams? What is it that you want? Who are you anyway?"

He looked deep into my eyes and simply said: "You will know very soon!"

Christian had his practice tapes lying all over the house. He sometimes shut himself into the bathroom to practise and sometimes in the large room when the children were asleep. He sometimes went out into the garden in good weather. I still didn't know why the cassettes were quite so great and I accepted the invitation from Christian to go along to one of these weekends. I had a very strange feeling beforehand. Perhaps it was because I wondered why I needed to know more, and maybe my progress as part of the Lichtenecker group would be enough. But perhaps I was able to feel something beforehand that was going to happen to me there. I was very curious to find out what it was that could affect my husband so and change him so much. He had taken part in many more weekend courses since then and he even used what he had learnt in his work.

I took Ilse along with me who was one of my closest girlfriends. She knew quite a lot about me and also happened to be my hairdresser. Unfortunately, I had set her off on this path and I was to "suffer the consequences" when, after many years of spiritual study, she also started to work as a therapist and I had to find myself a new hairdresser. I have never been able to find one as good as she was.

They held the weekend course in a very elegant hotel by Lake Zurich. I spent the whole weekend in the reflexology group. I really enjoyed staying in such a luxurious hotel and learning so many new things.

We arrived at the last minute. We had thought that the route was much shorter, so we arrived out of breath and excited. We were the last ones to take our places in the circle in the large hall. The group itself was enormous or at least it seemed so to me then. There must have been 40 or even 50 of us. I had only ever seen Harald at his two dream talks and I was keen to be able to learn more from him.

"I think that everyone is here now and so we can get going with the weekend. No, I've made a mistake! Gerald still hasn't arrived as always" said Harald and he started to tell us what was going to happen over the next two days.

"Is Gerald perhaps the man whom my husband has been practising with?" I thought to myself. I was happy that I was going to be able to meet him at long last. My husband had often told me that he was sure that we would get on well and that we would be able to help each other a lot in our work. Gerald was also involved in reflexology.

Harald must have been talking for about ten minutes when the door opened and the last member of the group stepped in. It was Gerald. I thought I'd fall right off my chair. The man coming into the room was my husband's friend and also the man whom I had seen in my dreams.

11

In a Storm
of Emotions

Gerald took a seat and looked around the room as if everything was perfectly fine. The smile on his face was by way of apology to the others for his late arrival. He fixed his eyes on me and that is where they stayed. I wanted to disappear, to be swallowed up or at least run out of the room. I could feel that my face was bright red and my body would get hotter and hotter with beads of perspiration running down my forehead. The young man looked at me in the same extraordinary way he had in my dreams and made me just as anxious. At the same time, I liked the fact that he was looking at me and it was the secret that he held that made it all the more exciting.

And now he was here, the blond knight from my dreams, larger than life. The blue eyes and blond hair were just the same. As well as all this, it was the radiance of his being which seemed to be so familiar to me. And now that I sat looking at him, only a couple of metres away, I realized that I knew him from somewhere. And not just from my dream.

I could hardly wait for the break and I rushed straight for the door. Gerald was quicker to his feet and he stopped me when I reached the centre of the room.

"Tell me who you are! Where do I know you from?" he asked me. This is exactly what I had asked him a short time before in my dream.

"From my dream," I answered suddenly. I was rather annoyed with myself as this meant that I would have to tell him about everything by way of explanation.

Gerald, as if it were the most natural thing in the world, took my hand and led me out of the room. It was made all the more confusing as the fact that he held my hand didn't seem in any way unusual. We looked for a quiet place where I could tell him everything that I knew. When I had finished what I had to say, Gerald let me into a little secret: he had also been thinking about me a lot.

"About me? And you didn't even know me?!" I asked back, starting to become increasingly curious.

"Not in person, no. But I tried to imagine what you are like. I practised in your house with Christian once when you had taken the girls away skiing for a week because Christian was only able to join you in the second week because of all the work he had from the office. There was a beautiful ball gown hanging up in the room, where we were, with a silk top and a lacy, net skirt. You know I used to be a tailor and I spent years making costumes for various performances at the opera house. The dress did more than catch my eye; I started to imagine the woman to whom the dress possibly belonged and how she must have looked in that gown. I imagined you just as you are now standing in front of me."

I could feel that I was starting to blush again and was happy to hear the voices of the others calling us back into the room because the break was over.

We went into another large room where everything had already been prepared. We practised on the floor and everyone had to wear a pair of earphones. I had Ilse lying on one side of me and Gerald on the other, and we lay in pitch darkness. Harald switched on the machine which produced interesting and unusual sounds: Hemisync vibrations. Harald began to direct us via a microphone and then he began to count. I was heavy one minute and light the next; it was hard to decide. These odd vibrations really did make me feel quite strange.

I could see a picture: England in the late Middle Ages. I say this because of the cloths but somehow I also knew exactly: I recognized myself in the picture; it was a long time ago. I stood on the steps of some or other church, in a beautiful dress. I was also very beautiful. It was obvious that I was a rich but also very cultured young lady. My brother stood next to me holding my hand, he had shoulder-length hair; it was Gerald. We were just coming out of the church where my brother had been sworn in and they had placed a crown on his dead as he had become the legal heir after our parents' death. Our parents had died together whilst hunting and they had allegedly been charged by a wild boar. We knew that this wasn't true and that it had been my father's enemies who had murdered our beloved parents. My brother also knew that there were many who wished him ill and could hardly wait to snatch his throne. We were of quite high rank, perhaps best translated as an earldom.

There was a crowd gathered outside the church waiting to greet myself and my brother. We loved each other very much indeed but the tragedy and mourning had brought us even closer together. We stood holding hands and welcomed this great display of respect and love.

Knights came galloping towards us from the crowd with their bows raised and they fired arrows in our direction. (Such arrows had also found our poor departed parents!) I could feel that I was flying, hand in hand with my brother, towards the light and across a scented meadow full of flowers. Then all that was left was to melt into the light.

"Come back, everyone come back!" I could hear vaguely in the distance. "Everyone make their way back to everyday consciousness and back into this space!" the voice repeated. It became stronger and began to have an effect on me.

I could feel the pressure of the floor on my prostrate body and I could feel it getting lighter and lighter in the room. All the lights had been switched on that at once blinded and forced us all to sit up. Ilse had already left the room and Gerald must have returned to his everyday consciousness because I could see that he looked very excited, as if he could hardly wait for the opportunity to tell me something.

126

"I went back to my previous life and you were my sister!" he said, waiting for me to react.

"I know, I saw the same life!" I replied. We sat on the floor and relayed what we had both seen one after the other. We described the events identically right down to the clothes that we were wearing and the headdress. We embraced and began to cry as we had no idea where it was that we knew each other from. Now I understood why it hadn't seemed strange to me when he had held my hand and led me out of the room a little while before. The old love that we had felt and our coming closer together as a result of the tragedy could still be felt in the air. After what I had experienced, I needed to be close to someone and he needed to be close to me again. We held hands as we went off to have lunch and we couldn't stop looking at one another and stroking each other. All the others stared at us with eyes as big as saucers.

We didn't lie down next to one another again after lunch. We tried to remove the chance that we might accidentally influence one another and lay in completely different parts of the room for the next exercise. Harald had only just finished counting and I found myself back in another previous life and another body. This time I was in France and I was a young woman promised to another. My husband-to-be was an older man of higher standing and I felt nothing for him at all. Two young musketeers were battling for my favour and my heart. I was terribly spoilt and rather proud of the fact that men found me so desirable and I had grown used to the fact that they were contending for me. I watched the rivalry of these two fiery knights with a similar sense of superior pride. My heart still leapt at the sight of the knight with the long blond hair and blue eyes. My blood began to run hot in my veins but his advances and contest with his companion still left me cold. The battle between the two of them eventually ended up in a duel and I was only informed at the very last minute. My carriage could not speed quickly enough to the scene as I wanted to be there when it happened. I was determined to put a stop to the duel because I had a very bad premonition.

I saw the reason for my sensing something wrong as I arrived. My secret love had been fatally injured. I was unable to stop myself running to his side, no longer caring for what any of the others might say. I fell, crying onto the bosom of my lost happiness, my lost knight. There was only the slightest glimmer of light left within him. I lifted his head and sobbed as I begged for him not to leave me because he was the only one I truly loved and I could never imagine being anyone else's. A fleeting smile was his response and he rose happily to heaven because the love could now be his for time in eternity. I was left broken and sad until the end of my days. I was no longer willing to accept my elderly fiancé's approaches after this and I joined a convent. I wanted to remain faithful to my one true love until my dying day.

The pain that I had felt at his loss brought me back to everyday consciousness without Harald having to say anything at all. The recollection that I had just lived through really shook me up emotionally, even now, in this body and in this time. My blond love was here in this life and laying just a few metres away from me in the very same room and was called Gerald. I had only heard his name spoken on a couple of occasions up until that point. His competitor was also in the same room and his name was Harald in this life.

"Could it be that this is how we are going to be reunited? Could it be possible that our meeting is not coincidental? But maybe this is all just the wild imaginings of my soul," my thoughts went on.

In the meantime, I could hear that Harald had concluded the exercise and he was calling all the participants back to the here and now. The lights went on. I shot a quick look in Gerald's direction to see if I could catch any sign of what he had experienced in this exercise.

Gerald just lay there still. I thought that I should go over to him. I was shocked when I saw that he was as white as a sheet, hardly breathing and that he didn't respond to my touch or my calling his name.

I called Harald over and he called on the help of a doctor who was also taking part in the group exercises.

They massaged Gerald's heart and someone slapped him around the face. I took his head in my lap and tried to give him energy in this way. Colour started to slowly come back to his cheeks and his eyes opened just a fraction. He looked at me and gently smiled. He asked: "Am I alive or have I died?" and his head fell back into my lap. We started to resuscitate him again but with much better results the second time around.

Gerald still wasn't able to stand but he just managed to say: "I fought for you and I died for you, and happily!"

"Unbelievable," I thought. We have just both lived through the same thing again but from our separate perspectives, via our emotions. Gerald also recognized his old rival in Harald with whom, even back then, he had been close friends before his love for me. They were just as good friends in this life and had been from the first moment that they met.

This had been the first course that I had attended of this kind, and it was true that it gave rise to paranormal experiences and opportunities. It also brought emotions up that had belonged to a previous life of mine and reawakened them in this life. I now had two new friends and all three of us knew that feelings, which must have been 100s of years old, had come back to life in our hearts. I was not promised to another in this life but rather struggled with all my might for the future of my husband and the future of our family. The path that I had started to follow years before and the one that my husband had now taken a few steps along meant more to me than anything in the world. I tried to build my old love and my old brother into my present-day life but in such a way that only the warmth of old memories should live in our hearts. Gerald was in a long-term relationship with his girlfriend and he didn't want to throw this all away for an old lost love either.

I love Gerald as a brother but his closeness always made my womanly heart skip a beat.

A very loving friendship also developed with Harald and he told me that he also knew of many of his previous lives where he had been in a closer relationship with me. In one life, we had been cousins but we had fallen in love with one another. Our love had been forbidden and I had been sent to live in a convent. Harald still managed to scale the walls and find me.

We had also met somewhere in the East. He had grown up there as a street child and I was a mother with a lot of children but without a man by my side. The adolescent boy somehow became attached to my family where he found warmth and he helped out wherever he could as my children were still all quite little. He grew up in time but I was always able to rely on him in return for his gratitude at being adopted.

All these lives popping up from the past made me very excited and they questioned a lot of the feelings that I had. I loved my husband and I had fought for him. I hoped beyond hope that the sudden change would remain permanent and that he would be able to accompany me on my journey at the same time as developing himself.

The opposite was to happen in the end, and just as unexpectedly as the other change had occurred. Christian started to get migraine when he was on courses and doing certain exercises. His head hurt and pulsated, his stomach grumbled. After several unsuccessful attempts, he announced: "This can't go on. I would have liked it to and I believed that I could make progress. A part of me is fighting this and doesn't want to carry on down this road. This is me finished!"

It was like hearing a death sentence. My hope in the future had been quashed. "What can I expect of the future? How can we go on living together if our paths are so far apart?"

We had been given an unexpected chance to spend more time together and to talk this all over. My husband was invited to attend a conference in Australia. We extended the usual two-week, child-free holiday with a further two weeks so that we would have enough time for all that we wanted.

Our trip to Australia was fabulous. We accepted kind invitations, saw beautiful countryside, and it was the end of the summer there while spring had only just begun in Switzerland. Our discussions, on the other hand, didn't take us any further forward and both of us feared that we had finally lost something that had been so precious to us both.

I suggested that we should spend a short time apart so that we could both come to terms with how we imagined our futures. I thought that it would turn out that we were still very much on the same path. From the outside, it appeared that we were together but we lived totally separate lives on the inside. My partner completely dismissed my idea despite the fact that I had imagined that this would all still go on within the four walls of our home. And for a period of three to six months. It would have been terribly important for me to get a final answer at least as far as my own emotions were involved.

Christian saw no reason or meaning for my doubts. He thought that everything was fine and that we were following separate paths but perhaps it was fear that made him think this way. So we took a month out of our lives and didn't move a single step forward.

I was left with no other choice than to wait for the next miracle: an external decision. I knew well enough that our life couldn't go on like this together. Worlds started to divide us. I prayed for help to come every night. My family was still everything to me. I would never have changed my children for anyone or anything. I couldn't just walk out of the relationship but the spiritual path that I had begun to follow strengthened to become a vital pillar of support in my life.

12

I Receive Startling Information About a Personal and Political Future

Back from our trip to Australia, our lives went on much the same as before. All of Christian's time was taken up with his new job and the poor thing had to prove himself all over again. I didn't like his new company very much and I liked his new boss even less. Ever since my dream when I had seen through the situation and the underlying intentions, I was scared by the knowledge that this would shake the foundations of our family.

In my dream, we had lived in our previous apartment as we had done in reality. The doorbell rang. I went out to see who it was. It was late at night and I couldn't think who could be coming to see us at such an hour. The owner of my husband's office was standing in the doorway. I didn't want to let him in, so I slammed the door and went back into the room. The man rang the bell again. My husband asked. I told him who was standing outside the door and that I really didn't want to let this man into our home. My husband still went out but I shut the door to the room behind him so that there would be no way this uninvited and rather unpleasant guest should come into the room. After a while, my husband returned. As it was getting late, we went to bed. Our living room opened off a corridor which led to our bedroom and the children's rooms. I was shocked when I looked into our bedroom as not only was all the furniture missing but the parquet floor had also been taken up and the raw earth was visible underneath. I looked at my husband in horror for some explanation as to what had happened. He was completely calm in his response as if what he intended to say was the most natural thing in the world.

"My future boss recommended that I should move our bedroom across into one of the children's rooms as he thinks that will be quite enough for us. I didn't notice them taking the floor up as well!"

Our bed really had been squashed into the smaller of the two children's rooms.

I woke from my dream in floods of tears. It was then that I told my husband of the bad feeling that I had about the new company and the new boss as well. As I have already mentioned, he laughed at my dream and also at my fear.

"There isn't the slightest reason for you to worry!" he said and he accepted the new post.

We moved into a new house in August 1986. I was the one most pleased about this. As I worked from home and I didn't have to take the children anywhere in thecar, so I got less fresh air and rarely moved out of the flat at all. The four-room flat had been getting very small but the fresh air was the main thing that was missing.

The story of our new house began at the end of the winter. We made the most of the winter sunshine. One afternoon, I set out on a walk with my husband around a local leafy suburb. We also lived by the edge of the forest but we looked for a new place to take a walk. We stood about two kilometres from our flat and stared at the splendid view and the elegant villas and family homes on the other side of the road. You could see that the area wasn't exactly populated by the poor.

"You see, it'd be great to live here!" The idea just slipped out of my mouth.

"Naturally, Mrs König, you can take our house right away! Please move in at once and we will set the rent to suit your budget," Christian retorted rather sarcastically and then he added: "I don't like this quality in you, always wanting or saying the impossible! Why can't you stick to normal things! I know that you'd like to move into a larger flat or even a house but we can only make a choice based on our means."

I was upset again. I knew that everything was possible, if only we give it a try unless we were to give up too soon. I always thought differently about the saying about only stretching as far as a blanket covers. It wasn't the blanket that was important, but me! I don't adjust to the blanket but the blanket is made to fit me. Yet I had long since given up debating such topics with my husband.

I could have well imagined that there was a house in the area where we were standing that was available and that we would be able to afford. I was an optimist and I wanted to prove that there were always other options to the ones that people believe and generally live by.

I had been looking through the small ads in the newspapers. It could only have been a couple of months after our walk that I found a house with seven and a half rooms, with an enormous garden and the price fell within range of what we could afford. I rang the number immediately and got an appointment for that afternoon. It might seem hard to believe but the house, with its massive garden and glorious views, was only a couple of doors away from where we had stood in the winter sunshine that day. I found it pretty hard to believe myself but that was the reality. The house was exactly what we wanted. The only problem was that there were a lot of parties interested and wanting to move in right away. So that night I reserved the house in my prayers and said that I really wanted to live there and how happy I would be if we managed to get it. I could work in the garden as well as in the office.

There were three families in the "final" and we were one of them. The owner lived abroad and he was the one who had to decide. He wanted to choose between two but in the end, he didn't choose in our favour. The news came two days before we were about to set off on holiday. The owner signed the agreement with the new tenant, I just couldn't believe it. I was so sure that we would come through. I had even furnished the rooms in my mind. It was hard to get to sleep that night. I didn't feel at all motivated to start the search all over again. Thankfully, we were just about to set off for beautiful Corsica!

We got an unbelievable call the next morning. The owner had changed his mind despite the fact that a contract had been signed. He had decided to give us the house after all. But what could have happened?

The original tenant, whom we immediately arranged to meet, told us what had led to the sudden change of mind. It turned out that there was a condition attached to renting the house. The previous tenant had only forwarded to the owner the telephone numbers of prospective tenants who were willing to take things over from them that the tenants had purchased while they had lived in the house. As this wasn't so much, and everyone wanted to get their hands on the house, we had all agreed. The new tenant had phoned the old tenant, who was still living in the house, to say that they had changed their minds about paying the price that they had asked. The old tenants then contacted the owner who had the contract cancelled. This meant that in the space of a single night we had become the proud new tenants of a seven-and-a-half room house. So we enjoyed our holiday even more than usual and, strangely for me, I was especially happy when we returned from Corsica to Zurich.

I really did get a lot of pleasure out of living in the new house. I had a separate room for an office and I just couldn't get enough of the glorious garden and the wonderful view. I planted a lot of new flowers and I tended the old ones. I had never had a garden before and now I saw just how much joy it could give. The children got a dog about six months later. We were finally living in a place and in a way that I had always wanted. Everyone seemed happy and satisfied. I had a load of work but I was happy to see an increasing number of people who were only coming to me for treatment. I wanted to take my exam with Mrs Steiner so that I could officially open my practice. I had only been practising massage on friends and acquaintances up to now.

We had been living in our new home for three years by 1989. We held a big garden party in August. We invited all of our friends and we wrote "White Nights" on the invitations and so everyone came dressed in white and all the decorations were white.

I was now giving my reflexology sessions in another place that we had converted out of a space in the basement. I was working with a good friend that day. She had a lot of complaints but I knew her well and I knew that the real reason lay in a bad marriage. She never mentioned it but she came to see me regularly for me to lessen her pain. Suddenly the VOICE spoke and he said: **"Why do you think that you are living in Switzerland?"**

I had never been "disturbed" like this when I was in the middle of my work and the question took me aback a little. "Why should I be here? I married here and my children are here. But I don't know how it's possible to ask such a question!" I reflected because the one who was asking me should have known all these things.

"That wasn't the reason, that was the solution!" I heard back.

"What? That wasn't reason enough but a solution? But for what?" I asked in return.

"When you grew up in Budapest and we wanted to teach you, we couldn't find a good teacher for you there. The old one's either left the country after the war or, if they carried on, they ended up in prison. Many fell silent but many more died. That's why we organized for you to come to Switzerland and find a teacher here. We had to wait for a long time for you to cure your childhood trauma with your current family. It was only after this that we awakened you and now we are soon going to need your work. We would like to send you to Hungary to teach. You have to go there to give back what you owe to your roots."

I couldn't stand it any longer and I spoke up: "Teaching in Hungary? But what? It's true that I have been studying for years but I really don't know enough to be able to teach anyone. And anyway, what I am learning about spiritual and medial development is banned in Hungary!"

"That is exactly what will make the difference!" I heard him say. **"You must write down what I am about to say and show it to as many people as possible! You will need witnesses as proof otherwise they will never believe you! Three months from today** (it was now August) **Communism will start to come to an end and great**

reforms will sweep through all the communist states and all without loss of life.

The transformation will begin in Hungary. The country will open her borders for the citizens of another country and that is what will set the whole thing in motion."

It was impossible to believe what the VOICE was saying. "Hungary and the other countries freeing themselves from Communism? Unbelievable!"

As I had promised, I wrote down everything that he had said. But whom should I tell? Everyone would laugh at me! I wanted to tell someone who was capable of believing what they had heard and I thought of Elisabeth Haich whom I had already met through the yogi, Mr Yesudian but also from her own classes. I was in awe of both of them for being able to preserve such spiritual freshness despite their advanced years. I called them on the phone and asked for a personal meeting saying that there was something important that I wanted to tell them.

Auntie Lizzy (as I was to call her later) was the only one at home but she agreed to see me that same afternoon. I told her what the VOICE had said and she looked at me lovingly and said: "My dear, the shadow that is there is so very dark that it won't be so easy to remove it. I shouldn't think that it will change in our lifetimes, though it might in yours. But God only knows: I really hope that your vision will come true!"

Mr Yesudian had a similar opinion when I told him after the yoga class which I had gone to with the specific purpose of relating this information to him afterwards.

However, three months later—despite what everyone knew and believed—the unimaginable did happen at last. The fact that Hungary opened up its borders to the East Germans led to previously unimaginable changes.

I went back to the Haich after this and I was welcomed accordingly.

Auntie Lizzy had tears in her eyes and all she could say was: "Who is leading you my dear? Who is the VOICE?"

I wasn't able to answer as it had never occurred to me to ask. The things that he told me were normally so amazing that I was always taken up with the contents of his message. I couldn't have ever asked as I must have been ashamed of such a question.

If he wanted to tell me who he was then, he would do so when the time was right. What he did have to say was always important and true. Whether I liked it or not, whatever he said did come true and would go on like this in the future too. This was the reason for my present fear.

The VOICE said something else in the August of 1989. In response to the questions whether or not I really did have to go to Hungary and what it was that my husband would do there because he couldn't speak Hungarian, he gave the following answer: **"You'll be going there on your own."**

"But why?" I asked, rather alarmed by what I had heard.

"Your husband won't be going with you. Your path isn't his path!"

"Oh, well I'm not going then in that case," I answered quite firmly.

"You know that will change in the end."

"In what? In my marriage?" I asked again but I answered just as quickly. "No, then I won't do anything. No, I won't do it!"

"Unfortunately, there's nothing that you can do about it!" came the final answer. I swallowed hard and was curious to see what still awaited me.

"Very well then, but the children?" What were they going to do in Hungary, they didn't even speak the language!

"You won't be going home straight away, it will happen after the change. The false teachers and false prophets will appear before then. The people's spirit will be so dry after Communism, like parched earth, and it will suck everything in. People will realize in time that this isn't what they were really looking for, what they were longing for. That is when they will find you and call you back home. Your return will take place step by step at first. By the time that you get there, your children will no longer need you!"

I wasn't so happy to listen to what the VOICE had to say and especially now after the political changes had taken place, how was my life and my marriage going to alter? As the VOICE had said, there was nothing that I could do to stop this happening. I heard him but I really didn't want to believe it.

13

Anger Sticks
in My Throat

The announcement of the change began once again with a dream. I had a book launch coinciding with the opening of an exhibition of my work. This was the book that I still had not written but I knew that I would write it in time. My paintings were displayed on the wall next to my book. These were the paintings that I only used to paint in my dreams. When I am awake I would not only say that I can't paint but that I am decidedly untalented. However, at night I paint the most glorious canvases.

My freshly printed book was on the table and pictures on the walls and I was surrounded by a mass of friends and acquaintances who were celebrating with me on the wonderful day. I felt really happy, especially because the book that I would have to write had been published and proved very successful amongst my friends. There was the slightest of shadows cast across the evening's festivities: my husband wasn't able to attend. He told me beforehand that the chances were he wouldn't have finished some important piece of work and that he would simply have to complete it that evening as the client was expecting it the following morning. I heard and I understood but still my attention was drawn to the entrance when another guest or celebrating friend arrived at the party.

Unfortunately, my husband didn't manage to make it. I tried my best to accept the situation and still there was a slight twinge of sadness in what was an otherwise very enjoyable evening. My friends all asked me why Christian wasn't there. I defended him and his precious work. Friends were coming over to me all the time offering me their heartfelt congratulations and hugs to comfort me and this only succeeded in reminding me that someone really was missing.

Then an unknown woman appeared in the doorway. She was alone and it was obvious that she knew no one in the ever-swelling and happy gathering. She started to look at my pictures on the wall; she went over to the table were my book was piled in two stacks with the visitors' book by the side. She started to leaf through the book but seemed particularly fascinated by the cover. I was curious to find out who this mystery woman was as I had only invited my friends to the evening. I went over to her and asked: "Welcome to my book launch party! How did you know about this evening?"

The woman introduced herself and produced a business card from her handbag to be sure that I understood her name. And it turned out that she worked with my husband at the new company.

"But how exactly did you know that I was having a party this evening?" I asked the woman again.

"The invitation has been on your husband's desk for weeks and when I finished work today, your husband mentioned that he would be taken up with work this evening and I thought that he wouldn't be able to make it. Being as I was interested in the event, I thought that I'd come along and see what the whole thing was really about."

"That's very kind of you; I hope that you enjoy the rest of the evening!" I said but I was thinking something else entirely.

This woman was curious to find out about me and my work for some reason. She thought that she would come as she knew that my husband wasn't going to be there but it never occurred to her that I would pick her out from a crowd of so many people. I busied myself seeing to those who had been invited but I kept a wary eye on the unexpected guest. She stood in front of one of my paintings for quite a while which gave me an opportunity of having a better look at her and especially her aura. Something suddenly became very clear. Her aura also included my husband's aura. This meant that they had a close relationship with one another. In other words, this woman was my husband's girlfriend. It really wasn't a pleasant realization and especially not on such an auspicious occasion.

Now I could hardly wait for the evening to come to an end and for all my dear friends to make their way home. This woman and the realization related to her had completely ruined my whole evening. Now I wanted to know the whole story and as soon as possible.

When I stepped into the house, I looked like I was making a delivery from a florist's shop. My arms were filled with wonderful, scented bouquets that kind guests had presented me with. My husband was waiting for me at home and he also had an enormous bunch of flowers in his hand. As always, Mrs Binder had arranged the bouquet especially for me.

My husband, flowers in hand, reeled off a long apology for not having been there on my night. He had hardly finished when I told him who it was that I had seen in the crowd at the party.

"Frau X, well, how did she get there?" he asked, a little taken aback.

"She had seen the invitation on your desk and thought that she would come along. She told me that she was your colleague but being as she was there, and I recognized her, something occurred to me."

"What?" he asked almost instantly but starting to sound a little unsure.

"Your aura was in her aura!" I blurted. My husband went pale but he didn't respond. "And that means that you are having an affair!" Now he looked an odd, waxy colour and all he could say was: "It's terrible that you always know everything!"

I would have liked to hear another answer. Perhaps that I had been mistaken or perhaps something about the fact that they spent so much time together during the day could have made their auras merge with one another in some way …

This obvious answer, and the pronouncement of the terrible truth, was final. What I had known at the party was suddenly totally reinforced. The thing had finally happened that I had wanted to never happen: my husband had a girlfriend!

An enormous change occurred within me in a matter of seconds. The battle that had been going on to save our relationship all these years came to my mind abruptly. The hope that our marriage would one day return to what it had been at the beginning. I could feel and see a red ball forming in my stomach that began to move up inside of me. It held the most terrible anger. I felt insulted as a woman at the same time as being helpless and not being able to change what had already taken place. I could feel the force building up inside of me and I was worried what would happen if I suddenly lost control and it would be free. I felt that as angry and hurt as I was, I was capable of doing anything. I wanted to rage around and smash everything or to beat my husband up. This feeling was completely unknown to me and it frightened me. "I have to run out of the house, into the forest where I can be free to shout this injustice and atrocity out loud!" The red-hot fire had reached my throat when I slammed the door to the house behind me but in a way that the whole house shook. I wanted to run to the ends of the Earth and never to come back!

Suddenly someone grabbed me from behind and shook me. **"What are you doing?"** came the shout.

"What I can! Didn't you hear and see what just happened to me?" I shouted back but I suddenly realized who it was that had been shouting at me and especially who it was who had lifted me up and shaken me, like some kind of rag doll. I couldn't see a thing but I could still feel that I was being held from behind.

"No, you can't do anything else! You have just behaved in a way that you have seen and heard other people behave in similar situations. This isn't you! There are always other solutions to a problem like this. Now, I want you to go back into the room and find another solution!"

It was as if someone had just thrown a bucket of cold water over me and I opened the door that I had just slammed shut. I still didn't know what had happened outside the house. I went back virtually automatically and told my husband what had just happened outside.

"Someone shook me in front of the house and told me to go back and told me to find an answer that suited me or rather us."

My husband could bear it no longer and he began to sob. "What an enormous heart you must have to come back after what you have heard and try to work out a joint solution with me!"

"No, no I haven't. I was frightened of my own rage that I saw boiling up inside me. That is why I had to run away. The 'one with the big heart' is the one who sent me back to find a better solution than our predecessors."

And now I was crying and I felt the tension beginning to lessen slightly in my throat that the rage had caused inside me. We sat side by side and cried for our past and for our future as we had no idea whether or not it was possible to imagine a future together anymore.

I woke to find that I was crying real tears. The dream had seemed so very true that I needed time to be able to calm down. My first reaction was to think that I was lucky because it was only a dream. But the very next thought was: "But what if ..."? That is the very same question that my girlfriends asked who I told about my dream at breakfast the next morning.

I was lucky to be seated next to two dear girlfriends at the breakfast table: with Mia and Ilse. Ilse was my hairdresser who I had brought along with me and it was Mia who had invited me to a beautiful, snowy village in the mountains for a couple of days' skiing. I had met Mia the year before at the Parapsychology Conference in Basel. Our meeting was terribly interesting. It was the first time that I had taken part in this annual gathering and it was full of interesting talks and information. The various presentation rooms held up to 1,000 people and this meant that there was a fair deal of coming and going in the lobby of the convention centre where I was feeling a little lost. I didn't have a list of events and so I was staring at a large board which had all the programmes listed for that particular day.

"Hi, you're here as well? I'm so happy that I've bumped into you here!" and it was with these words that an elder lady stepped towards me with a smile on her face and visible joy. She put her arms around me and continued: "It's the first time for me and I can't figure anything out! It's so good to see a friend at last! Have you been here before? Do you know what's on today?"

"No, I don't know this woman. Perhaps she has mistaken me for someone else," I thought. "But what should I say to her?"

I saw help on the way in the form of a very old friend who was walking over to join us. She waved and I was very pleased to see her again. My unknown friend also gave a smile and greeted my friend before I did. "Does she really know her or is this woman confusing everybody?" I chuckled to myself. My friend greeted us both and seemed amazed that we knew one another.

"Well, of course we know one another; we were all in Ascona at Chris Griscom's workshop. All three of us!"

"No, I wasn't there," I said at last, in an attempt to sort out the misunderstanding.

"Well, I never! I must have mixed you up with someone else who looks very much like you!" said my new friend and then laughed as she added: "Well, we know each other now and I must say that it pleases me."

This was the chance incident that led me to becoming friends with Mia, the friendship lasted beyond the two-day conference and we tended our friendship, the continuation of which saw the invitation to the mountains.

My two girlfriends waited for me next to a fully-laid breakfast table the following morning. Mia was a fine hostess and spoiled us in every sense. The table was packed with delicious food but I didn't have the slightest appetite.

I could hardly wait to tell them all about my dream. They both listened very attentively all the way through. It was mainly Ilse who had known the struggle that I had been going through with my husband in recent years, as well as my attempts to save the marriage and the shared hope that we had in the new direction that our lives had taken. I had also talked about personal things with Mia before now and she had shared her own secrets with me.

My girlfriends—after I told them all about my dream—both asked at the same time: "But what will happen if it is all really true?"

The sun was shining in through the window and the freshly fallen snow glistened in the sparkling sunlight. Any other time and I would have been struck by the beauty of it all. Now all I did was notice it but it didn't make me react in any particular way. It was as if the fear that the dream had caused me to feel had paralysed my emotions!

All I could say in answer to their question was: "I would be indescribably sad and it would be so painful. But perhaps this would be the solution?"

I suddenly thought of the many prayers I had said before going to bed at night for there to be some kind of solution because the present situation was just unbearable.

I realized that my partner did not want to follow the path that I had chosen for myself. I knew that I would never be able to leave my family, even if I suffered, and didn't find understanding and help.

Christian had never wanted to hear up to now about this idea that we should go our separate ways for a while. He saw no reason and he wasn't even willing to talk about it either. Maybe this was the answer: the solution to my prayers.

14

Flowers at
the Station

I didn't feel quite so good on the train journey back home to Zurich as I had done only a couple of days earlier when I had been travelling in the opposite direction. Back then, I had been looking forward to a couple of days of skiing, sunshine and relaxation with my friends. Now, however—ever since the dream of the previous night —I could feel pressure in the pit of my stomach and in my throat.

Ilse sensed my discomfort and did her best to keep my spirits up on the three-hour journey but with little success. I didn't know whether I wanted the time to pass quickly or whether it would have been best for the train never to arrive in Zurich. I knew that the dream had been a warning and to prepare me for something. All I wanted to do was to run away or hide somewhere. But maybe it was better if it meant that I decided.

We at last caught sight of Zurich, the lights of the city that I loved, and soon after the train was pulling slowly into the station. My husband came to meet me as he did on most occasions and stood waiting for me on the platform with a bunch of fresh flowers. Ilse said goodbye to us and I, taking the flowers from my husband, looked deep into his eyes. He gave me a loving smile but turned his head away and didn't want to look back at me. He started to look considerably uncomfortable. Had the dream been true after all?

It was really late by this stage and so we went straight home and told one another what we had both been doing over the last couple of days. I had been skiing while he had been working and our daughters had both been away at a skiing camp. I could sense a degree of tension in the air but wanted to give sufficient time to clear the situation. I was tired and longed for my bed and the forgetting that accompanies sleep.

I was fortunate as the girls would still be away for another couple of days and so I planned to sit down and discuss everything the following evening. I have always loved to cook but I prepared a particularly delicious supper that evening and decorated the table and the whole flat with beautiful flowers. I placed the bouquet that my husband had given me in pride of place at the centre of the table.

I also asked my husband to try his best to get home in time from work which he did in fact manage to do. He was full of praise for the decorated table and the delicious meal that I had prepared. Despite all of this, there was still a real sense of tension as there had been the previous evening. The candlelit dinner table and the delicious meal somehow made me think of a farewell supper and maybe he felt the same.

I served the dessert in the lounge and we opened a suitably special bottle of Spanish wine. We made ourselves comfortable on the sofa and I asked my husband to listen to the dream, which I had the day before, and not to interrupt me.

I started at the very beginning. I tried to describe every detail exactly as I had dreamt it. He was visibly shocked at the mention of his female colleague's name and the blood began to drain from his face exactly as it had in my dream. After I had finished explaining my understanding that a shared aura pointed to a sexual relationship, he went as white as a sheet. I waited for his reply and he said exactly the same as he had in the dream: "It's terrible that you always know everything!"

I was filled with the feelings that I had in my dream but now I was conscious and I felt these in my heart and in my soul, here in the room. I felt sadness and insult but I also felt the red orb appearing which began to move upwards in my body.

I had an overwhelming sense of my own helplessness but the anger that was building up inside me was more frightening than anything else. I really would have liked to rant and rave and run out into the forest and yell at the top of my voice.

I sadly continued my account to my husband and told him how I had run out of the house in my dream but had been halted by a force and told to go back and look for another solution.

I didn't notice the exact point at which the tears began to trickle from my husband's eyes but they were running in streams by the time that I reached this point in my story and he repeated the words that I already knew: "What an enormous heart you must have ..."

I replied in the same way as I had in my dream and I was crying too.

The dream ended here and didn't supply a solution. My husband stood up and knelt down on the floor in front of the sofa and said: "Do you hate me now?"

"Of course, I don't hate you but I am just terribly, terribly sad. I don't even feel anger any longer. It got stuck somewhere or simply disappeared."

"How did our glorious marriage end up here?" my husband asked, virtually talking to himself.

"I don't know how I am going to be able to answer that, here and now, and I think we would be better off working out what we should do from here on in. How do we imagine we are going to go on living together?"

My husband asked me to be patient; he said that he didn't understand how he had come to fall in love with his colleague and why he had ever agreed to the affair in the first place. He told me again how much he loved me and how important I was to him as was our family's happiness. He was very, very sorry for having caused me so much unhappiness and disappointment. "I'll end it all if that is what you want," he said or rather, I should say, he asked.

I was in a virtual trance. It was as if everything was happening beyond my control. I could hear myself responding: "I really don't think that would solve anything! You did what you did for a reason and it isn't me who should forbid you from carrying on."

The pain was so paralysing that I didn't feel a thing. (I must have been given some kind of spiritual tranquillizer.) I was sad as I thought back to when I had suggested our short separation, so that we could both clear our heads and put our plans and emotions in order. It had, of course, fallen on deaf ears. Now, when all looked lost and we couldn't undo what had happened, all eyes were on me for me to decide.

The night was short and passed without notice. It was already getting light when we finally went to bed. We cuddled up to one another like brother and sister who were afraid of what had or what was about to happen, and our bodies entwined under the blankets as we made love to one another bathed in tears—for the last time.

We tried to find a solution to the problem during the course of the night and we even went as far as writing it all down. We could see that our paths had started to move away from one another and so we didn't want to force what had not really been working for a good while. We decided to separate emotionally the following day and that we were each to live our own private lives. We would stay together like this for five years and then we would decide. If one of us should decide earlier then it would mean the end to our marriage.

I feel like laughing when I look back on this from a distance of some 13 years when I think about what we believed in and what we hoped would happen. In particular, we didn't take account of what effect our emotions would have on our bodies.

Our children arrived back from camp a couple of days later and everything appeared just as it had before they had left. I would do things so differently today!

To anyone looking on from the outside, our marriage didn't only appear not to have altered but it looked even more harmonious than it had before. My husband came home from work hours earlier than he had previously. He no longer brought work home with him and he did his very best to please us at the weekends. I received many more gifts, flowers and expensive pieces of jewellery than I would have done from a man who had fallen deeply in love. He was in love but just with someone else! The reason he was so kind to me was that he had such a guilty conscience and also because I didn't argue and make a fuss about his ongoing affair.

I really didn't pay anywhere near enough attention to the fact that I was suffering more and more internally. I really didn't know what to do for the best. I thought time was what I needed and time would bring the answer.

When my husband was away on one of his "free evenings" or "free weekends", I also tried to plan something for myself but I couldn't enjoy myself whatever it was that I did. It was impossible not to see his happy face when he came home. But he kept on asking me to be patient as he was convinced that he would soon get this out of his system and that he was already fighting it inside himself.

It was in this state that we all four of us set off to Sicily for the Easter holidays. The pain grew worse and worse and I was no longer able to reciprocate my husband's approaches. I became increasing withdrawn and, more than anything else, I wanted someone to help me. I wanted to be helped to answer whether or not I had made the right choice and how long I was going to be able to live like this.

My husband just kept reassuring me that his marriage was more important than anything else and by marriage he also meant me and the children. My situation became increasingly unbearable. I wanted to be truthful with him and I gave him the chance to wake up and see that he had to finally decide once and for all. There was no way that I could do this for him. I especially didn't want to make a decision that would cut me off from our possibilities. I was careful about everyone except, that was, about myself.

At the same time, I was afraid that I was going to have to raise the girls without a father that, in their teenage years, would be the worst thing that could happen to them and the hardest thing that could happen to me.

I also feared for my spiritual development surrounded as I was by so much pain and fear. I needed time but I really needed a little distance from it all. My husband completely rejected my request that he should move out for a couple of months until his emotional state finally cleared.

I was presented with an unexpected opportunity to go away myself for a little while. The dolphin research group, which I had met at the Basel congress, contacted me from Hawaii to say that they were holding a ten-day camp. I had put my name on a mailing list after their presentation and so that was how the invitation had found its way to me. The idea of travelling so far to be with my beloved dolphins seemed too great a temptation: being in the sun, swimming in the sea and camping on the beach ... and more than anything else, the chance to escape from where I was starting to drown (with no water!).

My husband not only thought it was good idea but perhaps the best possible thing, given the present circumstances. He was beginning to realize that he did need to decide, yet either he couldn't, or he simply wasn't willing to decide. His moving out would raise questions with the children, with his parents and mainly at his workplace. This chance meant that he too would win a little time as he obviously still hadn't finally decided what it was that he wanted to do.

I was to be away for a month while he was to stay at home with the girls. (And with his girlfriend, with no bad feelings whatsoever.) I hoped and he hoped that this month away from one another would bring the desperately needed answer.

Hawaii, and my time spent with the dolphins, was really wonderful. I had so many unforgettable experiences on that trip. And yet, I still wasn't happy. My pain and hurt accompanied me as did the veil with which I had been covered and protected for months. I knew that Hawaii was even more beautiful than I had found it to be but my vision was clouded by my veil. It did protect me from the absolute intensity of the pain but it also reduced my sense of happiness and beauty during the month there. I knew that I was familiar with Hawaii and it wasn't the first time that I had been there in my incarnations as I recalled so many places and sights.

The first surprise took place on the plane I had taken a book along for the journey that Elisabeth Haich had written called "Initiation". I had been planning to read it for a while, but I had always put it to one side as it was such a thick book. Now that I was going to be away from home for such a long time, and since the flight lasted several hours, I thought it would be the ideal companion.

While I was reading the book, I often caught a passing scent of flowers. I looked up to see who it was walking by with such delectable perfume, only to realize that there was no one there. I soon stopped looking up altogether, although the perfume appeared again and again.

The scent greeted me when I arrived in Honolulu and not only me but all the other travellers on the plane. It was the scent of the flowers of Hawaii and especially that of the pikake flower. Hawaii had appeared before me and even greeted me while we were still flying towards her. I knew that then, yet I didn't understand why. I can still recall the sweet fragrance

Since then, I have discovered that, age 16, I became the leader of my tribe following my father's death and that this was on one of the many islands off Hawaii. I also now know that I had been in contact with the spirits.

On the evening of my departure back to Zurich—in keeping with Hawaiian tradition—I lifted the flower garland from around my neck and threw it into the ocean. I asked and promised the following as I did so: "Wait for me Hawaii as I will return to you one day! Then I will be in full health and I will be able to appreciate your full and total beauty!"

I fulfilled this promise to Hawaii and to myself seven years later when I was able to spend a month there. I was happy as I was at last able to emerge myself in my Hawaiian past and knowledge. I was able to understand once more the secrets of the animals, flowers and the people.

15

Be Free

The whole family was waiting for me at the airport when I arrived home from Hawaii. They welcomed me but there was a slight chill in the air instead of the warmth to which I had become accustomed. I instantly sensed that the situation had worsened rather than improved.

The children had been fine with their father for the month that I had been away. They thought that I had simply taken a short holiday on my own and left their poor old dad with yet more to contend with. They had even done their best to help him with the housework.

The thing that interested me the most was my husband's decision. My dear husband was virtually laughing when he announced that he still hadn't reached any conclusions in the matter. Things were just fine for him and the one who should decide was the one who wasn't so happy with the situation. I was really unhappy to hear this and lost for words as to a reply. I really wasn't capable of believing that I was the one who was going to have to leave just because he was fine with the ways things were.

I was in great shape after a month away but my health soon started to deteriorate again. Up until this point, I had only felt something in my throat but now I was starting to actually choke. I kept having shaking spasms and on several occasions, I unexpectedly broke down in tears and found it really difficult to stop. It was completely impossible to get any sleep, I had a deep feeling of fear and my heartbeat became irregular. Being as I was the one who had been told to go, I was left to deal with the idea. But where would I possibly go? Beyond my family, I didn't have anyone! The qualifications that I had were meaningless after having run the housekeeping and looking after children for the previous 16 years. I had really cut down my work over the previous couple of years on my husband's request and I had spent more time becoming more familiar with my new path. The only thing that I now had left was my modelling agency that my girlfriend ran when I was away, but I really wanted to hand that over as well.

I was just running out of energy. I never felt like doing any exercise and perhaps I wouldn't have even been capable. The tiniest strain like walking up a flight of stairs had me clutching at my throat and I was left gasping for air.

I was in need of help. Dr Jenny came to mind as he had been such a great help all those years ago, and perhaps he would be able to come to my rescue now!

Dr Jenny hadn't changed one single bit. His kindness and humour were just as they had always been. He remembered me and sat and listened as I told him all about my present condition. First, he felt my throat and did an ultrasound and then he sent me to have an x-ray. "What have you been doing with yourself Mrs König?" he said with the test results in his hand. "The x-ray shows that you have a cyst in your thyroid gland. It can be seen from the outside but it has started to grow inwards and is not only a serious threat to your heart and lungs but it is also pressing hard on an artery and on your windpipe. I really can't begin to imagine how you have managed to get along in such a state. I am sorry to say that I have to recommend immediate surgery." Seeing the shock on my face, he carried on to explain: "You really cannot begin to imagine the severe danger that you are in and I mean your life and not simply your health!"

"Couldn't I wait just a little while longer? Maybe it will just calm down by itself. I have managed to regain my health in the past."

"What you are saying, I am afraid, is simply impossible. You really are not aware of the risk that you are playing with here. If you were my wife, I would take you to hospital straight away and operate immediately. Please believe me when I say that even though you know that I am the last person to recommend surgery, I really can't see any other way out."

I heard what I was being told and had to believe it. Yet still there was something resisting inside of me. I knew exactly why it was happening and I wanted to give my body the time that it needed to possibly heal itself or for things to at least subside a little.

Dr Jenny just shook his head: "No, I really cannot allow you to do that! You don't know the kind of risk that you would be taking!"

"Please just let me have one more attempt. You are the one who told me that it is our situation, emotions and our difficulties which lead our bodies to react in this way but that we can also heal ourselves if we take responsibility for our health. I want to have one more try. I know that I made major mistake by protecting everyone else and not bothering with myself. I thought that I was strong enough to stand everything that this entailed. And then my poor old body started to choke on it all! I would like to give it another chance and give it all the support that I possibly can. A kind of internal force is urging me to try again and win again!"

"I can do nothing other than to listen to what you have said. As your doctor, a fellow human being and as a good friend, I have told you as much as I know and warned you to the best of my ability. I can hear your decision but I am unable to accept it. I am here night and day if ever you need me!" and he handed me his home telephone number.

Dr Jenny was one of the most wonderful people I had ever had the good fortune to meet. He had given an answer which far surpassed all human and medical obligations. Perhaps somewhere, deep down, he too thought that I stood another chance of winning but he stuck to his medical belief that it was just impossible.

He only asked that I do one thing and that was to go to the university and have a biopsy so that we could at least be safe in the knowledge that the growth was benign.

I did go and have it done but only to please him. They pushed an enormous needle into my swollen thyroid gland. The whole thing left me in a complete state of shock. All I could do was to cry and shake for several hours. The girls were so worried that they phoned their father who came rushing home from work to see what all the fuss was about. The state that I was in frightened him just a little but he was no more able to do anything about it than they had been.

We had told our daughters the whole story soon after I came back from my trip to Hawaii who reacted to the news with what is perhaps best described as fear. They knew that there was nothing that they could do and they were frightened by the thought of our family disintegrating. Seeing me like this now only added to their fears. I felt very sorry for them both but now I concentrated all my energy on prayer and recovery.

My spiritual teacher, Mr Lichtenecker, gave all the spiritual assistance possible. I hoped that I would have enough strength to keep going until my husband finally came to a decision. The solution came in a totally different form. The girls woke up one morning to find me lying unconscious on the floor. My husband had come in late and slept on the sofa so as not to wake me and now came running in to see what had happened. They called a doctor who ordered rest and calm and that I should be shielded from all excitement and shocks.

I lay in bed, completely drained of energy, with my daughters sitting by my side. They looked questioningly towards my husband, with fear in their eyes. My husband knew that he had to leave immediately if he didn't want to be the one responsible for their continued anxiety. He packed his most important bits and pieces and left our shared home. Then all we had to clarify was that he was "officially" living separately. I thought, or we thought, that would be enough.

My condition started to slowly improve and my strength began to return. Despite this, every single time that I met my husband, I could feel my throat constrict and started to gasp for breath.

Then the VOICE intervened one Sunday morning: **"Be free and remain clean otherwise we will never be able to help you!"**

I awoke to these words as if from a dream that had been paralysing me. I knew that now I was the one who would have to act. That very Sunday, I posted the official application for divorce into the letter box of the county council offices. I felt as if I was slowly starting to regain full consciousness. The VOICE had an unbelievable effect on me!

I suddenly saw that I had been unable to accept the situation and I had been fighting against it with all my might. I would most definitely have paid with my life. I had understood what had been happening. Despite the fact that I had known full well that our marriage was well and truly over, and my husband had even fallen for another woman, there had still been a part of me incapable of dealing with the situation. It was the little child within me who was still so delighted at having a family that she wasn't willing to let it go. The other, spiritual part of me wanted to fly away. There were light years separating these two parts of me.

The spiritually developed part of me finally realized that the little girl within me had become paralysed and couldn't do a thing.

So I stopped the part of me that longed to fly and I took my poor, sickened and damaged, tiny being by the hand and held it close and I decided to nurture and heal this part of me that was in such critical danger.

I had gone a very long way and overstepped all boundaries of health! I needed a lot of time, care and attention to calm down and begin the process of recovery. Strangely enough, the divorce helped. I had my thyroid gland examined every year and had consultations with countless doctors. I even asked for Mr Yesudian's opinion! The consensus was irrefutable: operation!

It is now over 13 years since I divorced my husband. My thyroid has calmed right down and it is very nearly back to normal size. I go for a check-up once a year and the x-ray always shows that the growth has shrunk and looks set to shrink even further. I can't say that it has gone completely but it no longer gives me any trouble at all. It doesn't press on my artery or my windpipe. I long for calm and a sense of balance. I even left my spiritual development to follow its own path and to carry on at its own pace.

It is now no longer a question of simply accepting what the VOICE had told me back in 1989 rather than fight against it with all my might. He had protected me from a great deal of difficulty but he wasn't able to shield me then.

Ever since, if the VOICE tells me something, I always do my utmost to accept what it is that I am being told and strive to act in its spirit as soon as I can.

16

A Present-Day Cinderella

My parents didn't come to visit so often after we got divorced. They had been to see us every year up until then and we had always been delighted to see them. We didn't have so much money in the early years but later on things stretched a little further and we took them to slightly more expensive places to dine.

They didn't come together but with their new respective partners. I wasn't even three years old when my parents got divorced.

My mother gave birth to me when she was only 21 and my father was 27. Times were hard when I was born in Budapest in 1948. My father lost his job after the war with the Budapest Transport Company where he had worked as an official. He smuggled letters out of the ghettos that Jews had written to their families. He also managed to get food supplies in to them. There had been something to give back then but now he was unemployed. Days often went by with no food on the table.

Both of them were very hot-blooded types. My father was Aries and my mother was Leo. And they were both terribly proud people. The only way either of them could deal with being injured was with revenge. The poor things! But back then I was the one who fell victim to this situation.

They divorced and my mother soon found a job with the taxi company, and like the emancipated woman she was, she was very proud of the fact. She must have been one of the very first female taxi drivers. This meant that day-care and nursery school became my family. I was given lunch wherever it had been paid for. When I was little, I took food home from school but later on I took it back home from a local restaurant.

I made my own way to school from virtually the first day and got there sooner or later. I did have an alarm clock but my mother would always try to stop off by the house or she asked a colleague to pop up to the flat to check whether I had managed to get out of bed in time. I used to always set off or be on my way in time, it is just that I didn't always arrive so punctually. They had even become used to the fact at the nearby pre-school, that I would get there sure enough, although they were never quite certain when that would be.

The teacher complained to my mother when I was in the first class at primary school and said that classes began promptly at 8 am and not when I eventually showed up. It was only then that my mother found out that I had taken my good old habits along with me from pre-school.

I used to have to turn left to go to pre-school from our home back then and right to go to school. It must only have been a 10-minute walk (or 15 minutes at the most) to either school with my little legs!

There were loads of interesting basements on the way that were exactly my height. In one, people weaving by hand, while in the other a dear old cobbler was working away. There were just as many interesting things to look at in the other direction as well. There was a little place where they made plastic balls, toys and boxes and there was also the coal man's cellar. I was absolutely terrified of him as my mother always used to frighten me with him and say that he would take me away if I wasn't a good girl. So that meant I really had to watch him very carefully indeed. But perhaps the best thing would be to make friends with him, I thought, and all at the tender age of six. Every morning, like a little puppy running along to be fed, I always looked into all of these basements and I visited each of them daily. The minute they saw me peering through the window, someone would always wave to invite me in. They must all have known that I had to get to school but no one seemed to care and neither did I.

I always had to check how much carpet they had managed to weave compared to the previous day, what colour balls and toys had come out of the moulds. The most important thing was I definitely had to go and see the coal man. I sometimes gave him my sandwich as I thought that if he ever really did have to take me away, he would be much kinder to me if I had given him my sandwich!

Everyone liked the fact that I would drop in to see them and they were always worried if they hadn't seen me for a couple of days: "Have you been ill?"

I always liked to entertain them and I used to sing and tell them little stories.

I had tiny feet and I was tiny myself. I had gone from being an enormous baby (5.6 kg at birth) to being by far the smallest at kindergarten and then at school as well. I was so small because I was so terribly unhappy. I didn't belong to anyone; or rather, those who belonged to the family circle, in time, turned out not to belong to me.

No one seemed to realize that I needed love, care and attention.

That's why I always tried to make friends wherever I could. I used to go and stay with my father in Sopron in the summer holidays as he had gone back there after the divorce. My grandmother had been widowed and my father had to support her.

I used to enjoy myself there in the early days and I really did love my grandmother who was a wonderful woman. She was just like they describe grannies in children's stories. She was understanding, helpful and God-fearing. Everyone loved her just as much as I did. When I was small (somewhere between the ages of about three and six) I was always hanging on my grandmother's skirts somewhere in the kitchen.

I liked the trip that we used to make to the market twice a week but the poor thing often had to carry me home from the market as well as all of the groceries. She sometimes had to leave her basket at one of the stalls and take me home first, and if my father was at home he would go back to the market to pick up her shopping.

I also liked going to the cemetery to see my grandfather. It was rather a long way and my father would often come along and take me home on his bicycle. I adored the cemetery! I just couldn't get enough of the lovely gravestones with their pretty angels and I used to really love the ones that had a photograph on them. I was fascinated by who the person could have been, whether they were old or young and especially why the angels had chosen to take them.

Sometimes, I would wish for them to take me as well. My little prayers increased in intensity as we moved closer to the end of August. I used mainly to pray to my grandfather that I might have a family with a proper mother, father, sisters and brothers.

It is my birthday on 22 August. My mother was glad if my father had taken me back to Budapest by then. The trip home often had to be postponed as I always managed to get a sore throat around 20 August. In time, they also realized that the problem was always the same and that I had tonsillitis. The poor things, if they had only known how difficult it was for me back then to come away from my grandmother and grandfather. My father also spent a great deal of time with me. He also worked for the taxi company in the early days but later he started making shoelaces at home. He always used to start early in the morning, so that he would be free for the whole afternoon. We used to have dinner together, just the three of us.

My grandmother was a wonderful cook. She made all her own pastas and pastries and the most glorious cakes. The only thing that would upset me was that all my little playmates used to disappear from the yard. I simply couldn't imagine that someone had killed them all. They all had their own names and they were my "brothers and sisters" or that's how I used to think of them all. But who could they have been if there were no children in the area? They were animals, of course: a few chicks with mother hen, the cockerel, sometimes a few ducklings and my favourite was the new little piglet every summer. My father used to buy one every spring and by the time that I arrived in the summer it had grown a little but it was still just a "child". It lived in a little wooden shed with the chickens and all the other animals. The garden was quite large and so they would let all the chickens out and, after much pleading by me, they would let the pig out as well. He was always my best mate. Over the three months that I stayed there it would become as tame as a cat or a dog. I used to be able to ride on its back and if I lay down in the grass, it would lay down beside me. I always used to share my food with him just like the good brother and sister that we were to each other. He was always delighted by this but my grandmother could never find out as she would have been far less enthusiastic.

I always felt so sad when I had to set off home again to Budapest as there was no one at home to play with. The timing that made me the saddest of all was that I would never see my little friends again. They would have "outgrown" the garden and the little shed by the following summer.

I once discovered the most horrifying thing. I was able to go and stay with my father one winter holiday and was overjoyed at the possibility of seeing my little friends again. "They must be there as only a couple of months had passed!" There was no sign of the hen or the chicks but my pig was there alright! But only for a couple of days! I woke early one morning to see strange men and women standing around in the yard. It felt wrong somehow. And I ran out to see what was going on. Everything was covered in blood and the scene was indescribably terrible. No one had thought that I would wake up so early in the morning! I ran crying to the wooden shed but it was empty. I yelled with pain and the disappointment at what my father and grandmother had done.

They had murdered my very best friend and my only little brother! I was inconsolable. I closed myself in the back room and cried the whole day long. My whole world was in ruins. I had believed until now, yet I was never going to trust a single soul again.

I had always had difficulty in believing but there were people around me whom I had wanted to believe in. My grandmother and my father had been two examples and, earlier on, even my mother. But I no longer believed in her. I had realized that she didn't tell the truth. She took me to my other grandparents' all the time and said that she would be right back to collect me as she just had to run out to buy something. I believed her at the beginning but then she only came back days later. I was more suspicious the next time she did this. Perhaps now she was telling the truth! I so wanted to believe her. I started to look at the way she was behaving on the way there as we sat next to one another on the bus. I concentrated on her totally. I noticed that something changed in her whenever she mentioned the fact that we were going to visit my grandparents. The same thing happened when she left there to say that she was just running out to the corner shop. There was something that seemed to change around her head. I started to see when she said one thing but thought another. Whatever it was around her head, which had been calm up to that point, it now became agitated and its colour became somehow darker and unpleasant. I realized that I could see when she was lying. I tried to tell her this when I could have only been four or five years old when she said that she would be right back. She promised to slap me in the face for being cheeky. And she left and forgot me there again. So, she had lied again. It was me that she said was impudent.

The other great tragedy occurred because of the piglet being killed and I discovered that my father and grandmother had been lying to me year after year. They could have told me that there hadn't been enough money for meat and that they had bought the piglet; that the whey had been virtually free from the dairy and the grain had been free from relatives who lived in the country. I closed my ears and I cried inside although there were no longer any tears on the outside. I was disappointed in the people who had been the very closest to me.

I prayed to the angel now harder than ever to come and take me away. Later, I started to pray to the "Great Wizard" as I thought he would surely be able to help. He was the one who I knew was good and I knew that he helped good children who had no one and he loved them. The most important thing was that he would never ever tell a lie!

I extended my study of human behaviour to the nurse at kindergarten and then to the teacher at school and to my mother's friends. I also kept the concierge in our building under "close observation". Something always seemed to change around their heads when they weren't telling the truth. The children in the kindergarten seemed to tell lies as well.

Once I told my friend that the nurse at kindergarten had just told a lie. She gave me a solemn look and said: "But how do you know that?"

I told her that I could see it and she was horrified and replied in the must disgusted fashion: "The nurse would never tell a lie and you can't see it when someone tells a lie. You're the liar!" Then she marched over to the nurse and told her everything. She turned and gave me a strange look and I could tell that she stopped liking me from then on. My little companion then went on to tell all the other children about what terrible accusations I had made: the nurse had told a lie and I had seen it. Now they all hated me. My mother threatened me with a slap if I ever said such things about her and especially if I did this in front of other people.

I still didn't completely understand. All I could think was that being as my friend (Mari, the concierge's eldest daughter) had said it was impossible to see when someone was lying, the best thing would be to try it out. "I'll say something and then you look at my head to see if anything changes," I said. "You're going to see, you must see, when I am telling the truth and when I'm telling a lie."

It was just a game and so she agreed to play but she couldn't see anything. So then we changed places. She had to say things that were true and things that were a definite lie. "Say something like you hate Péter from the fourth floor!" when we both knew that Mari was in love with him. (I was five and so Mari was all of eight years old.)

She said it, and could see it. I asked her to tell me something that I didn't know. I told her that she should tell lies and tell true stories as well. Everything was as I had thought. I recognized absolutely every lie that she told. She still claimed that it was all just impossible. "You can't be able to see when people are lying! There's no such thing!"

But there was. I saw! And now that I had been really concentrating to see whether or not someone was lying, I noticed something new. I started to see or sense what was happening with people. Like when Mari or my mum (or people who were around me all the time) were ill, I told them that I knew from the beginning

Still more disbelief and: "You're lying, you can't see things like that!" was the reaction that I always got. The worst thing of all was when someone died in the building and I dared to tell Mari a couple of days before it happened that: "That old man is going to die!" Then she told her mother who told mine and they threatened me by saying that I was evil to ever think such a thing and perhaps the reason that the poor old man had died was because I had wished it on him.

I was no longer able to bear this as a small child and I decided: "I don't want to see and I don't want to know anything that other people can't see or don't know about."

It was impossible to go on living like this and to keep on seeing things that people said just weren't there. The worst of all was that they said I was lying and that I was a bad girl.

I begged and pleaded the "Great Wizard": "Please make me just like all the other children."

He always listened to children and especially sad children and I was definitely a very sad child age six. I was small because I was so sad and I lied because no one could see anyway. By the time I was six, my left eye closed entirely. The teacher noticed that I was sitting with my head tipped to one side. She told my mother that I would only look with my right eye when I was writing and that I would lie virtually flat on the paper. I was whisked off to the optician. They diagnosed one-sided blindness (birth deformity) and said that I would have to wear glasses for the rest of my life because my right eye was also very weak.

It was in this "half-blind" state that I started to behave like a normal child. Although not entirely. Even though I could no longer see when people were lying, I was still able to sense the character of an adult or a child and I would sometimes sense things related to the future. But this only tended to happen in the case of great tragedies. I remember one particular occasion when I was on my way home from school on the trolley bus and an ambulance came speeding past. And I suddenly said: "I think it must be going to fetch my mum." My friend gave me a stunned look.

"What makes you think that?"

"I don't exactly know, I can just feel something."

By the time that I had reached home, the ambulance men had taken my mother out of our apartment and rushed her off to hospital. She had to have an urgent operation for kidney stones.

There was something strange inside me and I also knew but—thank God—these inexplicable events happened less and less often and now I never made the mistake of telling another person.

The problem was that this meant that my tonsils and my throat were permanently sore. This didn't just happen at the end of August but was pretty much all the time when some sad thing happened to me that I didn't have anyone to tell about it.

The only things that I was left with were the angels and the "Great Wizard" himself. I had less and less faith in people. My mother married twice again after that. She always wanted me to call her new husband "daddy" which I never did and I was meant to instantly accept his children as my siblings. I didn't do that either. I became more and more withdrawn though nothing showed of this on the outside. I looked just like all the other children. I told lies, I was rude, I was kind and I was completely normal.

Despite the fact there always seemed to be someone else living with us following the divorce, my family just got smaller and smaller. My mother always seemed taken up with these new arrivals. I didn't only have to share my mother but also my home, my room, my desk and the few possessions that I could call my own. I also had to like those who shared these things with me. I did my best in the early days. Yet, by the time that I was starting to really get to know them they disappeared from our lives just as quickly as they had appeared. I never saw anyone ever come back again. Not daddy No. 2, nor daddy No. 3, nor brother No. 2, nor sister No. 3 and so on ... They had been erased from my mother's life. That is how she concluded relationships. And I decided that I wasn't going to open up. I closed myself up and I didn't let anyone near except, of course, for the fire fairies (more of them later), the angels and the "Great Wizard".

Things also changed with my father. Not only did I discover that he had lied to me but a new woman showed up there as well. She had a daughter from her previous marriage. I was pleased by this at the beginning, and that I would have a little playmate in Sopron over the long summer breaks. Now my father didn't only spend his free time with me but they were there as well. I accepted the situation. I really had little other choice. But something stuck out right from the very beginning. The girl was always telling lies. There was no need for me to "see" this as she lied about such completely obvious things that I knew could never be true. My father would sometimes notice that she told the odd tall story but her mother always responded with: "No, my little Zsuzsa would never tell a lie to her own mummy!"

This seemed rather odd to me at the beginning but then things started to affect me more personally. If we went to the swimming pool together and she fell off her bicycle and laddered her stockings or tore a hole in her trousers, she would say that I had pushed her off her bike when we got back home. It made no difference how much I protested my innocence and tried to tell the real story, the answer was always the same: "My little girl would never lie to me!"

My father started to believe her and they punished me. And anyway—as they were always saying—I was the bigger one and not only did I not watch over the little ones, but I was wicked to boot, and I'd hurt the smaller children when the adults weren't looking.

This all made me very angry: I was always being punished for things that I hadn't done. My father, instead of defending me, always believed them and punished me instead.

I no longer enjoyed my holidays in Sopron and this was despite the fact that I had to go there every summer until I turned 18.

My father married the woman in the end. She and her daughter moved in with my father and they all lived together in my grandmother's house.

The girl kept on telling lies and then she started to steal money and often larger things, from home. She stopped blaming me in the end but it was obvious that I was still a thorn in her mother's side. The unfortunate woman must have known what her daughter was like from the very beginning (I would think) but she wanted to protect her and that is what eventually led to the tragedy.

I was always a good student but her daughter just managed to stumble from one year to the next. I soon became a sporty and pretty girl with a sweet figure but her little Zsuzsa still had the big belly and fat figure that she had as a little girl. She was also very lazy and she herself told me that she hated exercise and that she couldn't do a thing and so she would pretend to faint in PE class and constantly complained of heart pains while her mother had her excused from these classes, protecting her from any kind of strenuous exercise. The girl never ate vegetables or fruit, and never did a stroke of exercise and so she was 18 with a big tummy and the type of figure that would be destined to put on weight.

She married a French man straight from school who already had a daughter of his own. His first wife had walked out of the hospital after giving birth and literally left her husband holding the baby. So Zsuzsa really did have her work cut out for her. She had never done any housework before and now she was left with the housekeeping and her own child soon appeared. They came to stay in Sopron a lot and they went on holiday from there, which my father always paid for. They had very little money as her husband worked on a boat as a ticket collector. Zsuzsa did work for a time but left on a pension following an illness of some kind.

My father and his wife travelled out to stay with them one summer and they came to stay with us the following year. We didn't like to go and stay with my father as it was obvious that his wife didn't like me. This feeling soon spreads to my whole family. She had a very strong hold over my father. There was a period when she decided that she didn't want to visit us at all and so we didn't see my father for quite a long time. His wife didn't like our happiness or the standard of living that we had managed to achieve.

It is true that things were financially much tougher in the early years but we still took them to restaurants, to the movies and the theatre and made trips to other towns in Switzerland. My husband soon became director and then managing director of a company. Then we were able to entertain them with a degree of luxury and took them to some of the better places to eat. We were happy to do it and it gave us pleasure to give what we had. Besides, my father was my daughters' Hungarian grandfather, and he was still my father despite any conflicts.

My father didn't feel at all relaxed when they stayed with his wife's daughter. Her mother tried to put the housework straight during the time that they were there and shopped and cooked for them. My father also had to pay for all of this. They never took them out and my father knew little or nothing about the town that he visited so many times over the years.

Things came to a head one time and my father announced that he was no longer willing to make the trip to France. From then on, his wife went to visit her daughter on her own and so my father decided to start coming to see us again. This pleased us very much and, despite all that we had been through, we resolved to turn over a new leaf and start things afresh.

The wife kept up her hostility towards us; she made it keenly felt when my father returned from his visits to us. My father started to notice and slowly began mentioning the differences between our two families, and his wife took this as a personal insult. Despite all of this, my father kept up his visits. I used to send him money every month because I had heard how meagre his pension was. I helped my mother as well. I carried on supporting them after the divorce and my father still came to stay with us.

We still hadn't divorced but we had separated when I tried to ease the tension by inviting my father to come and stay with us. I suggested that he go to France again and maybe that would ease things at home with his wife. He resisted at first but eventually agreed when I offered to tag along.

It was Whitsun and my daughters had gone off to guide camp and so I could act straight away. I really wanted to help my old father and to help solve some of the old family conflicts. It all got very interesting!

I called Zsuzsa to say that I would be coming with my dad to help smooth things out. They were pleased as they still had a good relationship with my father despite the fact that he hadn't been going to see them. They came to Sopron several times a year and their children often stayed over with their Hungarian grandmother and my father. I hadn't seen Zsuzsa since our eldest daughter's christening. I had had enough of Zsuzsa back in Sopron.

On the way, my father told me that Zsuzsa had been working again for a couple of months. She had a job in a small private bank and since then their financial situation had improved considerably. They had moved from their modest apartment to a house which they were paying for in instalments and they would soon have it all paid off. Their son had graduated from school and now worked with his father on the boat while he was looking for proper work. He had plans to go onto college.

I listened to my father and I thought that maybe this trip would solve the problem that had been causing me so much sadness for more than 30 years and had taken my father away from me. I had spent years working on myself and my feelings and I wanted more than anything to resolve this negative and unnecessary mood.

They gave us a very warm welcome and really did everything that they could to ensure that my father enjoyed himself. Zsuzsa still didn't do the housework and so she took us out to a restaurant. "Zsuzsa works and her husband and children eat at work and so she doesn't need to cook," they said.

Zsuzsa took us to the casino one evening and gave us both money for chips and she played as well. Neither of us had ever been to such a place so we were delighted by the change.

Her husband never came anywhere with us. He was tired when he came home from a hard day at work and so he used to sit and watch the television. Being as it was Whitsun, Zsuzsa was off work and she devoted all her time to us.

When I announced that I was getting divorced after 16 years of marriage, she seemed saddened by the news and thought the whole thing was unbelievable."But you two make such a wonderful couple. I really don't know what to say!"

"Could she really have changed so much?" I thought to myself with pleasure at what I was hearing. Could this really be possible after 15 years?

It was late in the evening and everyone else in the house was asleep when Zsuzsa came into my room and wanted to chat about why I was getting divorced. I tried to tell her as briefly as I could. She also seemed interested in my financial status after the divorce.

"Women in Switzerland are fortunate and are protected if they stay at home as a wife and mother and bring up the children as well as run the home. The husband has to pay support to his wife and children and the amount depends on the number of years that they have been together and the husband's wages. Thank God, my husband earns a decent wage. I have also got money of my own that I earned myself and is in a bank account in my own name. That will stay mine after the divorce," I told her.

Zsuzsa paid keen attention to this. "Have you got it invested or is it just earning interest?" she asked. "What is the interest like in Switzerland? You know that I work in a bank," she added.

"No, I haven't invested it and the interest is somewhere around 2% I think."

"I'd like to suggest something," Zsuzsa smiled. "I work in a small credit bank and I can get you a very good return there. I do it all the time with my own money and money from friends and relatives. The bank specializes in helping lending money to people in financial difficulty and business men and the interest rates are very high. What would you say to us lending your money out for a little while? You'd earn several 1,000 francs in just a few months. How much money have you got in the bank?"

"50,000 Swiss francs."

"Ok. If I lend that out three times at 10% (the bank officially lends at 15%) then you'd earn 30% on your money in just three months which is 15,000 Swiss francs. This is how I help all my family and friends in Hungary. I have got everyone's money here and I send them the interest whenever they want to travel."

"No, no, I don't really need that," I said. "I don't like the idea that my money would be lent to people in financial trouble and that I would make money out of them."

Zsuzsa laughed. "That's what banking is all about! But this means that you would be making money as well as the bank with my help. All your father's and my mother's savings are with me."

"Sure, but this is something that I wouldn't like to do," I concluded.

"Give it a bit more consideration. I know a little cash would come in handy and maybe you would even be able to stretch to a trip abroad to brighten up this otherwise dark period in your life or allow yourself some or other luxury that you wouldn't normally dream of buying for yourself."

"How kind she is by trying to offer me comfort," I thought. "I know that I won't have any financial problems straight after the divorce but then I'm going to be on my own after that. Although I know that I'll do well in my new work and that I'll soon be able to live from what I earn, I'm still not going to be able to spend my savings on luxuries. But I am still not willing to make a profit from the pain of others!"

We didn't say another word on the subject and we both went to bed for the night.

Three shiny and terribly stately beings appeared to me that night in a dream.

"Give your money to Zsuzsa!" they said.

"No, it just won't work!" I immediately objected. (But how could they say such things when they knew the terrific interest that the bank was charging borrowers!)

"No, I won't give her any money!"

I was saying all of this to them in my thoughts but they were no longer there.

I didn't think about the dream at all during the day. Zsuzsa had another go and I brushed her off by saying that I had already given my answer.

I dreamt the very same thing again that night and again on the third night. The only difference on the third night was that when I protested, they added: *"We wouldn't be telling you to do this if we didn't think that it was a good idea!"*

I was forced to believe what I was being told. After all they had gone to the trouble of telling me three times over and I was starting to realize that I was best to act on what they were recommending. The problem was that I simply couldn't understand how they considered such a financial arrangement to be good. I started to wonder what it was that was behind their recommendations. They obviously knew something that I could only guess at.

The visit went off very well. My father promised that he would start visiting his stepdaughter and her family again with his wife. When he told his wife this on the telephone, she responded by saying that she would now be willing to accompany him on his trips to Switzerland. (I must say that I wasn't so delighted by this news but at least it meant that we had managed to re-establish peace in the family.)

In the end, such visits never actually happened.

I mentioned Zsuzsa's offer to my father on the way home from Strasbourg and that she had told me she would earn interest for me on my 50,000 francs if I sent it all to her.

My father answered all my doubts when he said that he would never place money in that woman's hands.

I was rather taken aback by his response. Had he really said that he wouldn't trust her with money? And this was when she was holding all their savings for them and they used the interest to go shopping when they were outside Hungary. I was shocked! My father wasn't telling me the truth again!

I decided! I felt and I somehow knew that my decision—because of what my father had said—would set something terrible in motion. While I was still in the car on the way home, I resigned myself to transferring the whole 50,000 francs to Zsuzsa the very next day. I would never have done such a thing even though my wise advisors had gone to the trouble of telling me three times in my dreams.

I gave the instruction to my bank the next day and a couple of days later notice came back to say that the money had arrived on the Strasbourg account. I knew that I had started something that I wouldn't be able to stop.

It was the beginning of June. Zsuzsa had called several times to say that things were going well and that at the end of July she told me that she had managed to lend the money out three times and at a rate even higher than the one we had agreed. So, she would be able to send it back to me a whole month earlier than planned. While we were chatting, we realized that it was 1 August the following day which was a national holiday in Switzerland. She said that they would be delighted to see me, so I accepted her invitation. She said that we had to discuss whether she should transfer the interest separately so as not to cause complications for me at the bank. Perhaps they would ask how the original amount had managed to grow by 15,000 francs in only 2 months. I laughed and told her that no one would ever ask such a question in Switzerland as people's accounts jumped by millions in very short periods of time. We had to hand in our tax returns at the end of the year with an official statement from the bank but no one would ask why it was more than it had been the previous year. Those who had much more money simply didn't send this paper in or kept their cash in several bank accounts at the same time.

"Odd that she should trouble herself with such issues," I thought after she put the phone down.

I realized one or two things during the long drive up to their place. First of all, the milometer stopped in the car. Then the clock and next the speedometer stuck at one particular point, no matter how quickly I drove. I was driving a car where time and space had stood still. I moved with no kilometres and without time passing. I had a very ominous sensation! Clocks and similar devices had stopped in my presence before but that had been a long time ago and now three things had stopped all at once. I knew that something mysterious was happening but I had absolutely no idea what it was!

Zsuzsa welcomed me warmly again and, as I was only going to be staying for a day, she had taken that day off work. She nipped into the bank the following morning to see if my financial matters were being dealt with. She came back and pressed a bank document into my hands with a disappointed look. "See, I have organized the transfer of your funds. I signed it along with my department head but I didn't know that such a large amount—65,000 francs in all—needed to be signed by the bank manager who is off on holiday until Monday. But take the copy with you and your money will be transferred on Monday. You know that we are also going on holiday to Egypt on Monday and I really wanted to get all your finances sorted before we left."

As I listened to her, the sense I'd had as a child started to come back to me and I could tell that Zsuzsa was lying to me. But where was the lie in all of this information? I had the signed paper right in front of me and it was signed and stamped and had the equivalent amount written on it in French francs.

I couldn't stay any longer and they were busy getting ready for their trip but I had a strong sense that something was definitely wrong. Why were they going to Egypt? I remembered that during my visits there with my father, we had all of us gone to visit an exhibition on Egypt, including Zsuzsa. Strange that only six months after I had been, they were now all set to travel to Egypt! They had never been even as far as Paris. Perhaps it was the exhibition that had set their imaginations going? The trip home was a long one and I really had plenty of time to think things through in detail and analyse what was really going on. My car went without kilometres or time all the way home. I had to stop on several occasions because I thought I was going to be sick as my body started to react to the situation. I knew now that something horrible was casting its shadow over all these events.

My father and his wife were delighted to hear that I had been to see Zsuzsa. They were expecting them that same weekend as they were to fly to Luxor with Hungarian Airlines from Budapest. They were going to leave their car with my father and then stop off again on their journey back. It must have been cheaper this way but I am sure that I would never have travelled to Luxor from Strasbourg via Sopron and Budapest, but I guessed they knew what they were doing.

I didn't spend too much time thinking about their journey but instead spent the whole weekend trying to unravel the mystery. I could hardly wait for Monday to come!

Being as the document from the bank had the bank's telephone number written on the top, the first thing that I did on Monday morning was to call the bank. I first apologized for disturbing the manager and then for asking a personal question: "Have you been on holiday?"

"Yes!" he laughed. "But how come you know that and why are you interested in my holidays?"

"I have a relative, in fact she's my stepsister, and she works for your company. I transferred 50,000 Swiss francs to her a couple of months ago. I went to visit her last week when she handed me a signed document issued by your bank saying that only your signature was needed and I would have my money transferred back to me. I really am sorry to disturb you but I just wanted to check as the lady in question is on holiday at the moment," and I stopped to let him speak.

He asked what the lady was called. I told him Zsuzsa's surname which was greeted with s brief silence and then his tone changed and there was not a trace left of his laughter as he very seriously said: "I am afraid that I can't discuss this matter on the telephone with you madam, but I would like to ask you to come and see me in person as soon as possible. We are faced with a large problem as we have no one working here by that name."

My blood ran cold and I asked back: "Are you quite sure?"

"I have been head of this bank for ten years," he said, with a slightly warmer tone, "and our branch is small, so I know all my employees in person."

I put the phone down like it was a lead weight. Good heavens! What was going on? Zsuzsa didn't work there and she never had? So, where on earth had I sent my money to? The bank had sent notice that my money had arrived and the paper that I now held in my hand came from the exact same bank to say that the money was about to be sent back. The account numbers agreed. They were sending the money back from the same place that I had sent it to. But if she didn't work there ...? I daren't go on any further because I really couldn't imagine what could be behind all of this.

I didn't have any patients that day. I wanted to set off right away but before I did I thought I might try to catch Zsuzsa and her family in Sopron on the telephone. I would ask her to explain the whole situation to me. My father picked the telephone up and when I asked him whether his stepdaughter was there, he answered with a "no". "They left on the first train this morning and they could be on their way to Egypt by now."

I tried to carefully recount the conversation I had on the telephone with the bank to my father. My father was surprised at first that Zsuzsa had money of mine and then after a few moments thought he said: "Perhaps the manager wanted to draw your attention to a problem with the money and your bank but he couldn't do it on the telephone."

"But Dad, the bank manager said that no one by that name had ever worked at the bank!"

I could hear my father's wife standing by the telephone: "Yes, Zsuzsa told me that Dori had entrusted her with money and that she was now earning interest on her cash via the bank. And now she's trying to tell one of her stories like she used to do in the old days! Zsuzsa asked me not to mention Dori's money to you (my father) and she told me just before she left that the money was now all organized and that is why she could leave feeling relaxed as she had been able to handover all the paperwork to Dori. But that girl never alters and she's telling lies about my daughter again!"

My father was swinging back again: "Did you hear what my wife said? Everything will be fine and Zsuzsa told her everything! It must be the fact that the bank manager just wants to make sure that there'll be no problem with your money when it arrives on your Swiss bank account."

"But Dad! She doesn't work there!" I yelled in helplessness down the telephone.

My father's wife decided: "A bank manager wouldn't be able to give information like that out over the telephone. Zsuzsa has been working there for years and her financial matters have always been in order. Tell Dori to go and see for herself and leave poor Zsuzsa alone once and for all!"

I simply couldn't believe my ears!

The trip up to Strasbourg was awfully long and again I drove with no functional clock or speedometer. It was quite unbelievable to think what had happened in a matter of just a couple of days and all this apparently without space or time! They must have arrived in Luxor about the same time that I drove into Strasbourg. I would have so loved to have seen Zsuzsa's face now that I was back in Strasbourg. Perhaps that is why she had fled to Egypt as quickly as she had. Could she have gone on my money? I was sure she'd never stoop that low! Images and events from my childhood flashed before me and of all the things that Zsuzsa had done to me. (I pushed her off her bike. I was lying and not her. The money and the jewellery were gone from her mother's cupboard.) Could it still be going on?

Then I arrived at the bank at last. The bank manager was waiting for me. He had a very worried expression as he ushered me into his office and placed his copy of the document on the table with signatures from Zsuzsa and someone else.

"Madam, what I said is true. No one by this name has ever worked at the bank but I know of the woman and the document that you were referring to. The lady in question has been a client of ours for many years. I have seen the kind of document that you are holding about three times during the last week or so. I don't know how this woman got hold of such paperwork but she must have stolen a copy when one of our clerks wasn't looking, or she was somehow conspiring with a member of staff from the bank. The matter is now in the hands of the police and they are investigating. Your relative is also fully aware of this as she came in and virtually begged for a new loan before leaving for her trip abroad. The fact that there is a criminal investigation underway and her house is mortgaged meant that I was unable to be of help to her. I suggest that you go straight the police though I very much doubt that you will ever see your money again. I am terribly sorry to learn what has happened in this case and I know that it is even harder to digest that it is happening within the family as it has," he added.

I hadn't thought this would happen either! All I'd wanted to do was to help heal some old family wounds and I hoped that Zsuzsa had changed in the decade that had passed. Unfortunately, it appeared that she had grown more cunning as the years had passed.

My next trip was to the police station where they recorded my every word in a statement. They made copies of both the bank documents including the one that Zsuzsa had given to me the previous week. The policeman who was dealing with the case said that three other people had been in to register similar complaints within the space of a week. There had been a local taxi driver whose money Zsuzsa had been "handling"; there was a woman from Germany and one of Zsuzsa's neighbours. He also said that the bank had filed a complaint about the stolen paperwork and its unauthorized use. They had also put in their request for her house to be auctioned as the money that Zsuzsa had borrowed now exceeded the value of their heavily mortgaged home. This meant that it was rather unlikely that I, as the fourth complainant, would get any money back. So basically, all he did was to reinforce what the bank manager had told me.

I started to feel sick all over again. I was also feeling very hungry and so I dropped into a restaurant nearby. The sight of the menu and the smell coming from the kitchen sent me running straight to the ladies' room where the poisons left my body. Afterwards, I thought I might be able to eat a little warm soup as I still had the long drive home and it was starting to get dark.

While I was waiting for my soup, I called my father. They listened to what I said and then all his wife was able to say was: "No, it's impossible. My daughter would never do such a thing! I know that she will explain everything the minute she gets home and I refuse to believe what anyone has to say on the matter until then,—and especially anything Dori has to say about Zsuzsa!"

I didn't want to believe it either and nor did I want to believe what I was hearing on the other end of the line. My father didn't say a thing, although he knew full well what kind of state I must have been in! Or perhaps he was more concerned about the fact that all his savings had shared the same fate as mine!

I really have no idea when or even how I managed to get home that night. I was in an absolute trance with no time or space and I was "driven home": (they had driven the car as I was absolutely incapable.)

There was a message on my answering machine when I walked in. It was my father asking me to call him no matter how late it was when I arrived. It was terribly late but I did as I was asked and dialled his number in Hungary. They weren't asleep. This wasn't just because of me but because Zsuzsa's mother had found a letter on her pillow. It was a farewell letter to say that Zsuzsa would not be returning from Egypt as she planned to commit suicide there. She admitted everything in the letter and she also admitted that she had lost absolutely everything. She had lost the house and everyone's savings, including mine! She had lost it all in the casino. She admitted that she had lied her whole life and she also said that it had been mainly because of me and that she had always felt inferior to me. In fact, she wrote: "... Dori was always straight and I wasn't."

Now she had tried to put everything right with my money. She had put a larger amount than ever on a spin of the roulette wheel—and lost the lot. The rest (of my money) she had used to buy a car and she said that: "It was pretty, just like Dori." She had also paid for the whole family to go to Egypt (again using my money) because: "Dori said what a wonderful place it is." She had thought that she would like to die in such a glorious place. She also blamed her mother in the letter saying that she had always known that she was false and a liar, and why had her mother never put a stop to this behaviour? Perhaps this would have meant that her life would have turned out completely differently. She ended her letter by apologizing to everyone, including me.

My father finished reading the letter and a long silenced followed. My father was the first one to speak though I don't know what I would have been able to add.

"The only thing that I can say is that I made a great mistake and I believed her, in fact, I believed both of them before I believed you. And this was despite the fact that I always suspected something."

"Let's stop for tonight," I said. "I really have to get some sleep!"

All I wanted to do was to sleep and to forget the whole thing at least for a couple of hours. I mainly wanted to forget the question that placed an enormous question mark over all of my thoughts. Why had the spirit world done this to me? Why did I need to lose all my savings? Why had I been forced to make a sacrifice yet again?

I felt a little more relaxed when I woke the following morning. I took my car to the service garage and the guy said he had never seen anything like it before with everything switching itself off on the dashboard. I didn't say a word.

I called my husband and told him what had happened. I half expected him to blame me for having believed her in the first place, and that it was my fault for losing the money that I had asked to be kept specially in my own account. But no. He listened and then said something simply wonderful: "You know, if that was the price that had to be paid to put an end to the suffering you have endured caused by your father and his family over the last ten years, then it was well worth it! It has turned out at last who was genuine and who was the good one!"

I burst out crying and tears came pouring from my eyes that had been building up for weeks and months and quite possibly years. He also asked if he could be of any help at all. I thanked him but told him that this was the kind of situation where no one else could help.

However, everything turned out rather differently. Those above continued to help me but I just had to wait until the end. I will speed up my recollection of the events which followed.

Zsuzsa didn't go through with the suicide. Her husband got to know of what had been happening on their return from a wonderful vacation. Their house was locked when they got back to France. They were able to take their most personal belongings from the house the following day and then the bank auctioned everything off. Her husband took their son and they both moved back in with his elderly mother where his other daughter was living from his previous marriage. Zsuzsa had also managed to fritter away both the children's savings. The daughter had moved out a long time ago as they had never really hit it off. She had been saving money for a small flat of her own but that had all been lost. The husband immediately filed for divorce and Zsuzsa moved straight back home to Sopron. She had a massive amount of debt above and beyond the money she had owed the bank. She hoped that this wouldn't be taken out of her wages for years and years after the divorce. I don't know how that was all sorted out in the end.

On returning to Sopron, Zsuzsa was forced to move back in with my father and his wife as she had no money at all. Her mother said to my father: "Who else will stick up for her daughter if not her mother?" And my father couldn't do a thing. My father and his wife who had always been so bothered what the neighbours would think, were now the talk of the town. Zsuzsa had made contact with everyone they knew over the years and had helped them to "get money out" and "handled their finances". They daren't step out into the street now for fear of meeting someone they knew who had lost all their savings with Zsuzsa's "professional help". They also panicked that the authorities would somehow find out as it was illegal back then for Hungarians to keep money outside the country. That is also what Zsuzsa had been counting on. She lived on her mother's and my father's money as she didn't work. The situation had reached such a point between my father and his wife that she had decided to move out of the house with her daughter and divorce my father. But that never actually happened.

Zsuzsa disappeared for a couple of days from Sopron. She went to stay with her father and tried to secure a place for herself in another town. Her father knew about what had happened in Sopron and he knew all about Zsuzsa. He said that he wasn't able to help. He had also been very hard hit by what friends from Sopron had told him. My father got a call to say that Zsuzsa was in hospital after attempting to commit suicide. She had checked into a hotel with her French passport and it was there that she had tried to leave this life. She hadn't taken enough pills or perhaps she had just wanted to frighten her parents, it was impossible to tell. She wrote to her mother from hospital to say that she was going back to France where she was going to try to start a new life, and she promised that she would pay back her debts to the very last penny. If she had to, she would work until she drew her last breath. The poor woman really did want to believe this but her heart "saved" her from further disappointment. She developed an unexpected problem with her heart and passed away within a matter of days. She was at peace at last, or so I hope. The girl had killed her mother and it was only a short time afterwards that her father also sought peace in the hereafter because of the way that his daughter had behaved.

Now my father was left widowed after this terrible turn of events. He no longer kept in touch with his oldest of friends and he never really left the house. He completely withdrew into himself and became so terribly lonely. He was a broken man who was forced to worry about his health. He had no one else left in the world but me.

I was age 45 when my father finally rediscovered his daughter. He was now over 75 and I tried my best to help him wherever I could. I doubled the amount that I had been sending as he really wasn't able to live on the widower's pension that he received. I invited him to stay more often and, now I was visiting Budapest more regularly, either he would come to see me or I'd call in on him.

His stepdaughter and her family naturally came to his wife's funeral. It was then that she handed my father a list of her mother's jewellery to the last ounce and hallmark. My father now understood why his dead wife had wanted to invest as much money as she could in jewellery. She had wanted to save this for her daughter as her daughter inherited her jewellery after her mother's death. My father was hardly able to comprehend that his wife had conspired in this way with his stepdaughter. The jewellery was long gone as his wife had given it to me when she was still alive to cover the expenses that I had in connection with the legal process of claiming my money back. The cost of the lawyers had eaten up the value of the jewellery but, despite the fact that I won my case on all three counts and took it as far as the Strasbourg Supreme Court, Zsuzsa hasn't paid me a penny back to this day.

Zsuzsa didn't go back to work when she returned to France as there were four other complaints against her as well as all those from the bank and so all herwages—as she calculated—would have gone on paying back her debts. She managed to find herself a lawyer whom she instructed to challenge everything and we, along with the four other claimants, had to pay legal fees for years and were forced to prove that we had given her the money and that Zsuzsa had squandered it away in the casino. Zsuzsa contested every ruling but she didn't have any success at the Supreme Court. They sentenced her to repay the 50,000 francs, the interest over five years and to reimburse all legal costs. But this didn't change a thing as she wasn't working and it isn't possible to deduct anything from unemployment benefit.

I would have given up long before but my father and his wife insisted that I would get my money back one day. They covered the expenses with the jewellery but it wasn't worth all the effort.

One day, my father had a call from Budapest to say that the police were looking for Zsuzsa there. He was frightened by this and it turned out that Zsuzsa had been living in Budapest in a hotel as a joint citizen and disappeared one day without settling her bill. The police had traced her to my father's address as this had been their last registered abode and the hotel hoped that, being as he was her stepfather, he would pay the bill. My father had had enough and he was worried about what Zsuzsa would do next and so he decided! He transferred the deeds of my grandmother's house to my name and also paid all the taxes that I would have been forced to pay. When I received the letter telling me about this generous gift, I finally understood that I was now getting back all the money that had been taken from me through lies and cheating, and a good bit more besides.

The wheels of God's mills are slow to turn but turn they do. My helpers from above had helped to ensure that I would receive my rightful inheritance.

It is a very sad tale that so much adversity had to be suffered in order that a father might at last accept and love his daughter and be proud of her.

He still didn't know what to think about my work. He often asked me why I did this hocus-pocus because I had got a college degree.

To start over again age 45 after all these years? And besides I loved what I did and it was my all; my future.

But my father's way of thinking changed with time and I smiled at a dream I had when I was taking a course in reflexology in my home town. My father organized my first course!

I thought it was impossible but still it happened. My father came for his annual visit shortly after my dream. He was happy that both of his grandchildren were at home and the four of us did a load of things together. It was just the two of us together on the last day and we wanted to go to a special restaurant. My father got changed. He always loved dressing up in elegant clothes to go out for supper with his daughter to a swish restaurant. I heard a sudden noise and my father let out a yell. He had slipped on the rug and his left shoulder was giving him a great deal of pain. Instead of the restaurant, we ended up at the hospital with and an x-ray and his arm in a frame. He had broken his collar bone. He planned to travel home that day by train as there was no way he was going to be able to sleep strapped into that thing. So he was to leave a day earlier but I was sure that he would feel much better in his own home in the state that he was in. It was interesting that while we were at the station he told me that the previous night he'd dreamt that he would go home a day earlier. I pretended to be shocked: "Are you trying to tell me that you can now see the future in dreams?"

We called each other every day. His shoulder slowly mended. But he had some help. He took the dog for a walk with his arm in the frame when a woman spoke to him who was also out walking her dog and they knew one another by sight. My father told her all about what had happened to his arm. The woman offered to give him some reiki energy. When my father asked to explain what she meant, she happily told him all about what it was and how it could help. My father told her (without a mention of hocus-pocus) that his daughter did similar things. He already knew that the woman was a solicitor and so now he thought that what I had mentioned about these kinds of things might be right after all.

The lady treated my father on several occasions and he soon recovered. In time, he also accepted her invitation to attend one of her weekly meetings where they not only gave reiki treatments to those in need but held talks on various kind of alternative treatments and had meditation sessions. It was through them that my father wanted to learn more about my work. He met a lot of new friends and he was no longer alone and now happily attended the weekly sessions. He started inviting people to his house again. He came back to life and seemed to be rejuvenated. The next time I was in Sopron, he told me that he had been in hospital for a couple of days for something or other and that there had been an old man there (my father was nearly 75 at the time) and he couldn't sleep because of the terrible pain that he was in and my father had given him a reiki treatment (as he had even taken exams in the subject by then). The old man was able to get to sleep after that and I was proud of my old dad!

He asked me before my trip: "If I were to organize a course here in Sopron, would you come and lead it?"

Was I dreaming? No, the dream had come true once again. My father organized the course and he was my oldest student to attend. He wanted to know everything and to make up for lost time and it could be seen that he wanted to make good his mistakes. I was very proud of him and of our new relationship. I was happy at last! He even lit a candle when I asked him because my mother was ill in hospital and we didn't know if she would live or die. He had hated my mother ever since the divorce and now he was able to let everything go and in his thoughts, he asked my mother to forgive him for all that he had done to harm her.

I now had a father on Earth as well. Cinderella found the prince she had lost as a child: her father.

Times change but tales and stories don't. The white doves had helped Cinderella and had heard her prayers in the cemetery at her mother's grave.

The same had happened to Arjuna, in the Bhagavad Gita, the great Indian epic. With the help of Krishna, Arjuna defeated his stepmother and his seven evil siblings despite his father's impressionability.

I grew up on fairy tales! I believed in the love of the angels and the "Great Wizard" and I only ever trusted in their help. And now the fairy tale had come true! They had helped and I knew I could defeat anything with their help!

17

Catching a
Glimpse of Former Lives
Through Reflexology

I had often thought that patients went into some sort of trance while I was giving them reflexology. I generally work with my eyes closed so that I can feel my patient's points as thoroughly as possible, and so that I can fully concentrate on their energies and those that I give to them.

I noticed that my patients went into a deep dream-like state within minutes, no matter what time of day it was. They were not only refreshed and strengthened but often had no pain at all after the very first treatment. They said that they had been in a special sort of sleep and a different state of some kind. Those who had previously meditated compared it to that deep state of consciousness. Those without such experience likened it to being in some sort of trance, as if they had been hypnotized. They sometimes found solutions to problems, which had been a great worry to them before, and that they no longer thought about. Others, who not only had health problems, also came to realize that it wasn't worth worrying about them anymore. They found it hard to believe that the "big problem" was no longer important and they were able to let it go. Their illness was more often than not linked to this problem. However, as I saw that the patient wanted to primarily ease their headaches or the discomfort in their hip, I didn't consider that the time had yet arrived to discuss the reasons. This would have meant that they would have cancelled the treatments which they so desperately needed for they often arrived after a series of unsuccessful encounters with traditional medicine when the drugs they were prescribed no longer had any effect. There was no way that the medication could have helped as the personal problem simply didn't go away. Rather, it was their emotions that were having such a drastic effect on their bodies. The body complained: "Things can't go on like this; I can't carry on working as the environment is all wrong!"

I was delighted when they themselves realized what the solution was to the problem but if the pain came back after a while they would ask: "What is it that I am doing wrong? Where have I made the same mistake again?"

I could now start to work with them at a much deeper level as they had passed through a vital realization.

They had realized that negative thoughts and emotions lead to the body becoming ill and it was this illness that "warned" them of the underlying problem.

Interesting insights occurred as time passed. I not only sensed the reasons in this life for the problems that they had but also things that had happened in their previous lives. It was this that made me realize that some physical or psychological problems occurred because of something which dated as far back as an earlier incarnation.

I didn't know the word "karma" back then and the topic wasn't really so close to my heart. I wasn't particularly interested in the possible existence of a previous life and the fact that one probably came as a consequence of the other.

The first such astounding incident occurred when I was treating a pregnant mother. Perhaps it was the deep sense of understanding and a will to help which helped open the gates to this "magical palace". The woman had been sent to see me by a psychiatrist friend of mine who, along with the woman's GP, hadn't been able to make the slightest difference to her condition. She complained of the most excruciating back pain but she didn't want to take any painkillers, of course, because she was expecting. Back massage also proved to be a dead end and didn't improve the situation. So now she had come to see me for reflexology to see if massaging specific points on the soles of her feet would ease the pain that she was experiencing in her back. I knew the psychiatrist well and that was why she had thought that perhaps, by some miracle, I would be able to make her back pain disappear. Well that is what happened in the end.

My patient was a very appealing woman in her early 30s who already had a three-year-old child and, interestingly enough, told me that the pain had started with her first child but only when she had been in the fifth month of her pregnancy. It eventually became so crippling that she was only able to deal with the pain by staying in bed. The doctors thought that the baby was perhaps lying on a nerve and it was this pressure that was causing the pain which would have explained why it seemed to grow worse, the larger the little one grew in his mother's tummy. The pains immediately disappeared with the birth and were soon forgotten. They waited a couple of years before deciding that the time had come for their toddler to have a little brother or sister. She had no difficulties at all in the first two or three months of the pregnancy and had only just gone into the third month when she was stricken with back pain. The pain was so strong that the doctor again recommended that she should lie down and rest as much as possible and all this with a three-year-old and the housework! The woman was mainly concerned about what would happen if the pains got even worse. This was the state she was in when she eventually turned to me for help.

I totally empathized with what she was going through as I had been pregnant myself and I also knew that peace and calm was virtually impossible with another child around. Things were made worse by the fact that she and her husband didn't want the grandparents to take of their child for any length of time; they feared that this would cause the child more problems when the new baby arrived as he was particularly close to his mother. That is what they wanted to avoid most of all.

The therapy went just as it usually did. First, she sat opposite me in a chair and described her complaint, then she lay on the massage table and I covered her up as I did with all my patients. I sat at the end of the table by her feet and I started to switch my consciousness of and started to connect what I had heard to my feelings. The story really had touched me and I wanted to do all that I could to ease the pain or, "God willing", to heal her completely.

I had hardly finished my thought when a scene appeared before my inner eye; in fact, a "film" started to play. The strange thing was that I saw the "film" but I also knew who the characters were and what had happened beforehand. The scene was of a mediaeval jousting competition. I saw the gentry sitting on a balcony in wonderful clothes and the whole thing was in a setting of richness and bounty. I could feel that the highlight of the games was about to commence. The two finalists were about to joust against one another to see who would be this year's champion. The excitement could be felt buzzing around the crowd of commoners who had gathered around to watch the spectacle. It was a serious situation: who would prove himself to be the best knight in the realm?

The event was drawing to a close after several days but the two victorious knights showed no sign of weariness. Every nerve in their bodies was tensed and they both hoped for the same thing: victory. The images also told me that they had been very close friends for a long time and they both desperately wanted to be the "champion".

A sign came from the ornate balcony to indicate that the games should begin. The two horsemen really did have similar strength and it was obvious that they were both exceptionally skilled riders. This went on for a short while until a most unexpected thing occurred and one of the knights exploited the situation when the other was turning his horse. As he had his back to his opponent, he couldn't see what was about to happen and so was unable to defend himself. The other one lunged at him with his lance from behind and shoved him out of his saddle. I could see that the defeated knight was terribly upset. He wasn't so much saddened by his defeat as he was by the fact that his greatest friend and companion had done such a thing in order to win. Attacking from behind when your opponent is unable to defend himself contradicted all knightly ethics. And this had been done by his friend whom he respected more than anyone else in the world.

The other one managed to remain on his horse but he still lost the tournament, his title as knight as well as his best friend as he had been attacked by the "winning demon". He had done a thing that a true knight would never dream of.

The "screen" went dark again but a new realization opened within me. I recognized one of the knights as the pregnant woman who was lying in front of me on the table. She was the one who had been knocked off her horse. I also knew that she knew the other knight from this life. I sensed that he was her husband and the pain in her back was due to the spiritual injury she had received at the hand of her old jousting rival.

The story was so real and believable that it was if someone had shown this film in answer to the question that we had been asking. I was absolutely astounded: "What could it be that had caused this to happen all over again?" I thought.

I wasn't able to ponder this for too long as I didn't know how long I had been away on my journey back in time. Besides, I knew that I had to return to take care of my patient.

She was still lying on the table with her eyes closed and breathing very calmly just as she had been at the beginning of the session. She suddenly took a very deep breath like someone waking from a very deep sleep, opened her eyes and sighed: "Well, it's unbelievable, but I know that it's true!"

I didn't understand why she had said this and I asked: "What is so unbelievable?"

She went on to tell me that she had fallen asleep and had a dream and then she described exactly the same events that I had seen. It really was unbelievable, not least of all to me! We had both seen the same things or rather I had seen "her film" How had I been able to glance into her history and how was it that I knew it had been hers?

The woman went on to describe what she had experienced. She told me that she had felt the pain when she had been knocked off her horse now as she had re-lived it again just as she had in the past. This was the point that formed the centre of her pain; it radiated out to cover a larger area. She also knew who it was that had been jousting against her: her present husband.

She had already read several books about reincarnation and she told me all about how we meet people in this life who were our enemies in the last and with whom we still have a debt to settle. We meet them in this life to resolve a problem which has its origins in a previous one.

She now understood why she had subconsciously chosen this man as her husband: there was an old score which needed to be settled. She was intrigued by the fact that her spirit hadn't been able to recall this event until she had become pregnant. It was only now, when she was about to bring a new life into the world, that she was faced with the anxiety and concern as to whether she could trust her partner in this life. Would he not do the same thing all over again and abandon her with her child?

I was in a state of virtual semi-unconsciousness as I sat and listened to her. I didn't dare mention the fact that I had been shown the very same film. The only thing that I knew (but where from?) was that the story was true and that the old fighters had met once again. They need to meet again on a new stage so that the game could be played out once more, but this time with no mistakes.

After a while I asked: "What are you going to do now you know the background to the situation?"

"I am going to tell my husband everything," she replied. I will tell him all about my subconscious fears and the concerns, which I have about him, and as he also believes that we all had previous lives, I am sure he will help me to have faith in him again. This should lead to my full recovery.

I asked her to tell me how she felt when she sat up from the table but I could see all too easily that the pain had gone completely. She only felt slight pain in her left side.

She called me a week later to ask for another appointment. We had said that we would meet again if the pain reappeared. She was delighted to tell me that the pain had gone! Her husband had been open to what she had told him although he wasn't able to recall anything himself. He promised his wife that she could completely rely on him in this life and especially as he knew that this would perhaps redeem him for the mistakes that he had made in the past.

Is this a fairy tale with a happy end? No, it's reality which again led to a massive step forward in broadening my knowledge and deepening my understanding.

Incarnation, reincarnation! I wanted to know everything that there was to know. I found a pile of books on the subject in an esoteric book shop.

My curiosity only increased. I too wanted to relive my previous incarnations but I didn't know where to go for any further information (this was back in 1987–88!).

It is interesting that it was my husband who provided the possibility. Over supper one night, he told me that he had been working with a film director on a television advert and the guy had told him a load of interesting things. He had travelled to India because he had heard that a "Papyrus Oracle" existed there which had the details of everyone's incarnations recorded in it—not only past but also future lives. My husband was amazed to hear that such a thing might exist. He had never given the slightest though to the idea that he might have had a former life and he didn't believe in such things. The film director found his "own book" in India: they also read out his present life to him. He was warned about the relationship that he had with his elder brother and that he should try and settle matters between them as soon as possible. When he asked which of his incarnations this problem had begun in, he wasn't answered. He decided to go for regression therapy when he got back to Switzerland and when he revisited a previous life he discovered that he had been responsible for his own brother's death. Until that moment he had always felt that he would be incapable of accepting his brother as there had been a great many conflicts between them over the years. And, now, at last, he knew what had been the cause of his guilty conscience. Until then, he had always wanted to stay as far away from his brother as possible so that he wouldn't have to deal with these emotions. He was constantly worried that his brother would eventually have enough and break off their relationship with one another. But his brother—much to his annoyance—always remained very kind and friendly: he always forgave him and offered to bury the hatchet.

I wasn't so interested in this story and I could hardly wait for my husband to finish it.

"Who was the one who took him back?" I asked.

"I don't know but if you like, I'll ask him tomorrow," he replied. The next day, he came home from work with a name and a telephone number. He gave me a funny look but he didn't actually say: "You're not planning on going there are you?"

Sure enough, I made the first appointment available.

I didn't know what I was doing! I wanted to know everything immediately (perhaps at any price!).

I was given an appointment in three weeks' time. It was December and the weather was cold and snowy. The first snow had fallen a while ago and lay in grey heaps by the side of the roads coloured by the exhaust fumes of cars. The address I was looking for was at the other side of the city. It was late in the afternoon and the roads were still free of ice so I arrived in plenty of time. I was burning with curiosity! What was going to happen? Could they take anybody back? Would they be able to take me back? What was I going to experience? What previous lives had I lived? I also wondered what it felt like to be a criminal or what it was like to have been a victim. But all these feelings faded against my overwhelming curiosity.

I was welcomed at the door by a middle-aged man. (I deliberately don't mention his name!) He got straight to the point and began the therapy the moment that I sat down. I have to say that I no longer recall how he managed to take me into a hypnotic state and this has a lot to do with the fact that I did my very best to forget the whole experience!

He asked me to imagine a lift with buttons on the inner wall and that I was entering that same lift. I had to press one of the buttons and feel as the lift began to move. If it stopped, I was to get out at that floor and describe what it was that I saw.

The first "floor" that I visited was Africa where I was a woman. It turned out to be a very sad experience. I was leaving my village with a little pack on my back; I was also leaving my family as I had fallen pregnant to a man from another tribe. No one had wanted to believe me when I told them that the union with the man in question had been forced on me against my will. The man had raped me and I had conceived. As no one in our tribe had been willing to say that they were the father, I told everyone the whole story, which had led to the elders shunning me and my child as outsiders. I heard the beat of the drums and the yells of the dancers when the elders passed their verdict and I knew that death awaited us as we would never be able to survive alone out in the bush. The other tribe were our enemies and so I was sure to be killed if I dared venture into their village.

As I lay there, I could feel the absolute hopelessness and loneliness and fear of the death that surely awaited me.

I had no sooner started to relive this life when I could hear the therapist's voice: "Imagine yourself in the lift once more! Which floor do you want to choose?"

I no longer know how many floors I visited and how many lives I relived in one continuous dash from place to place without a break.

The session ended with me reliving my "birth" into this world. It was very interesting and gave me a lot of useful information. I recalled my joy and happiness as I established contact with the person—my mother—who provided me with the chance to come down to this Earth.

Things soon started to get very cramped (I weighed 5.6 kg at birth) and yet I still felt very good in the comfort and security of that warm nest. I was suddenly struck by pain on the right side of my head and I could feel it paralysing my left side. My mother was seven months pregnant and I decided that I didn't want to stay inside any longer and that I would leave again. I no longer wanted to stay on the Earth and to be born here. The pain saddened my whole spirit, I was unhappy and I wanted to leave.

Then some unexpected and unknown "Force" decided that: **"You have to be born despite all of this! This is something that you have to accept!"**

I didn't agree but I wasn't the one to decide. It had been decided! But who was it who had decided? I only relived the experience in this session but I had no idea who it had been who had become involved in my life and my fate. I recovered in the two months that remained leading up to my birth (or I was helped!), and I could no longer sense the paralysis in my left side or the blindness in my left eye. Whether I failed to completely defeat this blindness or whether something occurred later on, which I didn't want to see, I am unable to say for sure.

The injury that I had suffered in the womb troubled me and I asked my mother whether something had happened to me when she was seven months pregnant. She was surprised and asked me why such a thought had ever occurred to me. I admitted to her that I had taken part in regression hypnosis that had taken me back to my time in the womb and that I had suffered a blow to the head when I was seven months old.

She didn't answer that willingly, yet eventually she admitted that she and my father had argued a great deal around that time. (I was hardly three years old when they divorced.) On one of these occasions, my father had pushed my mother and she fell against the corner of the table. She had been in a lot of pain and was terribly worried that she would lose her baby. They immediately called a doctor, the bleeding abated, and the doctor said: "It looks like the baby has decided to stay with us after all."

When I told her all about this she was amazed that the time in the womb could actually be relived.

I heard the therapist's voice once again, telling me to walk back into the lift and come back down to the ground floor from where I had started. The lift descended and I stepped out.

He asked me to control my breathing and to use every breath to bring myself back one step closer to consciousness in my present life and back into the room. That was how I awoke again.

The therapist had no time to talk to me and he ran to catch his train. We quickly organized payment and he ran out of the door.

He brought me back; I paid and I left, going back down the stairs but something wasn't right. I did everything automatically as I still wasn't here in the present.

I stepped out into the street but I didn't know where I was. I didn't know where I lived and I didn't know how to get home. I had a vague memory of living with my family but I was still rather lost in the present. Zurich is a large city and we lived in a small suburb very close to a forest. I was able to summon up images of the place but I had no idea of which direction I should set off in. Cars came whizzing past me as I stood at the side of the road in front of the building. Then I remembered that I had arrived in one of those frantic machines myself. There were cars parked in a line on the other side of the road, so I crossed over in the hope that I would manage to work out which one was mine.

I did everything automatically. I honestly am terrified now by the thought of what I did then. I eventually recognized my car. I told myself that I had been perfectly capable of driving it only three hours before and so I should be able to drive it again now. That is what happened with the mechanical recollection that I was starting to perfect. I turned the key in the ignition and pulled out into the traffic in the hope that I would soon remember which road it was that I had come in on. It was completely dark and the snow had frozen and I couldn't feel a thing. I wanted to go home! I did eventually make it and I was more overjoyed and grateful to walk back in through my own front door than I think I have ever been in my life. I know that someone else was driving for me as I had been incapable of doing anything for myself because I hadn't completely returned to the present!

Thank heavens that my husband was in bed asleep when I got back. I wanted to forget the whole experience as I had managed to do with other events in my life when I had been unable to deal with or accept something.

I felt a great deal better the following morning but I was still terribly tired. My husband—on my request—brought my milky coffee to me in bed and he managed to get the children off to school. In the meantime, I managed to get up and sit next to the table. He sat and ate his breakfast and kept giving me strange looks until he eventually asked: "Just what is wrong with you? Your face keeps on changing! It is quite disturbing. One minute you look really young and the next you look more like an old granny! Then a Chinese man, an Indian, an aboriginal woman ..."

I was frightened. I was trying to regain myself at the same time as all the old images and faces were still living and moving within me and he could see this from the outside?! I didn't tell my husband about what I had gone through the previous day but all I said was that I had an odd dream, and I still hadn't fully woken up. I reassured him that I would go back to bed for a while and catch up on my sleep and so he was happy to leave me and go back to work.

I climbed back into bed and prayed to find my way back into my life and for my previous lives to close behind me. I fell into a deep sleep. It was nearly noon by the time that I awoke and I suddenly remembered all the things that I had to do. I happily got out of bed and made lunch for the children and I kept glancing in the mirror to see exactly who it was looking back at me. I gave thanks to my helpers who had been there for me once again.

I gained a lot of valuable information from my regression but the main thing was that I now knew that regression should never be managed in this way. It is extremely risky to turn the past upside down and shake all the experiences out of it with no specific reason. Curiosity isn't reason enough because all I was able to find out was who I had been and where. But what had I learned from all of this? I saw the greatest danger lying in the difficulty of finding the way back!

I thought it was damaging to take part in such therapy. In any case, I decided that I had had quite enough of this and I would stop trying to hurry my development. I wouldn't force things as then I was likely to make mistakes. Possibly, I could open the kind of doors that would otherwise stay closed to me as the time had not yet arrived for them to open and let me pass through.

Everything had happened according to an invisible plan up to now but there was someone watching me and watching everyone else as well. I shouldn't risk that again as it might lead to me endanger or lose contact altogether. I could see that I was slowly maturing and I didn't know where it was leading or where it would reach an end. I only knew that I was being led and protected. I could also feel this in my therapy where I was able to offer wider help to the increasing number of people who turned to me.

I decided to look for a group where I could discover more about the invisible forces and energies that are at work within us and, step by step, work through the school of awakeners. I enrolled and completed a course at the School of Medium Healers.

18

The Dead
Come Forward

It was many years later that I went back to attend the Basel Parapsychology Days. I would have liked to meet and chat again with the Plaamis. The previous year, when they had lived with us, I had helped them hold their courses in a painter friend's studio. We had grown quite close but then I hadn't heard anything of them for a while.

Mr Passián was also giving a talk, which I wanted to attend, and I hadn't seen Harald Wessbecher for years either. I was happy because I knew that not only would I come into contact with new and interesting things but also that I would have the chance to meet up with dear old friends.

Harald waved to me during the first break. He was also delighted to see me. We didn't really have too much time to chat as he was rushing off to the next talk but it turned out to be one that I had also picked out. An English medium was talking about her connections in the other world.

Harald and I set off together in the direction of the room and we were both pleased to be able to share this experience as afterwards, in the lunch break, we were able to discuss all that we had seen and heard. There was a very sweet blonde woman standing at the doorway. Harald led me over to her and introduced me with a warm smile: "This is Patrizia, my fiancée. But you two know one another really. She attended a course with you when you examined various different states of consciousness. That was the first course of mine that she took part in."

I could hear Harald's voice when he suggested that we should take a seat but my consciousness had already transferred. I didn't remember a single thing about the talk. I saw people going up to the stage where the speaker was standing—sometimes laughing, sometimes crying—and I guessed she must have been connecting these people with their friends or relatives, but I really don't know.

My memories took all of my concentration. I was remembering the course where Harald had spoken but I couldn't remember the blonde woman at all.

Then a picture suddenly came to mind. We were all lying on the floor and doing different exercises to reach a higher state of consciousness. The aim was to feel and experience different states of consciousness. Everyone was hoping that they would feel something different or experience something strange, including me.

I could feel my body relaxing to the music and Harald's calming tones. Within a short while, I couldn't feel my body or the carpet that I was lying on. They dissolved into me and then they evaporated. I couldn't sense my surroundings and I couldn't now hear Harald's voice. All I knew was that I existed and that all I could sense was my consciousness, which led me, and everything became lighter and shinier.

I suddenly realized that someone was standing to the left of me. The person must have sensed my thoughts and that is why they answered: *"Yes, here I am, by your side, and I would like to ask a favour of you."*

Then I noticed that there were two of them and the being added.

"Yes, this is my son who stands next to me. The course that you are on is also being attended by my wife and my daughter. My daughter has known the group leader for a long time and they needed to meet again. They belong together. I would like to send a message to them. I would like them to know that we exist and we live, but in a bodiless state. Unfortunately, I still haven't been able to make contact with my wife and my daughter as they have not yet become open to such thoughts. But the tragedy of our loss is what set them on the path of spiritual development. That is why we went on ahead of them that

we might help them. They will find what you have to say to them hard to accept but in time they will realize that love and help take many different forms to the ones that you know and experience on Earth. I hope that their search and their effort will be successful and—in time—that I can also contact them to tell them all about our lives here. Thank you for your help."

And then they disappeared. His parting words echoed in my ears, or rather in the part of my body which had heard him, as it wasn't a voice in the traditional sense of the word. We used a mutual language and it was more a question of accepting and understanding his thoughts.

The experience brought me back to my everyday consciousness and I could again feel my body and the carpet beneath.

The others soon started to move. It seemed that Harald had completed the exercise and he had called us all back to the here and now. I listened and looked around. The lights were switched back on. I looked everywhere. I remembered that Harald always used to talk to a brown-haired girl in the breaks and they sat next to one another at lunch. It seemed that they were important to one another but the girl also seemed to spend a lot of time with an older woman. They had arrived together and they lay next to one another during exercises. It appeared that the message was intended for them.

The room began to empty. The two women sat opposite one another and chatted about the exercise. I went over to them. "I hope I'm not disturbing you. Are you finished?" I asked them.

"Sure. Why don't you sit and join us?"

I carefully began what I had to say. I asked the younger of the two: "Is this lady your mother?"

"Yes," she said and laughed in her mother's direction. It was something of a rarity for a mother and daughter to attend an esoteric or psychology course together.

"Please don't be upset if I ask such a thing but have you lost someone in your family?"

They looked very sad and the mother answered: "Half the family: my husband and my son. They died together in a skiing accident. It was the most atrocious loss! I still can't accept it but I am slowly trying to come to terms with it."

Then it just slipped out: "They are alive and they send you their love!"

Well, you can just imagine their reaction. First disbelief: they understood and heard what I said but they were stunned by the news that they were alive somewhere.

I told both of them what the husband had told me from the other side. They cried and hugged one another as they tried to come to terms with what they were hearing. I sat with them for a while but I realized that they would much rather be alone.

I went over to Harald and asked him about the girl with the brown hair. We were good friends and so this wasn't an intrusion as far as he was concerned. He put his arm around me and as we walked along the corridor he told me that it looked as if things were starting to get serious between them. They had known one another for about six months and met regularly. The poor thing really was in need of his help as she had suffered a terrible loss two years before when both her father and her elder brother had died.

I didn't tell him that I knew everything and even more than he could suspect. I guessed that his girlfriend would tell him in her own time.

I hadn't seen Harald since then and so I was quite surprised when he introduced this woman as his bride-to-be. But where was the girl with the blonde hair? Hadn't the father said that they belonged together and that they had to meet again in this life? Perhaps it had just been for a short time.

In the meantime, the medium came to the end of her talk and the audience started to pack up and leave the room. Harald put his arm in mine and suggested: "Come on, let's have lunch together. Or have you arranged something with someone else?"

"No. I'd love to join you as we haven't seen each other for ages. I'm sure we've got so much to tell one another."

Harald and I used to be very good friends and we could discuss absolutely everything. We also met a lot outside class. My husband had also enjoyed attending his courses until he decided otherwise. When my marriage problems took up all of my time, I was in no mood to learn new things and I stopped attending for a while. Then Harald lived in Germany and so that is why we didn't meet again for such a long period of time.

He sat next to me at lunch. He was beaming with happiness and so was Patrizia who sat opposite me. The girl spoke first. "I remember you and I even remember where you were sitting on the course. I was sitting at the back with my mother. It was the first time that we'd attended something like this and we held back as we only really wanted to listen to what was going on. We came to see if perhaps we could find some help. You know, my father and my brother had died almost at the same time."

"Am I hearing correctly? Am I watching the right film? Something is going on here." I wasn't able to say anything because Harald spoke.

"Yes, it was the first time that Patrizia had taken part in something like this but she always takes things seriously and so she didn't just stop there. She has attended all the courses and she even came along to the "Dream Seminar" in Tenerife. I had broken up with my last girlfriend by then, you know the one."

"Yes, the girl with the brown hair and she had also come along with her mother on the course that we are talking about," I said but I wasn't able to go on because Harald wanted to continue.

"Such a shame that you didn't come to the seminar in Tenerife, the hotel is on the beach and the mood is always so uplifting in the group. I have always enjoyed holding courses there and especially now it's connected with getting to know Patrizia.

"Hm," I answered. "Getting to know? Who? What?" I thought.

"Perhaps it sounds a bit kitsch," he went on, "but that evening really would make a fabulous painting: the end of April, a warm evening and a full moon. All the members of the course went for a walk along the beach after supper. I was really taken with Patrizia's personality and would have loved to take a walk with her along the beach. I was overjoyed when she asked me whether I would like to tag along with her."

Patrizia was a beautiful girl. She had long, shiny, blonde hair, big, blue eyes like some kind of fairy. I also learnt that she had been studying law at the time and has since qualified.

"While we were walking," Harald said, "the moonlight fell on Patrizia's face and I had the strangest sensation, 'She's the one; I know her. She's the one, she's the one!'"

He told me of how he had dreamt of a fairy ever since he was a boy with long, blonde hair and blue eyes. As a child, he knew that this fairy realized who he was and would seek him out in this life. He got older and started to become interested in girls. The fairy disappeared from his dreams altogether and he couldn't even recall her face any longer. He had various relationships and was convinced that he had found the right one at least twice but something always spurred him on until he saw Patrizia in the moonlight that night: she was the fairy of his dreams!

"I know that it sounds like a fairy tale or some kind of slushy love story but that's just what happened! The full moon, the dream, the course and Patrizia," and with this he finished his story.

"Yes, Harald, you really have found the girl whom you have always known and whom you had to meet in this life. That is what Patrizia's father told me on that course; I told the girl you were seeing at the time."

Sometimes fate plays funny tricks on us. There were two girls with their mothers on that course. All the women were seeking solace in their deep pain and possibly some kind of message to say that their loved ones were still alive and had not died forever.

And that is the message that all four of them received.

The whole thing does sound quite unbelievable. Especially the fact that Harald seemed to sense that the one he was looking for had lost her father and her brother. Perhaps the spirit world had been testing him. "Have you really found your real partner or have you accepted someone similar who only appears to be the one you are looking for, but really isn't?" Those above do know who belongs with whom and help so that old companions can reach out to one another and say "yes" to one another.

Since then, Harald and Patrizia have married and have three children. Yes, such things happen!

In the next story, those who were left on the Earth will perhaps never be as happy as they were before the tragedy. It must be terrible to lose a child and especially if that child was murdered and possibly also tortured.

I was holding a reflexology course in an exquisite Swiss mountain village. My girlfriend had organized it and I had nothing at all to worry about. She had chosen the place and I was able to stay at her house. I didn't used to like the mountains. I felt like I was being crushed, and that I was so tiny in comparison. I think I must have been frightened of them. I grew to know them much later on in life as I had been a city child, but then I really fell in love with them. I was also very happy to go along this time and I hoped that the snow wouldn't fall as it was the beginning of November. Although the weekend was cold, we had no snow.

I didn't know anyone on the course except for my girlfriend. It was always interesting to see how the practical sessions would go on occasions like this; how people would find the whole experience. The first day went really well. Everyone reacted very well to sole diagnosis and on the second day—Sunday—we looked at the various reflexology points and the possible relief and even cure that they could provide.

The group worked in pairs with quiet music in the background. I walked around, helping out here and there, adjusted how someone was holding a foot or pointed out specific zones on the sole of the foot. I stopped next to one of the pairs and watched the work that was going on. I also took a good look at the sole. I asked the massager to go very carefully in specific areas as I could sense deep sorrow and the heart and lung lines seemed very tense and I was nervous that too deep a massage would awaken unpleasant emotions. The woman who was lying on the floor heard what I said and began to cry. I left them to keep working but I kept my eye on them to see if my help was needed. The crying stopped and they carried on working. I had the feeling that the crying woman was mourning someone whom she couldn't let go. I sensed the story. We chatted though our experiences at the end of the course and I gave some advice. I began to talk about fate and that sometimes the unexpected happens to those who are close to us that we never thought would happen, and how very difficult it was to deal with the hand of fate acting in this way. I also spoke about how important it was to work on this area spiritually otherwise we pay with our health. Nor do we help the one on the other side because they cannot comfort us. They cannot leave either because of our great sorrow and because we will not release them.

I didn't understand why I had said all of this. Now there were three other women crying as well as the one with the painful points on her feet. As the discussion went on, it transpired that all four of them had recently lost someone who was close to them. I offered to hold a meditation session for those who had died. Then I realized that it was All Souls' Day: 1 November. The meditation did seem to ease the pain and sadness of those involved. They thanked me for this little extra help. Meditation for the dead really doesn't form part of a course on reflexology, well, at least not normally!

My girlfriend wasn't able to take part in the course that afternoon as she had an appointment to attend that she couldn't postpone. I would like to have discussed everything with her that I had experienced that afternoon but I knew that she would only be home later that evening along with her whole family. So, I set off for their house alone and while I was walking it got dark. I was happy about the pleasant cold and the mild breeze. What had gone on that afternoon had also affected me. I was also surprised at the structure of the group. It had never occurred before that four members had all lost relatives or at least no mention had ever been made on a course before. Maybe it was the fact that it was 1 November, the All Souls', that had brought this out and that had led to the courses concluding with that extraordinary meditation.

The phone was ringing as I walked into the house. I thought that I had better take a message.

It was for me: one of my daughters. All she could say was: "Mummy, Pascale's been murdered."

"What? What happened?" I asked, hardly believing what I had just heard.

"Someone found Pascale's dead body in the forest this afternoon. They'd been looking for her since yesterday when she disappeared."

Pascale, just like my daughter, was a scout leader. They organized events for their little group every Saturday afternoon. The forest being so close by, they usually met up there and spent the afternoon together. We were all very close to Pascale and her family.

I couldn't believe what I was hearing and that such a thing could have happened. I knew that my daughter was at home and all on her own in that big house. I had lived there for years—ever since the divorce—just me and the girls. My other daughter was in the U.S. for a year as an exchange student.

"I'm coming straight home!" I said, and I put the phone down.

I would normally have driven home the following morning after a good night's sleep and I used to make the most of meeting up with my girlfriend to the very last minute as we always had so much to talk about. Now I left a short message to say that I'd had to go home urgently. I packed in minutes and jumped straight in the car. I was in a place called Klosters which is an hour and a half outside Zurich. I wanted to be there straight away, by my daughter's side. "What must she be going through? How is she dealing with having lost someone whom she knew and loved so much? The poor parents! Their situation must be even worse! How can a person survive something like that? The loss of a child!"

When I finally arrived back, Claudia was still awake and as white as a sheet. She told me everything all over again as if she were telling herself over and over. It was incomprehensible to her and to me. We couldn't really react. It was as if the whole thing had paralysed us.

"Let's go to bed," I suggested. "We can't really do anything else and maybe it'll calm us down a bit."

There was no chance of sleep as I was wide awake. I suddenly realized that what had happened to our friends could just as easily have happened to us as well. I would have lost my daughter! She had been in the woods at 2 am just like Pascale, waiting for the others to arrive. The mere thought sent shivers down my spine and my limbs were icy cold. I lay shivering under a warm blanket in a well-heated room in a safe house.

The thoughts just kept coming. How would I be feeling now if all of this had happened to my daughter instead?

It was then that I realized how we all live as if we are going to live forever and that's how we behave with our children. Had I given them absolutely everything that I could? Had they received all the love, understanding and acceptance that they needed to grow and develop as they should? Did I allow them enough of my time if they came to me with a problem or was I too taken up with my own things, and I said: "Yes, in a minute!" Did I say, "Yes, in a minute," to everything? When, in a minute? Perhaps when it was already too late? But the same was true of my partner when he came to me with his problems. "Was I always there for him? Aren't they the ones for whom I should always be there? Who could ever replace me as a mother and as a partner? Aren't they the ones I should be here for? They are the ones who chose me and said yes to me, and that's why it is so important that I should be here when they need me!" They are going to ask: "Did you do all that you could for those who were dependent on you?" My conscience will ask me the same question when and if they should depart depart, yet perhaps they'll also ask me up there when I move into my heavenly home.

I knew that this was the most important!

These thoughts kept bubbling to the surface. I just couldn't relax and so I got up instead. I put a warm gown and slippers on and threw a woollen shawl around my shoulders. I sat down at my desk and I just had to put my observations down on paper to remind myself with the title: "Is it too late?" Days later, I read out on the telephone what I had written to my girlfriend who worked for a local newspaper. She rang back a little later and asked me to take it into the editor's office as they wanted to print it in the paper the following day. They were pleased with what I had written as the Pascale tragedy had been at the centre of public attention for a couple of days. Especially as it soon turned out that the culprit had murdered several other women before Pascale, and had just come out of prison.

They had wanted to "rehabilitate" him according to the new "humanist" approach that was being pursued. That is why he was allowed out of prison once a week to meet a psychologist as his sentence was soon to finish and they wanted him to reacclimatize to the outside world. The psychologists in question lived in our suburb. The murderer's journey had taken him through the woods and that is where he had seen Pascale.

Setting my thoughts down in writing this way did help to calm me a little. I tried to get to sleep again and woke the following morning.

The depressing feeling didn't go away. Sleep had done nothing to ease it. The sorrow and tragedy still had a paralysing effect on me. I couldn't do a single thing. Thankfully, I had no patients booked for that day and I thought that I would just get something out of the freezer for supper.

I called Mrs Steiner. I thought that I might find some consolation if I talked through my emotions with her. Unfortunately, she was working and I only got an answering machine. That was still enough to make me burst into a sudden flood of tears. I had to sit down as it hit me with such force that I thought I was going to fall over. I sat by the table and cried and cried. The tears just streamed down my face. It reminded me of a terrible time in the past: I had cried like this as a child when no one had understood me and I felt so terribly alone.

The flood of tears didn't want to stop and it was just as strong as before. It was as if I was looking on from the outside (or the inside) and watching what was happening to me. It was if I was in dual consciousness at one time!

The person who was sitting just cried.

I asked myself while I was crying: "OK, this is the shock. It's the shock of feeling that just the same could have happened to us! Or is it for all those mothers to whom this has already happened? Or for those who suffer a tragedy like this and are unable to shed a tear. Or am I crying for those? ...", and an endless list began of whom I might be crying for. I thought: "It is good that I have tears for those who have not died or am I crying their stolen tears? Then, I should just cry!"

Something changed! Not in the shower of tears but in my consciousness. I could feel that the tears were melting my paralysis and my sense of helplessness at not being able to do anything at all! And the fact that such a tragedy could have occurred in the first place!

Suddenly, my tears were tears of anger. It was the kind of anger that could kill—to give the pain back to the one who had caused it to me. To kill them and to murder their children!

The feeling was terrible. I couldn't do a thing and just kept on crying.

Then a sudden jump—up or down?—and I was flooded with a totally different feeling. (And I was still crying.) Immeasurable sorrow! It was the kind of sadness which had no beginning and no end. Its depth and intensity broke all boundaries. Limitless. Now I was drowning in their feeling. Or was I myself the feeling?! Yes, I was the crying; I was the murderous anger and my being was also the endless sorrow.

Then it was as if I had been pushed again and reached another stage.

I dissolved in a sea of light. I became one with the light. I became the light and love. There was no room left for any other emotions now: no anger, no sorrow—only light and only love.

The crying stopped as quickly as it had begun. It must have just been there to show me the way.

I had a bath—I ate and radiated the state that I was in, and what I had become. Everyone was there, the beautiful and the good, but the bad and the ugly were there as well. And everyone was the same: just love and light. Whoever they were or whatever they had done, there was no difference and no discrimination. All beings bathed in this light and love flowed through them.

Someone touched me from the left. Pascale was standing beside me. Pascale who had died only two days before.

"How am I able to see you?" I asked her.

"Because you are in the same place that I am."

"Hm, in the other world.—Me? But I'm alive!"

"Yes, because you have discovered the route that leads here."

I knew what she was saying was true but the idea of actually being there was completely unacceptable to another part of me.

"I want your help," she continued. *"I have three requests and I would like you to carry them out."*

"Of course," I replied, "if I can!"

"First: find my parents and tell them that you have met me. Tell them where I am and especially that I am happy. I did what I had to do. (Me: Hm?!) The perpetrator is guilty on Earth and the victim is innocent. But you should know that often the culprit is innocent too! (The culprit innocent? I didn't understand but I went on listening.) *And sometimes the victim is the perpetrator. It is impossible to know down there what really happened and why. You know that I worked as a nurse in the children's hospital?"*

"Yes," I replied.

"I saw so much suffering there and I couldn't help enough. It hurt! The fact that I was a victim means that I can now do a lot. Perhaps I can help other people with my death. It wasn't the murderer who was the culprit but the situation itself. He couldn't help what he did and he should have been protected from himself! He should never have been locked up in prison and he should never have been released! He was ignorant. A little child still doesn't know what it is that they should

and shouldn't do, what is dangerous and what isn't. But a child is still able to learn and others aren't. In his case, if we are talking about culprit, it was the order that was incorrect and that allowed this terrible thing to happen. He should have been looked after so he would never have been able to do such a thing. Please tell my parents all this, and and perhaps it will help them to accept what has happened. Perhaps it will help them if they know that I am happy here and that they can do something for me. They are going to need strength. The situation needs to be used to point out the inappropriateness of the legal context and the laws need to be changed. In this way, they will know that my death and my sacrifice were not in vain."

The words echoed in my ears "MY DEATH? MY SACRIFICE?" Had she sacrificed her life for the lives of others? Isn't that the greatest thing that we can do? Wonderful!

"What I am about to say," she continued, *"you will also need to tell the Minister of Justice."* (She used the individual's name but I do not want to use it without his agreement.) *"He needs to know that this is my message to him! That was the second request."*

I had to respond to this:

"I don't think that I'll be able to do that."

It wasn't because I was afraid. The reason was that my younger daughter was in the same class as his son at school. I was concerned that if he told his son what I had told him then they would make fun of my daughter at school and say that her mother had gone crazy. No, I could never do such a thing to her. I wrote the letter in good time, but I never posted it.

Pascale didn't react to my objection or to my explanations. She carried on: *"The third thing I would like to ask is that you do not shut the door to our world! We need someone like you, rather like a telephone, to relay our messages to the outside world. This will allow us to reduce so much suffering and hurt. You would be able to offer comfort to those who mourn us. We sometimes have important messages to send about matters on Earth and to clear up very personal issues. The dying also need a helper like you who knows where they are heading for."*

"I will do as much as I can." ("If the door doesn't shut again all by itself," I thought, "because I don't know how to get a new door to open in its place.") I was no longer afraid and I didn't want to forget what had happened as I had just a while ago.
"I will accept this mission."

"Please remember to tell my parents not to be angry with my murderer!"

Then just an echo and a long silence. I was sitting in the chair next to the table. I had fallen back into the reality of the now. I looked up at the clock. It was nearly noon and I had to cook. I had the energy and I was very pleased that Claudia would soon be home from school and I could welcome her with my home cooking. I was still unable to talk about what had happened.

I summoned up the strength that afternoon and picked the phone up to call Pascale's parents. Then I hoped that they would pick up the phone, and that when they did so, they wouldn't slam it down again and be angry with me for disturbing their mourning with such impossibility. Perhaps they would say, "Well, she's definitely lost it!"

But I had promised and maybe they would believe me.

Pascale's mother, Jeanette, picked up the phone. I knew her well. She had helped me for years in the children's clothes shop. But we had also spent a lot of time together before then. We used to go to the lake together with the four kids, going on little trips together at the weekend or the two families had barbecued together in their garden.

I first expressed my sympathy and asked if I wasn't disturbing her at all as there was something important that I wanted to tell her. She said not at all and I told her that I thought that Pascale had been to visit me and that she had left a message for them. I didn't say I was the person who had gone to visit her as I thought there was no way they would ever believe such a thing. Then I stopped talking and waited for her to respond.

"Why don't you come over to our place now, if you can?"

Well, I never thought that she'd say that!

"I'm on my way!" and I put the phone down.

Although we had both moved from where we had once lived in the same street, I was able to get to her house in about ten minutes by car. The whole family was waiting when I arrived along with Pascale's boyfriend. Jeanette asked me to tell them everything. I did as she asked. No one laughed or doubted what I said. Pascale's father came over to me in tears, gave me a hug and he said:

"Thanks so much for coming. You have reinforced what I thought and what Pascale said to me."

Now I was lost for words.

"Until now," he went on, "I thought that the pain had caused me to lose my mind. This goes to show that the dream was real. I woke in the morning with love in my heart for my daughter's murderer and I could have hugged him. But then I shook myself to check whether I was awake or not as I could still hear Pascale's words in my ears 'Please don't be angry with my murderer.' And then: 'Do everything that you can so my death will not have been in vain.'"

"That is exactly what she said to me," I thought, but I didn't interrupt.

"And this was in a dream or maybe it wasn't a dream and she was really here," he said shyly. "But I promised my daughter."

His words were followed by silence. The relatives didn't say a word and Pascale's two siblings just stared at me, blinking their eyes.

Pascale's boyfriend broke the silence. "She also visited me and she told me the very same thing! I thought that I had just dreamt it. This must mean that she is living happily somewhere and sharing her thoughts with us. It offers me a little comfort in my loss."

His eyes filled up with tears.

I could see that the grandparents had been very touched by what they had heard. Could they really believe what had been said?

I felt sorry for Jeanette and wished she could have experienced the same as her husband but Pascale had chosen her father. Perhaps she had found an open door with him, who knows?!

The parents stood next to one another and they repeated what had been said: "Yes, we have to do everything possible to make sure that Pascale's death was not in vain. Perhaps this will help us survive the terrible pain."

I left shortly afterwards. I went to see them again after that but I saw that they were strong and capable of going through with what they had agreed to do.

Pascale's murder really did affect public opinion. Girls are killed every year (Pascale was only 21). After a short while, after it has been widely covered in the press, everyone, except for the parents, forgets.

That's not what happened with Pascale! Her parents didn't allow her death to be forgotten. They looked for those responsible and the reasons. The main thing that they wanted was to see the law changed and that this should never be allowed to happen again. It really did reach the ministry!

Suddenly, the Minister of Justice appeared on the scene. Yes, he was the one whom I should have passed a message on to!

He appeared on the TV alongside Pascale's parents, psychologists and the governor of the prison. They gave endless interviews to the radio as well as the television. The investigation lasted for weeks, months and years. But there was a result in the end! The Minister changed the ruling himself and he publicly announced: "I feel as if this all happened with my own child. It is important that the truth should be known. And then perhaps the death of this young girl was not in vain!"

"Has he heard the same thing? Has Pascale been to see him as well?" I thought at the time.

Pascale appeared to me on two further occasions and always when I was preparing lunch for my daughters in the kitchen and in everyday consciousness.

I always sense visitors from the other side on the left of my body. The first time she appeared was one year after her death. All she said was: *"Have you all done that you promised to do one year ago? Please ask all the others the same question."*

I thought that I would reach the largest number of people through the papers. I wrote an article on the anniversary of Pascale's death and I reminded the readers that it was at times like these that we see reality as well as what it is that we have to do and what our main tasks are in life. Nor should we forget what we have promised to do when our lives get back to normal.

Pascale then appeared again several years later. I was cooking lunch, as usual. I was stirring something on the stove when I could feel her and hear her voice. (She didn't need to speak as I could sense that it was her. I felt it with my unnameable sensory organ.)

"Call X!" and she mentioned the name of the Minister of Justice again.

"But they sorted everything out and modified the law."

"Yes, I know, but that's not why! It is important that he should know that I am thinking of him!"

"Well, he is just going to laugh at me if I say that to him, Pascale: 'The girl who died all those years ago, is thinking of you.'"

Pascale again didn't react to my disapproval.

She repeated: *"Please call him now."* And she emphasized the word **now**. *"This is very important for him."*

The echo: it's very important for him!

"OK, well, I'll give it a go and maybe it'll work."

Thank God, here in Switzerland, the telephone number of the Minister of Justice appears in the telephone directory. He is a lawyer and so I called his office. It must have been around noon.

One of his secretaries came on the line. I told her that I would like to speak to Dr X and that it was "very important!"

She would have dismissed me as a matter of course, and told me that the Minister was out of the office.

Then I repeated Pascale's message: **"But this is a very important message that I have to pass on to him."**

"Please hold the line, I'll try and see if I can catch him in the corridor," the woman said and she put the receiver on the desk.

No more than a minute passed and Dr X picked up the phone in person and introduced himself. But he did open by saying that he only had a couple of minutes to spare because he was just leaving for Bern where there were going to be parliamentary elections the next day and he was a candidate for his political party.

I quickly told him about how Pascale had asked me to make contact with him only two days after her death and what it was that I should have told him then. Then I finished by telling him that she had spoken to me again only ten minutes beforehand; that she had told me that I should call him and thank him for what he had done in this matter and to say that she was thinking of him.

There was stony silence at the other end of the line—I thought that he had put the phone down. Then someone cleared their throat as if trying to control their emotional response.

"Thank you so much for calling and telling me that. When all this happened, I felt strangely touched by the whole terrible situation. It was as if it had happened to me and my whole family. I wanted to do all I could and I did everything in my power to uncover the truth. (Very true!) Now, just before the elections, I needed strength because I know how important the role of justice minister is throughout Europe. I would be so pleased if I won the election. But now I have the strength that I need and I believe in victory!"

And that is what happened. The majority voted for him and he also had help and support from the other side. He became the head of state in the following election.

Yes, the threads can reach a very long way indeed and achieve a great deal.

My third job from the other side was completely different. A dear old friend called me on the phone and sadly told me that her sister had died. I also knew her sister as she had been to see me on one occasion because of her illness. She had lung cancer and had been ill for years. It was then that I sensed that she didn't want to get better. She never came again. And still she had to carry on living for a further three years. That is a terribly long time for someone with lung cancer! The poor woman must have suffered very much. I was pleased in a way to hear that she had died rather than saddened by the news. I wanted to be honest and so I told her sister what I thought: "The poor thing is better off now. She's free of pain at last!"

My friend reacted with a happier voice: "Yes, I am also very relieved. It was so hard to watch her wanting to die but not being able to."

My friend was also a therapist and she had a great deal of esoteric knowledge. And we were able to speak as we had done when her sister had been to see me. She had agreed with me back then that her sister had been seeking death and that is why she had lung cancer. She had a terrible marriage. She couldn't do anything to improve the situation and she definitely wasn't able to get a divorce. She chose the sickness and death as a solution to escape the cul-de-sac that she had found herself in.

"But that's not why I'm calling. I need your help. I have strange, inexplicable feelings about my sister. It feels as if she's in trouble and that somehow, she needs my help. But I can't contact her. Could you help me?"

"I don't know but I can try. When exactly did she die?" I asked.

"Two, nearly three days ago."

"Then I really have to hurry," I thought. They stay around the body on the Earth for three days and then it is difficult to reach them and, in fact, you shouldn't really disturb them after that.

"I'll see what I can do and then call you back."

I had finished work for the day and this was something that I urgently needed to sort out straight away, so I sat down to meditate. I asked the spirit world to help me to find her so that I could contact her.

The connection was successful and I got on to her wavelength. I'll try to use physical terms as much as I can so that it is easier to understand how to reach someone who is close to death. You have to go over to their frequency, to their wavelength just like with a receiver when you are using a radio.

She was in a tough situation. She had become stuck in the separation from this world. Her poor angel stood helplessly next to her but she couldn't help because this was the job of the dying.

I would like to help further to advance understanding of this process. The dead have 72 hours to extract their various fine bodies (there are six such shells) from their physical body and to detach them; they then take these with them to the other side where they live in them.

The poor woman looked like someone trying to pull her foot out of a boot, yet failing to do this because they have no energy left. She was virtually asleep and not really awake at all. I could sense that there were virtually minutes left before the 72 hours were up. I had to move quickly. I grabbed the foot of her physical body and tried to give her energy though this channel. So, I sort of held the boot, while at the same time giving energy to her foot so that she would have the strength to pull it out.

She freed herself with a sudden tug and she flew straight up with her angel and dissolved into the light.

I returned to everyday consciousness feeling much more at ease. I thought a lot about why she had been so tired. She was like someone who had woken late and been frightened and then lost all her energy due to the fright.

"What happened here? Why was she late?" And then I realized. The doctors—with the best will in the world—had given her too many drugs so that she could stand the pain. And the drugs still had an effect on her after her death. She was drugged up and still under the heady influence of the morphine. I really don't know how she would ever have managed on her own. I was happy that I was able to help and that she managed it in the end.

I called my girlfriend right away and the first thing that I asked about was the morphine.

"Yes, they gave her a lot virtually up to the point that she died. She had been unconscious for days and that's how she died in the end."

I told her what I had seen and what I was able to do. She also thought that her state must have been due to the amount of morphine that they had given her.

The reason that this was different from all the other cases was because I had to solve the problem all on my own. Up to now, I had always been told what I had to do and how to do it.

Another story also belongs here—this one is about Oscar. I would like to describe the help given to Oscar.

I am sure that everyone remembers the Luxor tragedy when terrorists attacked a tourist bus in Luxor: they shot everyone on board including young and old, women and men. The dead included three Swiss citizens. When it happened, the news was all over the radio and TV and pictures were shown of the terrible bloodbath. I knew nothing of the incident as I didn't have a television, I never listened to the radio and I didn't take a newspaper. I didn't involve myself with such things and I got to know everything important from my patients. I hadn't worked the previous day because I was preparing to give a course in Budapest.

I had been teaching in Hungary for a year by then and holding courses. I rented a flat in Budapest and I taught there twice a month. It was in a dream or during a meditation that I received the names of ten individuals whom I needed to help in their spiritual development. They had all taken part in my sessions at some point in the past or on the two-week camp held in the summer. They had all been working for years in the clarification and strengthening of their spiritual paths and many were talented as mediums. I wanted to help them further in the work that they had done so far. The group met in the flat once a week without me. They mediated and practised what they had learnt in my class the week before.

I travelled to Budapest once a month and held consecutive sessions on two Fridays with meditation and exercises. In the evening, I held a public meditation session that anybody was able to attend and both were free. I then taught reflexology and the chakras of the feet at the weekend as well as dealing with higher states of consciousness. I also held my first, fabulous "dolphin consciousness" course there.

The fact that I was away from home for ten days at a time meant that I had a great deal to prepare before I left as well as all the work around the house which involved cleaning, tidying, washing and ironing. I can only ever go away anywhere if I leave everything organized behind me. This stress accompanied me once a month for a period of two years.

I had a lot do on this occasion as I had to leave on Friday and I had only returned from Germany on the Wednesday where I had been teaching since the weekend. The thing causing me the greatest problem was that I had been hearing the VOICE since the morning repeatedly saying: **"Check your bags in at the airport"**.

"But why today when I don't even know how I'm ever going to be ready for tomorrow morning? And I only normally pack my bag the night before I travel."

I resisted because I only ever travel with one case and I would be able to take that with me the following day. I never checked my bag in the day before when I was travelling to Budapest.

The VOICE told me three times that day what it was that I had to do and so I was forced to accept the task and I had until 10 pm to check my bag in and I would have to make a pointless journey out to the airport. I grumbled but I did it because I was told that I "have to".

I arrived at the airport a couple of minutes before 10 pm—at the very last minute—and I checked my bag in. I did as I was told. "But why was it so important that I do this?" I asked myself.

On the way home, I noticed that I was low on petrol. The girls used to borrow my car while I was away and so I thought that I would fill up for them before I left. It was a self-service filling station where you had to go into the kiosk to pay. Or rather that was the idea because there was no one there. I was tired and I wanted to go home but I had to wait. While I was waiting I read the headlines on the news stand; all the daily headlines one after the other. There were bloody pictures of dead people all over the place and I guessed there must have been some terrible tragedy. It made me feel bad so I turned my head. Then the lady appeared and apologized, saying that she had had to go to the toilet. Well, you can only do something like that in Switzerland! The shop was open and she had run around the back of the building. I was happy to be able to pay at last but the VOICE said: **"Buy a newspaper!"**

"A paper? When I know that it is better not to involve myself with worldly matters? I can't do anything to change them after all! At least without all the negative things having an effect on my consciousness!" OK, so I bought a newspaper.

I got home and finished what I had to do. Then came a bath and bed. **"Read the newspaper before you go to bed!"** I heard again. If I had heard something about not forgetting to meditate or to spiritually prepare for the following day, it would have seemed quite natural. But to read a newspaper full of these atrocious images! Brrr, I was going to have sweet dreams!

I had forgotten all about the newspaper since I had bought it and pushed it in my handbag. I got up, brought it in and I read what had happened in Luxor. It was terrible but what was I to do? I thought that I would pray for their souls before I went to sleep. I must have fallen asleep at some point. I received the following message while I was sleeping: **"You have to go to Luxor, you have to awaken those who remained there because they are in shock!"** I thought that the part of me that travels at night had already set off.

The phone rang before my alarm clock went off. It was before 7 am. It was Mr Lichtenecker. "Dora, my dear, I'm sorry to disturb you so early in the morning but I know that you are going away and I wanted to catch you. Oscar's parents called me after 10 pm last night to tell me that the earthly remains of the Luxor victims had arrived back at the airport and one of them was identified as Oscar, and one of the others was his bride. Please, I would like to ask you to meditate for them both. I am afraid that the terrible shock will make it difficult for them to find their way home.

"I'll do all that I can," I replied.

"I already have!" I thought.

Now I wasn't upset any longer that the previous day had been so stressful. It turned out to be Oscar whom I had to help.

Oscar was a member of the Lichtenecker group where I had been meditating for more than ten years under the couple's direction.

Poor Oscar was so excited at the prospect of getting married. They had planned their trip to Egypt as a pre-honeymoon holiday. All the best Oscar! Be happy! I am glad that I was able to help you find the way home!

19

Healing Empathy

More and more people started to come to me for treatment. Men (although fewer of them), women and children as well as pregnant mothers. They even brought tiny babies to me. I actually had to go to hospital on several occasions, if the patient in question wasn't mobile enough to come to me or had just had an operation or was lying in a coma.

The suffering of little children touched me most of all.

The first of these tragic cases involved a one-year-old girl as the victim. It was virtually impossible to look at her without crying.

Friends of mine had recommended that the mother bring her tiny daughter to see me. She had an enormous growth between her eyes that distorted her whole face and pushed her eyes out to the side. She was terribly pale, just skin and bone and she had no hair at all. She did look a sorry sight.

The mother told me that they hadn't noticed a problem until she was nearly one, and it was almost on her first birthday that they noticed a bump at the top of her nose between her eyebrows. They waited a couple of days and it appeared as if the bump was growing. Only two months passed and the growth became the size of a golf ball despite all the treatment she had been given.

The paediatrician wasn't able to reassure them and had the child admitted to hospital for tests. The hospital specialists unfortunately diagnosed the growth as malignant and that it was growing at an incredible rate. They started chemotherapy immediately and then radiation therapy but still they weren't able to stop it growing.

The doctors decided that they would have to operate as they saw no other possible cure. They planned to operate in a month's time partly because this would allow the little one to recover her strength after the rigours of chemo and radiation. Her body was completely run down and it would be far too dangerous to operate on her in this state. They also still held out hope that the growth would eventually stop getting any larger. Operating immediately had about as much risk attached to it as did waiting for a while. If they were to operate on her in such a weak condition, it was quite likely that she wouldn't survive surgery. If, on the other hand, they waited, they couldn't be sure what changes and problems the growth would begin to cause in the young girl's brain.

The poor parents even had to consider the risk that their child might die on the operating table. The terrible thing was that if the operation proved successful, there would be a 50% chance that the child would have brain damage of some description and be disabled.

What it must have been like for that poor couple! It is impossible to feel such a thing from the outside and we can only ever guess.

The mother, who had told me the whole history of her daughter's condition, kept on asking why I thought this should happen to them. This caught my attention. She said that she and her husband had always been successful in everything that they had set their minds to and now they had realized that the only thing missing was a child, but then this had to go and happen. I kept on sharpening my senses and my inner ear.

The mother must have been nearly age 40 and the father, as he had built up a career, must have been about the same age. They lived well, had built their own house and now all that was missing to complete the picture was a child. They had everything and now this had to happen to them! How tragic!

It occurred to me that the mother never as much as mentioned the concern, which she felt for the child, and what she must be going through, whether or not she was in pain and whether something was frightening her when she cried. She never talked about how she must have felt when she had radiation therapy. How terrible it must have been for her when her mother "dropped her off" at the clinic and she only went to pick her up after she had finished vomiting following her treatment session. This was because the mother—as she told me—was repulsed by the smell of vomit. The child had vomited all over the car on one occasion on their way home and so now she went to collect her a little later. (The doctors decided to let the baby stay with the parents during the period before the operation due to the seriousness of the child's condition, and out of sympathy for the couple so they only had to take her in for her treatment sessions.)

I began to feel greater and greater sympathy for my tiny visitor. How much discomfort she was causing her mother! (This was all I could hear from what the mother was saying and it made me terribly sad.)

They had wished for a child and they were granted one as with everything else in their lives. And it happened to be their child who was "causing all of this for them". They couldn't go out in public with such a child as her appearance frightened people! And if she should be handicapped ... Well, I didn't dare guess the outcome.

"My poor little thing, you really are in a tough old spot. They aren't willing to accept you as you are and they don't love you for who you are. Maybe they no longer want to!" I was able to feel everything that the little tot was feeling. The mother's voice shook me back from my thoughts.

"Can you help?" she asked.

"I don't know but I'll try everything I can!" I replied.

I asked her to remain quiet and to concentrate on wanting to help her child. I asked her to try and imagine what her baby was experiencing. I asked her to try to pass her thoughts to the child that she wanted her to recover. I told her that I would try to give the child energy and while I was doing this I wanted her to think about her reactions to the child and how she would deal with potentially having to look after a disabled child for the rest of her life.

She looked at me with wide eyes. She was a little uncomfortable but she didn't completely understand what it was that I was trying to say.

"The main thing that this poor little girl needs is to be able to feel the love of her family and that you all accept what may lie ahead. The feelings of the child are the most important thing to consider."

I told her that I was sure that her own expectations had driven her away from her child. I felt sorriest of all for the baby who was all alone in this terrible tragedy.

The mother's eyes filled with tears for the first time! It was only now that she realized what had been happening during this last month. She had become separated from her child and she had pushed her away as she no longer accepted her.

As she closed her eyes and immersed herself in her thoughts and her emotions, I began to work with the child. The first thing I did was to take her in my arms—she was terrifyingly weightless. Then I tried to pass all my compassion and all my love to her so that she would have the strength to open up to me. At first, she stared at me with large, frightened eyes but with time she became more at ease in my presence. I started to stroke her little feet and I took them in my hand. I wanted to hold her heel but her whole foot was no larger than the palm of my hand.

I began to pray and I asked for strength to give to the child. I could feel soft, warming strength leave my hands. I turned to the baby in my thoughts. I asked her to take up this energy and to use it for what was best for her. I asked her to decide whether she wanted to stay alive and whether or not she would be able to accept her parents. If she was scared and tired and wanted to return to the place from where she had come then she should use this energy for that. She had to decide!

When I opened my eyes, I saw a completely different mother sitting opposite me although the tears were still running down her face. She had completely changed! Even her voice seemed softer when she spoke: "Yes, I can accept everything! The present situation is that I may have a lot of problems after the operation and I am also faced with the risk of losing this child. But I have realized that the most important thing is for the little one to sense that I love her, whatever happens! It was the trauma of the last couple of weeks and months which closed my heart and all I could feel was fear."

I recommended that they should hold the baby all the time. They should ask for help from the grandparents and friends and anyone the child knew and felt comfortable with.

The father should also hold her and love her as much as time allowed. If she had to go for radiation therapy then they should stay outside the door for the whole time and tell the child that they would be waiting for her.

I also recommended that I would send strength to my little patient every evening at 7 pm and I asked them to help me to do that. She should sit down with her husband at that precise time and they should ask all their relatives and friends to do the same and concentrate on the child and send their love and compassion to her.

They would not have to come and see me again as all the child needed was their love and compassion. But I did ask them to give me a call and tell me how they were going on.

Every day at 7 pm, I sat quietly and made contact with the child. I could see that she was in light and many beams of light were headed in her direction which bathed her whole being.

I hoped for the impossible.

The mother called about five days later to say that it appeared as if the growth had started to shrink and that the doctors had postponed the operation for a while.

I couldn't have wished for anything better!

She told me that everything had changed since coming to see me. She had the child in her arms almost permanently and she stroked her and petted her and she said that she had even stopped vomiting after her radiation therapy. Well done kid!

Two weeks passed before the next call. The mother didn't seem to believe what she herself was telling me: "The growth is half the size that it was and the doctors are full of hope."

A month later, the date of the original operation arrived and there was no growth to operate on either on the outside or on the inside. It had disappeared as suddenly as it had appeared in the first place. Of course, this is what I had hoped for all along but I was shocked to hear that it had actually happened! The love, caring and compassion of her parents and those around her had cured the child.

The parents and the doctors were unable to accept the recovery. They didn't believe in miracles and they put it all down to the medical treatment that she had been given. But they are best left to their own beliefs as they will change one day! They are surely never going to forget what happened and maybe one day they will realize that a miracle occurred.

I gave grateful thanks to those above for their help.

The child suffered no handicap as a result of her illness. She put all the weight back on that she had lost, her hair grew back and everyone was overjoyed that she was healthy again. Now she is 12 years old and a very happy and healthy little girl.

The swift recovery of the other baby was much more understandable. The mother called me on the telephone. She had been given my number in the children's hospital by one of the nurses and told that perhaps I would be able to help. It is interesting that it had been six years since the first case and the little girl's immediate recovery and she had remembered me and recommended me to this mother.

This woman's little girl was only three months old and had been lying in intensive care since birth. The poor little thing had been born into this world with an open stomach. It was horrific for me to imagine let alone what the poor mother must have been going through!

The child had been operated on straight after birth. The operation had been a failure and the infant's digestive system still didn't function properly. I had never heard of this illness but the mother told me that it was just like an open spine but in her case her stomach and chest were open all along one side. She asked if I would be willing to help.

I went straight over to the hospital. They allowed me into the intensive ward as a "close relative" where the mother was waiting for me.

I was surprised at what I saw. I found a rosy-cheeked and very pretty little baby lying in the cot. If the poor thing hadn't been attached to a mass of wires and tubes, it would have been hard to convince me that I was looking at a child faced with tragedy.

The mother lifted the blanket and I could see that the little girl's stomach was swollen like a child with dropsy and she had tubes trailing all over the place.

After the first operation, they weren't sure why, but she was still unable to absorb milk or formula to say nothing of processing it. This meant they had to feed her artificially through a tube and they had been doing this ever since birth. The second operation hadn't made any significant difference either and the surgeons decided to try a third time in the hope of achieving some sort of improvements. The operation was to take place in ten days.

I stared at the poor little tot as I sat and listened to her mother.

How much the poor thing had been forced to suffer since birth! Other babies were all now resting gently on their mother's bosom while this one had been whisked away from her mother at the very first opportunity and gone into surgery. Yet, they still couldn't be together as normal, happy, mother and child should.

It was interesting that, despite all this, I still couldn't see any fear or defeat in the child's eyes. This all appeared to me as if the baby wasn't at all touched by her own situation. I was allowed to pick her up. Her eyes sparkled and she smiled at me. The mother was amazed!

"It's as if she knows you! You really have cheered her up!"

Now I understand why the child had smiled so much when I arrived. Did we know one another? Did she know me? What was it that she could see in me? Or was there something surrounding me that had improved her mood so?

I held her in my arms and I started to talk to her poor little soul.

"Listen here! What do you reckon? Do you want to live or not? You can't carry on behaving like this! I will try to help you if I can. I'll give you energy and I want you to use it and decide! If you want to stay then you are going to have to start working on your body. If you only came for a short time then it is yours to use to get home again. The doctors aren't able to work out what's wrong with you and this will mean that they can go on trying until they succeed or ..."

I gave her energy and the baby shone with happiness.

The mother knew nothing about our conversation and our agreement. I asked her to keep on stroking the baby's feet and to massage them. I showed her the stomach reflexology points. I also suggested that the father and the grandparents should stroke these points when they sat by her cot.

I wanted to hope but I wasn't the one who could decide as I didn't know what was best for the baby. I didn't know what the family background to the illness was and its karmic origins.

I asked and I hoped, and the parents hoped too.

I went back in a couple of days as we had discussed.

"Yesterday, one of the doctors noticed that her swollen tummy had started to go down a little," the mother said. "Today they are certain that something has started to happen as it wasn't swollen at all this morning."

They postponed the operation.

I started to work with the little one again in mind and spirit at the same time as I continued to massage her feet. The mother sat in the waiting area while I did this and looked on with concerned faith.

I went again a couple of days later just as the doctor was examining the child and he said: "It looks like her digestion has started to work. It would appear that she wants to cooperate after all. But what could have caused this sudden turn around?"

The mother smiled at me and the doctor said that he had decided to start pipette feeding the baby every hour.

I went to see them again two days later. The baby wasn't being fed through tubes anymore and neither was she being given formula but she lay in her mother's arms taking milk (her own mother's milk) from a feeding bottle. The mother had been expressing her milk for three months and freezing it. Now the baby was drinking that milk and smiled just as warmly at us both.

The doctors didn't know how to react to what had happened. They hadn't done anything and they hadn't altered anything. It really was little short of a miracle.

Perhaps "something" had happened but they weren't to know that.

I told the mother that I thought everything would be fine and that I wouldn't have to come back to the hospital again. I asked her to let me know if anything changed and when the baby was ready to be released. I also said that if anything disturbing occurred, they should not hesitate to call me at once.

I happily left on a trip to the Ticino for a couple of days to the old Yesudian-Haich yoga school. The school only ran in the summer and it was the beginning of July, so there was no one around but me and the invisible ones. The school wasn't run by the old lot any longer, they had sold it and new people ran the summer yoga courses. I had been there for the first time the year before but as I had realized that the most important thing had been missing—the old spirit—I didn't attend the yoga sessions anymore. The new director of the school died unexpectedly a year later.

I arrived back in Zurich five days later and spoke to a delighted mother on the telephone: "We are at home and the little one is fine! She is taking milk from a bottle and her intestines and kidneys are working."

I was overcome with joy and gratitude.

The mother asked what they owed me for the treatment. I laughed and told her that it didn't have a price attached. I had only been there three times in all and they were to accept this as a gift from me. They sent me the most wonderful bunch of white roses the following day.

There is no point trying to explain or understand what had happened as it was completely impossible. My spirit was filled with gratitude and thanks.

I would like to describe a third incident where both the doctors and the family had given up all hope. The patient had been lying in a coma for ten days after having had a heart attack.

The patient's daughter contacted me by phone. Again, it was someone I knew from the Lichtnecker group and this girlfriend had given her my details in case I could help.

I corrected her by saying that all I could do was to try but I was more than happy to do that.

It turned out the woman was Hungarian and her father was called Jankovich; it was the same Jankovich who had twice come back from the other side. He had written about his experiences in several books and had been teaching as well as painting and writing ever since.

I was really interested in this one!

The woman told me that they had been considering her father's wish that, should he ever fall into a coma, then he didn't want to be artificially kept alive by machines. He wanted to be left to die as this was his third life, after all.

"I am happy to do anything that I can. I will try and make contact with his spirit now but I will go to the hospital at five tomorrow afternoon," I told her.

We said that we would meet at the main entrance and go in together as if we were sisters, speaking Hungarian. They didn't let strangers in to see coma patients and he was in the intensive care ward.

I contacted his spirit during my evening meditation session and I asked him whether he wanted to cooperate with me. The next day, I stepped into his room with his daughter by my side. He lay motionless and lifeless covered in wires, tubes, clips and sticking tape. I had never been on a hospital ward like this before. Everything was being watched by monitors with machines clicking and whirring in the background. All his organs had to be directed from the outside and this included his heart, his lungs, his kidneys—his whole body.

It was rather an odd feeling but I tried to separate myself from the surroundings. I sat down on a chair by the side of his bed. I had never seen him before despite the fact that we were both involved in much the same things. I hadn't had the opportunity until now.

A voice awoke me from my thoughts: *"You made me wait long enough!"*

Who was speaking? Could it be him? I didn't know whether I had heard the voice from the outside or from within.

But it was his voice: an unfamiliar male voice. Why had he said that? Had he been waiting? Did he know me?

I returned to another world and I was being led. I heard what I had to do and he continued: *"Hold my hand!"*

I did as he asked but I didn't really believe it. Time and consciousness came to a standstill and he spoke again: *"Release my hand and now you can leave!"*

I let go and turned, confused, to his daughter and asked her to walk out with me as "my job was done".

It was only now that I looked at her. She was staring at me. What had she seen? "Did you hear it as well?"

She answered with little more than a sigh: "Yes."

I could hardly wait to get back out into the fresh air because I thought I was going to faint trapped inside the hospital. I stood in front of the entrance. I had forgotten to ask if she had heard the voice from the outside or from the inside. I was still no clearer about where I had heard the voice. I had simply heard a man's voice that had told me exactly what to do. Had I heard it with my ears or another inner sense?

I no longer recall how the rest of the day passed. The next morning, I got up and went to the surgery as if nothing had happened. Jankovich's daughter managed to call me there. Her voice sounded a little choked as if she had been crying. All she could say was: "They took him off the machines."

I felt very sorry for the poor woman. "Oh, I am sad to hear that."

"No, he's alive!" and she said the unimaginable.

I didn't know what to say in reply. She was the one to break the silence and she asked: "Are you still there?"

"Yes, what happened? When did it happen?"

"I was in such a state when I walked you out that I didn't know what day it was," she said. "As the door closed behind you, I turned and walked back to my father's room but people were running down the corridor shouting to switch the machines off because the patient in the room had woken up.

I ran the last part because it was my father who was in the room. By the time that I got there, they had taken all the wires off him and he lay in bed with his eyes wide open like someone who had woken from a deep sleep. I burst into tears and fell on his chest."

I still sat stunned at the other end of the telephone, listening to what she said: "Thank you so much for what you did for my father. How can we ever repay you?"

I was able to answer at last: "I only did what he told me to do."

"Oh, I nearly forgot," she added. "The first thing that my father asked was who came to see him, and I told him that it was Dorothea König, a healer."

Jankovich had thought for a while to see if he remembered a healer by that name but he didn't know who I was.

He didn't remember who I was when he was awake, only when he had been some other place. That was also very interesting.

He called me a few days later from the hospital and thanked me for bringing him back to life.

"Why me?" I asked. "What makes you think it was me?"

He told me that he got stuck in a long dark tunnel and he couldn't move forwards or backwards. There was just darkness and a terrifying timelessness. He didn't know how much time had passed there but it seemed to last forever and he was frightened the whole time. He didn't know how much had time passed when a light being just appeared who took his hand and started to take him back to where he had come from. Then he noticed that it was getting lighter and so he opened his eyes and asked who had held his hand and pulled him back.

"The doctors listened to the story in disbelief," he added. "But the only thing that is important to me is that I am here. Thank you again!"

His daughter called me a couple of days later to tell me that her father had made such a swift recovery that they were transferring him to a convalescent home where he would be able to rest his heart and build his strength back up after the heart attack. She said that he would be there for about a month.

Jankovich himself called me a couple of weeks later to say that he was in Zurich as he had been allowed to go home earlier than expected because he had made such a swift recovery. The doctors were completely baffled by the whole thing and especially by his startling recovery.

The answer is surely not on this Earth or in this understanding.

We arranged to meet the following day. He invited me for lunch and I chose a large Indian vegetarian restaurant.

The old man sat waiting for me when I arrived. I felt very odd to be sitting opposite someone who had been floating between life and death only a couple of weeks before.

He handed me a red rose with the following words: "I have my mother to thank for being born. They sent me back twice because the time had not yet come for my death. But the fact that I can now live and eventually complete what I want to in this life is thanks only to you. I would like to give you this rose to symbolize my thanks because a life cannot be paid for."

I listened to his kind words. What could I have said in reply? I hadn't been able to understand a thing for weeks now. All I was able to do was to accept everything I was given with deep gratitude. Just like the red rose.

I did receive a large gift later on, although not from Jankovich, it was connected to him!

His reawakening from the coma had been in August. I held another fast between Christmas and the New Year as I had done many times before. On 26 December, I heard the VOICE say: **"Call Jankovich!"**

I knew that there was no point in pretending that I hadn't heard because he would repeat it twice. (I only often responded after the third time of being told as I didn't dare resist after that.)

Something miraculous always happened if the VOICE asked me to contact someone at this time of year.

I went straight over to the telephone and called Jankovich. He was at home and very pleased that I had called and wished me a Happy Christmas. I told him that I wasn't calling of my own accord but that the VOICE had told me to. This seemed to please him. He started by saying that he would like to invite me to his spiritual centre if I was able to go the following day. I said "yes" because I was curious as to what would happen.

Their centre was in a completely different part of Zurich from the area that I lived in. It got dark rather early and the snow had started to freeze. It had been falling for days. There was a fresh blanket of snow on the road and it glistened in my headlights as I made my way there by car.

The talk wasn't so important. I just sat and listened to Jankovich's voice and I asked myself: "Just why is it that he was given the chance three times? Will he manage to finish what he wanted to?"

I had the impression that the man had once known a great deal. Did he remember everything? Was he able to transfer his knowledge to others?

He will only be able to know that on the other side. Now I write these lines he has moved to the other side for good. I hoped that he was successful in what I was able to help him to do.

Listening and the discussion made me tired as this was the third day of my fast and I grew weary more easily in the first couple of days than at other times. I said goodbye and went down to my car which was in a street and in an area that I didn't know at all. As the street was long, I decided to turn around and drive back the way that I had come. I didn't feel like getting lost. I wanted to get to bed and go to sleep because I was cold as well as tired.

I drove back along the road and something appeared in my headlights that twinkled on the road. I had seen it as I was about to turn around: I thought it must have been a piece of silver paper and now I saw it again. Interesting! I had hardly completed my thought when I heard the VOICE: **"That isn't foil! Stop the car, reverse and go and pick up your gift!**

I had no energy or will to contradict what I was being told. I thought that I must have been tired because I was starting to see things. Just for my own peace of mind, I reversed and picked it up. It wasn't foil but a large ring with a red stone.

Then I came to my senses. The ring was pushed down in the snow and it couldn't possibly have caught my headlights. So what had been shining on the ring? Who had been shining a light on it that I might see it and pick it up?

I stood in the road in front of my car and I realized that I was right outside Jankovich's house. I parked again and went up to see him with the ring in my hand. In the light, we could see that the ring was very old. It was so big that it even fell off my thumb when I tried it on. It was an unusually thick, gold ring with a large red stone set so deep that it seemed to be dissolving into the gold. It turned out to be a ruby.

I told Jankovich that the VOICE had spoken to me a couple of minutes beforehand and told me to pick up my gift. He wasn't able to say much, so all he added was: "They must love you on the other side! It looks like they have just presented you with a gift for what you did for me!"

All I wanted to do was to go to bed and get a good night's sleep. I was still frightened by the thought that something extraordinary was happening to me.

I shoved the ring in a drawer where it lay for years undisturbed. I couldn't and I didn't want to know what it was that I had experienced. Then one day I decided to take it out and have a look to see what I could do with it.

I recalled that this had been given to me as a gift.

I couldn't wear it because of its size but if I had it adjusted to fit then I could. This was my gift to myself on my next birthday: I had the ring adjusted to fit. The goldsmith was smitten with it and tried to establish its age.

"It must be very old. I have never worked with a ring like this before," he said.

He measured my right ring finger and told me when the ring would be ready. He called a couple of days later to say that he couldn't adjust the ring as it was made of an alloy that neither he nor his colleague recognized. He suggested setting it in a more modern gold alloy.

I said yes and put the phone down. A gold alloy that they didn't recognize? Where had this ring come from and who could have worn it before me?

I have worn this ring on my right hand ever since; this inexplicable gift.

Perhaps I was given it for my help, for my cooperation or for the compassion that I felt for my patients and those who turned to me for help.

I have no way of knowing. But thank you for this as well!

20

It's Hard to Deal with Not Always Being Able to Help ...

Ilse, one of my oldest girlfriends in Switzerland and the one who used to do my hair, became a therapist and no longer works in a salon. I "gave her the bug" and so I ended up having to find a new hairdresser!

It was a long while ago now that I first noticed her in the street. It wasn't her hair that caught my eye but rather her feet. I was attending reflexology class back then with Mrs Steiner and I found every pair of feet that I saw a source of fascination. It was the middle of the summer and women generally wore sandals with no tights.

I was shopping in Bellevue Square in the department store there and I wandered out and into Corso House, which is just next door, as someone stepped out of the door and set off in front of me. I noticed this woman's feet and how she placed them in front of herself. I had to practise my personality diagnosis which involves looking at the way a person walks. This wasn't what caught my eye in Ilse's case but rather the fact that her left ankle bone appeared terribly swollen.

I had to have a closer look! From observing her, I thought—I formulated as I walked behind her—that her problem was likely to be with her left ovary, and most likely the result of a cyst. I didn't much like the look of the inside of her ankle either because that also looked a little swollen. Could the problem have been with her womb?

In the meantime, we walked over the first crossroads and stood by the tram stop. We both got on the same tram. We stood next to one another on the platform. I had been rather taken up with my diagnosis until then, but now I made the most of the chance and looked up so that I could inspect the owner of these feet. She was a woman of about my age, somewhere between 30 and 40, dressed fashionably and with absolutely immaculate hair. I could hear myself saying: "You have got the loveliest hair. Who cuts it for you? I have been looking for a good hairdresser for absolutely ages but still haven't managed to track one down. I used to love the hairdresser whom I went to when we lived back in St Gallen but I have found no one to match her since we have lived in Zurich."

The woman laughed at my complement and my dilemma. She smiled as she replied: "I do my own hair because I haven't yet found a better hairdresser. I am a hairdresser myself. Back there in the square," and she pointed through the tram window. "In the Corso Cinema building. My place is on the second floor. Why don't you drop in and I am sure we will get on just wonderfully."

Well, that is exactly what happened. I went to see her that very same week and she did appear to have a gift. She was even better than her predecessor in St Gallen. I was more than satisfied with the result. People talk about all kinds of things with their hairdresser and not only the women but men as well. I heard a lot of things from Ilse but I told her my fair share as well.

Several of my girlfriends started to go to her and this included my old Hungarian friend Judit who had just moved to Zurich herself from St Gallen. This is the same girl who had come along with me on my first reflexology course with Mrs Steiner and to whom I had sworn I would never have anything to do with the subject again. Yes, time goes on and people alter their opinions according to the circumstances. Judit hadn't carried on attending courses. I had now been studying for a good many years, I'd even gone back to see Mrs Steiner and I had worked on countless feet but still only those of friends and family.

I had perhaps been going to Ilse for a year when one day she said: "That Judit was here yesterday, and she told me that you do reflexology and that you can give a precise diagnosis by looking at the soles of someone's feet."

"No, I'm only a learner!" and I blushed slightly.

"Well, I've got a terrible problem with my left ankle: it's permanently swollen. It is only the left ankle, though I am standing around all day but just the same on both legs. If that was the reason then surely both ankles would be just as bad. It isn't from any kind of injury. What do you think could be causing it?"

I now recalled how I had come to meet Ilse in the first place. It had been through her feet and I had noticed her left ankle in particular. I had completely forgotten!

I laughed as I explained the run-up to our meeting. She thought it was very amusing and she responded with her usual humour: "It looks like my ankle has done its job and brought us together. Now it's more than time for it to get better!"

"If you like, you come over and see me. I have my suspicions but I wouldn't like to say anything when I am not completely sure. I need to take a closer look at your foot and feel the swollen area."

"Is it likely to hurt?" she asked.

"Well it might but it shouldn't be that bad."

The instant diagnosis that I had made on the street proved to be true. Ilse came to see me on her first day off and when I pressed certain points on her foot, she felt pain in her lower abdomen but she also complained of a lot of discomfort on the points around the swollen area.

When I asked her about the last time she had been to see her gynaecologist, she just shook her head.

"I really don't like going and I haven't been for a good few years now," she replied.

I asked her to go all the same as I thought there might be a problem with her left ovary and with her womb. She went along and we had a good chat afterwards and she told me that the doctor had established that she had a problem in both areas and had even gone so far as to recommend an operation. Ilse called me on the phone as she was terribly worried. I calmed her down and I told her all about what I had been through. She asked me to accept her as my first official patient. As I wasn't willing to take money, we agreed that she would do my hair for me in exchange.

Strange how people make friends and what it can lead to!

Ilse came to see me once a week for treatment and my hair always looked great. She asked a lot of questions while she was having her massages. She drew knowledge into herself. Something has awakened in her; something that wanted to awoke to the conscious.

Both of Ilse's complaints faded with time and she recovered fully. She asked to borrow all of my books and she read every single one. We started to go to talks and attend courses together. She slowly became independent and she wanted to learn all about reiki and even completed a course on Swedish massage. She made a load of new friends who all helped on her path of discovery.

I still went to her to have my hair done but now only once a month as I had in the old days. We still meet now and then for a chat.

We bumped into one another once by Lake Zurich and while we walked together she told me what a great trainer she thought Rhea Power was—she was an American healer and teacher. She specialized in a form of reincarnation therapy which she had developed herself. It was like a red rag to a bull! I was reminded of the terrible experience that I had a couple of years beforehand and the fact that I had promised never to go near reincarnation therapy again! I also knew that it was a very dangerous form of therapy and that it required a great amount of knowledge and sensitivity on the part of the therapist. I told Ilse all of this. She told me that she had heard of similar incidents herself but that Rhea's work and teachings really were very different. Rhea was a seer and a healer and that was why she had received the gift of developing this specific form of therapy.

"That sounds more like it!" I thought.

Ilse said that Rhea's therapy wasn't focused on who you had been or what you had done in a previous life but she used this therapy to locate the cause for a specific illness or a recurring personal problem. An example of this would be if someone was fixatedly jealous or had a fear of fire and this fear was very apparent, yet with no apparent cause evident in this life.

Rhea's method sounded more and more credible to me as it seemed to be exactly what I had thought and found lacking when I had attended a session myself. I was more concerned as to why I had lived the lives that I had, what was the task they represented or what was it that I was meant to learn from them?

"If you have faith in me, as that is important when people are working together, then I thought we could try this out together. Maybe it will change your mind about this sort of therapy?"

"OK!" I answered.

I found an appointment that suited us both about a month later. I have to admit: I had my doubts, but my doubts but I had maximum faith in Ilse. Despite the bad experiences of the past, I was open to the idea of revising my opinion.

We did the regression. It was quite phenomenal and I gained some of the most important information in my life. This new experience completely altered my view of the whole thing, and I thought that Rhea Power's method was just wonderful. I wanted to meet her in person and I was soon presented with the opportunity as she was about to hold a weekend course in Ulm in Germany. It didn't matter what the course was to be about, I was much more interested in the woman herself. I was taken by her manner as she interacted with people or simply by the way that she looked at them. She knew! She had been on this road for a long time and I could trust her!

When the course was finished, she called me over, put her arm around my shoulder, looked deep into my eyes and said: "We have met many times before."

I was also convinced of this and soon after that I enrolled on an 18-month course where we not only studied reincarnation therapy but also clearing and channelling. But the most important thing was getting to know ourselves and the development of our finer senses.

I was able to do this the moment that I stepped through the door! My old abilities came back to me after a very long break.

It happened on the very first day. I arrived at the absolute last minute after an excruciatingly long journey to get there. I had trouble finding the venue. When I entered the room, everyone was sitting on the floor up against the wall. There must have been 50 of us in all. I looked along the line of people and was stunned to hear the VOICE and I saw two warning arrows floating in the air. They were pointing at two men whom I had never met before. **"You will have to beware of these two individuals! One will go mad and the other is still capable of killing!"**

This was all too much for me. How could someone possibly know if another person was going mad or if another would kill? What were two such guys doing in a group where the spiritual stakes were so high? Perhaps they subconsciously sensed these dangers and they were looking for a way to release this negative part of their characters? Could what I have heard been untrue or could it possibly be turned around? Could I perhaps be of some help now that I had been warned of the danger, yet help in such a way as to keep this information to myself?

I really would have liked to! I decided that I would do my best.

All these thoughts were going through my mind when Rhea entered the room. Her radiant being filled the whole space. I hoped that her power would have an effect and so I would be able to achieve what I so wanted.

The members of the group introduced themselves one after another, as is typical on these courses. This was all very usual but Rhea's presence made it all different. We were all hungry in the search to acquire knew knowledge. The request or demand included the fulfilment of the task. I hoped my personal matter belonged to the group of requests that would gain a hearing and be solved.

The first weekend and the long weeks that I spent with the group and Rhea led to endless events in my development and great steps forward.

I made many new friends. I dedicated most of my time to these two individuals whose secrets I had been let in to. I spent a great deal of time with them on the course and in our free time. I gave them therapy with all the methods that I had acquired. They also let me into their private lives where I was also able to help them with a lot of issues. We went through their childhoods and did a lot of clearing and then used careful regression to try to uncover the reasons that lay behind the problems that they now had.

With one man, we discovered lives in which his personality intensified his emotions to such an extent that we realized that it had caused death and wild abandon. He still had problems with losing control in this life and we worked on ways of trying to deal with that.

Fortunately, the other man didn't live so far away from me and so I was able to work with him a lot. The key to his life appeared to be believing in a theory and doing anything that it required of him, even if it went so far as killing another person. We cleared many incarnations where he had gone to war as a fanatic believer and where he had killed young and old alike in the name of religion with no qualms at all. I worked with him to try and discover if there was a motive in his life which required this total dedication from him, that would lead him to such extreme acts of violence. We couldn't find a thing.

But we soon got results. As we spent so much time in each other's company we soon revealed our most intimate secrets and I became a very important figure in his life. He saw his complete recovery and perhaps his total happiness in me. He made several attempts to make our friendship closer than it was and he would have liked our private lives to be shared. I couldn't imagine anything like that between us or so it seemed.

In the meantime, I took a foreign holiday where I met an Italian man who appeared to understand me—and I him in return. It was summer, so I had fewer patients and we were having a break on Rhea's course and so we met up a lot. He lived in Milan but the journey to Zurich was a relatively quick one by road or even train. I was also able to go and see him and did so several times and stayed for a couple of days.

I was happy when Rhea's course started up again and I was happy to meet back up with my fellow students. We arranged to work at my place after the first weekend. It happened to be the turn of the other guy. Before we began, we told each other about our respective summers. He began, though I can't recall exactly what he said because what happened made me forget everything in seconds. I happily told him that I had met a man, that we spent a lot of time together and that the relationship meant a lot to me. On hearing this, my friend's face appeared to turn to stone. I made as if I hadn't noticed a thing, but I was prevented from carrying on as he had his hands wrapped tightly around my throat. Fortunately, I was able to yell at him with all my might: "Wake up! What are you doing?"

He released me at once and, like someone who had committed an awful act, ran from the room, out through the front door and down the street. I sat stunned. It had all happened so suddenly that I had no time to be frightened. The greatest shock was that what the VOICE had said had been proven true and that I had been able to do nothing to prevent it. What has to happen just has to happen! I couldn't help in something that he had to solve! It was a great lesson to me.

We met again the following weekend on the course and all I said to him was: "Unfortunately, I know that this danger is real with you but I can't help you anymore than I have. I just hope that the fact that you nearly did it will prevent you from doing anything similar in the future."

I no longer felt like practising separately with the other man either so I cancelled our meetings. I left fate to decide what would happen in his case as well.

The year and a half passed and the course drew to a close. I had learnt an unbelievable amount. Beyond the reincarnation therapy and all the old tools that I now had at my disposal again, this lesson had an incredibly deep effect on me. I was forced to accept that I couldn't interfere in the history of others even if the knowledge of what was to happen to them caused me pain. What had to be had to be. Perhaps if they could recognize the dangers and do all that they could to avoid them then their current karmas could be pointed in a slightly different direction.

I now remembered why it was that I hadn't wanted to see and had lost my sight in one eye in my childhood. Back then, I hadn't been able to deal with what I had. I couldn't stand seeing what was happening to people and what they were capable of. It was simpler to be half blind and not to know.

One of the women from the course called me a couple of months later and asked: "Did you know that Willy has died?" That was the name of the other man whom I had spent so much time working with. "Well, actually, he just went mad and hanged himself. He went to study with a famous teacher abroad straight after Rhea's course ended," she continued. "He became so disturbed by something that happened there that they couldn't calm him down. Not even the teacher was able to help. They said he was behaving like a madman. They had to call for an ambulance and they took him to a psychiatric hospital. No one knows how he managed it, but he hanged himself. I don't know anymore," she said and she hung up.

I had finished! The course had eventually come to an end that had started the first day that I stepped through the door—and for me right there!

I decided that it was much simpler not to see and not to know, but now I was going to accept my sight and accept the knowledge that accompanied it. I was also going to accept that there might be cases when I wouldn't be able to help. I accepted my fate. I knew that this would strengthen my teaching: my teaching of recognition and accepting what was destined to happen.

21

The Long Road
from Egypt

I wasn't at all hungry that morning. I still didn't feel hungry by lunchtime either. Nor was I hungry by the evening. It was interesting as it had happened a number of times in the past. My body (or some other part of me) didn't want to eat. It was just the same the following day. So, it looked like I could fast again. Sometimes my body just decides that it wants to fast out of the blue. Other times, when I decide that I am going to fast, it gets really tough around the third day and then, when I have passed the third day, my hunger leaves me and I am filled with energy. I don't even feel at all tired and I need much less sleep. I try to do a one-week fast at least once a year but sometimes I do two or even three. I only drink water when I am fasting, though I do tend to drink tea in the winter. If I have been very tired beforehand, or in the winter when there's a flu epidemic, I drink fresh orange juice. I always feel great when I'm fasting and I would be happy to go on but I have only ever gone as far as two weeks. I have often thought how much time I would save if I didn't have to shop for groceries, prepare food, cook, eat, wash up and then tidy up all over again. I don't have to do any of this when I'm fasting and I have loads of free time which I generally use to meditate.

This time, I lost my voice completely on the third day. I was taking a shower when I heard the phone ring. By the time I had clambered out of the shower and made my way to the phone and spoken into the handset, it had stopped ringing. I have to correct myself: I didn't speak! I opened my mouth but nothing came out. Well, nothing like that had ever happened to me before and I didn't even have a cold. I wondered what my patients would say if all I did was to point. I thought it best to switch my answering machine on as I wouldn't be able to say anything anyway. I had just switched it over when the phone rang again. It was the same caller as before who wanted to cancel a massage for that morning as she was a little unwell. I was also quite pleased as it meant I would have fewer patients to deal with in this condition. I only had three patients that morning and so that now meant I'd only have two people to point at. I found the whole thing quite ridiculous. The next two patients didn't come either but neither of them bothered to cancel. I made a note of all of this and wondered what it could all possibly mean: "I haven't felt hungry for three days and now I've even gone and lost my voice. My patients haven't turned up. It would seem that I need to be alone for a while and to meditate," I drew the obvious conclusion. Although I liked both things very much, it is true that I had less time to sit quietly and so meditation was starting to be skipped in my daily routine. Now the unknown powers did absolutely everything to ensure that I made up for lost time and they presented me with the gift of a day off.

I spent virtually the whole day meditating. A beautiful image appeared to me during my evening meditation: it was a heart with wings and a shining, six-pointed star above it that was made out of two triangles. I knew the six-pointed star as the symbol of the risen masters. One of the triangles represents man and the other shows the power of God. These two connect in the symbol and form one. I meditated on the image before me but the VOICE spoke: **"This is your symbol."**

"But what does the heart with wings mean?"

"Your work, expressed quite literally," he went on. **"You help others to rise up with the love of your heart and this happiness under our guidance, the risen masters. You do on Earth what we do from above. Draw it and use it!"**

I did as I was told. I have had this on my business card ever since. It was hard to "bring light into the paper" as the symbol I had seen had been bathed in light.

I had another vision that same evening. I had to go into a cave in the side of a hill where there was a gift waiting for me. The cave was full of gemstones and everything sparkled in a rainbow of rich colours. I was told to carry on going. There was something sparkling in the dark depths of the cave. And then I heard: **"Take a look at this!"** There was a six-pointed shining star inside a dark thing. And the VOICE spoke again: **"You can take it, it's yours."**

The light blinded me when I came back out of the cave. I closed my eyes for a short time and slowly reopened them to get them used to the light. It is then that I looked down to see what it was that I held in my hand. I had a black crystal lying in the palm of my hand but I couldn't see the shining star in the centre—outside in the light. Now I heard the explanation. **"This is a black diamond that has a six-pointed star at its centre. It is this that lights up in the dark. Other things need light to be able to shine and they do not sparkle in the dark. This is a gift from us as it is one of the talents that you possess."**

I thought, "Black diamond? There's no such thing! To say nothing of the six-pointed star that lights up in the dark! It's impossible!"

I didn't work with anyone the following day. I was happy to have so much time to myself. My daughters were away on holiday so I used the time to write letters and my voice slowly started to come back. But I didn't talk to anyone and no one called me on the phone. I suddenly remembered that I had promised to give a copy of one of my pictures from Egypt to a German girlfriend and so I went along to the local photocopying shop where they made very high-quality colour photocopies. I had to wait. An old man stood in front of me and fished papers out of his bag that he wanted to have copied. I couldn't believe my eyes. There was a black diamond in one of the pictures with a shining, six-pointed star at its centre.

"Impossible," I muttered and then I turned towards the old man.

"Is there really such a thing? A stone that lights up?"

He was happy to show me the picture and gave me a friendly smile.

"Isn't it beautiful?"

"You're simply not going to believe this," I said, "but I have seen a similar stone in a dream I had recently." (I didn't want to say that I had seen it while I was meditating the previous day.) "I thought it was just an intriguing dream as I didn't think that black diamonds really existed, to say nothing of a six-pointed star in it! Unbelievable!"

"No, there really is such a thing as you can see. I work with stones. (He was called Mr Uhl and he wrote and published the most exquisite books on stones.) Not many such diamonds are known of around the world, and they are priced accordingly as you might well imagine," he added. "Would you like to have a photocopy?" he asked.

"I'd be delighted!"

We chatted a little after that, but all I could think about were the two black diamonds that I had seen in the space of just two days.

My voice came back the following morning but it wasn't accompanied by my appetite. It was now the fifth day that I hadn't fancied a single bite to eat. It was just as if food didn't even exist. But that was nothing new. My hunger would come back again soon enough.

I was really looking forward to this day as I thought the unexpected fast and the black diamond must be leading up to something. I was expecting Ilse that afternoon so that we could do some reincarnation therapy with the Rhea Power method. I was happy to see her and soon after she arrived I laughed as I told her of all the interesting things that had been going on in the last couple of days. Then we went down to work in the basement which I had converted to house my practice.

"First, we have to discuss what it is that you are thinking about at the minute and what it is that you would like to be answered. Then we will construct a short sentence. Then I will take you into a semi-hypnotic state and I will repeat this sentence to you so that you might seek out the answer. For example: what causes fear when I am closed in a small space with a large number of people?" said Ilse starting the session off.

"I would like to know what life I was living when I learnt to heal. I haven't got a problem with this but I am always keen to know more about what methods I might have used and whether I can put them to use in my healing in this life."

"Yes, that's doable," Ilse said. "So we are looking for the life from which your powers as a healer stem. Yes, that'll be great!"

She also explained to me the difference between total unconsciousness and the conscious hypnotic state. In traditional, total hypnosis, the hypnotist (doctor, psychologist, therapist, etc.) takes their patient into the hypnotic state using various methods where the individual is unconscious of his or her actions. They do as they are told, but they know nothing of what they do and they remember nothing of what has happened afterwards. The experience takes place outside the conscious mind and that is where it stays. It is just like going through a door, doing something and not being able to remember a thing when you come back out of the door.

"Now, you are going to enter a semi-conscious state," she said, and added: "So now you will also be able to direct events as you are the one who has to open that door and the consciousness to that particular life that we are looking for. Now everything will be clear to you throughout and that you are doing my bidding based on what we have previously agreed. When you come back—with my help—to this life, you will be able to remember everything. You will experience everything during the regression both physically and mentally. You will also feel pain but this will only stay with you as a memory when you return rather than a physical sensation."

I was getting more and more interested by all of this and I trusted Ilse completely but I was more excited by the fact that I might be able to offer new help to my patients by what I was about to learn about my past.

We started to work. Ilse's kind and calm voice had an immediate effect and her words helped me to unwind and relax. I soon found myself standing in the place from where I was going to be able to enter a previous life. I stood and waited for the agreed sentence that would decide which life I was to step into. Then I heard it:

"Look for your life's origin!"

Ilse had made a mistake. It turned out that she hadn't noticed it either. I heard the instruction and I asked the same: that I should step into the life that was my life's origin rather that the origin of my healing!

I looked for myself or rather I searched for the place and the body into which I had arrived. It wasn't there: only my consciousness. But my consciousness knew the job that it had to do.

I had arrived in a place where nothing else existed other than us. We were the Ideas. We were all Ideas but each with our own individual consciousnesses. Each Idea knew what its aim was. We had to raise our resonance. How we did it, I didn't see but it could be sensed. Each Idea worked on itself. When it reached a certain level, it drew the idea towards it that was at the same level of resonance and they joined, melted into ONE and went on resonating together. They stopped being one and another and just became ONE. The aim was for all the Ideas to continually combine until at the end there was nothing more than ONE. I can still feel that generous excitement and joy in the work. I worked on my resonance as an Idea and felt the joy of soon being able to draw another one towards me. (How many could there have been in me by this stage?) Then there was an unexpected surprise. A voice spoke, but not audibly. We all, Ideas, could sense what it "said": *"You are now entering material and you are to strive there and live on what you have begun here. The aim will live on within you. Work on yourselves with your resonance and continue combining until nothing is left but ONE."*

Then I (we) began to sink down. It was a very strange and unusual sensation.

I suddenly felt a tugging. Or more of a jump! And I leapt out of the water as a dolphin! I lived happily in this space and this matter for a while. I also felt attached to the other Ideas but I felt the looseness and friendliness of the dolphin community in the infinite ocean. I was as happy as a dolphin and all the others were very happy.

Then there was another sudden jerk and I was on dry land. I was surrounded by pomp and riches. I recognized myself as a female of high birth and I was the daughter of the Pharaoh in Egypt. I had a very high consciousness. It was a good feeling. I knew that I had learned all that there was to learn and this filled me with happiness. I was happy to study as I wanted to know everything. My father and I were not the children of the Earth. I knew that we had come here to learn and that afterwards we would leave again. There were others learning there though not very many. There were an awful lot of ignorant people around. Their mind hadn't yet opened and they lived like ants.

I only concentrated on my own development as this was the only thing of true importance to me. I soon wanted to be on my way again. I longed to return to my original home once more where I could be among my own kind. It was beautiful there but there were too few of us. My only happiness lay in the acquisition of knowledge! My father led the teaching. I loved him entirely and it was his voice that I heard: "You cannot return with us because you still have much to learn!"

"That's impossible for I have learned everything."

"No, you have not yet learned the most important thing of all!"

"It cannot be true. I have learned everything!"

"The most important thing for you to learn on Earth is love and you do not know how to truly love."

I became very agitated. "How could you say such a thing? You are my father, whom I love so dearly. I love you. I revere you because you are my father and my teacher. You are the wiser and the most magnificent. It is impossible to love more than I love you!"

His answer was softer than it had been up to now. "Yes, my daughter, you love me, everything in me but just me. All your love is directed only towards me."

I didn't understand what he meant by this.

"True love is when," he continued, "your love is not only towards one person or one thing but for everyone and everything."

"That's impossible!" And I thought of all those ignorant ones whom I paid no attention to whatsoever. I was fully aware of their existence but they were nothing to me as they lived in the world of their instinctive boundaries.

"It is impossible that I have to love them as well! Impossible!" I repeated.

My father's announcement was final. "Not even I can alter this law," he concluded. "You have just chosen the quick route and really there was little missing for you to transform yourself from here, but it didn't succeed. Now you have to die."

"Die? But I always thought that death didn't await us!"

"Yes, but you MUST DIE TO BECOME AN EARTHLY MORTAL and you have to start everything all over again from the beginning."

The words echoed in my head but I really didn't want to believe my ears! I had lost my companion and I would have to stay here and I would have to know death? It seemed unimaginable. My father's will was my command. It was his loss that caused me the greatest pain as he was everything to me. He was my love and the purpose of my life.

I longed to have his knowledge and I wanted to enjoy his might. I wanted to learn from him and for him to let me into every secret and to return with him to our galaxy, our old home, from where we had originally come. But what would happen now?!

"You will be buried alive surrounded by pomp and ceremony as best befits my own daughter ..." and that was the last that I heard. Suddenly, all pictures disappeared. I was overcome by a terrible sensation. Something started to leave me. I became heavier and heavier. I knew and I could feel that I had lost my knowledge. The pain was indescribable. It was like the death of all deaths! There is no physical or mental pain to compare. I died in this pain and I became a true earthly mortal.

I became a dark entity and everything left me and this was all that was left of me. Heavy and dark. It was awful to feel and to know this. This black orb suddenly began to roll and I was hidden inside it. A lot was going on the outside but I hardly took part in things at the beginning. And then I started to pay attention as time went on. Everything became much brighter. The orb just rolled and rolled until it came to an abrupt standstill. I could hear a voice which seemed somehow familiar but I couldn't remember where it was coming from and whose voice it was.

"You have arrived in your present life. If you learn everything that there is to learn, you will be able to transform yourself in this life! Never forget that the Earth will only release you if ..."

I suddenly remembered: "If you know how to truly love!" Then the orb burst open and I saw a sparkling, six-pointed star.

The experience was such that I felt as if the floor were pressing me where I lay; I could hear that I was breathing. I could feel the blood as it was beating in my heart and flowing into my veins. I could feel my body. Ilse could see that I had started to drop back into my present-day consciousness a little, all by myself. She led me back and I fully returned to this life with her gentle guidance.

We weren't really able to talk about what had happened. The image and the task in hand were so clear. I now also understood the past week and everything that had happened. It was for this day that I had needed to fast. I had needed to be in quietness for days at a time without a sound. All the interesting experiences and the six-pointed star had been part of this.

"Yes, now I know what's at stake! I would like to do all I possibly can and not simply to fulfil the desire I have been carrying for so many 1,000s of years (4,000 years!) to make my way back to the others, but for more reasons than that. It must be a glorious thing to love everyone and everything through love of the ONE."

The whole experience stayed in my mind for days and days. So many images and deeds had collected in the last few days and I didn't know why I had done them and what they meant.

The first trip that I went on after the divorce was to Egypt. I had to go there as soon as I was "free". I felt truly at home in Egypt. I loved everything about Egypt: its people, its cities and even the dirt itself. I was brimming with love. I didn't know why, but I felt just so fantastic and full of such a wonderful feeling. It was as if it had made me feel freer. Coming away from Egypt was really tough. She didn't want to let me go either. The flight that I had printed on my ticket didn't in fact exist.

I felt the best when I was in Luxor. I walked among the towering columns of stone with the sure sensation that I had been there before.

I had never been quite this sure that I had actually been in a specific place in a previous life. Hawaii was similar but somehow different. There the connection with nature was so strong. Here it was more difficult to pinpoint. The feeling was familiar but I just couldn't quite explain what lay behind it.

The Pharaoh's pyramid at Chefren had a particularly strong effect on me. It was the same unknown feeling: I can remember something but I don't know exactly what.

I could have spent weeks wandering around the Egyptian Museum and then I realized that I had felt exactly the same as a child in the Egyptian rooms at the Museum of Fine Arts. There was something "eternal" there for me. Like a child, I felt that there was some kind of hidden secret.

It must have been a good six months after my return from Egypt that the VOICE spoke again after rather a long silence. **"The proud Chefren Pharaoh buried his daughter all in gold."**

His voice and his message hit me like a bolt of lightning. "The VOICE, I know the voice!" It had never occurred to me before that I might know it. He said "Chefren" in a very old-fashioned way so that it sounded almost like "Chepheer". I had always known that this was the way that it should be properly pronounced.

And now this regression therapy and the experience ... Could I have been his daughter? Otherwise, why would I have received that message?

He had contacted me again! This must have meant that I was on the right path! This was the first time that this had happened! It was a couple of days later on a Sunday morning that I heard: **"Now the only thing that is important for you is Thot!"**

I jumped straight out of bed and dashed over to the bookshelf. I took down my book on Egypt. "Thot is the God of knowledge and literature." (I suppose he would be referred to a patron saint in modern parlance.)

So literature! Writing down what I have known and what I have learnt! He had said the same 18 years ago: **"Write everything down that happened to you. In time, you will have to write everything in a book. It is to teach others through your example."**

Learning and experiencing things for others?! Perhaps even suffering for others? Love can be expressed in many forms. This is one of the many different kinds.

So, as he said, now only Thot was important. I had done everything else that I had promised to do. At least I had done all that I had managed to recall.

The VOICE gave me a task a little later on that I couldn't fulfil.

"Send your daughters abroad to study for a year. The time has now come for you to concentrate all your time and energy on your own development. You are using energy up on them that was never intended for them."

"Impossible!" was my reply. "What on earth would my husband say if I were to send the children away just like that? And they wouldn't go anyway. And how would I ever be able to afford something like that?"

I didn't receive an answer to my question—not that I ever had done when I hadn't been able to accept what I was told.

My daughters had, in fact, caused me a lot of trouble and a fair amount of sorrow. They were teenagers ages 15 and 17. They were forever battling with me despite the fact that I was their mother and the same mother who had been their role model up until this point. They also thought that everything that I was doing was a load of rubbish. I came back once from a talk: Claudia had stuck a note on my bedroom door which read: "People who give talks are stupid; and people who go to listen to the talks that they give are even more stupid." So that was the way things were going at the time. I felt terribly alone and even when I was able to contact familiar spirits during meditation or in workshop groups, I was still left to deal with everyday life on my own. I had also been taken ill with my thyroid gland and my neck was quite swollen. My practice was still very new but friends were already asking me to teach them and hold courses on the secrets of meditation.

The question of the girls studying abroad sorted itself out, or perhaps it was helped along from above. I had already forgotten that there was something that I should have organized. I moved with my daughter, Toncsi, from the big, old place to a smaller one and from eight rooms into five. I was no longer able to afford the rent on the old house but nor did I really have the strength to move. I knew that the answer would come from the outside. I knew? I knew because I had been told. The rent was a lot to pay out every month. I had sat down and gone through the small ads in the newspaper several times since the divorce. And all the time I could hear something within saying: **"The time isn't right. You're still not strong enough!"**

I eventually had to stop taking a paper as I would automatically flick through the section on places for rent.

I needed three years of peace for my health to right itself. My practise and my meditation group were both going well. It was the owner of the house who eventually asked me to find somewhere new because his daughter was about to get married and they were going to need somewhere to live. I managed to find a lovely big flat in the area and the rent was really unbelievably reasonable. They'd helped me again!

I came across my diaries while I was packing (I had been keeping a diary for a good ten years by then, as I had been asked to) and they fell open at a page in 1991, when I had been asked to send my daughters to study abroad. Claudia had been living with a family in Brazil for about a year. It was a student exchange with study. I read a few of the things that I had written and was reminded of how impossible I had considered the whole idea, and so I had completely forgotten that task. It was as if I had never heard anything in the first place.

Now, I went back over how it had all come about. Claudia had heard something at school about an opportunity of travelling abroad as part of a student exchange. It wasn't a condition that someone should come and stay with us but they still called it student exchange. Claudia asked what I thought of the idea. I didn't think that it was at all bad and it would be a great way of experiencing another culture, another family, another language and even another religion. It really was a chance not to be missed at her age! They only let the best ones go and Claudia was a good student. Now, the only question was where would she like to go? The main place that she talked about was South America; Ecuador or Brazil. She had always been interested in South American Indians. She found a family in Brazil, in Bahia, with a doctor couple who had four children. The mother was black and of African descent and a paediatrician involved in homeopathy. The father was from a Portuguese family and worked as a psychiatrist. The family lived according to the ancient religion of reasonable. My daughter was presented with the opportunity of discovering a completely new world. She was attending one of the best private schools in the whole of Brazil.

I was ashamed to read the proof of my lack of faith in my diary. I had really no idea that such exchange programmes existed. However, the fact that I didn't know about something doesn't mean that it doesn't actually exist! What the VOICE had said had come true yet again along with the fact that it really was the best thing that I could do—just as it had been for most important figures from my story.

Antonia, according to her sister, also wanted to try the student exchange programme. Only a year before she had said that she would never go anywhere foreign, speak anything foreign or ever eat anything foreign. Claudia had only just returned and she left.

The fact that my daughters had gone still didn't mean that I was able to devote all my strength to my work and my health because there was always someone at home who needed to be looked after. I had learnt a lot again!

So we moved house and it was a big job. It tired me out because my health was nowhere near what it had been. My thyroid was going down by this stage but any strain tended to have an effect on it. Moving wasn't only about packing and unpacking a houseful of things but also about packing up a place we had moved into as a family of four with so much faith in our future and now three of us were packing up and leaving. I held our 16-year-old marriage and whole history in my hands. I still had the love letters that my husband had written before we were married and I also had the replies that I had sent to him. I cried when I found them and sat down and read them through. It was just the same with the gifts that we had bought for one another back in the early days. Everything had stayed with me in that house. My husband had only taken his own personal things and a couple of pieces of furniture but the past had stayed here.

I held a little ceremony that evening and I said a loving goodbye to everything. Then I placed all the paper in the fireplace and put a match to the lot so that I could be free. I didn't want to take a past with me that had become redundant. Everything that was important stayed with me and was inside me. This was still living on in my daughters.

I had a terrible fever that night but everything was clear again by the morning. I was full of strength the next morning and I even lent a hand to the removal men getting everything into the truck. I was happy to take it all off again at the other end and I took everything up to the new flat.

The place had been freshly painted and the wooden floors had been newly varnished. The whole place was full of a new and fresh energy.

We eventually got everything into place and popped a bottle of champagne and drank a toast to the new flat. This was a new beginning! And the champagne was fabulous! Neither I nor my friends had ever drunk anything like it before and the colour, aroma and mainly the taste were unbelievable! We looked at the bottle and it was nearly 20 years old. We must have been given it when we got married or when our first child was born. We'd never opened it and it had always been passed over in the cellar despite the fact that we had moved five times. Well, it was certainly worth the wait as it really was nectar in a bottle! It was still full of fizz and sweet like a liqueur without being over the top. We savoured every last drop. I was grateful for being able to thank my friends for their help with such an exquisite gift. I put the bottle on a shelf in the kitchen, in pride of place in the new flat.

I was tired but happy as I went to bed in my new bedroom in my newly christened home.

The house-warming carried on at night. My friends stayed with me in my dreams and the champagne bottle was also there but this one was much smaller than the one that we had enjoyed. It didn't occur to me that it would be too small for all the thirsty people in the flat. We couldn't open it. It had a double seal on it. There was the usual champagne sort and then one that looked like a beer cap. I still didn't realize that this was a special bottle of champagne. I went out into the kitchen to fetch a bottle opener. I thought that this would help us take the cap off and then we would be able to get at the usual champagne cork.

That's not what happened though. I had hardly raised my hand with the bottle opener, when the bottle burst open all by itself. The pressure in the bottle blew the cork out with such force that it flew up in the air and went straight through the ceiling. We all looked up in surprise and saw that it really had ripped a hole in the ceiling above our heads. I was more surprised to see that the hole began to grow. Then my everyday mind cut back in and I suddenly thought, "Good heavens. The man upstairs isn't going to have a floor left to walk on!"

It stopped when only the outside walls were left. Now, the flats weren't separated from one another as no one was left with either ceiling or floor. In reality, I only had the owner of the building living above me but in my dream, there were several floors above me and now with no divide between us. The people above me just floated in the air, waved, smiled and raised their glasses to toast me. They were celebrating as well. There were no walls between us and the little bottle was enough for all of us. It really was manna! The contents of the bottle kept on growing until everyone's glass was full: "But how will I ever convince the insurance man that this was all done by such a little bottle? They'll never believe me when I tell them that I was just trying to open it!" and my everyday Swiss consciousness cut in when I thought of the smashed ceiling.

I laughed when I woke up the following morning and looked up at the bedroom ceiling. It looked perfectly intact despite having had a champagne cork burst through it in the night. There was no longer any "division" above me. Perhaps my father from 4,000 years ago had been right up there somewhere raising his glass to me. I smiled to myself. "There was so much force in such a tiny bottle!" I thought in amazement.

They had known what they were doing when they had put a double top on it! That is what had made it grow so strong and the pressure and force had built up inside it. A 4,000-year-old bottle really would have been worth a lot!

22

India Calls

The inauguration (initiation) was followed by day-to-day work. Claudia had already returned home and now Antonia had left for the United States to live with a family on the shores of Lake Michigan as part of the student exchange programme. The father was a music teacher and the mother a manager. The whole family followed the teachings of the Jewish faith and they were generous enough to allow my daughter to take part in all their festivals. What a coincidence: the father had visited Switzerland some 20 years earlier and had gone to the violin maker's in Brienz and bought a violin for his music school. That was where my father-in-law had worked! Our families still keep in touch. My daughters go to stay with them whenever they have the chance and they have been to stay with me several times—together and individually. Lina, the eldest daughter of the Brazilian family, stayed with me for a while after she finished her medical degree and she had the chance to take a look at what goes on inside a Swiss hospital. This all meant a bit more housework but I was always delighted to welcome any of them into my home.

My work made me very happy. I was doing what I had longed to do for such a long time: I healed and I taught. I also found a place for my practise in the large flat which meant that I won the time back that I would have spent travelling to and from work every day. My patients all liked coming to see me and said it was just like stepping into a "home of light": everything was glowing! Everything was lit in a very special kind of light! And that was what it was like. They could see, though they weren't seers.

I now started to take weekend courses as well as weekly meditation groups in both Switzerland and Germany in a "spiritual development" school. I worked, I shone, I was happy.

One day, an old friend called and we arranged to meet by the lake and drink a coffee together. He had previously lived in Germany but then had moved to the United States and that was why we hadn't seen one another for such a long time. This was even though there were deep threads which connected us from another time. He had rented a room from me when we had still been living in the house. He had always organized his work from Switzerland whenever he was in Europe although, strangely enough, we had never run into one another here and whenever he stayed at our place, I was always away from home. Five years later, when I was on a Gabriella Roth course in New York, I wanted to go and see him and his wife who were living in New Mexico at the time. The only trouble was that they were in Europe, yet they had been sweet enough to leave me the key to their place. Now, I was curious to see how things were with him. I wanted to know everything there was to know, as is typical between such good friends.

It ended up being rather a swift chat because, as usual, he had to run off somewhere. He was organizing a seminar the following day where he was going to talk about his guru.

I always kept track of what had been going on his life as we have known one another for nearly 20 years. The road that he had chosen to take really didn't appeal to me. I had my own leader from the very beginning: Mr Lichtenecker, and through him those who lived and worked in higher regions who had already become masters and spiritual teachers.

The VOICE had provided sure and protected leadership. My inner voice had also become heightened and so I sought no other route or other master for myself. I was, however, always interested in everything so I was more than happy to say "yes" when Wulfing invited me to attend the seminar to be held the following day.

I was running a little late on the Sunday morning as I had meditated after waking. I made my way there as fast as I could but I still managed to arrive late. The seminar had already begun. There was a woman standing at the door who greeted me with a forgiving smile and pointed to a seat near the side so that I wouldn't disturb the others. It was the first one. "I would be here," I thought.

Wulfing was speaking and all those gathered in the room listened attentively. There were quite a few young faces in the crowd, which I was pleased to see. "I wonder if there's anyone here whom I know," I thought, as I glanced around the room. Then the pictures on the wall caught my eye. Impossible! I had seen the exact same, unknown, Indian figures in my meditation that exact same morning! But there had only been three of them. They radiated so much strength, peace and love. While I was meditating, I had realized that I wasn't alone. They had been standing in front of me. They noticed that I had seen them and all they said, or rather transmitted, in my direction was: "It is time that you visited India. Rediscover your ancient roots!" And now they were here! They had appeared, despite the fact that I didn't know them at all. (Well, at least not from this life.) I thought that they must be Wulfing's masters. Unfortunately, I can't recall a single word of these seminars as this took up all my thoughts. I was already on my way to India. I was on my way to another ancient homeland and the roots of ancient wisdom.

I already knew Wulfing's response. The pictures showed his masters' ancestors. I simply asked: "I know these people too. They visited me in meditation and told me that it was time for me to go to India."

How fascinating fate can be! I arrived in Delhi during my travels around India, and who was waiting for me at the airport but Wulfing! He just happened to be there at the same time as me. I was on my way to Dharamsala to hear the teachings of the 14th Dalai Lama that were to start in a couple of days. Strangely enough, Wulfing was also there because of the Dalai Lama as he had interviewed him along with his master, Rajinder Singh. I seem to recall that he had recorded it on video as a spiritual congress had been held there with the living leaders of various faiths. I accompanied Wulfing on a visit to his master whose home was just outside Delhi at the same time as a group of Hungarians arrived. I was overjoyed by this meeting and I saw it as a sign that perhaps Hungary would be the next destination on my journey. Would she call me?

I needed to wait for Antonia to arrive back home before I could set off for India. Six months later and it was my turn to tell my daughters that I wanted to go on a study trip to India! To India! The mere thought of it filled me with joy and the girls were just as excited as I was.

"She's come to life at last!" they said to one another. They had seen my long sadness and they knew all about my dangerous thyroid illness. They were sure that India would be my cure and they were right!

I excitedly prepared for the trip. I planned to stay for five weeks but I was on the road again just a couple of months after I had arrived back. I organized everything at home so that, this time, I could stay for three months. I had centuries of catching up to do and a vacuum to fill. I wanted to learn and see so much.

I have put the two trips together as they belong together.

I was given plenty of addresses and ideas by friends—and from the other side—while I was preparing to leave. There was a master whom I deeply respected and whom I had never dared to approach. I knew that he was wonderful. I had always planned to read his books but I had only read about him once by then. I had absorbed myself in books on Egypt after my time there, and books by Paul Brunton that he had written based on his experiences in Egypt. Now, I was about to go to India and so I bought my first book on his first experiences there in which he wrote about his master and teacher, Ramana Maharshi. I had already seen pictures of him and I was stunned by his simplicity.

I was given books by friends while I was preparing for my journey between the two trips and they had told me that I simply must read them before I set off. There were three books in total and they all dealt with Ramana Maharshi; two of them featured pictures of him that I already knew. I knew, from Paul Brunton's book, that he always called his pupils to him when the time came. His ashram was to be the last stop on my second trip; I am going to describe the experiences that I had there at the end of the chapter.

I had also promised an important visit to my girlfriend in India; she had been a patient of mine for a long time. Through her feet, I had come to realize that she hadn't been living the life that she wanted to. The pains in her feet disappeared on the second day of the course as if they had been blown away and she said: "You are so right! I never have been able to accept the fact that I really want to live a spiritual life. My parents have always been against it (she was over 50 at the time) and they always said that I would end up in a cult. The truth is that true Buddhism has always fascinated me. I have always longed to meet the 14th Dalai Lama."

"Well, what's stopping you?" I provoked.

"Nothing now! I decided last night that, from now on, I am going to live the life that I want and not the one that others would have me live."

Well, she really did it, and two weeks later she was on her way. Her destination: Dharamsala, the home of the 14th Dalai Lama and the University of Tibetan Buddhism. Monika, as she was known then, is now an initiated Buddhist nun.

Three weeks later—and she only stayed in Zurich as long as it took her to give all her possessions away—and she set off for the mountainous, Indian peaks to follow her dreams. I promised her that, if she did live there, and I was ever to visit India, I would definitely pay her a visit.

She was delighted when she got my letter confirming that I was to arrive. She asked me, if possible, to come at the end of winter. It wasn't only because of the weather getting better but also because of the 14th Dalai Lama's three-week long teaching. She thought that I would be happy to take part. She was right! Without doubt, I wanted to arrive at Dharamsala during my journey at the time when His Holiness teaches in person and blesses all those present.

My first trip led to the Indian Ocean. I wanted to feel the sea and the sun of southern India on my skin after the long, long winter. I arrived in Trivandrum with Air India and I went to Kovalam Beach to relax and mingle with the Indian people. I loved everything! The people who live there are open, helpful and believe very deeply in their gods. It was a little difficult to get used to so many deities but I soon switched over to be able to understand. They have one main god: Brahma. The others simply bear his important qualities in a similar way to our Father, Son and Holy Ghost, angels and archangels. (This is just a comparison to help you understand what I want to communicate.) They also revere Jesus, Mary and the Apostles. I felt this way when I was in a temple of Vishnu or Shiva, Shakti or Krishna. I tried to feel the strength with which the local followers of the faith believed in these gods. So I didn't enter their temples as a stranger but with openness and I was taken into places where not only Europeans rarely visit but also Indians never see unless they happen to be a devotee of that particular deity. Accident or good fortune?! No! Openness and deep respect for other faiths opened doors that remained closed to many. Secrets hid behind these doors and I was able to take part in magical, healing ceremonies. I would prefer to keep events there to myself. The main reason for this is that I didn't know their rituals and I don't really want to pass on my incomplete knowledge. The fact that they allowed me to take part and they asked me to help them in their healing was much more than I had ever dreamed of experiencing in wonderful India.

I did, however, have to provide healing throughout my whole journey. Things, or rather people, were always falling into my hands. I had been on the road for several weeks and I decided to visit the deeply respected Sri Sri Sri Satchidananda Yogi in Madras. I arrived at Madras airport and took myself straight there by taxi. Yoga Ashram was written in my information exercise book which I had put together back at home. I gave the exact address to the taxi driver.

It was late, getting dark; Madras is unfathomably large with more than 5 million residents. It is mainly populated by Tamils who have very dark skin. The taxi found its way into the centre of Madras. There were people bustling to and fro in their 100s with cars and buses trying to weave through the crowds, packed to the limit with people hanging out of the windows and clinging to the roof often accompanied by the odd goat or two. The whole thing stopped dead for a couple of minutes when a cow happened to want to cross the road and everyone waited patiently for it to go on its way. But, they often had no intention of completing their journey and rather lay down right in the middle of the road. It was like some enormous joke. The traffic came to a standstill in all directions, the important crossroads was no longer and people had to make their way around the holy animal as it is forbidden to disturb them. It made an interesting spectacle for a European onlooker, like some kind of surreal film. 100s of people stop and that means buses, taxis, rickshaws: the whole lot. It is as if the cows sense that they can do exactly as they like, and they lie down in the most inconvenient place imaginable.

Eventually, we set off again and arrived in the little alley. I guess you could say that it was a market. There were hawkers in the shops but they were also selling from barrows and all kinds of vehicles. They were surrounded by a mass of animals such as cows, goats, dogs and the odd chicken and all of this was in the centre of an enormous city.

The taxi simply couldn't go any further. The driver said it was only a couple of streets away. Was this where I would find the Yoga Ashram? And, amazingly, it was right there down a couple of narrow little streets. He got out and said that we had arrived. We were immediately surrounded by curious children but there were also grown men and women in the crowd. It was completely dark by this stage and I really couldn't believe that the Yoga Ashram could be in such a place. The driver was stunned when I opened my little book again and showed him the address of the Hotel International. It was really close to the bus station as I planned to leave for a small trip from there. Well, I was in charge, and paying the bill, so, despite vigorously shaking his head, he climbed back into the taxi and we started to pick our way back out through the narrow alleyways.

I rested well that night and tried again with another taxi the following morning. The result was exactly the same and so I gave up. This time I got out and, in the light, I could see the words "Yoga Ashram" written on the wall right there in the middle of the market.

The noise was absolutely deafening but the smells also took a bit of getting used to. I made my way up the stairs and soon laid eyes on the holy man who had been three-times enlightened and had lived in silence for several decades. His hair was bundled up on his head like a mountain and they said that it would reach the floor if he were to let it down. His simplicity was sublime. His whole being radiated knowledge and humility. He waved that I should sit down. In time, he placed photo albums in front of me when he thought that I had managed to calm myself after my journey. They had old photographs in them which showed him as a young Yogi. He looked wonderful even in his younger days. The *asanas* couldn't have been done more beautifully than he had done them in the photographs. The only difference between then and now was that now his hair was completely white and the skin wasn't quite so smooth over his muscular body as it had been back then. But the devotion and faith with which he had welcomed me was also in the pictures.

We sat there all day as he worked. This was the place where he both worked and lived. He only lived in one room in the building. He brought me information from time to time or wrote something for me on a little blackboard and handed it to me.

The house had been a gift and this was where the Yogi ran a school for the children of the very poor. Everything was provided for free, even the food. In fact, that day was *pudja,* when parents could also come along and were provided with something warm to eat. The reverential Yogi quietly prepared the room (his room) for the celebrations. I was also able to take part in the work. He would call me over from time to time to help but he was the only one who could decorate the altar. He also slept just in front of the altar.

Sometimes he left me for an hour or two and he went off to meditate but in the same room as me. And so I decided to meditate as well. In his presence, I sensed that my being, born in another faith, began to lift up. I could no longer hear the noise coming up from the street or the chatter of the children running around the school.

At the end of the day, when the time arrived for his *pudja,* I was there in his silence but I was also there in all the flower garlands that were placed around his neck or laid at his feet. He also blessed a garland himself and placed it over my head. I was scented that evening by the sweet smell of jasmine but there was also something deliciously scented in my soul that was indescribable. It was the scent and the breath of silence, holiness, devotion and the perfume of the gods wafted through my whole body and carried its beauty deep into my soul.

He placed a blessing on my head that evening for my onward journey and I left the touch of his hand, the scents and the experiences of the day and dissolved back into the bustling Madras night.

I had decided to visit Amma, Ammachi's ashram, in southern India with a very nice couple I had met in Kovalam. My new friends lived in Provence and spent several weeks in India every year and were happy to go and visit Ammachi when they were there. I had never heard of her before but I have discovered that she comes to Zurich every year when she is in Europe. I didn't know what went on there but I was happy to go along because everyone who visited her always spoke with such love and devotion. I was curious to see for myself...

I was surprised to see something that looked more like a little palace than an ashram. We were told that this was necessary to accommodate the 100s and sometimes 1,000 of people who flock there. Everyone sat on the floor. They waited for the "ceremony" to begin. The Ammachi appeared at the appointed time and there were steps leading up to the throne where she took pride of place. The expectant crowd had been waiting for her arrival and all set off on their knees towards her. I didn't feel good and most definitely not at home despite the fact that they were playing the most blissful music in the background. I really didn't like all the pomp. Amma embraced everyone and each individual came away smiling making a place for the next devotee.

I saw a familiar face and I knew that it was a guy who used to make frequent visits to Sai Baba's ashram. But now he lived here as he said he felt much better in these surroundings. I respect the feelings of others but I have always followed my own convictions. I really wasn't enjoying this but I stayed because of my new friends. They were virtually glowing with happiness at the thought that they too would be "embraced", which they had been waiting for, a whole year. I let them go in front of me, on their knees, and I went up after they had been embraced. It was only now that I saw Amma from close up and she rather reminded me of my dear, old grandmother. She seemed very pleasant but it was the atmosphere of all this ceremony which I didn't like.

Now I stood before her and she embraced me before releasing me and embracing me again. She really was like an amma or a nanny, for all those who sought solace and love found it in her bosom and her embrace. She embraced me one more time and gestured that I should stay. I wondered why this should happen to me. Those who actually lived in the ashram looked on with what I would call "devout jealousy" and signalled that I really should stay, where I was, if that was what Ammachi wished. My friends waved at me to see if everything was alright and then went back to their places at the back and waited patiently. There were those who joined the back of the queue and waited in line to be embraced a second time. Suddenly Amma signalled to say that she had finished. She had called a small circle of people around her as well as me. She spoke to us all in person so that no one else could hear what was being said other than the young girl who translated. I went closer to her in order to hear what it was that she said. She turned to the young girl who turned to me with eyes wide open and said: "She wants you to embrace her."

"Me, her?" I asked back.

Amma tilted her head to one side which means "yes" in India.

I felt really strange. All eyes were on me. And she requested that I should embrace her?! I could do nothing else, I thought. She had embraced me and now I would embrace her. It was difficult but in the end, I did it with joy because now I felt the great amount of love that came flooding from her. I was reminded of my grandmother again. She signalled that I could now release her and she turned back to the interpreter and asked her to tell me that I had a rare and beautiful strength within me and, if I had not realized so far, this was to be used to heal and teach people which I should do with all my time and with all my strength.

I looked on her with love but I wasn't so willing to look around at everyone staring at me. Many pairs of eyes looked on me with jealousy and radiated much worse than that. I waved to my friends to tell them that I wanted to leave right away. They didn't ask a thing and I was more than grateful. I wasn't so happy to talk about the feelings that I had in the ashram. I felt sorry for the people who were there and who were not able to leave their negative thoughts behind them and, I guess, not for the first time. If they had managed to do that, then one embrace from Amma would have been more than sufficient for them.

I was really looking forward to the next stop-off on my trip. I was headed for Pune as I was on my way to the ashram of the famous (notorious in the world's press) Bhagwan Shree Rajneesh, who later became known as Osho. I had read and heard so much about him in previous years. I found the starting point for his journey, his philosophy and his teachings interesting and saw them as representing some kind of reform. They proclaimed freedom. They questioned the form of religion and his followers were promised freedom via the new doctrines which he represented. They offered liberation from sexual restriction and he proclaimed and introduced complete and total freedom in his ashram. 100s studied under him in Pune and became his pupils. They called themselves the sannyasin.

His fame led to a build-up of criticism and objection to his ashram in Pune where there were several other yoga ashrams. Opinion was completely divided. The Baghwan had a mass of followers but the number of those opposed to him grew with equal speed. They wanted to solve the problem and continue the mission at the same time and so that is why they moved out to Oregon, in "free America" where there was more space and greater freedom. They were sadly mistaken! The local farmers and members of religious groups met them with just the same amount of hostility that they had suffered back home. From what I have read, and from speaking to the people who were sannyasin back then, I know that the situation became just as unbearable inside the ashram as it was on the outside. The Baghwan didn't speak for years and so the real story of what forces came to the surface there only became public through the newspapers after the whole thing collapsed. The deeds of many of the leaders came out into the open when everything came before the courts and the whole movement came under mass, public criticism. Osho, as he had started to call himself in Oregan, spent a good deal of time in American jail before he was deported along with the whole of his ashram. They all returned to Pune and Osho died soon afterwards. Many of his followers claimed that he had been poisoned while still in prison in the U.S.

For me, Pune and the free expression of sexuality (up until the appearance of AIDS) were somehow part of the history of the 20th century. I knew a good few sannyasin personally. There were very few among them whom I would have been able to love or respect. I am only talking about the ones I knew in person! At the very beginning, those who arrived back with new names behaved really very arrogantly. I didn't have anything to say to them. They grew more approachable in time as they seemed to "come down off their high horse". This was especially the case when the reason for criticism and the allegations proved to be true. Many suddenly forgot their sannyasin names and past and went back to being plain old Peter and Martha.

However, many new types of therapies were developed in Pune and Oregon. I was interested in them but I was also fascinated by Pune, where the whole thing had been born in the first place. I did have a few friends who admitted their past in Pune and recognized what they had learnt there but they proved to be sufficiently mature and straight to say what it was that they hadn't agreed with now or even back then. These were the kind of people that I considered Gayan Winter, Kutira Decoster and Rhea Power to be. They learnt a great deal and they refined these teachings and then passed them on to others.

Pune had so many surprises waiting for me. The first problem was that they were not willing to let me in, or at least not on the first day.

"You'll need to have a new AIDS test done," they told me.

"Here it is and it isn't even a month old," I said.

I knew that since they had made the use of condoms a prerequisite to a free sex life in the ashram; that they only allowed people to enter with a negative AIDS test and so that was why I had one done before I left home. I knew that it had to be less than a month old and so my irritation was understandable at not being let in.

"You can only do the test here. We no longer accept results from other labs."

"What a nerve!" I thought to myself, especially when it turned out how much they intended on charging me. "I should have known: it's all about money! Unbelievable!"

"OK, so let's do the test!" I said.

"Not today because the lab is only open until two," came the answer. "But you won't be able to go in straight away because we only get the result the next day."

Well, now I was ready to burst!

"I am only here for three days and I only arrived this morning!" I explained, thinking that I might get a little sympathy. The answer was neither spiritual nor did it show too much understanding: "Well, that's your problem!" and the door was already closed.

I was stunned and hopeless and all I could do was to sit down. I sat down by the side of the road on a stone. I didn't have to burst as I was able to swap stories with all the other angered, would-be visitors. It wasn't even 3 pm and now I had wasted a day for one hour's late arrival. Pune started to live up to my expectations without me having even stepped inside the ashram. I sat, chatted to the others and looked around. I was given addresses as I had rushed here straight from the airport and I didn't have any alternative accommodation lined up. I hoped that I would find a room in the ashram's hotel, which was relatively close, but I was mistaken. I was told that I could only get a room if I had already been admitted to the ashram or, in other words: if the blood test was negative. Well, that was all I needed! I sat there and had a stronger and stronger sense of the vibrations of Pune and the ashram. I was sitting on a stone between the two entrances and the ashram was on both the left and right of the road. One must have been completed and then they decided to expand and extended with the second building. Those who lived there—the lucky ones who had accepted AIDS tests—were able to pass back and forth through both entrances as they pleased and all they had to do was to show an ID card with a photo on it. A bad feeling started to well up inside me, especially when I took a good look at the people who were coming and going. They didn't even bother to look at the people who were sitting outside. We didn't belong among them. True, we weren't wearing purple clothes, as everyone needed to change into purple when they entered the ashram. They seemed to look down on us and I didn't know if this had happened when they changed their clothes, whether they had learnt this behaviour inside the ashram or whether they had been like this before they arrived. I had plenty of time on my hands. I was only interested in the ashram in Pune as three days later I was going to Delhi and onto Dharamsala where Monika and the 14th Dalai Lama were waiting for me. I saw little happiness on their faces and no special light in their eyes but was more convinced that they knew they were seeking something in vain. It appeared to me that many of them had the following written on their faces: "I have looked everywhere and tried everything and I have grown tired of the search and I still haven't found it."

Perhaps I even felt sorry for them as I knew they weren't going to find what they were looking for. Or perhaps they only said that they were looking for something and they had really only come to this famous ashram for something completely different.

I would have happily left but my plane and all the onward connections only came to life three days later.

I knew what Indian airports were like and the chaos that filled such places and I thought it better to try and get into the ashram instead. It had happened often enough that my prepaid ticket had only been greeted by the shaking of heads at the airport. "There is no flight there today, only tomorrow. So, you can only go to this place in eight hours' time and you will have to take this and this flight ..." and in the end, I would arrive there at virtually the same expense and in the same time that it would have taken me to find a hotel for the night and fly direct the following day. That was India! Yet you soon get used to it if you spend weeks and months on the road.

I decided! They weren't going to get rid of me that easily! I was determined to see what was going on behind those closed doors and high walls. I really did want to see the secret for myself that I had heard so many different opinions about. Now, I had heard with my own ears and I was beginning to become convinced with my own eyes. Despite all of this, there were still a couple of things that I did want to see and to experience for myself. One of this was the "Samadhi", the home of "great silence". This is where Osho himself had once lived and now you could take part in quiet meditation. The other was the Buddha Hall that I had heard so much about. I had brought a wonderful, white, silk dress with me as my friends had told me that everyone had to wear one who went there in the evening. It was a floor-length gown and I had brought it along for especially this occasion so I had not even considered wearing it before then. I wanted to respect the person (and the place) whom I thought worthy of it.

The large meditation hall—the Buddha Hall—really did live up to my expectations and fully deserved the christening of my white, silk dress.

It was late and getting dark and I had to look for a place to stay. The crowd waiting outside the closed doors, if anything, seemed to be growing and so I had to be quick in order to be sure of finding accommodation. There was a girl standing next to me who had been there before and she recommended a place that I had read about in my guidebook which was called the German Bakery and apparently not so far away. I was told that I would find answers to all my questions there. In the book, it said: "Make new friends and buy any kind of drugs you like." Some said that there were those who used to visit the ashram, and now only went to this place, as they were just as able to get there what they had been looking for inside. At least: that is what some people said! As I was only looking for a place to stay, I thought I'd go over and see if they had a noticeboard or something. I was new to the place and so everyone looked at me a little strangely as most of them had been coming here for years and they all seemed to know one another. I sat down quickly and thought that I would ask the waitress when she showed up. She still hadn't appeared when two men came up to my table and asked me if the two other places at the table were taken. I wasn't too pleased about it, but I said yes. "Off to a good start," I thought, "Hardly sat down and I'm already being harassed. They're not interested in the free places but me, the new arrival," I thought to myself. My suspicions proved to be correct. I pulled a miserable, unsociable face. This was a habit of mine from childhood whenever I thought that those around me were overstepping the boundaries that I set. I especially disliked pushy men. They both seemed to start off at once and in a very informal tone!

"Hi! You new? We haven't seen you here before! Are you sannyasin? Where have you come from? Can we be of any help? We're old hands here you know. We really know our way around and can help with anything you might need."

I didn't know whether to slap them, scream or just keep up the grumpy expression on my face. It was unbelievable, the nerve of these two and they didn't even appear to realize that I hadn't answered them. They were like programmed robots. Not only did I not reply to them but I wouldn't even look at them. I decided that they were just air! But definitely not the sort of air that I was prepared to breathe for fear of catching something! I was revolted by their impertinence.

I realized that the elder of the two only asked questions at the beginning and the younger one continued on his own but soon got bored and went over to another table where two—supposedly new —girls had just sat down. It seemed that I had managed to get rid of one of them. It went rather quiet, so I slowly looked up to see if the other one had also given up but no, he had gone for the silent approach so we continued to sit there without saying a word. Then, at last, the waitress arrived. I asked for a tea, the type of real tea that you get only in India. I was quick to ask her where I would find a noticeboard before she disappeared again as I had waited for a quarter of an hour for her to turn up in the first place. The guy sitting at my table beat her to it.

"You looking for somewhere to stay?"

"Here we go!" I thought. And I gave a rather agitated sigh.

"Yes, but I am more than capable of finding a place myself!"

"I wouldn't be quite so sure of that. There isn't a free room in the area!" he replied.

In the meantime, the girl had come back with my tea. I asked her again about a noticeboard.

"If you are looking for accommodation, there isn't any!" she said.

"Doing well here. Ashram? Niente! Accommodation? Forget it! And now I have been sniffed out by this hyena!"
But the man didn't give up. I was wondering what I was going to do because it was getting dark and I had left my suitcase and my bag at the gate of the ashram. I would either have to get a taxi from here or from the hotel, trust the driver (though this perhaps wasn't the best idea) and find a room that way.

The interfering voice spoke up again from my left: "Won't you tell me what your problem is with me?"

"Won't you just leave me alone?" I cut straight back with no consideration for politeness.

"But I really did only want to help!"

I turned towards him to laugh in his face but was surprised that he appeared quite appealing, or at least he would have done if he hadn't been quite so pushy. He made use of the momentary silence and added: "I have been living here for nearly seven years, or at least for most of that time, and I know how hard it is to find your way around Pune and I also know that you are new."

"How can you be so sure?" I asked, trying to sound as offensive as possible.

"Because I saw you waiting outside the ashram earlier on, sitting on a stone for hours on end. I was standing talking to an old friend and I kept my eye on you the whole time.

"Now this!" I thought, but all I did was raise my eyebrows.

"Hm?"

"I simply couldn't take my eye off you and I stared at you the whole time without you ever noticing. Then I just followed you when you came here. I know you must think that I'm very rude, but I pushed my way over to your table as well."

I must have given him a very strange look. Had he really done all of this on purpose? But why? He could sense the question and began to explain straight away: "You look exactly like my dead wife."

I'm afraid to say that this made me laugh.

"Aha, is that a typical chat-up line here in Pune?" I asked. "Where I come from they say a girl looks like their mother."

"He really is a cheeky one," I thought. He didn't reply but reached for his bag and pushed a photograph in front of me. Now I was the one to look amazed. The woman in the picture, besides being virtually white blonde, could easily have been my sister. She had a round face and strong cheek bones with light blue eyes, just like mine.

"She was the love of my life and she left me forever seven years ago," he said as I stared at the woman in the photo.

"Are you joking or telling the truth this time?" I said, my voice taking a much softer tone.

"Do you really think that people joke about such things?" he asked back.

I took a good look at the man sitting opposite me. Perhaps that was why he was dressed in black from head to foot. But for seven years? He really stuck out in a place like the Bakery where the crowd was brightly dressed in all the colours of the rainbow. I turned to face him and asked: "Does that explain your attire?"

"Yes," he replied. "I'm still mourning."

It was tough enough to believe him but I did my best. "And where was she from?" I asked, trying to lessen the hardness in my voice.

He started to tell me their story but then suddenly stopped and asked me a question: "Would you let me help you find a place to stay? Because, as you've heard, it is hard enough to find a room and sometimes to even find a bed."

I agreed in the end. He promised to tell me the whole story later or perhaps the following day. I thought that I would have an empty day the following day, anyway and it was perhaps just as well to have someone to chat to and who could show me around.

He really did know a lot of people. I got a room in the first place we went to, but only for that night. I agreed and the stranger came with me to go and fetch my bags. I was getting pretty hungry by this time and so I didn't resist when he suggested getting a bite to eat together. It was dark by now and I was quite relieved to have someone by my side to guide me around the place. He told me his story as we sat and ate. His name was Kish and he came from a rich, Afghan family. He had attended school in India and then gone on to university in the U.S. He had worked as a film director and producer. He had met a Swedish girl called Anna, while he was still at college. She was the only daughter of a rich industrialist. Kish knew that she was the girl he wanted to be his wife. Anna didn't seem at all interested in the beginning (strange that I had been just the same) but Kish didn't give up and eventually he managed to seduce her. He gave her everything: he bought them an enormous house on the coast in Hawaii and he fulfilled her every dream and wish. Anna had been used to this kind of treatment when she had been growing up but his ongoing struggle for her love really was like something out of a fairy tale. Kish must have been a really good-looking young guy. I looked at him in some detail as he spoke. His hair was now completely white and his dark skin was accentuated by his bright blue eyes. His eyes smiled in a way that lit up his whole face and convinced his mouth to join in. I reckoned that he must have been somewhere in his late 40s.

I could easily imagine the shock in Anna's family when they found out that she was living with a dark-skinned Afghan. But Anna had fallen deeply in love with Kish by then and she told her family that she had already decided to marry him. Her family gave in and gave their blessing. Kish was overjoyed at attaining his goal and he and Anna flew off to Hawaii. Now, the Muslim man in him began to speak: "She is mine, only mine." Despite the fact that he had attended university in the West in the States, he would have been happy to make Anna wear a veil and he admitted as much to me there and then. She was so outstandingly beautiful that he couldn't stand going shopping with her or dining out with her and seeing other men staring at her beauty.

"I didn't let her go anywhere on her own, of course. I didn't want to risk her being 'molested' by other men."

("Well, that really is the limit! And now here he is molesting me!" I thought to myself. "He besieged Anna for years on end with his love, then she was his and everything changed.")

"Anna was happy," he said. "I read her every thought and wish and did whatever she asked. I adored her as a goddess. I loved my work but I only lived for Anna, and Anna for me."

("That would have been too much for me!" I thought.)

They never had children and I forgot to ask why not. So they lived happily on like this for years. Anna had often complained of severe headaches. No one had taken her seriously at the beginning until one day she passed out. Kish called a doctor immediately who sent her into hospital for tests. He said that he wanted extensive investigations to be carried out as there was something that really disturbed him about her condition. She had a blood test right away which showed an abnormality. The tests showed that Anna had a brain tumour that needed either radiation or chemotherapy to halt its growth. The other option was to have an emergency operation. I don't exactly recall the sequence of events. They gave her radiation treatment and then she was operated on—I don't know. And she died within only a couple of months. "That was seven years ago and Kish is still mourning!" He also said that the first thing that he did was to move out of the house in Hawaii. Now it was being used by his rather large, extended family and he made the key available to friends, but there was no way that he was even able to place a foot inside the house where they—as he said—had lived in such limitless happiness together. He had come out to Pune after the funeral and sought solace in spirituality. The look on his face and the clothes he wore led me to believe that he hadn't had the greatest success.

I listened sadly to Kish's story but I wasn't completely convinced that Anna had been as happy as Kish was telling me, and as he believed totally. Why had a tumour grown in her head that had taken her away from her "happy life"? I had my doubts about all of this, based on what I had experienced with those around me and my patients back home. I had no right to question his belief and so I neither said nor asked anything.

I was starting to feel rather weary. The long day with the disappointment at the ashram and now this long talk with Kish had all taken their effect and I could feel my bed beckoning me to sleep. Kish took me to my lodgings on his motorbike and offered to take me for my AIDS test the following day and then help me to find another place to stay. Now I was happy to say yes as he felt like a friend through the story that he told me. I had even got to love Anna, unknown as she was to me in person.

I really longed to stretch out in bed as I was starting to feel a little unwell. I thought it must be all the excitement, the long day or perhaps even the supper that had affected me this way. I was in bed within seconds and I wanted to go to sleep straight away. It was simply impossible. I felt increasingly ill and my temperature started to rise rather drastically. My body just got hotter and hotter. This was rather a familiar scenario as it had happened several times to me in the past when I had sensed something uncomfortable in my surroundings. Could the food really have been off? But would the reaction have been this swift?

I knew that I had to get out of bed and rush to the bathroom. I only made it as far as the door and the inevitable happened. All exits at once—everything came gushing out of me. I had to lean on the wall as I suddenly felt terribly weak. When all the poison had finally left my body, I crawled back into my bed and, ashamed as I was, I called the porter to send a cleaner up to my room to clear the mess up in the bedroom and the bathroom. I wasn't ashamed any longer, I was just glad to be alive. The wave of illness that had flooded my body told me that the place I was in was poison to me. It felt as if the air was poisoned. I wasn't even pleased any longer by the fact that I had met Kish and we had become friends. I traced everything back to my present state while they cleaned my room in silence as they do everything in India. They brought hot tea to my room and asked if they should call a doctor. I told them that all I wanted to do was to sleep but that I would call them if I was taken ill again.

This had happened to me several times in the past but normally with a little less force. It tended to happen when I spent a long period of time with a group of people or one person in particular whose energy was poison to my body. I always ran a fever and often vomited or had diarrhoea. Then I fell into a deep sleep in a matter of seconds and woke the following morning as if nothing at all had happened. That was what I was counting on now. Despite the fact that I had this spasm and such a high temperature, I actually hoped that I didn't have food poisoning.

I didn't have time to think it all through as I soon fell fast a-sleep. I slept through the whole night and was woken in the morning by a strange noise. There was a knocking on the door and it got louder and louder. I shouted to say that I was just coming and I climbed out of bed like a person who recalled nothing of the previous night and as if nothing sad had happened to me at all and I opened the door. Kish stood there next to the porter who had been on duty that night. It was long past the time that we had agreed to meet in front of the hotel and Kish had asked the porter if he had seen me and been told that I had been taken ill the previous night. He had also told him that I had just wanted to sleep and not to disturb me as I would ring if I felt any worse. This news sent Kish running up to my room with the porter running behind him. Now I stood at the door well-rested with rosy cheeks as if nothing unusual had happened at all.

"You OK? You sure you're feeling alright? Should we call a doctor just in case?" the questions came raining forth out of Kish's mouth. But he did look quite concerned. I guessed that the porter must have told him what state they had found me in the night before.

"No, everything's just fine," I replied. "Give me 15 minutes and I'll see you down at the entrance." I took a shower and fixed myself up. I really felt no weakness from the night before which is exactly what I had hoped for. So my body had managed to expel everything that had been so poisonous to me.

I needed to leave Pune right away. But I was pig-headed: "I am still going to go in and see what is behind closed doors and high walls." My body has already defeated everything! Now I wanted to know as much as there was to know. I didn't give in. But why? I wanted to know what it was that I had suffered such an extreme reaction to.

All I said to Kish was: "Thank God, everything that had been poisonous has left my body." I knew this reaction well by now.

He didn't ask what the cause could have been and I wouldn't have told him even if he had. I wanted to make sure for myself first.

Kish gave me a tip on the way to the ashram: "If you don't want today to go to waste, and you want to get in this afternoon, there is a trick."

"Trick?" I asked. "What kind of a trick?"

"Ask for an express lab test and although it's a good bit more expensive, you'll have it this afternoon and you can be in before two."

I was irritated to think that it still turned out to be a question of money. I would get an extra day this way and the price was more irritating than it was frightening so I decided to go for it. I was at the entrance at 10 am and, like some sort of old hand, I said I'd like an express test. I paid the ridiculous fee and we were soon chugging along on Kish's motorbike looking for some new accommodation. Kish said he knew of a place a little further away where someone rented out one of the rooms to their villa. "As we are such good friends," he said, "I'll take you and fetch you every day on my motorbike," he added with a laugh. "Because the memory of Anna comes to life within me if I am able to look at you."

I still wasn't sure what it was that he wanted from me but I needed his help if I was to stay so far away, and I decided that I could stand it for a short period of time. So I accepted his generous offer. He said he would take me back to the ashram for 1 pm but he wouldn't be going in himself. "So what are you doing living in Pune?" I thought. "Aha! He is another one who finds everything that he needs at the German Bakery! But another two days, and I'm going to be out of Pune."

He helped me again to take my bag and case over to the new place. He dropped me off at the ashram for 1 pm, and we agreed to meet up later that afternoon at the German Bakery, as he had already agreed to meet two friends there. I told him that I would make my way there before or after the meditation. I really did want to take part in the meditation session in the Buddha Hall, accompanied as it was by live music. I got my negative test result back at 1 pm and was forced to wait for another hour while my photo identity card was made which would eventually open the doors that had barred me from entry up until now.

This was the ashram of Osho, the ex-Baghwan. I was there at last and going to see the truth for myself! What was the secret that had been so closely guarded behind closed doors? The whole thing had been an incredible challenge not to mention the vast amount of paperwork that I had to fill in to get into the place ... Bureaucracy! But now I was in!

The ashram covered an enormous territory. You couldn't see anything from the outside because of the wonderful vegetation. I had found myself in the Garden of Eden. There were flowering trees and shrubs with little streams and lakes with white swans (which were Osho's symbolic animals). It was just like a magical wonderland. The first thing that I had to do was to swap my outside clothes for the purple ones that they wore inside. It looked something like the nightshirt that my grandfather used to wear but his had light blue stripes. As the colour was the only set thing—it had been orange when Osho had still been known as the Baghwan—many of the women wore their robes very short with them held up very high by a belt. There was a swimming pool as well where, in the good old days before condoms, everyone had been free to swim together in their birthday suit, just as they had been born into the world: gloriously naked. There were no signs of those times now and just white bits of flesh showing at the edges of purple bikinis and shorts on the bodies of tanned Europeans by the side of the pool.

There was to be no swimming for me though: not enough time. The most important thing was the Samadhi and I read on an information sheet, if I remember correctly, that you could go in at 3 pm and at 10 am. I was delighted to realize that it was not yet three. I looked on the board to see where the Samadhi was. It wasn't that far from where I was standing and I managed to get there just a couple of minutes before three. There was someone standing in front of the door. This wasn't the Samadhi, but the first barred door that I wanted to pass through. He said that it was to the left where a woman was sitting at a desk and I'd be given a piece of paper, and only then would I be able to gain entry. I said that was OK and I went over to the girl in the purple robes. She searched a list which she held in front of her.

"But you're not on the list for this afternoon!"

"What list?" I asked.

"The list that contains the names of those who can go in at 3 pm this afternoon."

"Did I need to register beforehand?" I asked, virtually crushed by this unexpected news.

"You mean to say that you didn't know?" she asked back.

"No, but I'll register now."

She pointed to an office that was close by.

"Good, I'll hurry," I said, dashing off. "So that I am back in time for three."

I could say that it was laughable, or at least that she and the other lucky ones with their names on the list laughed as I dashed off.

"Well, you're going to have to wait a while!" I was told rather spitefully by the boy standing behind me. His tone was more than a little condescending. Novice that I was, I naively asked why.

"Because, in order to get in—along with the other 50 happy faces who go in at the same time—you have to wait for days." (I don't recall exactly but I seem to remember that 50 people went in on each occasion.)

"Well, that's impossible!" I said, automatically and rather loudly. "I'm only here for two days!"

Shoulder shrugging and "Well, that's your problem!" was the response. I'd heard that the day before as well. How good it felt, for a novice like me, to feel such sympathy from the crowd of fortunate ones who had been waiting for ages to get in themselves and to meditate in Osho's old, earthly residence in such great silence. It was the same big-headedness that I had experienced from sannyasin in the past, even back home in Zurich. This seemed like some kind of special quality of theirs. I was never going to feel good in such a community. So then, what next? I would go to the office to register and it was there that I met the first person who had any sense or sympathy for what I was feeling. I knew that I was going to have to to do my utmost to get in as I only had two days. I started by saying that all I wanted to do was to get in to the Samadhi and I had two days rather than three because of the AIDS test and to help if they could.

The guy must have felt pretty important as he was the one who could help. He told me that he could put me on the waiting list for the day after tomorrow at 10 am. He said that he would first have to let in the 50 on the list, and only if someone didn't turn up would he be able to let anyone else in and then that would have to be according to the order that they appeared on the waiting list. (It was just like the airport, yet even there, this degree of regulation and regimentation didn't apply.)

"OK. Well I'll be here and I'll just hope."

"I really have had enough of this treatment! I'm going to go to the park and take a walk." I thought, and that's what I did.

The park was wonderful and was made up of many separate parts. There was an area like a tropical rain forest, a Japanese garden with parrots in enormous cages and there was even a banana plantation. I walked the whole day and the beauty of nature and the delicious scent of the flowers lifted my mood. I wasn't so happy to be surrounded by people in purple anymore!

I was getting a little hungry so I thought that I would go out to see Kish, as I had arranged at the German Bakery, and get a bite to eat there. I didn't want to burden my stomach too much before meditating. I had plenty of time. I had brought my beautiful white dress with me in the morning and I had put it in a locker together with my outside clothes. Now I walked out of the ashram and I was one of the many purple-robed figures who populated the streets that led to the German Bakery and back. Kish was sitting there as he had promised; accompanied by a very thin girl with long, black hair and a young man. They were speaking English but when it turned out that the other two were Italian, I started to speak to them in Italian. "At last, two likeable figures," I thought. Sampati—that was the girl's name—said that she was also going to attend the evening meditation and then they were going to meet up with another couple and go on to have a meal at an Italian restaurant. They invited me to join them if I liked. I looked at Kish who I was dependent on because of my lodgings being so very far away. The others all lived in the ashram hotel. Kish winked at me, as if reading my thoughts, and said that he would come along too and then take me home afterwards. "Hm, he understood what I was thinking," I pondered to myself. "What abilities did he develop while he was living with Anna? It really is something of a talent and he would make a good therapist. That is if he wasn't stuck here all day long." He knew everyone and everyone knew him. It was obvious how many women smiled at him and how many would come over to him for a kiss on the cheek or a simple smile. I could see and sense how much he was loved and liked. Then I remembered that he had mentioned how rich he was. No one had a motorbike here and I thought that it must be quite an expensive one as every time he parked it a small crowd would form around to take a better look. I hoped that it wasn't his wealth that attracted so many people. He really did appear to be a helpful and kind individual.

I thought that perhaps the time had come to get back as I still wanted to have a shower before I put my white dress on and go into the long-awaited Buddha Hall to meditate. I had been told that, when Osho was still alive, they had smelled everyone before they went in to check that they were clean but also to see that they hadn't used scented soap or deodorant as Osho was terribly allergic to such things. Sampati and I went back together. Her clothes were somewhere else and so we didn't shower together but agreed to try to meet up before the meditation so that we could sit next to one another. She had been there for two years and I was pleased to find that she was so kind and was a new friend. She was just like many of my other Italian friends who I really love for their kindness and directness. Freshly showered, I happily took my place in the queue, dressed in my white wonder. Everything was made of white, transparent glass and sparkled in the sunset. We had to put our shoes on a stand first of all and to carry on along a carpeted path. I didn't see Sampati as there were so many of us. "No problem," I thought, "I'll have plenty of time to look for her." And, with this, the procession started to move slowly forwards.

Now it was eventually my turn. There were people standing at the door to check and see if everything was in order and especially to see that everyone was wearing a long, white robe. I felt quite pleased with myself at how good I must have looked in my beautiful white, silk dress. I was standing quite proud as the robes that the others were wearing didn't look anywhere near as good.

"Stop, you can't go in!" The queue came to a standstill and we all wondered who the poor unfortunate was who wouldn't be allowed in after such a long wait. I was being shoved from behind and I looked around to see what they were pushing me for only to discover that the guy at the door, with an unkempt beard and odd stains on what looked like a white nightshirt, was pointing to me: "You, you can't go in!"

"Me, but why not?"

"Because your clothing isn't right."

"What? My clothing?" And I was already being pushed out of the line. I stood in front of the door and wanted to know what on earth was wrong with the clothes I was wearing.

"You can only get in here in a robe and you are not wearing a robe!"

"So what is a robe then?" I asked back.

"Like mine!" he said pointing to the dirty nightshirt that he was wearing. I still didn't understand. What was wrong with my beautiful, white, silk dress? It was a floor-length, white skirt with long sleeves tied at the waist in a bow of the same lovely material. The top was completely closed looking rather like a kimono. So the cut couldn't have been a problem. I asked again what the problem was as, according to my English, "robe" is the same thing as a dress. All I knew was that I had to wear a "white robe" and that is what I was doing.

He looked at my dress in virtual disgust and said: "It's in two parts," and he pointed again to his filthy white shirt. "This is a robe and yours is not." I tried to talk to him about this but he wasn't willing to listen and he gave an agitated wave to tell me to go away. I thought that I'd try just one more time.

"Listen, I am only here for three days and I already lost a day yesterday because of the AIDS test ..." but I just got the usual Pune reply: "Well, that's your problem but you are not going in dressed in that thing!"

This was just unbelievable! The bureaucracy and unkindness that I was experiencing and now for the second day. I saw a clock somewhere and saw that there were still 12 minutes to 7 pm. I had 12 minutes to think of something. This man-eater was never going to let me in dressed like this, I knew that now. I remembered a place on the corner near the German Bakery that sold clothes in white and purple and thought that I had seen something there that looked a little like a nightshirt. I had bought my purple clothes from a similar place but they had been new and packed in cellophane. They also had used clothes there from the sannyasin that no one had gone to the trouble to wash out. They were also very cheap and cost no more than three or four Swiss francs. And there were some even cheaper than that. They sold them in the same state they had been left by their previous owners. I thought that I would rush to the changing rooms for money, buy one of these things, go back to the changing rooms and swap my white dress for one of these unwashed "ROBES" and go back to join the queue. I needed to do all this in less than 12 minutes in order to get back and be allowed into the hallowed Buddha Hall. I didn't want to and I couldn't give up now. I wasn't going to let them do this to me! I was going to win! I wasn't going to give up all the joy with which I had prepared for weeks and months to meditate in the Buddha Hall among—as many have described them—an army of angels. I was beginning to doubt the humanity of this "army of angels" to say nothing of the level of their spiritual development. I was going to win! I simply would not give in now!

I ran back along the queue towards the entrance, not forgetting to pick up my shoes with my photo card inside. Over to the other side and I showed my ID. Then the locker. Where's the key? Here! Money. Ran back to the entrance and showed my card again. I sprinted the 200 or 300 metres to the shop, grabbed the first filthy, once-white robe that I could find and handed over the couple of rupees. Then back to the ashram. Showed my card again no more than five minutes after I had run out of the place to the same face who was still standing there. But I knew there was no way I would be allowed back in without my card. Changing room, locker, dress off, "robe" on. The sweat was running down my face in rivers and the white wonder was virtually completely transparent from the moisture. There was nothing for it other than to use my beautiful dress to wipe the rest of the sweat from my body and to slip into the nightshirt which had been last worn by God-knows-who. I was disgusted by the idea but this goes to show the extents I was capable of in order to be allowed into the Buddha Hall to meditate with the others.

My face was bright red from all the rushing around and I took a look in the mirror and caught sight of a clock which told me that I only had three minutes left. I knew that they wouldn't let me in if I was any more than a second late at the door. I ran out and showed my card at the entrance opposite and now I was there. Everyone was inside and I arrived out of breath but in time. The guy in the dirty clothes and tangled beard looked me up and down and said: "Now, you see. This is how you need to go in: in a 'ROBE'."

I didn't want to believe what was going on inside. I eventually found myself inside the "LONG-AWAITED BUDDHA HALL" in my smelly, disgusting, once-white nightshirt.

My joy vanished within seconds. I was ashamed at what I witnessed. Not for myself but for the fact that this was the Buddha Hall and for all that was sacred to me. I sat among the meditating white angels (all dressed in robes, of course).

I didn't meditate but rather prayed for a lot of things and a lot of people; I mainly prayed for happiness not here but at home in my group that I held twice a week—after work and not freshly showered and not in a white robe—that I would be able to meditate with those who surely were angels to me.

The evening had deeply saddened me and I was happy to go with Kish, Sampati and the other Italian guy and eat a pizza and be among kind-hearted, helpful people.

The others could see that I was unhappy and so I told them what had happened earlier on. Sampati and the Italian boy were both sannyasin and they didn't really express an opinion but nor did they say that this was my problem. They knew that this wasn't simply my problem. After the restaurant, we went to listen to music in a hotel lobby where Sampati was suddenly taken ill. She was chatting away and suddenly couldn't catch her breath, went ghastly white and collapsed in a faint. There were few other people there and no one seemed to notice what was going on. The other two in the group seemed quite calm and said that this often happened to her. Her heart was quite sick and she had an incurable condition. I wasn't so calm and I placed my hands on Sampati's heart and on her forehead and radiated energy into her body. The other two said that she would regain consciousness in a couple of minutes. I was terribly concerned about what it was that she would be going through for those couple of minutes. She probably put the question forward on each of these occasions as to whether she would actually wake up or not. They said that she carried medication with her which, if she took it in time when she felt one of these spasms coming on, would actually prevent her from fainting. "Poor Sampati," I thought. "What is wrong with your little heart?" Sampati started to slowly come around. I kept my hands pressed to her body. She opened her eyes and smiled at me. Then she said: "I didn't feel the terrible fear this time that I was going to die. I was filled with a sense of safety for those endless minutes and I was sure of the fact that I would return."

She said that her condition was very rare and it had already taken her sister from her. She simply didn't wake up again after one of these fainting fits. The doctors had given her only a couple of months to live but that had been two years before. She had wanted to make the most of the time that she had left and that was why she had come to Pune to live life and to discover all that she could in the precious time she had. India and Pune had given her the gift of another two years but she was far from happy in herself.

"There is no point going home as there is nothing I could expect to find there. Perhaps it's even better to die here," she added sadly. I offered to treat her the following day as I had no intention of doing anything inside the ashram. She was delighted by the idea and the other guy said that he had terrible asthma and would like to be treated as well if I had the time. I was happy at having something useful to spend my time doing the following day and especially because it meant that I would be able to give something real to two such deserving people.

They both lived in the ashram so that is where we met, in the nearby forest. I worked on Sampati first. Her body had completely changed as a result of the illness. The first thing that I noticed was her long face and her unbelievably long fingers. Her limbs were also very thin and seemed somehow too long. She said that this was all a result of the illness. When I held her shoulders, I was able to feel the whole cause of her illness: her shoulders were turned inwards and her whole chest was pressing in on her. So she was actually squashing her own heart. The process could be neither stopped nor altered. Doctors recognized this illness but they didn't know the cause and nor did they know how to cure it. Her back was rounded and all bone, while her chest was virtually concave due to the constant pressure that it was under. Sampati was really very beautiful despite all of this. Her whole being seemed airy. Her white skin and long black hair made her look like an angel in this late stage of her illness.

I worked on her on a bench. She sat and supported herself on the backrest. The boy sat opposite her a few steps away on the grass. He asked whether he should leave and I told him that all I needed was silence and, anyway, there were just the three of us there.

I asked Sampati to close her eyes. I stood behind her and felt her upper body that was no more than skin and bone and I could feel that she was finding it difficult to breathe. Her collapsing chest was pressing on her lungs just as much as it was affecting her heart. "Poor Sampati, I will do whatever I can to give you relief for this last stretch," I thought, I wished, I asked.

Then the miracle happened which I can still feel in my fingertips to this day. Sampati's deformed back and closed-in shoulders moved in my hands and they kept on moving until her shoulders were completely straight again and the curve in her spine was no longer visible. I could feel what was happening with my own hands but it really didn't make it any easier to believe. Unbelievable! A back that had been bent for a decade couldn't just straighten up like that! But it did! It was impossible to explain! When the movement finally stopped, I removed my hands and sat down next to Sampati. The first thing I did was to pray and gave thanks for what had just happened. The boy, who had been sitting opposite Sampati, slowly started to sob in silence. He had known Sampati for years and he knew how much she had suffered from the terrible pressure that her own body had put her under. He also never knew whether or not she would wake up again the next time she fainted or finally find herself on the other side. I was inexpressibly touched by what had happened. An unimaginable thing had just taken place both physically and medically. I sat next to Sampati and just looked at her. She sat fragile and almost transparent with a beautifully straight back and horizontal shoulders. What must she have been feeling? She just sat and sat and sat for what must have been half an hour or maybe even longer than that. We sat there, too, like witnesses in stunned silence. She slowly began to open her eyes and they were filled with tears. She didn't dare alter the position of her head and instead she just moved her eyes to look at me and she asked: "If I move now, what will happen? Will everything go back to the way that it was before?"

"I don't know, Sampati, but I don't think so. Please try and believe in what has just happened and ask to stay this way for as long as you possibly can."

She closed her eyes again and began to pray. She asked for the impossible in which she wasn't able to believe and yet she still sensed was possible. She asked that things should stay just as they were. She slowly opened her eyes and stood up. She turned her head in one direction and then the other. Then she slowly moved both her shoulders. What she must have been feeling was beyond words. Straight back, straight shoulders, free heart and lungs with no more pressure. She began to walk, a few steps forwards and then back again. The boy and I just sat there, hardly daring to move and then she asked: "How long do you think it will last?"

"I don't know Sampati. And nor do I know how it happened in the first place. You have been given a gift and I was just the courier.

All I did was to hold your shoulders. The strength that I gave you through my hands wasn't of my making but was given to me to give to you. I am sure you will stay this way for as long as you are able to have faith in what has happened."

The three of us went along to the German Bakery where Kish was waiting for us. The Italian boy hadn't said a word about the fact that I had agreed to treat him for his asthma. That had been more than enough for one day. Sampati's friends stared at her as she walked into the German Bakery as they could see that something had changed in her appearance but I don't think that they were able to say what it was. I stayed with Sampati and my new friends for the whole day and I was indescribably happy. If I had come to Pune just to be part of this miracle, it had been more than worth it and I was willing to accept all the bad things that had happened and move on.

I still had a day left as my plane only flew the following afternoon. I wanted to be at the Samadhi Hall for 10 am. Kish agreed to transport me again but this time it was to be by car. He went to Bombay that evening to fetch his new car but promised to be back in time to leave the following morning. He was also very pleased at being able to see the "new" Sampati that afternoon. I could sense that there was something that he wanted to ask of me. He wanted to ask whether I was able to contact the dead. I told him that I did not request or look to make contact with them and that there are mediums who did this but that I didn't agree with it. I didn't know whether or not it was such a good idea. They had looked for me up until then and so I knew that contact could be made. Kish told me that he had been to see many famous and some less famous mediums and no one had either been able to contact Anna or make her come forward and speak. I felt happy about this as it suggested to me that she was at peace now.

There was something else that he wanted to ask me but similarly didn't dare. I thought that it couldn't be so terrible. But it was! He asked me, with a blush, whether I would agree to be his wife and to fill the vacuum which Anna had left inside him. He said that he thought that he could truly love me and that he could be happy with me again.

I didn't know whether I should believe what it was that I was hearing. He added that then we would go back to Hawaii and move back into their beautiful house together. I could no longer hear what he was saying as all I could think about was me suffering the same fate as Anna and having the door to the golden cage locked behind me. But there was no question of this happening as there was nothing more than a pleasant friendship between us as far as I was concerned. I thought more and recalled that Anna had also resisted at the beginning of the relationship and Kish had still managed to persuade her. I knew the end of their story and I knew that I could never become another Anna. I didn't want to hurt him so all I said was: "But we've only known each other for two days!" and then I changed the subject.

I went into the ashram in a taxi the next day as Kish had gone to Bombay to collect his new car. I stood at the door to the Samadhi at exactly 10 am. "Open Sesame!" All the doors opened at last. The room was a little cool but it was really beautiful. The other room I had passed through on the way in hadn't looked so nice. It had been one of Osho's rooms and was a little like a museum and housed his favourite car, which I think was a Rolls Royce, and there was also a dentist's chair. But that was just the entrance! The real Samadhi was very impressive. They sat us in rows as we followed one another in. The side of the room was all glass and behind it there was a tropical jungle with bamboo and a little stream trickling through. There were also quite a few observers in the room but I can't remember what it was that they were observing. I guess that it must have been the order and the silence. All I wanted was silence! Everything that I had been through the last three days had been a lot; in fact, it had been a little too much. I just longed for quiet and all I wanted to do was to meditate. And then I would be out of there, out of Pune and out of Osho's ashram!

There was an enormous photo on the wall opposite us of Osho-Bhagwan in a knitted hat. I didn't even want to see; I didn't want to see anyone—all I wanted was quiet.

Silence at last on the outside and now on the inside. Everyone was seated in a silence that you could literally feel, when someone touched my left shoulder. I turned with my spiritual body and I saw: Osho standing at my left shoulder. "But he's in front of us on the canvas," I thought. But now he wasn't wearing a hat and he looked like he had in earlier photographs which I had been looking at for decades. He spoke and said: *"All is true that you see here, all is true that took place here. What began in the ashram, despite the fact that I now see where it is leading, I wasn't able to stop. I took a vow of silence although I had to speak but only when it was too late! I would never have thought that what I began with such faith and hope would end up like this. The situation and those I believed in were not as mature as I thought. I placed dangerous things and knowledge into their hands."* (I guess he was talking about sexual powers.) I sat in silence and just listened.

I couldn't believe what I was seeing and hearing.

"But I am asking you to leave, as this place really is poison to your system! Thanks for being here and for listening to me." And that was all.

He disappeared into the silence. I dealt with it by deciding that I had been imagining things and and—that was that! Then I felt another touch on my left shoulder. I turned and saw Anna. I knew who she was despite only having seen her in photos. I knew it was her but I asked all the same: "Anna, is that you?"

"Yes!"

"But why have you come to me? Why is it only I who can see you? Kish has told me how many mediums he has been to see and not one of them has managed to contact you."

"That's because there was such a great difference between their resonance and mine but you are not only like me on the outside but our resonances are also very similar. I would like to say a few things to you and ask you to be sure to tell them to Kish. I know Kish from a previous life. I was his wife but one of many. Kish was also very rich

back then, and he was able to afford the luxury of a large number of wives. I can say nothing bad about him because we wives lived a good life and he treated us very well. But we were all just his property and he kept us for his own entertainment. I loved him very much and I did all I could to make him notice me. He did for a while as he was flattered by the fact that I wanted to impress him and show him my love and adoration. This was natural to him and no more than he deserved. But as new wives came along, he was distracted by them as they all brought something new into his life. The fact that they were all young and pure only went to boost his male pride. That is when I suffered the most. He took no notice of me, whatever I did. He was my every wish, my every desire, and I lived for a moment of his attention, a second of his love. I begged in my prayers that he should love me and I imagined how happy we would be if there were just the two of us and I was his only wife. Maybe then he would love only me and he would be all mine. As I got older, I was the same as all the others to him. We no longer demanded either his love or his attention. I was so sad and in such pain that I lost the will to live and so I died. My last thoughts were of him and that if there should be another life after that, I wanted him all for myself and that I should be the only one for him.

I got what I wanted, yet not in the heights above but on the Earth in my last incarnation. I wasn't able to recall my previous life then but I saw the thread after my death that ran from my old incarnation to my last. I attached myself to Kish and my prayers were answered. It had been my endless prayers that had created this. Kish became mine and I was the only one for him. I resisted at the beginning as he wanted me with such force that it scared me a little. It was natural to him from the very beginning when he first saw me at the university and he decided that he had to have me. I could only be his! I protested and I was quite upset by his behaviour. He was a man of the East though he was living and studying in America. Neither I nor my girlfriends could explain his bizarre behaviour. We were modern, emancipated women who had been born in the West. We were accustomed to directing our lives as we thought best and we were more used to selecting our partners rather than them us.

My resistance to Kish didn't do a thing. All it seemed to do was to strengthen his will and make him battle even harder than before. I don't know how or when the situation changed. I started to miss him. I started to miss him if I didn't see him for half a day at the university. I started to think about him all the time and I began to worry that perhaps he'd had enough of my resisting him and would go off and fight for another girl's favour. It was just unimaginable! Not the fact that he would do such a thing but the fact that I might lose him. The hours that I spent worrying and doubting became unbearable. I became devoted to him within a couple of months and that is how I remained my whole life. He seemed to think it completely natural when I finally said yes to him as it was he who wanted me and had done everything he could to make me his. This wasn't only at the beginning when I had resisted but it went on this way. He not only fulfilled my every wish but it was his specific "talent" to sense what I was thinking. I was happy to have such a husband, the likes of whom no other woman would ever have. His love and loyalty was as sure as mine. It really was a marriage made in heaven. We lived our lives here on the Earth, in the West, in America where everything is transient and unsure.

I thought about when I had been a girl or rather the things that I used to read. I started with stories and went on to the great legends but I adored love stories. I was a teenage girl and I too wanted a fairy tale love. Perhaps I had wished for this and it was my wish that came true? I asked myself this question a couple of times and later I put the same question to Kish. We didn't find an answer only that we had been meant for one another from the very beginning.

I still hadn't finished university but even afterwards, when we moved to Hawaii, I never had to do a single thing. We had staff and I had wanted to cook and to prepare something for Kish with my own hands but he was of the opinion that I was meant for better things. I couldn't even work in the garden because that was the gardener's job. He always came with me if I ever went shopping or rather I only went if he was available. He did almost everything from home with the help of modern technology and he had good people working for him who were all able to work very well unsupervised. He did have to travel on the odd occasion that he had to attend a meeting somewhere but he didn't really like doing so as it meant leaving me, you see. He never said so but I knew that he would have preferred it if I didn't even go out shopping alone for the couple of days that he would be away. He'd always say: "You can order whatever you want by phone or ask the staff to organize it for you." The days that he was away were just terrible. It was as if half of my being was missing. I couldn't even eat without him. Neither of us altered these habits as the years went by. We simply couldn't. We were slaves to one another but mainly I to him. He had his own links with the outside world but everything stopped for me. We had a very small circle of friends but if we ever went anywhere, we spent our whole time with one another. Perhaps it was fear that the other partner would discover someone more interesting. This led to a lot of friendships breaking down. People weren't able to get to know us as we really wouldn't let them come close to us.

I was only able to see all of this after my death and that's when I realized. I also understood the reason for my illness. It was my spirit as well as my head that was wrapped tightly in bandages. Kish's love and protection as well as my constant fear of losing him all became a sort of sickness. They drove me out of my head, if you like, and that's why I ended up with a tumour. My condition worsened very quickly but I was still only able to think of Kish. What would happen to him now? Would he manage to survive losing me? Yes, he did survive but he carried on living the love that had bound us so tightly together. I did leave the physical life but I never really left him because I couldn't leave him and he couldn't leave me.

I have learnt a great deal in the years that I haven't been physically there. I also knew that my devoted prayers had come to life. I had been given the man whom I had prayed for and really was all mine. That was my ruin and it cost me my life. I have learnt from it. You can't, you shouldn't love like that. We kill ourselves or the other and sometimes each other. That is why I am so pleased that I can talk to you now and ask you to give this message to Kish. He should accept what has happened and let the past be the past. He really is a good, *kind man. He has closed himself in his mourning and that is how he has been living for the past seven years. The fact that he noticed you and has said that he wants to spend the rest of his life with you is only because you look so much like me, not only externally but also on the inside. He would like to pick up with you where he left off with me. First, he should put down his black mourning clothes and learn. The first thing that he should do is to study our lives and the cul-de-sac that we were stuck in. Then the last thing he should do is to find a wife to fill the gap but instead he should make the most of the fact that he is a free man. Kish has a noble spirit and he has the kind of qualities that would stand him in good stead for working with people and teaching them. Kish could become a really good spiritual leader: all he has to do is freshen up his old knowledge. He should really leave Pune now. He is never going to find what he is looking for there and what he really needs. I believe that if he lets me go, as I've done him, then he stands a very good chance of finding happiness on Earth and it will allow me to eventually find peace here. It would make me so happy if he threw away his black clothes and I could see him again in his white suit and blue shirt that he used to wear. All he has to do is to open the other side of the cupboard that he closed tight shut seven years ago. Thank you for listening to me and for helping us."*

Silence returned. I could feel the cool air in the room again which now felt really good. What had happened this time? First Osho and then Anna? Anna's story was stunning, tragic and beautiful all at the same time! Would Kish ever believe me if I told him? I hoped that I hadn't hurt him and that he would do what Anna had asked. If Anna had really appeared to me, and I was sure that she had, this also meant that Osho had been and I didn't know why he should have chosen me.

I didn't have much time left to put questions to myself as the silence was broken. They had somehow signalled that the period of meditation had come to an end and the people sitting next to me started to stand up and leave the room. "I will appear to leave the room as I entered it," I thought to myself. "But I would like to see all their faces if they ever find out who I have been talking to!"

I hurried to the German Bakery as I had arranged to meet Sampati and the Italian boy there. They also wanted to come out to the airport with me. Kish wasn't there. I couldn't speak about what I had just experienced. I thought that I would have a bite to eat while I waited for him to show up and then I would tell him all about the message.

There was an obviously expensive car parked in front of the Bakery. Its blue-grey paintwork glistened in the Indian sun. It must have been a rare beauty as people were stopping to take a better look.

"I reckon it must be a Bentley," I heard one man say on the next table. It had dark windows so I couldn't see who was sitting inside. You really didn't see cars like that in India and the ones you did either belonged to maharajas or Osho himself. All eyes were fixed on the car. Eventually, a car door opened and a man stepped out. He looked like something out of an expensive advertising campaign in white suit, blue shirt, white shoes and a hat. He threw his white gloves back into the car with a leisurely movement and looked at us. It was Kish! A new Kish! He had thrown away mourning and was now his old, happy self. Everyone stood up who knew him. They knew all about the seven years of pain and that was why they all stood to greet him. I remained seated as if I were paralysed. I looked at Kish, and along with all the others gathered there, I wondered what could have happened. They were all struck by the outer changes but it was the inner difference that amazed me and how he could have known what I knew. Had he read my thoughts or had I forwarded them to him? Or had Anna appeared to him after seven years? I couldn't do or say a thing.

It was as if Kish could only see me and he walked right up to me. He lifted me from my seated position and gave me a big hug. Then he whispered: "Anna appeared!"

I fell back into my chair. He sat right next to me and told me all about it: "Imagine, as I was driving back from Bombay, I suddenly felt as if someone was sitting next to me in the car. I knew with every bone in my body that it was Anna. I didn't see her but I know that it was her," then he paused. "Now we have to go and get your bags and I'll tell you the rest on the way to the airport."

Sampati and her friend sat behind us in the car. Only Anna existed for him and for some reason I was the one he wanted to tell all about it. The other two were just passive listeners.

While we drove, he excitedly told me that Anna had told him about one of her incarnations where he had been the husband but that he had many wives other than Anna. He told me the exact same story that I had been told by Anna just an hour before. She had also asked him to change his clothes.

"She told me to open the other side of the cupboard that I had closed seven years ago."

"That's exactly what she said to me," I thought to myself as I still hadn't had the chance to speak. But I didn't want to. I was glad to let him believe that Anna had appeared to him and him alone. "His Anna" had appeared again. He had done as she had asked without even seeing her but by reading her thoughts as he had when she had been alive. ("Kish really does have talent as a medium," I thought.)

Anna filled Kish's whole being. I looked at this beautiful, happy and unbelievably rich man. Had he asked for my hand in marriage only the day before? Yes, but that was a man in mourning who had wanted to fill the void left by Anna and I seemed like the best one for the job. I was curious to see how the "new Kish" would behave with me.

We arrived at the airport. The next surprise: there was a group waiting for me with flowers and gifts. Kish's mother and siblings had arrived to see the woman he had asked to marry and whom he had described to them as Anna's successor.

Again, I stood in silence. Kish fetched gifts for me from his car. (Jewellery, silk scarves, cassettes and I can't remember what else.) He handed them to me with the apology that he had only bought them that morning and hadn't really had so much time but that I would be on the road for weeks to come.

"But, I'll make up for it!" he said with sparkling eyes.

"Yes, he must have bought them in the morning before Anna appeared to him," I thought.

His mother and the others all looked at me like a new member of the family but then the announcement came for all those travelling to Delhi to board the plane. This is how I left Pune and I never saw any of them ever again.

There was already a letter waiting for me from Kish when I returned home from my travels. He asked if I would like to join him on a trip around the world. He made no mention of whether I had considered his proposal of marriage. I wasn't able to reply as he had given no contact address and the letter appeared to have been sent from a hotel in Thailand. I didn't know why there was no address but I was happy because this meant that I wouldn't have to reinforce what I already knew: Kish only had one true love in this life and he would go on loving her despite the fact that he had put on his white suit as Anna had asked.

Kish made mention of Sampati who also wrote to me on several occasions. She said that Kish was still living in Pune. He travelled quite a lot but he was unable to put down roots anywhere else. Understandable! Hawaii had been his island of happiness and Pune the home of painful mourning. He had no other home here on Earth. Both of them tied him to Anna. The letters came less often and went unanswered until they finally stopped arriving. I think that Kish must now be happy in the belief that he will meet Anna again when his life on Earth comes to an end. But who can be sure? And then there was Sampati. I never saw her again either. She phoned me about four years ago. Sampati on the phone! Fantastic!

"I'm in Turin with my mother who is very ill and she wanted to see me one more time. So I thought I'd make the most of the opportunity and come to visit you in Zurich."

What a surprise! Sampati was alive! Alive and coming to Zurich!

"Wonderful! I'm so happy! I can hardly wait for you to arrive! We've got so much to tell one another!"

We organized for her to come the following weekend. She said that she would let me know which train she would arrive on as soon as she managed to get a ticket. I thought of so many things that we could do to welcome Sampati to the West after spending six years in India.

She didn't call and she didn't come that weekend. She hadn't given me a telephone number or her mother's address and so I wasn't able to contact her. I started to pray for little Sampati. A week went past and I received a letter from her mother to say that Sampati hadn't opened her eyes one morning a couple of days before the planned meeting. She had passed so gently like the light and airy being that she was. She was sure to have come to visit me over the ether but I was too busy waiting for the telephone to ring. I cried as I said farewell to her beautiful soul.

The plane took me from Pune to Delhi where Wulfing was waiting for me and he had a great deal to tell me. I was happy just to sit and listen as I really wasn't in the mood to tell him what the last two hours had contained and the intense experience that I had been through back in Pune. It's really only now that I have managed to reach a stage where I am able to tell anyone else about that time.

Wulfing filled the time that I spent in Delhi. He took me everywhere and when he was busy making his video, he always told me where I should go and what I should see. The two days just flew by and then I was on my way again but this time by train. I was going to see Monika in Dharamsala and His Holiness, the Dalai Lama.

The train eventually reached the end of the line and I transferred to a bus where I shared my onward journey with a load of people all speaking different languages. Nearly all on board had the same goal in mind and that was to meet the 14th Dalai Lama in person and to listen to his teachings.

Monika must have been waiting for me for a long time as her face was ice cold when I leant over to give her kiss. We must have been delayed by a good hour and the snow had only just started to melt up there in the mountains. It seemed so odd after having spent two days in Delhi trying to avoid the midday sun. And this is only one example of the unbelievable variety that is to be found in India.

The first thing that we did was to drink a real tea but not like in India, with milk, but this time according to Tibetan tradition which meant that we drank it with melted yak butter and salt. I drank it because Monika and her friend had greeted me with so much warmth but it was the first and the last occasion.

"That'll warm you up!" they encouraged. I must have pulled a terrible face as I sipped the concoction with all the enthusiasm that I could muster.

I only took a couple of bags with me into the mountains and I left the rest in a locker at Delhi airport. Monika had warned me in her last letter to bring warm clothes as it would still be very cold there. And cold it most definitely was. There were all kinds of surprises awaiting me in the hotel room that Monika had reserved for me. The best of all was a warm pair of flannel pyjamas which Monika had placed on my bed with a selection of other gifts. I had never thought that I would be so pleased to see a pair of warm pyjamas in India!

The teaching, as it was called there, that the Dalai Lama held, had started several days before. 100s of foreign, Indian and Tibetan pupils had come to attend. The foreigners had come to study and to listen, while the Tibetans were there to see the greatest representative of their religion. They had come from the distant Tibetan mountains and travelled 1,000s of kilometres for this once-in-a-lifetime experience. There were old people walking with sticks and little babies wrapped in blankets. They had come or been brought for their greatest dream to be realized and to receive the personal blessing from His Holiness, the 14th Dalai Lama.

They amazed me! They fascinated me for the whole time that I spent there. It was their humility, dedication, love and togetherness in their faith with which they accepted everything and lived according to the direction of their religious leaders. Their faces shone with joy, gratitude and the flame of inner faith.

I looked for the same expression on the faces of the other visitors but I didn't manage to find it on a single one. This was despite the fact they had also travelled 1,000s of kilometres to see and hear the Dalai Lama. And yet the quest for faith and hope that they would find something there reflected the difference between the two worlds. I saw this manic quest in the ashram in Pune and many other places like it. It was the hope of finding something there and understanding something at last. I have no way of knowing whether the 100s of foreigners who sat for days and weeks and listened to the wise words of the Dalai Lama ever found what it was that they were looking for. I was sure that the Tibetans had found it long ago. In fact, they had come for the Dalai Lama to reinforce what they all already knew and not the other way around. That is why they amazed me and why I loved them so much. I felt sorry for the others who had travelled so far and would have to leave at the end just as they had arrived. They were the ones who were waiting and looking for the answer from the outside but had forgotten to knock on their own front door. I felt sad for them. I finally managed to unpack my bags on the second night in the hotel and I found the book that I had brought along with my guidebook, which was Adelma Vay's diary in which she wrote about her travels. She had been in India at exactly the same time of year as me but a century earlier.

This book had wanted to come with me. But I was also curious to see what would happen and what it was that I would experience in India on the same days as her. I will relate how this book came into my possession in the chapter about Hungary. The only thing that I will say at this point is that, naturally, it involved the help of those from above.

The day that I decided to go and investigate the differences between the foreign visitors and the Tibetan Buddhists, I found the following written in her diary (in short): "A relative explained that she had gone with a sibling to see a famous healer in the south of France because her sibling was ill. They had no idea how many times they had to change horses on the coach on the way there. They were happy that they were making this trip and that they were able to afford to do so. The famous healer had a completely different opinion of the whole matter: 'I was sad to hear that you have travelled from so far away and also because I am unable to help you. What you seek here is in your own home. You cannot find the faith here that will cure you.'" Adelma also wrote: "Yes, the poor things. I feel sad for them too!"

I had written just the same in my diary only a couple of minutes before. The only difference was that I had been writing at the end of the 20th century and Adelma had written her thoughts at the end of the 19th century. That really was the only difference! I fell asleep with a happy feeling of warmth in my heart and gratitude for the gift of Adelma's diary which she had "given to me".

Sadly, the days in Dharamsala passed all too quickly. Monika showed me so many interesting things and, thanks to her, I got to meet people with deep faith and great knowledge. Through a quirk of fate, I was examined by the Dalai Lama's personal physician and he was the one who gave me the famous "diamond pills" wrapped in a silk scarf, which is one of the most effective medicinal treatments known to Tibetan medicine. We had gone to find one of Monika's friends who was a female doctor who taught and practised at the local medical university. But His Holiness's private doctor saw that we were looking for someone and he offered to examine me himself. My friend didn't dare respond and said that we would come back the following day. I butted in: "Thank you very much. That would be wonderful! I would be delighted to accept your offer of an examination!"

Monika didn't believe her ears but I was indescribably happy to be part of such a great honour.

Monika also introduced me to the deacon of the Buddhist University one evening, in a popular Tibetan restaurant. It was a fascinating experience to sit at the table with him and other local, highly respected religious and spiritual teachers. It was wonderfully refreshing. They were humorous, direct and straightforward. I could only like and respect them.

The deacon spent several days in Zurich a year after we had met, invited by Monika and accompanied by his English interpreter. I dearly wanted to invite them to visit me, and so I did, when I met them in a restaurant in Zurich. Before Monika could say a word, the deacon showed his unquestionable delight at my gesture. He even added that if I had friends whom I would like to invite along then he would be happy to hold a talk on a subject of our choice. I could have flown up in the air with the joy and honour of it all. The day that they came seemed to go on and on. They arrived for lunch at noon and stayed until late in the evening. The wise, old, Buddhist professor took a nap on the sofa in the afternoon and the woman interpreter asked me to treat her eyes. I had offered to do this, while I had been travelling in India, but we had run out of time there. I had grown to like her humility and devotion in her support of Tibetan knowledge and its greatly respected representatives. The treatment was quite special. A lot of "visitors" were in attendance. My surgery was full of Buddhist spiritual beings clad in red robes. They all wanted to see what I was going to do and, although I suppose they were always present around my two guests, it was only now that I noticed them as I closed my eyes and concentrated on my female patient. They smiled benevolently and were all visibly curious and showed their approval. The woman had experienced a great deal of trauma in her life and it was this that I was seeking to lessen. Many of them helped and so I think we must have achieved something.

The evening was quite delightful. My meditation group came along and we received the kind of glorious gift that we would have never dared to hope for.

Dharamsala was the last stop on my first trip to India. On my second trip, it was Tiruvannamalai, the ashram of Ramana Maharshi whom I greatly revered. I was always being given addresses and ideas as I travelled around India but I knew before I arrived that I must definitely go to this place in the heart of India. I had read all three of his books that had been given to me by a friend and my respect for this indescribably humble and modest, enlightened yogi was infinite. I respected a lot of knowledgeable people but Ramana took a different kind of place in my heart and my soul. I had a lot of role models but I could only ever hope to achieve greatness such as his in my dreams. He outdid all those individuals I had read about or whom I had known in the last century. I know that there were other highly knowledgeable teachers besides him but I still felt something more for him and I couldn't explain. It was something that I just felt. I had been looking for role models ever since my childhood and I had always tried to model and direct myself according to their teachings. If I met someone new, I would always put them in my role model album and do my best to learn from them. When I decided that the last stop on my trip would be Tiruvannamalai, I had planned to stay there for quite a while—at least for Christmas and New Year. I wanted to spend at least two weeks there and to fast for the whole period. This is how I wanted to show my deep respect for this holy man. By this I mean it was his spirit, as he had been living in the worlds on high for more than 50 years. I had a white, two-part, Indian dress made in the meantime but I only wanted to put it on there, and it was what I intended to wear for the duration of my stay. The dress was made up of a pair of trousers and a long, white tunic with a white scarf. These are the clothes that Indian women wear when they don't dress in a sari.

I left one of the ashrams earlier than intended as I had felt uncomfortable there.

I had recognized one of the teachers as a figure I had known some 2,000 years previously. He had taught Veda philosophy in the ashram and I had reacted very conservatively to him from the outset. I wasn't able to accept what it was that he taught. This was despite the fact that the Vedanta was holy to me, but it seemed sacrilege coming from his mouth. He suddenly raised his hand in the middle of one of his teaching sessions:

"Listen here! They can kill you, torture you but they can never kill the truth, it will survive you, everyone and everything. The truth is in God and in faith. Never forget that!"

He had just started to continue when the picture in my mind changed. I was in Rome, in the bloody years of the persecution of the Christians. I was standing in the Colosseum with my fellow Christians and I was shielding my two young daughters. They were pulled from my arms and the strength of a she-lion filled my body. I turned to face the tribune where prominent figures sat with Caesar at the head. I raised my index finger and shouted: "Listen here Caesar. You can kill each and every one of us ..." and then I continued with the words that the teaching yogi had used. Now, I knew who he was! He had served the punishment for his crimes of 2,000 years ago and this had eventually taken him to India. It was this that he wanted to pass on to us. The VOICE asked me to forgive him in the name of the others. I was frightened and I couldn't do it. But I was helped. I felt something hit me in the middle of the chest while the yogi was still speaking and I could see a silver arrow, like a laser beam, cutting through the air from my heart to his. I lost my outer consciousness after this. I don't know how long I was in this state. When I opened my eyes again, the large figure of the yogi just sat clutching at his heart with tears streaming down his face. He stood up slowly and asked to be excused. He really wanted to leave the room as he had been hit by a sudden feeling that he could not describe. He retired to his room and I left the Yoga Ashram the very next day.

The young girl from Munich joined me again whom I had been travelling with for more than a month. I was pleased by this as it meant I had a pleasant travelling companion with whom I was able to share my experiences. I still wasn't able to discuss what I had gone through in the last days of my stay at the Yoga Ashram with her. The whole thing had been far too much of a shock to me as well. I had seen my life in Rome several times and many blurred faces started to become clear to me. I was really taken by the fact that I had seen Caesar again here in India, in a Yoga Ashram, after a period of more than 2,000 years. I stayed quiet for a while and my companion found company in her books. We travelled for days and the road was terribly long. I lost my appetite again. My mind and body wanted to fast. I had wanted to start at Christmas but my body wanted to start a week earlier. I was left with no other option than to start my fast there and then. We eventually arrived at the long-awaited ashram after a tortuous journey by train and bus. We were distraught to hear that there wasn't a single free bed in the whole of the ashram. My guidebook had told me that, albeit simple, accommodation was always easy to find. When we asked at the information office at the ashram where we would find a place to stay, we were told that there was absolutely nothing available. Nor was there any free space in the nearby town. My companion was bitterly disappointed and I was hardly my strongest after having fasted for two days. But we still didn't give up. We left our bags in the office and set off to look for somewhere to stay. In the end, we found a place. Believe it or not, it was directly opposite the ashram. It was in a rather strange place though, on the roof of a tea merchant's house who had an eye for a business opportunity. There were two rush mats on the floor and a curtain that concealed a hole on the floor (it isn't so difficult to think what that was for), a tap and a pipe in the wall which also provided water. It wasn't exactly the height of luxury but we had a roof over our heads which we desperately needed as the midday sun was terribly unforgiving in that part of southern India. Our little shack was pretty hot inside but at least the sun's rays weren't beating down on our heads. There was no way that we could sleep from the stifling heat and the rush mat didn't act as the best "sleeping pill" either. But at least we had found something and it was just across the road from the ashram. We took a shower and donned clean clothes. Naturally, I put on my new white outfit as a sign of my respect for the ashram.

Every step that I took in that place was one of devotion. I was there where he had lived; I was walking where he had walked and praying where he had once prayed. I was overcome with joy and I no longer felt my hunger and tiredness. It was pleasantly cool in the temples inside the ashram and so that is where we spent most of our time. I was happiest of all in the room where Ramana had lived and taught. There was a picture of him seated on a couch wearing only a loincloth. He had no use for anything else as he had everything he needed. I sat for hours in front of the same couch with my eyes closed and time stopped for a while.

My companion was taken ill the following day and, as she could no longer abide the heat in our rooftop shack, she decided to see a doctor and return as quickly as possible to Europe.

I was left alone and I enjoyed the silence even when I had to leave the ashram in the evening.

It soon transpired that the reason that all the free rooms had been taken was that the faithful had come from all over the world to celebrate the 100-year anniversary of the birth of Ramana. They had come from China, Korea and Africa and I heard many languages that even I wasn't able to identify but I really didn't want to talk to anyone anyway. All the information was displayed on a noticeboard in front of the information office. The following day saw preparations begin for the enormous celebrations. They started to put tents up and the kitchen for the whole event was situated in a courtyard to the rear. They were expecting several 100 visitors as the Indians were to arrive for the festivities the following day. I didn't like all the frantic preparation going on around me as there were far too many people. Ramana's room became so crowded that it was not only difficult to move, it was virtually impossible to breathe. The heat was completely unbearable especially with so many people sitting packed so closely next to one another. I had another problem above all of this and that was my fast with the great festival to be held the next day! "Everyone will be eating, drinking, singing and who knows what else. Should I break my fast?" Then someone spoke to me: *"You need not fast because of me."* It was Ramana speaking—not his picture but the man himself. He sat on the couch where the picture had been. I blinked my eyes but he continued to sit there with a warm smile on his face.

"Yes, I said that there is no need to fast for my sake."

"I am not doing it for you but for myself! How could I ever compare my fast to yours? You didn't eat for weeks and months and you were sustained by the pure glory of devotion. I am doing this to cleanse myself and as a sign of respect for you. Please look on it as a gift," I concluded. He smiled at me again with that indescribable inner smile of his.

"Very well, then I accept."

Tears came streaming from my eyes and my whole being and spirit wept from happiness. He, this great holy man, had accepted a gift from me of my own humble fast! I was the one who had been blessed with a gift!

I no longer recall how the evening passed. I suppose that I walked around, slept, spoke to people here and there but not a single scrap of the events of that evening stayed in my memory.

The festivities began at 10 am the following morning. By 11 am I was the only one left sitting in Ramana's room. I sat right in front of him. I had rarely managed to find such a good place. The music, and who knows what else, began to start up outside. I was there, sitting in the room. I closed my eyes and began to meditate and I hear his voice again: *"Who is it who truly celebrates with me?"* He asked and then went on: *"The one who sits with me in silence fasting of all food and drink. They drink, dance and eat outside to celebrate me but there is only one individual who is truly with me. She sits and celebrates with her silence and her fast. It is you!"*

I wanted to die. I had never experienced such great joy. Then he added: *"Thank you, Sister, you are among us. But what are you doing here? Please return and teach people with the help of your faith and knowledge. I will now bless you!"*

He touched the centre of my forehead and it was as if I had been struck by lightning. My whole body shook and the energy filled me completely, right down to the minutest cell. Beyond my physical body, I was able to feel that I was surrounded by an invisible shield of light.

My tears eventually began to subside and I peered out from behind this watery curtain. Only his picture was there; his spirit had dissolved and there was perfect silence. I couldn't move and closed my eyes again and lost myself in it all.

I was being touched and touched again. This started to bring me back into the room and my everyday consciousness as people started to file back into the meditation room. Perhaps the celebrations were over, or this was just a break. All those who passed me, touched me and smiled at me. This was strange as no one had consciously touched me up until this point other than accidentally nudging me when taking their place on the floor. Now, they were coming in through the door and touching me on my shoulder or on my arm as they passed me. Perhaps they felt something and were touching me although they weren't sure why. Perhaps they also wanted to get a little of the gift that had been given to me at these birthday celebrations.

I stood up and felt no strength at all in my legs. I must have been sitting on the floor like this for hours. I turned from the door and smiled at his picture, gave thanks and said farewell.

I was on the road the following day as Ramana had asked me. I didn't return directly to Europe but to where my Indian journey had begun in this world: I went back to Kovalam Beach. My airline ticket was for the New Year but I wanted to go back to my life in Zurich. Now on the south coast, I started to eat and drink again and bathed in the sea and sun. I chatted to the people and I welcomed the New Year in, dancing in the sand on the beach. I was glad to be going home and teaching again.

It was interesting that Mr Lichtenecker, and through him my brothers and leaders from above, had directed me to go to India and said: *"Take light from West to East."* And now I was being sent back from the East to the West.

But I was a different person returning home than the one who had left a couple of months before. This journey had been destined to happen. I had to accept my new task of teaching those who came to me and passing on the light to them that I was able to bring down on my first Christmas meditation. I was to teach them with the same love, humility and faith which Ramana had strengthened within me.

Thank you, my eternal India; and thanks to my old friends, my brothers, my teachers in the higher regions!

23

My Higher Consciousness Is Born

When I lived and worked in that wonderfully bright apartment that my friends from above had blessed and filled with such pure energy, another inconceivable thing happened to me.

Everything was going well with my work and my teaching and my relationship was really good with my daughters. It all happened when I was preparing mentally and spiritually for my trip to India but there was still something that was bothering me.

I couldn't explain it but I had an odd feeling inside myself. It was like a secret that wanted to be discovered.

I was nervous that I might have lived in India in a previous life and that this held unpleasant memories and perhaps was disturbing me in this way. It would have been good to know if this was the case or not and what would happen to me when I got there. Or perhaps it would have been better not to know! My inner anxiety was growing and I needed help.

Ilse was now living abroad with her husband whom she had met on a course given by Rhea Power or rather that is where they met again. They knew that they also belonged together in this life and they knew that there was something that they had to complete.

I had trusted Ilse more than anyone ever since her first regression. I didn't know anyone else whom I could turn to with this odd inner sensation.

I had never come across any great crime committed in my lives up until that point. So I didn't know what I would do if it turned out that I had committed a terrible crime. I wanted to sort everything out before I left for India and not just everyday chores and my home.

I thought of Mrs Steiner again. I thought that as everything had begun with her then I wouldn't be frightened with her and I wouldn't be ashamed if it turned out that I really had committed a terrible crime in a previous life.

She was happy that I had called and we soon found a date that suited both of us. She lived several hours away from me on the train, and I didn't want to drive as I didn't know what sort of shape I would be in at the end of the day.

We hadn't seen one another for several years and so she was keen to find out how I was doing after the divorce. I told her everything quite quickly and her sympathetic presence made it impossible for me to hold back my tears.

"Yes, I know that you really wanted to keep your marriage alive and I know that it meant everything to you as you always used to say. But you see, we sometimes need to make sacrifices as big as this."

"Yes, I know," I sniffed like a little child. "I came to accept everything and never even suspected that it still hurt so much. I thought that I was over it and that I was really coping with everything. But it seems that the pain is much deeper than I ever suspected."

We started to work. I didn't tell her why it was that I had come to see her as I thought that it was bound to turn out during our session together. I lay on the massage table and she stood at my feet and took hold of my heels. I started to cry again. I tried to pay attention to the emotion that was rising within me and to see if I could work out what it was that was still causing me so much pain and that I hadn't completely dealt with.

I had my eyes closed and a glorious Madonna appeared on my left side. Mary with the infant Jesus! She was smiling and looking down at me. My crying became even stronger because of the love and sympathy that was shining in her eyes.

She moved suddenly and offered me the baby Jesus.
"I am giving him to you!"

"How come you give me your child when he is yours?" I asked almost in anger.

"Why shouldn't I give him to you?" she replied.

"Because a child is everything to a mother and she can't give her child to anyone else just like that!" I reprimanded her.

"That's not true. If it is to help someone and that is more important, then you can and you must give your child!" I felt great love as she continued to smile at me.

"Didn't you exactly say before that you had to release those who were dearest to you in the interest of your further development?"

"Did I really say that?" I thought but I didn't mention a thing.

"There are completely different standards in the spirit world. I am giving my child to you now in exchange for the ones who you had to let go of."

This time she didn't just offer but placed the glowing infant on my lying body. I was flooded in light and I started to cry again from the emotion of it all.

I slowly started to relax and the light dissolved but I could still feel her touch in my whole being.

I was just starting to feel calmer when an image appeared on my right side. It was a field of swaying corn baking in the midday sun. I was also in the picture and I was lying in the field feeling the warmth of the sun's rays all over my body. I was filled with calm and peace.

I was watching something. As if made from fire, a red bull was coming towards me. I didn't feel at all frightened but a sense of curious wonderment. It was a beautiful presence and more of an energy than something that could be called an animal. It was glowing with the redness of fire.

I started to feel pain. But the reason lay in my body on the table and not my body lying in the sun in the cornfield.

I started to feel pains in my abdomen: cramping pains. The picture of me with the bull in the field of corn disappeared. All I could feel was myself and my pain as the cramps grew stronger.

Now I was back and fully conscious in the room on Mrs Steiner's massage bed. "I've got really strong pains. My stomach has stated to hurt!" I told her.

"Then concentrate and follow the pain!"

I have related and described what I felt up to this point but now I can't describe where this terrible pain came from.

All images and previous sensations disappeared and I was left with only the pain and the cramps that were growing ever stronger. There was a short break and I thought it was over and then it came back. Then there was another break.

"This is impossible but I am having birth pains!" I suddenly announced.

"OK, well keep following them!" said Mrs Steiner who remained perfectly calm.

"But this is just impossible! I'm not pregnant!" I said in virtual agitation at her calm responses.

"Then where are the birth pains coming from?" she asked.

"Well, this is unbelievable! It's exactly the same sensation as when I gave birth to my daughters!"

I had no time left to think as the break between the pains grew even shorter and I was completely absorbed by the flow of pain that is felt by all women when they are giving birth. Everything happens instinctively at times like this and is beyond human control.

The pain was totally unbearable by this stage and then the pushing began. The cramps stopped and my whole body began to concentrate on the process and that I was about to give birth ... but to what? "I cannot believe what is happening to my body!" I suddenly saw a light appear between my pulled up legs. Mrs Steiner was still holding my heel. I could feel this quite clearly. "I must be conscious!" I thought. I could also feel the contraction pains in my body. "Then this light must also be real!" One more strong pain. I used all my strength to push out whatever it was and the whole room was suddenly filled with light. There was a light being standing between my legs, it was indescribably beautiful and giving off a light not known on Earth.

"Well, what or who is that?" suddenly slipped out of my mouth. The light being was radiating love and a feeling not felt for a very long time.

I asked mentally again.

"Tell me, who are you?"

"I am you and you are me. I am your higher being from above. You call me your higher consciousness. The person that you know from the mirror is just a set of clothes that you wear. I am within it but you live life."

"Tell me, have you, we got a name?"

"Yes, you—I—am called GLORIA above."

"Well, that's unbelievable. That's what they called me in the beginning—at the Christmas meditation with Mr Lichtenecker's group—when I left my body! Then they greeted me with 'Welcome Gloria'. Then I said that they were confusing me with someone else as my name isn't Gloria."

"So perhaps I am!" I have always somehow known that they never confuse anyone but the name was still baffling. Why had they greeted me with this name?

Writing this whole process down, it all seems very long but it all happened in less than a minute. The glowing figure of the higher me still stood between my legs where I had given birth to it or it had given birth to itself.

"There is still something that I would like to know. What happened here exactly? Why did I have to and how was I able to give birth to you like a flesh and blood child? Just like my daughters?"

"This had to happen so that you would finally believe who resides within you and who you really are. Don't forget and never hide YOURSELF or ME away ever again. Accept us both at last! You and I are ONE!" And with this it dissolved into the wonderment that was within me.

I was still lying, as before, on the bed with my feet pulled-up and I could feel that my body was still working away. I could feel that my womb was beginning to contract exactly as it had after the birth of my daughters.

I tried to sit up but I had no strength and I couldn't sit on the open wound as I felt an instant jab of pain shooting through me. I really did have everything that accompanies a real birth!

Mrs Steiner helped me up and I couldn't speak. I have no idea what she saw of the whole thing. I wasn't able to speak about what I had just gone through. It was incomprehensible and indescribable. It was a little difficult to get down from the bed which was at the height of a table as Mrs Steiner stands to work.

She asked me whether I would like to drink something.

"Oh, yes please. That would be great! Now I can feel just how dry my throat is," I replied.

She offered me a place to sit but I couldn't sit at all as everything below was throbbing with pain.

Taking wide steps, like a mother who had just given birth, I left the "delivery room" without saying a word.

I couldn't sit down for a good week and my womb carried on contracting for a good while afterwards.

I am quite sure that what I have written here seems quite unimaginable. There was a time when I would have had trouble believing it. But it was true. My higher being gave birth to itself so that I would be capable of accepting it, MY-SELF.

24

The First Steps

My relationship with my old home, Hungary, changed after my divorce. When the children had been small, we used to go back for Easter and Christmas and we even went to Lake Balaton a couple of times. As the children grew, they joined the scouts and Easter and Whitsun was the time that they went on camps, so my husband and I used to make the most of the opportunity and take ourselves off to somewhere nice. The children loved the sea, so every summer we would go camping in Corsica and surf all day long.

After the divorce, I spent the first Christmas and New Year in Budapest as the girls, age 13 and 15, went skiing with their father. I thought that this was a good idea as they met very rarely because my husband was working more and more. I couldn't stay at home in the empty flat and my mother and her husband were delighted that I spent Christmas with them after so many years. A couple of friends came to stay from Zurich for the New Year and we celebrated together.

The same happened at Easter as the girls were leading a scout camp and I still wasn't able to celebrate alone so I went back to Budapest. My mother's friend said that her son was coming to visit from Munich who had a Hungarian wife and I was glad to see them as we hadn't seen each other for some years. The interesting thing was that my mother "inherited" her best friend from me. I had a boyfriend at school and just afterwards before we split up but I kept in touch with his mother for years. She and my mother became the greatest of friends. We used to meet when I came back to Budapest with my husband and that not only meant the mother but my old boyfriend as well. They were like members of the family. We liked the woman so much that she often came to visit us in Switzerland. The boy was called Feró and he had quite a few relationships after me but he eventually found the girl he knew he could spend the rest of his life with. Csilla lived in Germany at the time as her mother had married a foreigner and she had taken her daughter out to Germany with her. Feró went to live with his wife in Munich and they were also going to be coming home for Easter. They were officially invited for breakfast on Easter Sunday by Csilla's brother and they asked me to come along too. Béla, Csilla's brother, was very hospitable and he said that any friend of his sister's was a friend of his. This is how I happened to spend Easter Sunday with the Ernyei family.

There was another couple there called Kata and Péter. Both of them worked in TV and they had both studied at the Film Academy. Feró had also worked in TV before he left to live in Munich. They soon started chatting about their favourite topics of theatre, actors and films. Mari, Béla's wife, was an actress herself so she soon joined in the discussion

Béla, as the host, soon realized that, although not meaning to, they had closed me out of the conversation as I didn't know anything or anybody related to these topics at all. He politely apologized and said that he would like to know more about me because he didn't know anything other than that I lived in Zurich and I was friendly with Csilla and Feró.

I started with my family and then I told him that I had now become involved in reflexology. I also mentioned that a lot of unusual things had happened to me over recent years and, despite the fact that I couldn't or I didn't want to accept them, things always happened as the VOICE had described them or as they had appeared in my dreams. They seemed really interested in this and especially what I told them about reflexology. They wanted me to diagnose all six of them by examining the soles of their feet, and for me to tell them everything that I could see. I laughed and told them that it would take a whole day.

"OK, so we'll all get together again tomorrow and carry on with the soles of our feet. So now you can tell us everything that the VOICE has told you: what it said about the liberation of the country, when it happened and whether or not you really do have to teach here in the future.

They were curious about everything and I was warmed by their curiosity and open-mindedness. Book titles and the names of authors, whom they had also read, flew around the room, but now they had someone sitting among them who had experienced all of this in person. No one showed the slightest doubt that what I was saying was true. It would appear that their fine artistic senses were in tune with my spiritual being. It was already dark before we said goodbye for the day. Kata and her husband took me home as my mother lived close by. The following day was filled with analysing soles, explaining the significance of specific points and massage sessions. By the time that everyone had massaged the feet of a companion, the day had gone. Kata and Péter took me home again that night and they invited me to go to theirs for lunch the following day as we had become quite good friends. I was happy to go as I had also grown quite fond of them. Kata asked if I would agree to do a TV interview with her the following week. She was involved in women's programming and she said that she would like to do a piece on what had happened to me. I wasn't as confident about the idea as I wanted to be a little surer in myself and in the things that the VOICE had told me. But I wanted to make Kata happy and so I eventually said yes.

The weather in Budapest was beautiful. It was a glorious spring day at the end of April. Kata managed to organize everything in a couple of days and we started recording the interview in her lovely garden. Kata was both reporter and director and was accompanied by a staff of around four others. The situation felt a little alien as I had only told my closest friends about what had happened to me and now I had to do this in front of strangers and I wouldn't be able to see the reaction via the television. I wasn't feeling too good but I didn't want to ruin it although that's exactly what I ended up doing.

When we went out into the garden, I thought Kata and I would sit on the grass and have a friendly chat as we had done a couple of nights before. The other director and cameraman decided that we needed to have furniture so they brought out armchairs, a little table and even a cupboard. They snapped a couple of roses off a beautifully scented shrub and plonked them in a vase with no water.

"Now, that's just lovely. We can start!"

I suddenly felt like I was the furniture or the roses as I wasn't in my natural environment. I felt strangled in the deep armchair and I felt that the rose must feel the same in the crystal vase on the little ornate table surrounded by the glorious green scented garden. Everything changed. I didn't feel as free as I had done a couple of moments before. I had also become one of the props.

"OK, let's start!"

Kata took her place in the other chair and put forward her first question. All she asked me to do was to introduce myself. The camera started to buzz; the guy came closer and waved his hands to say that the lights needed to be moved to the other side. All I could do was stare and wonder what all the lights were in aid of on such a beautifully sunny day. But now I had to concentrate and answer Kata's question. I had just about begun—I could hear that my voice sounded about as artificial as the surroundings—and I couldn't say another word. There was a loud bang and the transformer blew up. There was a burst of swearing and cursing as only Hungarians know how to do on such an occasion. They went to get another one and we had a short break. All those standing around me used this interval to smoke a cigarette. The guy soon came back with another transformer which he plugged in and we were ready to roll again. And everything started from the beginning again. We only managed to say the same as we had before and the transformer blew again. The level of swearing matched the frustration that they were all starting to feel. Someone had to go back to the studio to fetch a third one. I was happy for the break as I had started to feel really hungry and thirsty. Kata came to my rescue with a slice of bread and butter with chives from the garden. I sat and talked to Kata and her little boy who had the loveliest curly hair. I was starting to feel a little better as the mood had become more human and natural. We escaped from the heat into Kata's room, the men stayed outside smoking and the first bottles of beer appeared. The TV studio wasn't so close and we had to wait more than an hour for the next transformer to appear by which time we were being treated to a little April shower. The gang of men started to curse and say that they had never had such a day. The first two converters had blown and the third one arrived to be greeted by lightning from a sky that had been clear blue only minutes before. Kata suddenly asked: "You've done something, haven't you?"

"No, well at least not consciously. It was true that electronic equipment sometimes broke down (clock, TV, camera) when I wasn't feeling too good or I didn't want someone to take my photo. Perhaps I wasn't feeling so good because everything seemed so terribly artificial."

The surprise changed cursing into laughter. Kata laughed most of all: "We should have recorded that but it's too late now!"

Everyone hauled up all the equipment back in the room as the rain started to pour down. The walls were covered in pictures of old relatives and bookshelves and everyone felt very comfortable. They started to ask questions, yet this time not only Kata but also the cameraman and the guys that did the lights. There was a great atmosphere and I could feel their overwhelming curiosity. I now began to answer their question with natural ease, the director waved his hand and the film was made late into the night in the intimate surroundings of Kata's study.

Kata became a very close friend of mine.

My mother and her husband moved to a place called Békésszentandrás (Peaceful Saint Andrew) from the following summer and Kata insisted that I stayed with them whenever I was in Budapest. I accepted with pleasure as I visited Budapest so rarely.

I was back within just two months because they needed to take a couple of last shots to finish off Kata's film. They decided to do this on the grassy slopes of Gellért Hill, free of all interferences. The cameraman made the kind comment: "We wanted to find a place where you'd feel comfortable!"

Well, they managed alright; they had understood and I was able to speak freely as it would have been impossible otherwise.

I was staying with Kata and her husband. We were sitting eating our breakfast in the kitchen when the old lady arrived who took their son Peti to kindergarten and then she came back to discuss something with Kata. We were still hanging around in the kitchen for some reason or other as we were deep in conversation. I seem to remember that I was telling her about Dr Hermann and Gaye Muir's justification.

"I have my own story about the ability of mediums to see," said the little old lady who was called Erzsi. "In fact, I personally knew the greatest Hungarian medium."

I was all ears "Hungarian medium?"

"There used to be really talented mediums in Hungary between the two wars and there was even an organization known as the Spiritual Investigators. This was where the medium called Eszter worked and I knew her quite well. My sister was her housekeeper and so I often went to visit her. I have got a lot of books about organizations and people involved in the occult and spiritualism.

"Hungarian mediums? I would really like to know more about them! Would you be so kind as to let me borrow a couple of your books?"

Erzsi reacted as if she'd been stung and her reply was rather sharp: "No, I won't let a single book out of my hands. When my sister left Hungary, she left me her library and made me promise to look after it until people were free to discuss such things again. I looked after them all but I lent one out a couple of years ago and they never gave it back to me. It was then that I vowed never to lend anyone a book ever again."

She became rather agitated and looked hurt and so I saw that there was nothing to be gained by asking her anymore questions. I accepted the situation and forgot all about it as the day went on.

She came again the next morning to collect Peti and we were in the kitchen again. Erzsi popped her head around the door and gave me a very kind smile and said: "If you would like to come to my place Dórika, and look at the books, you can do so this afternoon with pleasure."

I laughed as I asked: "But what caused you to change your mind in less than 24 hours?"

Erzsi blushed slightly and admitted: "The medium Eszter appeared in my dream and told me that not only should I let Dóri look at the books, I should let her take as many as she wanted because she was going to need them. So I promised that I would do exactly that."

I was very happy that I had been helped from above again otherwise Erzsi would have never given me a book. And now she was going to give them to me as a gift which is more than I could have ever wished for.

I went to see her that same afternoon. There was a cupboard which formed a door to a small room with 50 esoteric books inside which had been meant to stay closed until now. I felt very honoured to be allowed to look at the books of these spiritual people and mediums. None of the names meant anything to me. Then I heard the word: **"This one and this one and this one ..."** I eventually selected 13 books which I had to take down off the shelf. I didn't even look to see who had written them or what they dealt with. The VOICE had surprised me once again. Yesterday the medium in Erzsi's dream and now a list of books from the VOICE. "This must be something important," I thought. Erzsi insisted on giving me a couple of photographs from her treasury of the medium Eszter in a state of trance with the spirits also in photograph who appeared and spoke through her. I had never seen anything like it before!

I travelled back to Zurich the following day with my new treasure. This had been all too much for me to deal with and so I tried to forget about the books by pushing them to the back of a bookshelf and this is where they stayed, unread, until they were pointed out to me again.

A couple of years passed and I was given another telephone call to make (26 December 1994). This time I had to call Mr Passián. I blushed a little when I said that I was fasting again and the VOICE repeated his request for me to call this man. (The VOICE had often asked me to call some or other person on the telephone and interestingly this usually occurred at Christmas of Easter. Something important always happened after one of these telephone conversations.) Mr Passián asked me how things were going with Hungary and I told him that I had made a lot of new friends and that I and a girlfriend of mine had held several courses and meditation sessions.

"Dórika, it would be lovely if we could go to Hungary together some time! The next time you plan a trip, please call me and I'll come along with you!"

"That really would be good but what makes you want to come to Hungary?" I asked.

"I am still looking for the last clues in Adelma Vay's life".

"Who? Who is this Adelma Vay?"

"The greatest Hungarian medium and also perhaps the greatest medium of recent times. But, Dórika, are you telling me that you know nothing about Hungarian mediums?"

This rang a bell and I asked him to hold the line for a minute or two. I put the receiver down and ran to look for the 13 books at the back of the bookshelf which I had hidden away years before. I seemed to remember that this name was among them! And it was! It was the diary of Adelma Vay covering many years of her life, the original two-volume story of the Spiritual Investigators by Dr Grünhut, books about Eszter ... etc.

I picked the phone back up and told him that I actually did have books about Adelma Vay and also several diaries. Mr Passián hiccupped.

"Dórika, how did you get hold of these books?"

"From above!" and I was rather ashamed as I told him that I had been given these books years before but I hadn't dared touch them."

"Well the time has come my girl!" Mr Passián laughed.

The girls wouldn't be back until the New Year and so I buried myself in these books and read them day and night.

Mr Passián was to join me much sooner than I had thought and it happened to be thanks to the Spiritual Investigators. But first I had to get to know Erzsike better or Dr Erzsébet Tusor whom I have known as Tusika ever since, which is what all her close friends call her.

Kata had to go and see Dr Tusor about some problem and, as she said: "They started to talk about all manner of things". Kata told her something about me and Tusi asked for my telephone number the very same day and called me. She said that when she mentioned my name, she sensed that we knew one another without ever having met. I had the similar feeling that I had known her for a long time. She had a personal problem and as she asked whether I would be able to help her. I said that I would give it a go, and then I would call her back. It was she who called me about a quarter of an hour later and said it was as if she had just received the answer from the sky. She had been unable to solve this problem on her own. I was happy that I had been able to help and that I had made such a nice new friend.

Tusika helped me on my path which led to Hungary. The next time I was in Budapest, we met and she invited people to her flat a day later so that I might be able to meet them. I also held a short meditation session. They asked that we should hold a similar session every time I visited Budapest when we could discuss a topic and meditate together. I happily said yes. There were so many people on the following trip that we had difficulty fitting into Tusika's room. We agreed to meet the next time at her clinic where we could make use of the waiting room which was considerably larger than her living room. There was a TV presenter at one of these meetings who asked whether he could film an interview with me the next day to be shown on the TV programme called "Aquarius". Again, I was happy to say yes. I hadn't done a thing and again the doors had opened before me and presented me with a new opportunity.

They made the film the following day and they mainly asked me about the VOICE and especially what he had told me in 1989 about the changes that were about to take place in Hungary and Europe as a whole.

I stayed with Tusika on my next visit because she had not only organized the meditation session in her waiting room for the Friday evening but also a reflexology session for some of her friends on the Saturday and Sunday. These included Kata, András, who ran an esoteric publishing house, Victor who was a Ukrainian healer and came along with an interpreter, another doctor, a lawyer and several alternative practitioners. The course was a great success and I had met new friends once again.

In the meantime, my mother had heard about what I had been doing through the Aquarius TV show. She knew that I was involved in alternative medicine and mainly reflexology but she wasn't aware of my other experiences. I hadn't told her because I knew what she would say. What she saw or could take hold of she was able to believe and the rest was just superstition and bunkum to her. However, after she had watched the broadcast, she said something that really took me by surprise: "Interesting, the VOICE that you talked about on the television. While I was watching you, I remembered that you could virtually say that you owe your life to a voice. I had completely forgotten about it and I still feel uncomfortable having to talk about it."

"But what are you saying? What do you mean when you say that I owe my life to a voice?"

"I have decided to tell you what I had hidden from you to now. When I realized that I was pregnant with you back in 1947, your father and I decided that it was going to be impossible to raise a child in those conditions when there was no work and often no food either. We made an appointment with the doctor to go for an abortion. We had decided and we were quite happy with our decision. We went by tram. I heard a voice from nowhere but not from outside with my ear but with some inner organ. The voice was rather frightening and it was if an ancient being had spoken with terrible severity: **"You cannot murder this child! This child must be born!"**

This scared me so much that I told your father: "Gyuszi, I can hear a frightening voice and it says that the child has to be born!"

Your father laughed: "Well, you really are scared of the curette aren't you?"

My mother answered him in a hurt tone: "I'm not frightened of anyone, not even the devil himself and this voice does really scare me. If I were a believer, I would say that God has just spoken to me in the child's interest. No, I really daren't get rid of this child! Perhaps I'll end up paying with my life. I can't say no to that voice! I can sense it!"

"Your father kept on pushing me about this and that and in the end I simply got off the tram. Your father reacted rather strangely to this. It was from that moment on that he didn't want you and he couldn't accept you. And then you ended up being a girl! When he found this out at the entrance to the hospital, he turned and left saying that he didn't want to see you or me for that matter. When we got back from the hospital, he saw that awfully big child and just laughed: 'Well, I'd like to see you find a husband for that one! You'd better start looking for a giant!'

Well, I have told you at last. Are you angry with me?" she asked shyly.

The only thing that interested me was that the voice had already been directing my life when I had been in my mother's womb. He decided for me. I had wanted to leave in the seventh month because of the blow that I had taken to my head.

My mother wanted to say something else and so I stopped the inner conversation that I was having with myself.

"That's why I chose your name, Dorothea, because it means "gift from God". "Doro" means "gift" and "Thea" stands for "God, Goddess". I thought that I hadn't wanted to let my child live and that is why someone spoke on the child's behalf and they wanted that you should be born. This is how the VOICE saved your life and you became God's gift!"

I didn't know what to say. I was 45 and I had only just discovered this secret.

It was Tusika who organized the next meeting. We arranged to meet in August 1995 so that we could be together for a whole week. We did quite a few regressions with each other. It was there that I recalled my life as a Christian in Rome that came to its end in the Colosseum. It was there that I said the words that I had heard, word for word, from the yoga teacher in the ashram in India and I recognized his face and especially his eyes. I recognized one of the men, who had been Caesar's right-hand man in persecuting the Christians, in one of my patients. The woman had fantastic powers of healing which I had discovered before when she took part in one of my courses. I brought her attention to her gift and I gave her a careful warning and said that if she didn't use her powers for healing then they would turn against her.

I didn't hear anything from her for about six years. The next time that she got in touch was when she had her left breast removed due to breast cancer.

"Victoria!" I told her. "I wanted to save you from the route that you have taken!"

"Yes, you were right and I knew that I was here to heal people in this life and I have known since I was a child. A seer woman told me that I had the power to heal and she told me that I had to use it to make good my past crimes."

When Victoria said this, the scene at the Colosseum appeared to me and I saw that terrible, Christian-hating man on Caesar's right hand who was called Victoria in this life. The image evaporated and tears started to form in my eyes and Victoria cried along with me.

"Do you know what the seer said to me when I was in England?"
"Yes."
"Did you see who I was and what I did in Rome?"
"Yes!"

"Don't tell me that you were there as well."

"Yes, I was!"

We hugged one another in floods of tears.

I was staying with Tusika when I discovered Philomena. I had the feeling that this was the selfsame angel who had contacted four young people in the 1940s and prepared them for the terrible times that were to come.

As chance would have it, I sat meditating the day before setting off on my August trip when a book fell from the shelf which was "The Angel Answers" by Gitta Mallász. I am ashamed to say that this was one of the books that I had hidden away. Some years before I had been given virtually the same book twice within the space of a week. The same book twice. One edition had been in German and the other in Hungarian. These poor books suffered the same fate as the ones that I had been given by the medium Eszter or the ring that I had found in front of Jankovich's house: I shoved them all to the back of the bookshelf. It was the Hungarian version that fell out the day before I was due to leave for Hungary! Unfortunately (or thank God) this happened to me quite a lot and then I immediately read the book in question. Now the same happened with "The Angel Answers". It came back to Budapest with me and I had already read quite a bit of it on my journey back.

I used to sleep in a room in Tusika's flat where she keeps her books. I noticed a tiny little book on a shelf above my head: "Saint Philomena". She was pictured as a child on the cover with her arms open wide and staring up to the heavens with devotion in her eyes. "She's an angel too!" I thought and then I took the book down from the shelf and read and read until I eventually fell asleep. The other book which I had brought with me stayed on my pillow. I saw the two of them lying next to one another the following morning when I woke. I had the feeling that Philomena was the little saint whom the book described and that she had helped me before in Hungary and something told me that that she was the angel in Gitta Mallász's book. I asked Tusika to tell me what she knew about Philomena.

"A dear friend of mine wrote that book and I was planning to introduce you to her tomorrow. After all, tomorrow is 9 August which is the festival of Philomena and my girlfriend is helping to organize a small celebration in a nearby church."

I wanted to find out more about her. Tusi took me to another church the same afternoon but unfortunately it was closed. Instead, we went into the Pilis Hills to visit a small chapel and then we tried again a little later on in the day. This time it was open. The picture on display of Philomena was breathtaking. But something rather unusual caught my attention. It was the scent. I had smelt the same scent that afternoon in front of the church.

"Can you smell that fragrance?"

"Yes, I wanted to ask you earlier what perfume you use because it is really very delicate and suits you perfectly."

"But Tusi, I'm not wearing perfume. The scent isn't coming from me!"

Tusi disagreed: "Yes, it is. This morning when we were outside the church and you were sad that it appeared closed and you walked down the side to look for another entrance, the scent went away and it came back when you did. I wanted to ask what you used then but you were so concerned about getting in that I forgot all about it. But I can smell it again now that we are standing in front of the picture.

It was interesting that I could smell the scent here, and I had then, but I never thought that it might somehow be related to me. In the evening when I was lying in bed in Tusi's room, I started to read the little book again and it said: "Wherever she appears or offers help, people say that the scent of an unknown flower fills the air."

I put the book down and I fell asleep with the name of the little saint on my lips.

The little Philomena celebrations were held the following day in the church. We were late to arrive and so we were forced to sit in the front row. For some reason, I would have been much happier if we had found a place in the last row but Tusi insisted that there were only free spaces right at the front.

We had just sat down when the ceremony began. They brought in a relic of the little saint and we were able to go and kiss it at the end of the mass. I sat glued to the spot from the moment the whole thing started and my heart was beating at a disturbing rate. Tears ran down my face and I started to visibly shake. Everyone in the congregation made their way to the front to pay their respects to the little saint. I was the only one who remained seated because I simply couldn't move. I must have known something or been afraid of something happening if I stood up. I started to shake so violently that I thought I would faint and pass into another consciousness just sitting as I was. They took the relic back to its normal position in the church and the ceremony came to an end. And people started to slowly file out of the church. It took me a little while to recover my composure both spiritual and physical, although I had no idea what had happened to me or why. Tusi went over to a very pleasant woman to whom she later introduced me. Her name was Judit Zipernovszky and she was the one who had translated and adapted the Philomena book. She, along with her husband who had already moved to the other world since then, had visited the faraway corner of Italy where the relic was taken. On the way to, and before Mugnano del Cardinale, a lot of miracles and recovery happened. I thought: "And ever since then."

I asked Tusi and her friend to go on without me as I wanted to have a few words with the priest. "OK," they said. "We'll wait for you outside."

I went to look for the Franciscan priest and asked if I would be allowed to take a look at the relic some time. I told him that something had happened to me and I was unable to stand but that I would really like to see it and kiss it myself.

He smiled kindly and suggested that I go back at 10 am the following morning. "Thank you. That will be just fine!" and I said goodbye.

"Wonderful timing," I thought. Tusi was going away somewhere the next morning. A friend was going to take me out to the airport for 12 noon and I would ask her to come into the church with me on the way.

I was walking out of the vestry and through the empty church when the organ suddenly struck up and started to play AVE MARIA. I started to shake again but this time from joy. Something was happening and it is interesting that I had often heard AVE MARIA at such times, wherever I might be in the world whether it be Budapest or Rio de Janeiro. They are telling me something at times like this. But the secret is not yet revealed!

I was back in the little chapel the next day at 10 am where the brother was waiting to greet me. He handed me the relic and watched with emotion as the tears ran down my face. Afterwards, when he placed it back, he asked: "I can see that Philomena means a great deal to you."

"Yes, indeed," I sobbed and he offered me a handkerchief so that I could wipe my tears away and blow my nose.

"It is interesting that we should meet like this," the brother said. "She means a lot to me as well. My parents desperately wanted to have a child but fate didn't offer them that gift. My mother was a deeply religious woman. She had heard about Philomena and she prayed to her. She asked to be blessed with a child of her own. I was born nine months later. They were happy when they noticed that I had a religious devotion and they helped me to become a Franciscan brother. They gave me a book at my initiation with a picture of a saint in it, and it was Saint Philomena. She has followed me throughout my career. You see that she is here with me now—and with this he produced a much-used prayer book from his habit and from within it a picture of Saint Philomena. He looked at me and said that something or someone was asking him to give me the picture that he held in his hand that he had been given at his initiation. Would I accept it?

All I could do was to cry. The brother wrote a message on it which said he wished it to accompany me on my journey. We said goodbye and he added: "If you take this picture in your hands, please include me in your prayers."

My friend had been standing next to me throughout and was a-mazed by what she had seen. She was Jewish. We sat quietly in the car out to the airport until she said:

"Dóri, it is strange that when I stood with you both in the church, I had the same feeling that I had when I first visited Israel and I went up the Golgotha steps!"

I couldn't add anything to that.

At an earlier meditation at Tusi's, I met a man whom she called because she knew that he had to meet me! The man was the head of the newly reformed Spiritual Investigators Society (Szellemi Bu-várok) and he was called András Liptay. He listened attentively as I told him about my travels in India and especially when I spoke about the VOICE. He asked me to give a talk or talks and he said that I could set the topic. Tusi had also told him that I did sole diagnosis, which I had developed myself, and he also wanted me to teach that at their meetings.

While we were talking, I mentioned that I had a very good old friend who would be delighted to give a talk about one of the found-ing members of the society, Adelma Vay. Mr Passián had already published one of Adelma's works in German.

András Liptay was delighted by this and they did invite Mr Pas-sián to give a series of talks in Budapest.

The two of us travelled together to Budapest to give our first joint talk on 6 October 1995.

25

Hungary Finds Me

The day was a very special one but so was the date: 6 October 1995! It was exactly six years since the VOICE had first told me that I would run courses in Hungary.

A lot of people came along. The room was so crammed full of people that we had to open up the corridor and still there were plenty of people left with no place to sit. Most of the participants were (as yet) unfamiliar to me as there weren't any other familiar faces in the room beyond Tusi and the people I had met through him. In fact, there was one other person and that was my goddaughter whom I hadn't seen in years and we knew virtually nothing about one another. It came as a surprise but I was delighted to see her there. We were only able to greet each other briefly before the talk and to arrange to meet in the coffee shop next door. The Spiritual Investigators' Club was in the centre of town, very close to Elizabeth Bridge on one of the floors of a large tenement building. Tusi took me along as I stayed with her whenever I visited Budapest. She had been to the club before, and so I just tagged along and didn't really pay that much attention to where we were going. I was full of joyous excitement. I was going to be giving my first talk! My name was listed in the programme. I was curious to see who would come along and how many people would turn up. It was a good feeling to see the room fill up and even overflow along the corridor. It wasn't just because I saw so many people who were interested to hear what I had to say but mainly because the prophecy had finally been fulfilled: **"They are going to find you and you will return home to teach!"**

The help of the VOICE and the spirit brothers and sisters really did have an effect on me on this day. Yet another thing to have come true! But how had this all come about in the first place? All I knew in 1989 was that I wouldn't be going home straight away when the borders opened but I'd make my way back one step at a time. Seven years previously, I didn't know any of the people who had so far helped me on my way. The information passed by word of mouth while they held my hand from above and led me all the way.

I began the session with tears in my eyes. I knew that even though they were paying very close attention, there was no way that I would be able to fully communicate the emotion, the gratitude and the thanks that I felt at being able to work in this wonderful, invisible art! They had chosen me and accepted me as one of them. They had allowed me in on the secret and I did as much as I could with the tools that I had at my disposal.

I started my talk with the memories I had of 6 October. I spoke of martyrs and heroes who had made a sacrifice from the very beginning despite the impossible circumstances. All that they had done, they did for the country and for the improved fate of others. This sacrifice had meant lack of understanding, rejection, all forms of torture and perhaps even death. That is how I felt as well. I asked everyone to close their eyes and to give thanks to those earthly and spiritual powers who had made it possible for me to be standing in front of them giving this talk in 1996.

Then I told them all about the appearance of the VOICE and the work that I had been doing. I also told them how difficult it had been for me at the beginning to accept those things that I would have liked to have gone a different way. Now, I was not only fully able to accept the decisions of those above but, after six years, I could see that it was best for everyone concerned including my husband, my children and, of course, myself.

I also told them all about the dream that I had the night before. I had been walking home to Budapest. It being late at night, the streets were empty. I was walking past a famous statue on the outskirts of Budapest when an angel appeared. It wasn't a spirit but a big, shining, white angel and it had enormous wings. It stood waiting for me. As I walked up to it, I was handed a plant pot filled with soil.

"I entrust you with this," and it disappeared. I held the plant pot in my hand and stood frozen to the spot with surprise and emotion. I simply stood there with this earth in a pot, the soil of Hungary, on the outskirts of Budapest. I knew that I had to keep going because people were waiting for me and I had to arrive in good time. It was only now that I realized the pot that I had in my hand was virtually new and had only just been made and hadn't yet been fired. It was still quite soft to the touch and so I took great care of it. The vibration caused by my steps was just a little too much for it and it started to crack. Before I could do a thing to stop it, the earth started to trickle out through the crack. I stood helplessly and watched it come streaming out. It was quite dark by now and I could see that there was something glinting in the soil that had fallen on the road. I bent down to see what it was and it turned out to be gold. The soil was full of gold nuggets but there were also coins mixed in with the earth. I tried to press the pot back together again so that I could pour the soil back inside again along with the gold but the clay was no longer pliable.

I knew that this was a prediction of the time that was to come. The soil had valuables in it, the gold, which wasn't initially apparent whereas the plant pot still hadn't been finished. It had been moulded but there still hadn't been sufficient time to fire it.

I had to keep on going as I was expected at a certain time and I was on foot. I buried the plant pot, along with the gold, in the ground and marked the spot.

I can also remember the second half of the prophecy from 1989:

"You won't go immediately. After the opening of the borders (this could have many meanings) **the soil will be craving for the touch of the spirit. The earth is dry like a sponge. It will soak everything up. Unfortunately, the false prophets will be the first to**

appear and those who represent false faiths. People will slowly come to realize that this is not the spirit that the soil longs for and they will begin to look for the true teachers. It is then that they will find you and invite you home to teach."

Now, standing on the outskirts of Budapest, what exactly was this vision to mean to me? I wasn't to know but those above already did.

All I knew was that I would do all that I could and that a great many things would change in the meantime. Perhaps the plant pot would eventually be fired and it would at last be able to hold the soil that the angels had placed inside it.

There was silence in the room. Everyone was pondering what they had heard and looking within themselves. They were perhaps thinking that they themselves were little pieces of clay and considering whether or not they had been fired and whether they had done everything they could to make sure that the soil remained inside them.

I could sense the dramatic mood of the silence and as I had finished saying what I had planned, I concluded my talk with the question left open. I thought that the audience would be able to attach their own thoughts to it in the break that followed.

I longed for a breath of fresh air and I walked to the other end of the room where double doors opened onto the street. I opened one and stepped out onto the balcony. We were quite high up so I was able to look down on what was happening in the street. I saw the Kárpátia Restaurant over the road and a dream came back to me which I had been having for years.

Intermezzo

I only had a couple of weeks before I was to give my talk at the Spiritual Investigators and I had an important dream. Although I had already met them, the people who would be giving talks reappeared and they were in a room with 100s of people in the audience. I had a spirit standing behind me offering me protection—Elisabeth Haich. The talks were long and there were breaks in-between. I went out to the balcony for a breath of fresh air and to recharge my batteries. After the break I was going to be answering questions and healing. I could see the Kárpátia Restaurant from the window. In my dream I thought: I went into the building for the talk on Ferenciek Square. There was a neon advertisement in the air between the travel agent's and a grocery store. It said, "Light Centre" but what it really meant was "House of Light". Written in light above it were the names: Selva Raja Yesudian and Elisabeth Haich.

It was the "House of Light" in the spirit of Yesudian and Haich! I had this dream again and again after I went to see them and told them the message that the VOICE had given to me in 1989. But I couldn't see the sign from the balcony. I had seen it when I entered the building but I couldn't see it now. So I saw the sign in lights when I entered the building but not when I went out to the balcony in the break. The only thing that I could see was the Kárpátia: it was as if the entrance had been from a side street. Because I couldn't see the sign in lights from there!

26

After the Break

I had to go back into the room as they wanted me to continue my talk. After the break, I answered their questions as I had promised. Even though it was getting pretty late, we still managed to fit the healing session in that we had planned. I asked that only those people should stay who had a very great need for help because I wanted to form the chairs into a circle. I guess about 30 people stayed behind. The others left either because they had come a long way and had to set off home or to give those in greater need a better chance than themselves. The room eventually quietened and I asked everyone to meditate for a moment or two. We all gave thanks as we had at the beginning of the previous session and then we concentrated our minds on placing all our energy into our work. We asked our spiritual leaders and brothers to help us in our own development as well as the group's, and for the spirit to defeat matter. The resonance changed completely and lifted. It became clearer. I knew that everyone—just like me—was trying to do their absolute best.

I had planned this session to last for no more than 15 minutes but there were a lot of people who needed healing and it took a good half-hour to get through. I close my eyes when I heal. I give myself over to my higher self and ask to be taken to the individual who is in greatest need of healing. I didn't have to go over to all of them but I had to touch some part of almost three quarters of the people gathered there or I had to work on their individual auras. When I had finished everything and I was sitting in the room, there were quite a few who wanted to speak to me alone or ask me a question.

My goddaughter came over, took me by the hand, and led me out of the circle of people that had formed around me. I was very grateful to her. It wasn't just because I was tired, although I was still too excited to fully feel it, but I really didn't want to have to say anymore. I was very interested to find out more about my goddaughter. I wanted to know how she happened to be there and whether she was involved in similar things herself. She started to tell me without me having to ask. We were out on the steps when she told me that her girlfriend had recently lost her husband and since then she had become very interested in all things to do with parapsychology and what happened after death, and she was looking for ways that they might be able to establish contact with her dead husband. This is what had brought her to the Spiritual Investigators meeting. She had seen my name in the programme and as my goddaughter had mentioned that she had been to see me a couple of times in Switzerland, she thought I might be the same person who was going to be giving a talk at the club. My goddaughter only knew about my work in reflexology but when she heard the name, she was certain that it was me. She planned to surprise me by turning up in the audience. She managed well enough and not only with this!

"Godmummy! Now that I have heard your talk, I am sure you will believe me when I tell you what happened to me. In fact, it involves you too!"

She had made me curious. She told me that she had read a couple of books about developing spiritual powers a couple of years before. She had wanted to find out more about herself and how to handle her own spiritual powers. She heard that a practitioner of alternative medicine held a group where they practised such exercises. She signed up to go on the course. Everything went well at the beginning but then one evening in the middle of an exercise, she found that she wasn't able to catch her breath. Within a minute she was having an asthma attack, which she thought she had grown out of in her childhood. The attack was so severe that they had to stop what they were doing and help her as she had started to suffocate. They put her straight in a car and drove through every red light until they arrived at the nearest hospital. Thankfully, there was a place close by—less than five minutes away—but she had suffocated by the time that they had arrived. The young doctor who greeted them was able to establish that she had died but still they rushed her to intensive care so that they could try everything possible. Perhaps shock her heart? The doctor found it hard to come to terms with what was happening: "She's a young girl, maybe we'll be able to bring her back!"

The first thing they did was to drain the saliva from her windpipe when they noticed that my goddaughter had "switched back on" and started to breathe again and her heart started to beat. They were all delighted that they had been able to deal with this more than life-threatening situation!

"I am so grateful to the doctor that he didn't give up but I am very grateful to you as well!"

"But, why me?" I asked, rather surprised.

"I really did die and I saw myself from above with all those people scurrying around me. I was happy that it was all over and I started to lift up towards the light. I eventually arrived and there were a lot of people waiting for me and you stood at the front of the crowd in a white dress. You looked just like an angel but you didn't have wings. You shone brightly. You came straight over to me and you said: "Your time has not yet arrived. Here, take my hand and I will lead you back."

I opened my eyes on the hospital bed and there were people standing all around me. "Fantastic! It worked! We managed to bring her back to life!" the doctors shouted. I didn't say anything to them as there is no way that they would have believed me. I was pretty amazed and wondered how this could have happened and especially how you were up there. As soon as I could I called your mother and tactfully asked how you were. I was frightened that something might have happened to you that I didn't know about. Your mother told me that you were fine and she promised to tell you to call me when you were next in town."

I laughed and thought, "Yes she did get in touch but not from Budapest!"

"The whole story shocked me and I couldn't bring myself to believe what had happened. I didn't tell anyone because I was scared that they would say that I was lying and they would think that I was being big-headed. And now I have told you. It feels so good! It was a terrible secret that I don't have to keep to myself any longer. But you do believe me, don't you?"

"I do but I can't tell you how it all happened, I'm afraid."

I started to feel tired and so we said goodbye and I went home with Tusi in a taxi.

"So many experiences and secrets in just one day!" I thought. I was grateful to get into bed as I was at the point of complete collapse. I hoped that I wouldn't dream that night.

The talk at the Spiritual Investigators Club turned into two courses and then I had to do it all over again as so many people wanted to attend. I only used to work with a maximum of 15 people but I now had to raise the numbers to about 20. And then there was still a waiting list. A lot of people wanted to repeat the course because they were learning so many new things and they simply couldn't take it all in the space of a weekend. The request soon emerged to take a group for a whole week in the summer. I was happy to be asked and I was happy to take it on.

We began to organize things. The people who had already taken part looked for somewhere to hold the course because we wanted it to take place outside somewhere, sleep in tents and so use all the hours of the day and night. In May, I had not only the weekend courses but I also had to teach in the evenings, five times a week. That was the time when I could have some free time only between courses to look for a potential venue. The best place that I came across was a clearing in a place called Búbánat (Sorrow) Valley. The area belonged to a small guesthouse where they used to hold theatre workshops for children during the summer. The place was ideal from absolutely every point of view. We could camp or stay in the hotel or one of the little wooden chalets they had along the edge of the woods. Everyone chose a place according to their needs and to match their budget. There were tourists, second-class and luxury guest. We were given breakfast and supper in the restaurant which left us with the whole day to arrange as we saw fit. The clearing was as if it had been created especially for us. It was surrounded by tall trees which meant that, even though it was July, we were always able to find a spot in the shade where I could work together with the group. There was a wooden stage in the centre of the clearing with three or four steps leading up to it. This provided the ideal spot for our "sunrise meditation" followed by a yoga session when everything still had a layer of morning dew on it. We also held our evening "sunset meditation" on the same stage. We spent the rest of the time on the grass or the nearby banks of the Danube and we swam in the river several times.

The number of people wanting to come on the summer camp kept on growing and so I was forced to limit the number to 40. I also had to agree to teach for two weeks rather than the original one. The size and responsibility of the whole thing just kept on growing. Now, I was going to do a two-week course with 40 people and for 24 hours a day. I really had to prepare and prepare well!

The topic that I chose was elemental forces: earth, water, fire and air. I had the running order for the whole thing set in my head a good two weeks before we started. I thought it important that the people on the course should know about, love and respect the elemental forces and ask for their help in their everyday lives just like the Indians did and other peoples who had lived out in the open.

But how did I come to have this knowledge in the first place?

27

Elemental Forces and Secrets
of Their Earthly World

I became familiar with one of the elemental forces, fire, when I was still only a small child. They let me into its secrets and they sought me out. I spent an awful lot of time on my own when I was small but also between the ages of 9 and 14 because my mother and her husband at the time worked nights on the taxis. They left in the evening and came home to sleep in the morning just before I left for school. This meant that I was at home alone in the evenings. I was frightened at the beginning but there was very little that I could do about the situation and I was forced to come to terms with it. All this time on my own created a very special situation. I liked to sit in the quiet and study and read but I didn't like lying in bed. Something frightening always happened there. My mother would often return to find me sitting at the table fast asleep.

The same thing always started to happen in the quiet of the flat. Something changed around me. Everything became sticky as if I was pulling myself out of something but it wasn't an unpleasant sensation. I tended to get the most scared when the room started to move away from me and everything went very small until it finally disappeared. I didn't know back then that it wasn't the room that had disappeared but that I had flown out of it. The fire fairies were waiting for me on most occasions. This is what I called my little friends who came to visit me in the evenings. They lived with me in the room but I could only see them at night in this state when they could approach me in perfect safety. They lived in the tiled stove that heated my room. I soon became not only a friend but also a member of their family. They lived in family groups just like humans. There were tiny little sparks among them and ancient flames. Of course, I spent most of my time with the children and they showed me everything that I didn't know. Their external appearance, if it can be called that, was constantly changing just like a tongue of flame and yet still they each had their own personality. Their colour was that of fire varying from a light carrot colour to a deep dark red. It is really quite hard to describe it in words; perhaps I should paint it one day!

My relationship with them lasted a very long time. Unfortunately my mother and her husband decided to give me more space in my room by removing the stove and putting an electric contraption in its place. There was absolutely no point to my protests and I would have never told them my secret. They wouldn't have deserved it and they would have never believed me.

I told my girlfriends in kindergarten and later at primary school all about them but they could only deal with this as an invented fairy story. I let them think what they wanted to think. The years passed and I also forgot all about the fire fairies and decades went by with no contact at all.

One day, I attended an interesting talk as part of the Basel Parapsychology Conference. The following programme was listed under the name of Dr Sigrid Lechner-Knecht: "Connection with the Elemental and Natural Forces". She really intrigued me and was a multi-talented individual who had studied biology, geography, ethnology, philosophy and psychology and graduated with summa cum laude. Why had she come into contact with the natural forces and how?

An old woman walked up onto the platform in front of an audience of about 100 people. She looked just like the little old lady in children's stories, all that was missing was the small hump on her back and it would have seemed completely natural to have met her deep in the forest of fairy tales. She spoke genuinely about the relationship that she had enjoyed with fairies and pixies from early childhood. These tiny people, some visible and some not, were the wardens of the woods and protectors of the flowers. She told us that she not only saw them but that she also consciously communicated with them. Everyone sat in stunned silence including me. I believed everything that she said although perhaps not everyone did. She also spoke about the spirits of the air and the wind, the spirit of fire and those who live in fire but she added that she only knew of these from what she had read in books and what other people had told her. I put my hand up and asked why she thought it was that she only saw the "inhabitants" of the water and the earth and why she didn't see those who lived in the air and in fire. She said that this was because she had an affinity and that these signs were very strong in her horoscope. She said that she had absolutely no air in her chart and only one indication of fire. I suddenly recalled the fire fairies and when I used to visit them at night in the stove. I went over to her at the end of the talk (she was easily well over 70) as I wanted to ask her a few questions. She suggested that we go and sit in a coffee shop where we could chat in comfort. We sat together all evening and she was the one to ask the most questions. She wanted me to tell her all about my own experiences. She had very little information about fire before she met me and she knew nothing of the beings that lived in it. She partly explained my link with these fire fairies by the fact that fire is very dominant in my horoscope. I was born in the sign of the Sun; my Moon is in fire in Aries and my other three signs are all in fire. She then presented me with a dedicated copy of her book, which she had written about "her beings".

I gained more information about my special relationship with fire while I was on the Rhea Power course. We had to do regression therapy on ourselves to at least 20 previous incarnations. I wanted to find out where this trait of mine had come from which meant that I was capable of doing anything, even giving my life, for something that was close to my heart. I was amazed to discover that I had in fact been an elemental force. Fire! But this was a different kind of fire to the one that I knew in this life. My fire had come down from on high to the Earth to help people. I was the fire that could warm anything, bring anything to life but also the inner fire that would push people to achieve anything but could also burn anything. I can still feel that elemental force, that joy and will with which I arrived in the form of a comet's tail which had no beginning and no end. I came rushing towards the Earth like a "chariot of fire". People saw me and ran screaming: "Fire! Fire!" And fled for their lives and I went after them yelling: "Wait. I came for you. I came to help you all!"

They didn't hear me but their fear deafened them to my cries. They ran and I went after them asking: "Why do they run from me? I only want to help them!"

The VOICE gave the answer: **"Because you are great and dangerous in their eyes."**

"Yes, but that is where my power lies!" I replied. I then asked: "What should I do now? How will I ever be able to reach them?"

The VOICE answered once again: **"You first have to make contact with the other elemental forces, get to know them and make friends with them."**

"Me, fire, with the other forces of nature? But I am the greatest and the most powerful. Should I lower myself to the level of all the others?" I asked shocked by what I had been told to do.

"Yes! If you want to reach people then this is what you must learn to do!"

The desire in me to reach people was so strong that I was forced to accept.

"Very well, then I will do as you say," I replied although I still thought that the whole thing was degrading. I, fire, had to lower myself to the level of water and air and even earth! But I had to do what I had been told if I was to ever achieve my goal!"

I first made contact with the air. I was still angry and so I threw a great burst of flame into the air. I became enormous. "Not a good idea," I suddenly thought. "I don't want to be bigger; I want to be much smaller. This will only frighten the people even more."

I tried to make myself smaller. It wasn't so unpleasant. I knew how large I was and this was just a game that I was playing in order to reach my goal. Then I noticed that my fire had nearly gone out because I had made myself so small. But the air appeared and helped me. I now knew that the air could be dangerous as it could make me roar with a giant flame and I shouldn't do that now. I also realized that I needed air if I fell to the other extreme and neglected myself and let my flame die down. Air had to constantly be by my side and I could control my size with its help.

This was more interesting than I had thought!

Water was the next. I didn't think that water was an equal partner to me either and I lashed out at water which lashed back and I had to jump back because it came at me with such force that I was frightened that it would put out my flames. "I have to be careful here!" I realized. "This is totally different to air. Air helped me and could make me grow larger. But if water is larger than me, it can put me out if I'm not careful enough." Now I tried with a smaller stretch of water and I moved inside it and warmed it up. Hot springs appeared and people came along to bathe and to use the water for healing. I mixed with other water but with more force this time and we created the element of steam. This was interesting as well. Now I knew that I had to keep a safe distance from water.

Now there was only earth left. I had kept this until last as I had a very low opinion of earth. It couldn't move and was passive and so I thought it was impotent. It let people and the forces of nature do whatever they wanted with it.

I was capable of doing anything to eventually achieve my aim. The earth was covered in a white blanket when I approached it. I could still feel the shame of hiding inside it so that no one could see me and the earth let me do it. Something next to me started to slowly flow and the snow and the ice started to melt. Everything changed in the earth. The little seeds that had slept, protected under the snow, began to wake and come to life. My heat made them struggle to the surface and push their little green heads out. People were amazed to see this as everywhere else was covered in snow but everything started to become green and lush where I had buried myself in the earth. I tried to show my greatness here as well and only succeeded in frightening the people away. I pushed flames through cracks in the earth, which was easy with my immense power, and they all fled all over again.

I practised and continued to make friends with the other elemental forces but I knew that I had to make serious efforts to control myself. I spent all my time on this and I tried everything that I could.

The VOICE spoke to me again and said: **"Good, now come up here and see what has happened."**

I took my old form again, my old greatness, and moved up to the heavens and looked back down on the Earth as a planet.

All I could see was that there were little fires burning all over the place and the VOICE spoke kindly to me: **"You see, you managed to readjust yourself to people, you accepted the other elements and you made friends with them. Now you have achieved what you set out to do: a sea of fire made up of millions of tiny flames. None of this would have happened if you hadn't gone down to Earth and done everything that you intended to do."**

The other forces of nature had all appeared to me earlier. While I was still living with my husband and we were flying back from our trip to Australia when I sat on the plane listening to music through headphones. I must have been very relaxed as I suddenly felt as if I was soaring through the air but I was still touching something. I could feel that my whole being was free and that I no longer existed as a bodily power. The thing that I was touching was the aeroplane and I was flying on the outside of it. I was the wind: the air that was moving! The speed and the indescribable power appealed to me very much. The plane could have done nothing to help itself if I had shoved it. But I was only playing with my power. I could push the clouds along or disintegrate them completely. All this was just a game. All I was doing was showing and feeling what it was to be me and what I was capable of. All the time I knew that I was the wind and I was the air. And that is all I was! Yet still I had a consciousness that was playing with me and experimenting with me.

Then I dived down to the seas and I flew above the waves as I tried to entertain them. Now I was a wave in the vast ocean but still moving all the time. I was the water and the wave moved me and my whole being moved. No! I was that movement. I enjoyed the constant soft, rhythmical movement. I knew that the wind and the water was also somewhere with me then another sudden change as a wave crashed on the shore and ran into the sand. The way I ran through the sand then out and away made me happy. I did it over and over again. I gave myself over and drew back again. I was soft but so was the sand. My senses changed again. They were flowing into me and draining from me and softening me. I opened and closed: I was the earth and the sand. Now I was all things at once. The wind and the moving air, the water and the wave on the ocean and also the earth—but all at one time. Then the Sun entered our gathering. It gave light and warmth to everything including the air and the water and the earth and my being and consciousness. Now I was Sun; Light; the Eternal Light. I disappeared from all consciousness and only the Light remained.

Something was shaking. Someone was shaking me. This was something new. I could feel something new. I slowly picked up my human consciousness and I could hear. "Wake up. Your dinner" I could smell the food but I didn't want to eat a thing. I liked being in the light and the universe and I wanted to stay there forever! And now they were waking me up!

The experience that I had with a rainbow is also related to aeroplanes. I was on my way back from a regression session that I held with Ilse, and I had to go to Potsdam. This was where the Visions Congress was to be held in 1991. A Native American called Sun Bear had said years before on a previous visit to Berlin when the Wall had still stood: "I can see this Wall falling and the time is not so very far off." That was back in 1987. I would have liked to have been at that congress as he knew what I also knew. (The difference was that I knew the exact month and year.) I went there by plane. There was a terrible storm and just before I left, my daughter Claudia asked me to take her to the library in my car. She wanted to take some books out but she didn't want them to get wet. I had enough time and so I took her and waited for her. We drove home and she showed me what she had borrowed. They all dealt with rainbows. She was going to be taking a scout group the following day and she wanted to talk to them about rainbows. They were going to paint and talk all about rainbows. I was happy to hear that she was doing such interesting things with her little friends.

It was the Saturday before Whitsun and the congress was to be held over the two days of Whitsun. I didn't eat anything on the plane as I had only just completed a week-long fast and I was trying to slowly reintroduce my body to food. I sat with my eyes closed and enjoyed the sensation of flying. I thought of my daughter and of rainbows. "It is a long time since I did a rainbow mediation," I thought and I started to visualize the colours. I didn't let the individual colours go but instead linked each one to the next. In time, one colour blended into the next and I became those colours. Now all the seven colours were together. The rainbow had been made and I was that rainbow arching across a blue sky. The time on the plane passed very quickly. I prepared for the plane to land. I had to walk along a labyrinth of corridors as one does in all airports. My good friend, Johann, stood for me—I will write much more about him in the chapters that deal with the dolphins. He gave me a warm hug and we were both pleased that we could meet up again like this. He came to collect me by car and he was staying with a friend who also offered me a bed for the night. He, unlike me, had been to Berlin many times before and so I was glad to have someone to show me around the big city. He threw my bag in the boot of his car, looked up to the sky and said: "Unbelievable to see a rainbow over the airport that has been there so long and doesn't seem to be fading. It appeared at about the same time as your plane arrived and seemed to fill the whole sky. I waited for your plane to arrive out on the viewing platform and a whole crowd of us stood there and stared at it. The strange thing was that it wasn't raining and there didn't even appear to be any mist about either. So, how could a rainbow have formed?" and with that he looked at his watch. "It's just an hour since it appeared and it's still there. The whole thing is quite amazing."

I didn't exactly understand it myself either. I sat in the car and closed my eyes. I gave thanks for having experienced the rainbow and I asked to be taken back up into its colours. I now went through all the colours again in turn. When I took a deep breath in and opened my eyes again, I looked in the mirror and saw that there was nothing left but the clear blue sky.

The rainbow was a glorious gift to the Visions Congress. It greeted us and waited for the earthly participants to arrive along with the heavenly powers.

28

Surprises
at the Camp

I really wanted to deal with the four elemental powers at the summer camp. (Three days each.) The sun was at the centre of our consciousness as we greeted it in the morning and said farewell to it at night. We also greeted the Earth everyday as the place where we lived and as Mother Earth.

I could write a really thick book just about what went off at the camp but I will have to make do with mentioning a couple of very special episodes. I would ask those who were in the camp to respect the anonymity of those involved. I will make no mention of names as long as they don't name the individuals I describe. I hope those whom I mention have learnt their lesson from what happened!

People with all types of backgrounds attended the camp. It was a spiritual yoga camp and so had a great many interesting things to offer. Many already knew me from the talks that I had given, various courses that I had run and even from my appearances on television. They had great expectations as so many interesting things had happened over the course of a weekend, and now we had two weeks to look forward to!

Before the camp got underway, I asked everyone to explain what lay behind the ideas that they had. I warned all those taking part not to expect anything from me or from the camp! I, on the other hand, put my heart and soul into ensuring that we would spend two weeks together that they would have only ever dared to dream about.

We opened the camp with a ritual celebration on the Friday night. Around the campfire, which burned bright every night, four people—born under the signs of the four elements—greeted the spirits of the elemental powers and asked them to support us in our learning and realization. We asked them to share their secrets with us.

And that is what happened. They accepted our request. The four elements showed themselves in all their glory during the two weeks and helped us wherever possible. The rain halted one night when we asked it to during a meditation session. A rainbow appeared above one of the houses and doubled itself before our very eyes while we were meditating. One arched over us in the meadow and the other soared above the building that we were staying in. They also prepared many more surprises for me. Where there is so much beauty and goodness and especially life and light, the other darker world sends its representatives to do their dirty work.

I started to watch several individuals from the very beginning to see what they would be unveiled as. It happened on the day of fire, which was the ninth day. That night we placed all those personal qualities and events from our past in the fire, which we no longer wanted to carry with us, and had been storing deep down. I first called everyone's attention to the contrast between the sexes—that we had been looking at over several days when we had dealt with earth and water—but I also talked about the contrast between generations. Fire is the greatest help to us to release and burn and transform. The whole camp could hardly wait to let go and give to the fire and disperse what we had been preparing for several days. The energy burned in all those gathered around the flames. We went one after the other in silence to place our "sacrifices" into the fire. A young guy did the same and the whole camp span out of control. A man grabbed at his throat and he yelled: "Golem! Golem! He is strangling, me!"

We immediately closed the circle and asked for help from our spirit leaders. We asked them to help us banish the negative force which had just appeared out of the fire to purify it. Calm slowly returned and the energy was restored to what it had been before the incident. As the evening came to a close, I asked all those present to ask for their own personal safety that night and that we would continue our discussions the next morning.

I don't know what happened! I didn't see a golem and I didn't feel the negative forces that were at work but a load of the people there did see and recognize them! It must have all depended on affinity. We are only able to recognize those things that we already know.

I finished the day with prayer and a request for help.

I waited expectantly the following morning to hear what the folks had to say about their experiences.

The man started who had been strangled. He said that as the young man had walked towards the fire and symbolically placed something in it, he had seen a spirit of sorts that grabbed at his throat and started to wrap itself around his neck. He was only released when we formed the circle and we helped and asked for help with prayer. Two or three other people gave the same description of the golem and the rest of us were amazed to hear what they had to say.

I turned to the young man who had been quiet up until this point. I asked if this being was in contact with him that the others had called a golem. He said yes. He had created this being with the help of various books dealing with black magic and the golem had been his slave. It was forced to do his bidding as he had created it and he had brought it to life. However, the golem had started to turn against him and he had thought it a good opportunity to burn it in the fire. The golem had other ideas and had thrown himself on another person who had seen it.

I was stunned to hear all of this. The boy's father was the next to speak: "Yes, they sent us here. You have all been coded incorrectly and we are here to recode you during the night."

I didn't want to believe my ears! What? Recode us? The father had caught my eye on another course that I had run. He had suddenly become transformed during one of the exercises and had spoken like a man possessed about the retribution for sins, about judgement day and purgatory. The whole thing had only lasted a couple of seconds but several people had changed in a similar way on another course. I had laughed on that occasion and told him that he worked for truth and purification. (It was really difficult for me to accept all of this as there was neither love nor understanding in the words of the previous being, and it had been more a case of fighting against all those who didn't believe with fire and steel!) I felt rather uncomfortable when I saw him on the list of people who had signed up to go on the camp. I spoke to him personally. He said that he was having problems with his child and that his son had been mixing with a bad crowd that was having a bad influence on him and he hoped that his son would see a good example in the camp that he would be able to follow. The boy had come to see me a couple of days before the camp about a wound that he had on the sole of his foot. There was a growth that kept appearing on his right big toe next to his nail which was inflamed and septic. He had tried everything and even been given laser treatment to burn it off but with no success. The growth simply reappeared and the process began all over again from the beginning.

I knew that something was wrong in his consciousness and what we had just experienced on the fire day only went to support my suspicions. The big toe represents the head and the nail the face with the right side being conscious action. So I knew that there was something present in the conscious side of his brain that was confusing, unclean and infectious.

They admitted what they had been doing and where their allegiance lay. I asked them to leave the camp within an hour but the father wouldn't give up. He made threatening remarks and said that he would teach us all a lesson! He said that those who had sent them were able to control us from a distance and that they had only wanted to help us as we had taken the wrong path. He said that those who did as they were told were rewarded and those who resisted ... I didn't allow him to continue spewing forth such poison.

"Leave the camp immediately!"

They laughed as if they had won and then they left us showering us with curses as they walked away from the clearing.

I held a break. The camp fell into disarray. Many sprang to their defence and said that we couldn't just send them away like that in such a state. If we didn't help them then who would? I just listened and I could sense that the camp was splitting into two factions.

"Very well," I replied, "but who will take over the leadership of the camp? Yes, negative forces do really exist just like weeds in a garden. If the gardener feels a misguided sympathy for the weeds and leaves them to grow then they will soon take all the nutrients and space away from the beautiful flowers. The same is true with animals and people. There are those who try to push themselves forward in a parasitic fashion but we shouldn't allow them to multiply.

Even the softer ones soon saw—after several people described what they had experienced—that the safety of the camp was sacrosanct. Many had seen serpents, witches and devil figures in their rooms in terrifying putrid colours with large eyes.

The boy returned to the camp after several days. He brought all those things along with him that he had used in his black magic and he asked us to help him rediscover the way of light. That night we all sat around the campfire and prayed for his release (from the negative forces) and he threw everything that he had brought along into the fire. This time nothing unpleasant happened. I very much hoped that he had been telling the truth and so I offered my help as well. When the camp came to an end, I asked all those who had taken part to carefully follow the boy's progress. We selected several individuals—as godparents—who would be in constant contact with the boy and would be able to rush to his aid at any time, day or night. We also provided him with material support. We dissolved the circle of helpers a year later and passed the boy to the spirit helpers. If they think it is good and if the boy is willing to cooperate, they will give him every chance he needs for a new start.

I would never have thought that the camp would have presented us with such a test of strength but that wasn't the only such incident. I was forced to accept that where light appears and grows so does the eternal antithesis and it tries to operate with its own opportunities and powers.

I knew what a challenge this was for me but I also knew why it had happened. It was at times like this that my strength multiplied. I was cleansed in the night and reinvigorated. I had my usual high fevers every night of the last week of the camp and awoke again the following morning refreshed and ready to work. We had to help nearly 40 people and we managed it!

We closed the camp with another ritual and no one wanted to leave and return to their everyday lives. But I knew that the powers of help would go with us and remain with us all.

29

My Dolphin Brothers
and Sisters

The success of the camp and the enthusiastic response of those who took part led more and more inquisitive students to my door with a desire to learn. The same year, I decided to find an apartment that would not only provide me with a quiet retreat but also a venue for courses. When I teach, I always give so much of myself that I can neither speak nor am I in the mood to listen to anyone. Those kind people who had acted as hosts to my courses up until now, always wanted to know how the course had gone and they had trouble accepting that, although they could see me, they couldn't get through to me. At times like this, I always feel a happy emptiness and then I like best to be alone. Sometimes I mingle with people outside in the street or I go into a restaurant. Other times I long to go to the cinema or my body demands that I do nothing more than simply sleep.

Chance led me to a spacious, sunny, four-roomed flat on a tiny little street in Buda. There was a bus stop close by and I was able to do all my grocery shopping on the corner of the street. The price was quite high and I had to pay 100,000 Hungarian forint a month but I was teaching in Germany at the time and I was able to fund my teaching in Budapest out of these earnings. The money that I earned in Budapest was just about enough to cover my food bill and incidental expenses. I had something in the region of 30,000 Swiss francs saved up at the time and I thought that I would just "throw this in the pot" and see what happened. My new commitments meant that I was only able to work in Zurich two weeks a month, or even less, and so these savings meant that I was able to carry on teaching in Hungary for a year.

I soon had a "little group" of ten gathered together and I met them twice a month. I often told them about the experiences that I had had with dolphins. In time, it became clear that they too would like to come into closer contact with dolphins and get to learn more about dolphin consciousness. But how did I come across this knowledge?

My first encounter was in Basel at that first parapsychology conference where I had met Mia. I have already mentioned Mia in the chapter where I described my dream about my husband's girlfriend.

That conference is really quite enormous and often has as many as 1,000 people attend it. It is held in two or three larger and nearly ten smaller rooms and they hold a constant, parallel stream of presentations and workshops. They publish a guide every year and list all the programmes, where they will be held and when. I was a beginner back then and I was only able to leave my children with their Swiss grandmother at the very last minute. And I really didn't have enough time to properly prepare. Their grandmother lived several hours from Zurich but still she came to our place for a couple of days simply to look after the children for me. My girls always loved to go and stay with her in Brienz and they were just as pleased that Mutti was coming to visit. I was pleased that I was going to be free for a couple of days and that I would finally be able to attend that famous parapsychology conference.

After I got to know Mia and we realized that neither of us had been there before and that we didn't have a copy of the programme guide between us, we studied the display board which had all the details of that day's events posted on it. We both caught sight of a shaman workshop. I had heard about their work and I might have even read something about it. But Mia was virtually "initiated". She had been on a retreat for a fortnight with a Peruvian shaman from the Sun Dancers. We decided to go to the room where we would get to learn a little more about shamans. There must have been nearly

50 of us and the room was pretty small. Mia and I ended up at the front quite close to the leader of the group. The man was, in fact, Swiss but he had spent years in South America and Tibet studying with shamans of various beliefs. After his introduction, he told us that we would have the opportunity, in this session, to discover our totem animal or rather that the animals would find the people. Now, that made us really curious. I loved my dogs and we had always had a very intense relationship and the same is true with my cats. "Are they perhaps my protectors from the others side?" I pondered, as the teacher had already begun to lead us in a relaxation exercise. He told us that the consciousness started to open up when an individual was in a state of hypnosis and it is then that we are able to tune into the vibrations of other beings and other consciousnesses. This was all quite new to me but I did everything that he told me to do. I let myself relax. There was silence for a while and nothing or no one appeared. And then, pop! There was a jump and a dolphin came out of the water. It tumbled in the air and then made a wonderfully elegant dive back under water.

I could feel the touch of the water on my skin but also the closeness of my brothers and sisters. My whole being was filled with a sense of joy as a dolphin. The contact that was just indescribable seemed so natural at the time. It was the harmony, helping one another and the sense of a shared goal. It was also a sense of lightness and the joy of the moment. I jumped out of the water again and it was as if my body was completely weightless and I flew just like a bird. I was high above the water and I twisted in the air, did a somersault before succumbing to the force of gravity once more and allowing myself back into the softness of the water. The others did the same as I did in perfect synchronization. If one was happy then all the others were happy. We were having something of a jumping competition and we each tried to outdo the show that the last had put on and our joy just multiplied. When we were eventually full of the joys of jumping, we began to swim. We swam under, over and around one another and tried out every possible variation. It was as if I had always known this sense of each and everyone looking out for the other: everyone looked after themselves in the same way as they did for the ones who were around them. Seeing the baby dolphins swimming alongside their mothers and rubbing up against them gave me particular pleasure. I could be somewhere where I was truly happy and in a space and environment with those whom I love and among whom I belong!

"Please start to make your way back to today's consciousness and into this place!" I could hear coming from somewhere far off in the distance but I didn't pay any particular attention to what I was being told. Another dolphin was just approaching me whom I particularly liked. It came over to me and touched me, and my whole body was electrified.

"Everyone, come back! Come back. Come back ..." echoed in my ears, preventing me from staying where I was and from where I really didn't want to leave.

The voice still had an effect on me and much more strongly than perhaps I would have liked. I could now feel the hardness of the seat and the weight of my body. I could feel the dryness of the air and the unpleasant smell all around me. The most disagreeable part of all of this was the isolation that I now felt from all the others. I was surrounded by people and they not only closed themselves in but also closed me and all the others out. I knew that I had arrived back in this body and into this consciousness, into this place, and it didn't please me in the slightest! Now everyone stood and tried to get out through the door to the room which seemed virtually impossible. There was a crowd on the other side of the door who were all keen to come in as they were all eager to attend the next presentation. Everyone seemed to want to sit in the best place possible and they pushed and shoved the one in front of them, while all we wanted to do was to get out. I let myself be pushed, prodded and elbowed by all these people who were so inquisitive and keen to learn. In my thoughts, I was still in that place where all the members of the group looked after, respected, protected and loved one another.

I was eventually pushed and pulled back out into the corridor because I still wasn't "in myself" in the same way that the others were. Thank God! Mia also pushed and shoved her way out and the minute that she caught her breath she said: "It's as if you're not here! Come on, let's go and have a refreshing drink!" and she whisked me away to find a drink. I simply drank and stayed quiet. "It was so great there!" The loudspeaker suddenly broke into my silence and my feelings: "The talk about dolphins living in the wild is just about to begin in such and such a room, including a film and a demonstration of work with dolphins and all the possibilities that it offers. Two ladies from Hawaii are going to share everything that they know on the subject."

I didn't know if I had heard well and whether I wasn't just "on my way home" again, so I asked Mia: "Did you hear what they just said?"

"Yes. Something about a film on work with dolphins is just about to start."

I grabbed Mia's hand and pulled her along with me.

"Come on. This is something that we just have to see! I'll tell you all about why when it's finished!" I answered as I rushed hand in hand with my brand-new girlfriend.

The film had just begun all about the islands of Maui and Kauvai where a group had gained a great deal of new knowledge via dolphins. They monitored their behaviour, the togetherness of the group and their movements, and they tried to sense their consciousnesses. They approached a family of dolphins with telepathy who took up contact with them. After that, the two women (they were both European) talked about the institute in Maui where they tried to make use of this knowledge and teach others. They had previously studied the Tantra and now they realized that the dolphins lived according to this in the water. They learned the movements from the dolphins and this is what they practised in the pool in the grounds of the institute. The work is referred to as Oceanic Tantra. They wanted to reach the sensation of ecstasy with this knowledge and they led us through an exercise in the room. We all stood together—men, women, old and young—and we tried to take up the harmonious and wave-like movement of the dolphins on dry land. I felt strangely shy and I was hardly able to move. I thought back to what I had experienced no more than half an hour before and the movement, lightness and softness and the electric, tingling shock that I had felt at the touch of another.

The presentation came to an end and everyone applauded and I just sat there staring at the images on the screen without saying a word. There they were still swimming wild and free, jumping in their togetherness: "my dolphin companions". As we left the room, we had the chance to give our names to receive a copy of the programme from the Hawaiian group. Mia and I both wrote our names down. "When will I ever make it to Hawaii to swim with wild dolphins?" I thought to myself as if it was some kind of unattainable dream.

Yet fate had different ideas and it was only half a year later that my dream came true and I was able to swim with the dolphins in reality—as a person—and learn from the members of the group in Hawaii what they had learned from the dolphins. I sometimes had the feeling that, although I don't live on the island as they do, it was still as if I knew a little more about these wonderful inhabitants of the world's oceans! But I didn't say a thing as I had travelled there to learn. Five days later, I made a decision; I left the group that split up that day. Up to that point, we had been on Kauvai Island and lived in tents on Secret Beach. We did a lot of interesting things but I had come for something a little different and I was sure of that. I simply followed my nose and the same day I went to Maui for two weeks. I learnt a fantastic amount and made very important friendships.

I was having supper one evening when I heard some very interesting music and I wanted to know straight away what it was and who was playing it. The owner of the restaurant was called Casanova (the same name had been given to the place) and he also said that it was the first time that he had heard the music and his girlfriend, who was sitting with him at the table, had composed it herself based on inspiration that she had received from the dolphins.

They invited me to join them at their table and they gave me a copy of the cassette that same day.

The month came to an end and I had to go back home to Zurich and see how my situation had changed with my husband. Nothing at all happened on the flight back other than that I drew further and further into myself.

The past was waiting for me back in Zurich. Nothing had changed in the slightest. I could remain just as I had been as a wife, in the knowledge that my husband had a girlfriend, but that seemed to be impossible. I suffered a great deal but I didn't know how to solve the situation. I only had faith in that my spirit friends would be able to help, and so I constantly prayed to them. My goitre grew and grew until it was nearly suffocating me. Sometimes, I could hardly catch my breath. And it was right in the middle of this atrocious period in my life that I received a gift that I had never expected.

Gerald and I had not really kept in touch over the years. I called him on the phone when I got home from Hawaii. I wanted to tell an old friend about the pain that I was suffering. He still remained my darling brother and secret love from times past. As we hadn't wanted to revive the past, we had gone our separate ways and led our own lives.

We met when he invited me to visit him in his new flat. All I could do was cry. He sat me in his lap, like I was his little sister, and stroked and kissed my head. I let him as I really needed to be held and loved. Somehow, I was able to calm down with the help of this familiar intimacy from the past. We decided to pick up on our relationship and continue our interrupted friendship. He also described the problems that he had been experiencing inside his present relationship.

We agreed to meet up again a couple of days later. There was to be a full moon and we were going to meditate on the shores of the lake. We said that we would meet at 7 am. It was glorious July weather. I quickly told Gerald all about my trip to Hawaii and all that I had experienced with the dolphins. We went to a nearby Mexican restaurant and then, when it was already dark, we made our way to the lake because the moon was now high in the sky. I was happy to be by the water and to be able to meditate with my understanding friend and brother. We had hardly put the blanket down when we felt the first raindrops. And, literally out of the clear night sky, a summer shower began to fall. We grabbed the blanket and ran with it over our heads to the car along with a whole crowd of other people made up mostly of young lovers. We were soaked to the skin by the time that we got back. It was my car and so I recommended that we go back to my place. We would be able to dry ourselves there and, as the rest of the family was out, it meant that we would be able to continue with our meditation there. It was also quite likely that the rain would soon stop and so we would be able to sit in the garden under the pergola for a little quiet reflection.

We were shivering with cold when we got back to the house. The heavens had opened by this time and lightning was crackling in the sky. What had looked like a brief shower was definitely going to last for a while. We could hardly wait to get our sopping wet clothes off, so when we arrived back, I ran to get towels and asked Gerald to try to light the open fire as there was always dry wood ready stacked by the side. I hoped that the heat of the fire would warm us through a little more quickly. I switched my Hawaiian cassette on which I had been playing constantly since getting back from my trip. The fire was now going strongly and the sound of splashing dolphins and inspirational piano music was flowing freely from the loudspeakers. We eventually undressed and dried ourselves with fresh towels when something completely unexpected happened. The glimmer within us both burst into flames again. We fell into each other's arms and everything else disappeared. I held my dolphin love close to me with my flippers and his touch sent my body into a state of scintillating ecstasy. We let the waves carry us away and our bodies moved with the ocean. We dissolved into one another in this reality of ecstasy and also into the waves, the ocean, the others, with everything which is kindness, love, acceptance and giving. The wave carried us further and further. A little later, I sensed that I was alone and it was no longer the soft water but the velvety carpet below my body. I opened my eyes and Gerald was lying beside me. He soon woke up again in his body, turned to look at me, smiled and held me in his arms.

"I could say what I have just experienced but I know that exactly the same happened to you too. I recognized you and found you again my dolphin love!"

It was getting late and he had to get ready to go home. I went and fetched a blanket for myself and carried on sleeping on the carpet which had been our soft seaweed that evening. I put the dolphin tape back in the stereo and I fell into a deep sleep to the sound of dolphin calls.

I didn't see Gerald again for several years after that. We both knew that what we had experienced was a one-off, that old memories had come to the fore and that if we had continued, it would have caused a great deal of pain. The joy stayed with us both in the memory of that marvellous evening.

It helped me to realize that I could love a man again just as much as I had loved my husband at the beginning and that the world was still full of wonders that I would be able to discover. My husband soon realized that he had been the one who had found a new partner for himself and it was he would have to leave the family home. Three months later and I was living alone in the house with my daughters and my goitre had started to go down a little.

I very much wanted to pass on what I had learned in Hawaii to my friends in Zurich and anyone interested in the subject. I received the film of the dolphin project from Maui and I showed it to the Parapsychology Society at one of our meetings. It raised a lot of interest. I wanted to know more about this and so I invited Kutira over from Maui to give a talk and hold a workshop. She was accompanied by Sophia who played the lute when Kutira sang in our workshops.

Nearly 400 people must have attended the talk and the list was soon full of those signing up for the weekend workshop. We were only able to provide places for 16 people. I introduced the talk and

I was delighted to see that so many people had an interest in the dolphin topic. This was back in 1990 when there wasn't so much information available on the spiritual strength and help that dolphins can provide.

A small group formed after the talk who still wanted to know more about the subject and a lot of personal questions and experiences were discussed. There was a very tall and inquisitive German guy on the course who said that he was also a member of a dolphin consciousness group back home and there were similar groups in Italy. They would camp on the beach from where they were able to make telepathic contact with the dolphins.

There was something disturbing and unpleasant in his personality. I couldn't explain why but I felt terribly uncomfortable in his presence. The dolphin workshop started two days later and I was sad to see that the German man was one of the participants. He was kind to everyone and wanted to be on good terms with us all and especially the women in the group, but he always seemed to go one step closer to people than they were really comfortable with. Obviously, he didn't notice this at all. Kutira ran the day perfectly and Sophia's lute playing and singing easily lifted us all up to a higher state of consciousness. There was an important exercise that we did on the afternoon of the first day. We lay in a circle on the floor with only our heads touching like a 16-pointed star and Kutira asked us to try and establish contact with the dolphins. A dolphin appeared to me within minutes and it brought a message. It told me to go and hug the person after the session who was in a line with my head. I should say "welcome" to him and this person would prove to be very important in my later development. I listened to what I was told and started to wonder who it could be who was in a line with my head. Then I suddenly thought: "I am willing to hug anyone at all but not that horrible German man!"

There is no need for me to say that he was the one and I didn't give him a hug but I kept a constant eye on him and wondered why he would be important in my development. In the last exercise of the evening, we made a snail formation and we wove ourselves together with everyone hugging the person next to them. Needless to say that he was the one who was hugging me! There was nothing that I could do about it because I was just one member of a group. I held someone in front of me and the German man held me from behind. I would have been sure to push him away if I'd had a spare pair of hands. However, I was left to put up with the situation against my will. I was convinced that I would feel repulsed but actually the opposite happened. There was a warmth and vibration radiating from him that I was completely unable to resist. His energy entered every bone in my body and every cell down to the last atom. I was unable to move as I made up part of this living snail formation and so I passively noted the changes that were taking place within me. His whole being dissolved into mine and I didn't know where I began and where he ended. I wasn't even able to concentrate on the person in front of me as all my attention was focused on the German man, whom I knew was called Johann. What I was feeling would have been pleasant if I had also wanted it but I was still fighting it. Kutira's voice woke me from my thoughts.

"Now turn out of the snail formation and turn back in to face the other direction." This meant, whether I wanted to or not, I would have to embrace the German man whom I simply couldn't abide. "Terrible!" I thought. The human ring began to move and turned to face the other direction and turned inwards again. I was faced with the German man whom I really didn't even want to touch. Unbelievable! Now I was giving out that warmth and softness that he had given off a short while before. Something changed and something affected me differently. The group broke the formation and we all sat around on the floor again and I was looking straight at that horrible man. His eyes sparkled as he looked at me and the light of happiness covered not only his face but his whole being. Well, that's just what I needed!

Kutira finished the workshop for the day and we all got ready to go home. Johann was by my side in a flash and he put his arms around me again but this time without Kutira asking him to do so and he whispered something in my ear!

"I've fallen in love with you!"

"Me too!" I whispered and I couldn't believe my ears. I didn't understand how this could have happened when I had so strongly rejected him, kicking and biting him in my mind and yet ... "Why did the dolphin want this? What do they know that I don't know?"

This was all too much for me, I was totally confused and we soon said goodbye and all I wanted to do was to go home and sleep.

The next day, the whole group sensed and knew that we had fallen in love. Everyone was pleased but I still didn't want to be pleased by any of this. That had also changed by the time evening came. I stopped fighting and my emotions broke through.

We went down to the lake after the course. We began to talk about what we should do about the way that we were feeling as we lived a long way away from one another. He smiled and said that was the least of our problems. I didn't understand what he meant by this. He said that he had been living with his girlfriend for years and they had a little girl who was just one year old. I started to get annoyed and asked how he imagined that we could have a relationship!

"We, that is Sabina and I, live in total freedom with one another."

"What do you mean by total freedom?" I asked back.

"Well, it means that we each follow our own emotions with no attachments."

"This means that you can have relationships with other people?" I asked.

"Yes, love can't be forbidden or tied down. When Sabina and I met we agreed to give each other total freedom. Our only condition was that we should tell the other if one of us were to meet someone and to fall in love."

"Do such things exist?" I carried on pushing but I had my doubts.

"Can't you feel that it really does exist?" he asked and laughed as he threw his arms around me.

"OK, OK. But what do you feel for Sabina?"

"I love her as well. She is the woman whom I live with and she's the mother of my daughter."

"But won't it be painful for her to discover that you have fallen in love with someone else?"

"I don't know why it's never happened before. I have been close to other women in the past but I have never fallen in love with anyone else while I have been with Sabina. It's only ever happened with you. She will understand because I didn't do this by choice. Love and loving is a gift that has to be accepted and no one has the right to forbid it."

"Hm. Well that's a totally new idea to me. I have only ever been able to imagine myself in a monogamous relationship up to now," I admitted. "So what you are saying is that you want to carry on living with Sabina but you want to maintain a relationship with me."

"That is all I desire! But could you imagine it? Could you accept that I am not entirely yours?" he asked.

"I can't answer that at the minute because this is all so unexpected. I have never thought about such a thing before as I would never have been able to imagine it. I have only got bad and painful experiences of such things."

I told him all about the last year of my marriage when I suffered so much because of my husband's girlfriend. I would have liked to come to terms with it, but it just didn't happen. I would have liked it if my husband's affair had not caused me pain but things worked out very differently. "Is this love that I feel for Johann a chance for me to realize that open relationships can really work without pain, jealousy and the constant fear of loss?"

I told Johann about all my doubts and fears and he said again: "Man has no right to forbid or restrict whom a person should love."

I didn't know what to say to that. He went on: "Sabina is coming back from her holidays tomorrow. She has gone to see her girlfriend in Holland with Suzi. I'll tell her everything right away and then I'll give you a call. But you can be sure of one thing: there is no way that I am going to lose you. The love that I feel for you is unique and I have never felt anything like this before although I always hoped that I would."

"You are going to say all of that to Sabina?" I was starting to panic.

"No, that is my secret. I will definitely tell her that I have fallen in love but I have no intention of mentioning that I love you more than I do her."

"Of course," I thought. "New love: fresh and fiery!" But I didn't say a word.

And so we parted with very different feelings and I could hardly sleep from the excitement of it all. Is it possible that we can love more than one person at the same time and that the other partner can deal with this feeling without any pain at all? I didn't know the answer but I was unsure about a positive result.

Johann called the following evening. He told me how he had collected Sabina from the railway station and his girlfriend asked him: "Have you met a woman who is older than you with light hair?"

"Yes," replied Johann. "But how do you know about that?"

"I dreamt it!" she replied. "I also sensed that you are in love. Is that right Johann?"

"I told Sabina everything about the weekend workshop and also about the fact that I have fallen in love so suddenly that I hardly noticed it myself!"

"Just like me," I thought. "The difference was that not only was I unable to come to terms with it but I couldn't actually stand you!" I finished my thought but naturally only to myself.

"Sabina asked me to organize a date with you as she would like to meet you."

"OK, I'll come over to your place. That would appear to be the simplest thing," I recommended.

I went to see them the following weekend. Sabina opened the door. An exquisite angel was standing in the doorway with little Suzi standing by her side. Sabina was about a head taller than me and must have been at least 180 cm tall if not more. She had long, blonde hair and bright, blue eyes. She was not only beautiful but she had an inner radiance. The little one looked just like a tiny version of her mother. The young woman embraced me and ushered me into their home. Johann took Suzi for a walk and left the women alone to talk. Sabina reinforced what her boyfriend had told me about their agreement. Her voice carried no tones of hurt, pain or jealousy and her whole being appeared to be free of such emotions. She also said that she loved Johann very much and had hoped that he would not fall in love with someone else. I took her words to mean that news of Johann approaching other women had never reached her before or the fact that Johann had never fallen in love before meant that she had never concerned herself with the subject.

Listening to her, I thought that this really was a new generation or perhaps I was hearing the voice of an especially big-hearted person. Sabina and Johann were both only 27 and I was already over 42. The thing that struck me most was that I didn't feel at all like an outsider or that I was interfering and nor did I feel any older. In fact, I even thought that they were more mature if all that they were telling me was indeed true. Sabina said that she wanted us both to try and reach an agreement on how we would manage our relationship now that there were three of us involved. The fact that we lived so far away from one another left no other option than that Johann should travel to stay with me at the weekends. Sabina agreed that Johann should spend every other weekend with me. We also agreed that we two women would also stay in touch and that if either of us should have a problem, then we should sit down and come to a joint decision on how it would best be resolved.

I listened to her and I thought how different this was that she accepted Johann's emotions and feelings compared to when I had discovered that my husband was having an affair. There I was, cut off and left alone with the pain and my fears. I was curious as to whether what we had come up with would work in reality. "Can I live like this? Can I deal with the fact that Johann lives with Sabina for two weeks and that he only sees me for a weekend every other week?" I was grateful to them for giving me the chance of trying out something new and real with them.

Johann came home during all of this and Suzi was tired so he put her to bed in the centre of the room on a sheepskin rug. We both sat on the floor and told Johann all about what we had agreed. He looked at us both lovingly and it was impossible to sense any difference in his emotions. We agreed to meditate before we parted. I closed my eyes and so did they. After a while, I discovered that the centre of the room was becoming lighter and lighter and that the four of us where enclosed in a tent of light that was protecting and strengthening us all.

Sabina came with me to the door and put her arm around me like an old girlfriend. But I also felt a deep love and sense of wonder for this radiantly beautiful young woman. She said: "You know, I wanted to get to know the woman whom Johann had fallen in love with. Now, I have met you, not only can I not forbid it, I can so easily understand why it is that he has fallen in love with you. I hope that the love I have for Johann will allow me to live with this and I will continue to be as happy with him as I have up to now."

I wanted much the same but I was even more curious to know whether it would work.

A rare and beautiful love affair began with Johann but there was something mysterious in it from the very beginning. It was as if the dolphin, that had asked me to embrace him on the course, had not only started something new but something that was limitless and indescribable. The first time that Johann travelled up to see me, and we could embrace once again, the same light appeared in us both that I had noticed when we had all meditated. The next thing I saw was a strip of light leaving my body and from above I looked down on two bodies holding and in love with one another. Then all I could feel was my body melting into the light. I have no idea how much time passed when again I felt myself approaching my body. The strip of light re-entered my body where it had left through the top of my head. Then another strip of light followed it and this also entered the top of my head. Then I was conscious again. I knew that Johann knew and sensed many things and so I asked him at once: "Did you notice something?"

"Yes, you suddenly left your body."

"Yes, and after that?"

"I saw you as a light something returning."

"Did you see anything else?"

"Yes, it looked as if you were being followed by another light."

"That's it! I saw it as well. What do you think it could be? I hope that a new little soul didn't come back down with me!"

"I think we should meditate and ask," he suggested.

It was as I had feared. A little dolphin being appeared and expressed its joy that it was going to born as a human. It also said that it had been close to me for a very long time and had hoped that it would be able to establish contact with me.

I was not only unhappy about this, I was very disturbed.

"No, that's impossible! I don't want another child and especially not now and not from Johann." I was in the middle of the divorce and I had been living apart from my husband for less than a year. I was just about starting to feel free and breathe fresh air. Johann loved me but he lived with his girlfriend and their daughter. "Impossible! I just can't accept this!" Johann had said that he would accept anything and it would make him happy if we were to have a child together. This little soul, which had just introduced itself and was still a dolphin, wanted to be born as a human ... and definitely wanted us to keep it but it trusted me with the decision.

I made contact with the little dolphin being again. I asked it to understand and accept that I was completely incapable of accepting it. Now it reassured me that everything would be fine and that this had been approved from above, otherwise it would have never been allowed to come down to me. It also told me that we would be able to speak to one another, as we were doing now, throughout the whole pregnancy. It would join me as we both experienced new things and acquired new knowledge.

"Perhaps I can believe all of this and I can see it actually happening but I am not strong enough! I am worn out. The last couple of years, with all the problems with my marriage and carrying my whole family on my back, have used up my last reserves. I can't fight now and accept the challenge of something new. I want to calm down, sort myself out and be healthy. Nor do I want to complicate my daughters' development with this relationship."

The little being explained again that it would cause no particular problem and all I had to do was to accept.

"No, I can't accept!" I responded.

"Very well. Then I am forced to accept your decision. Please relax and I will leave. I am very sad that you have decided this way but your decision is the important one!"

I closed my eyes and I not only relaxed but also prayed that this little soul would be able to leave and to be given another chance with another mother who would welcome it with love and open arms.

The light left as it had arrived, through the top of my head.

The relationship with Johann had lasted several months. There was someone who loved me and I tried to live freely with a person whom I loved. When we love we would like our lover's being to be ours and only ours for ever and ever. It had been the fracturing of this image that had caused me so much pain in the last years of my marriage. I knew from the very beginning of this relationship that I didn't want to keep or take anything. Still, I sensed the shadow of jealousy but I was able to deal with it.

Johann handled these two loves very interestingly. He said that when he was with Sabina and the little girl, he was happy with his family and could be there completely. In the meantime, he knew that I existed and that he also loved me and that we would soon meet again. I was curious to see how our story would go on.

I spoke to Sabina quite a lot on the telephone and she said that she was still happy and, if anything, she was happier as her partner now loved her even more. I was happy to hear this and I hoped that it was true. I received a call about six months later to say that they were going to be holding a course with an Indian shaman. I had an old girlfriend who lived in a little town nearby whom I was able to stay with and so I was happy to accept the invitation. I also wanted to see Sabina and Suzi again. I could hardly believe my eyes. In the time that I had been seeing Johann, this stunningly beautiful woman had lost an enormous amount of weight and was pale and weak. I waited for the break and I called her to one side to ask what was the matter. She didn't want to talk about it at first and she said that everything was fine. I asked her to tell me the truth and she broke down in tears and flung her arms around me.

"Dorothea, I'm so ashamed of myself! I didn't want it to hurt but still it hurts very much! I really can't cope with the fact that the man I love loves another woman. I would so like to be different and to be able to stick to what we decided with Johann when all this began and I don't want to own him and I would like him to freely express his emotions."

I listened to what she said with love and it hurt me too. I could feel that the same thing was causing her pain that had been so painful to me when I had found out about my husband's girlfriend. Even though the three of us had been honest and open from the very beginning, we were forced to realize that our idea and our attempt would not work. I didn't want to and I couldn't love if it meant causing pain for another person. Sabina said that Johann had loved her more and been much more sensitive towards her since he had loved me but that she had become more and more withdrawn in her reactions to him. She always thought that the reason her partner was happier was perhaps because he loved the other woman more than her. I told her to stand up for her feelings and not live her life the way that her partner wanted it. Johann had always said that he would never have any problem if Sabina were to have fallen in love with someone else. Sabina had thought the same but when it happened, the pain and the fear broke through which she had wanted to keep secret even from herself. She thought that she wasn't strong enough, and that she wanted to own, and wasn't capable of living in a modern relationship. I completely sympathized with her. I promised that although Johann and I would remain friends, that I would put an end to our intimate relationship. Compared to what this young woman had given me, this was the least that I could do for her.

Now I felt that I had not been possessive and unjust when I had suffered as a result of my husband's affair. I wanted to be understood and to be spared. Perhaps, despite all of this, there are relationships where one party can handle the fact that their partner loves another, perhaps more than they love them, and they can live with this. Sabina and I weren't like that.

Johann was outraged by our decision. He thought that we were both weak and not determined enough. I kept my promise to Sabina. Their relationship didn't improve after this but came to an end. Sabina soon moved out of their home and she realized that the agreement that had been reached with Johann didn't concur with what she really felt, and she had just tried to go along with the wishes of the man she loved. We met a few times after that. Her love for me had remained constant. In fact, she was grateful for the fact that she had been able to see her relationship and her feelings so early on. She has now found the partner who thinks and feels the same way that she does and since then they have had two little boys.

I stayed friends with Johann as we shared many interests and I also knew a number of his girlfriends but none of them was willing to accept his idea of open relationships.

After this, I was able to go back to my own, good, old idea: we have to love but when we can no longer love or we feel that we are not loved, we have to let the other person go.

I had a vision a couple of years later. My friends from above showed me a way of living in the future as part of a couple and part of a community where couples with similar thinking will seek the connection to allow them to form a new kind of community. It is possible that they will choose a simpler lifestyle which is closer to nature. In exchange for greater freedom, they would give up most luxuries and the opportunity to earn large amounts of money. Family will be important once again as will community. Each family will live in their own little house but there will be a lot of communal spaces where they can cook and eat together and they will raise their children together. By this I mean that the children live in a children's community within their own little families. They will spend most of their time with their parents but they will also have strong links with the other families and all the children will be able to move freely from home to home. Although the children will love and respect their parents, all the other relationships they have will mean that they will pick up fewer of their parents' bad qualities. They will know more individuals from a closer perspective and so be less dependent on their parents. These children will be also able to freely express their will because there will always be someone keeping an eye on them and protect them whenever necessary.

The adults live in pairs for as long as they love one another. Love and mutual respect are what attract them to each other. Faithfulness is natural. They don't need to swear an oath before man or God. They simply promise each other and themselves that they will love and help each other. If their feelings change, they are given help by the community. Their friends listen to them and give them advice. When their feelings completely alter, they separate but they remain within the community and they remain the most important figures in the lives of their children. This reduces the damage to their children to an absolute minimum or removes it altogether. The ones they love stay close to them and they do not have to experience any hate or scheming against one another.

After the vision finished, I thought: "Is this perhaps how the dolphins live? Is that why they are all so happy and helpful? Perhaps they live here in the ancient oceans in the same way that they live from where they were born."

"It would be so wonderful if we humans were able to live in such love, happiness and lightness. It would be fantastic if the vision were to ever come true!"

On the request of my students in Budapest, I finally gave my first dolphin course. Many of the participants were able to establish contact with the dolphins and they received a lot of information and a great deal of love from them.

Many felt high vibrations during the exercise and they hoped that they were coming closer to experiencing ecstasy. There were still secrets that I would have liked to pass on. I knew and I believed that a teacher is able to pass on what they know and have experienced to those students who understand. This is what it was like to experience ecstasy.

30

Ecstasy—the Body's Great Secret

My first experience is connected with Rhea Power and I experienced it in a dream. I had just finished my "lightworker" course with Rhea which had lasted a year and a half. She said that I and two others had matured to the degree that we should be initiated. I was delighted to be one of them but I can't remember who the others were.

Rhea showed which hill it was that we have to climb where the initiation was to be held. It was very high. "But I have to do this! I have to bear it!"

We climbed and walked for the longest time but at last we reached the summit. Then Rhea pointed down into the depths and she said: "Now you have to jump down from here!"

"Jump down into the depths? But I always thought that we had to reach the peak!"

"Yes you do, in order to jump off. To see if you dare jump off: that's the initiation."

"Well, no one has said anything like that to me!" I thought. Everyone had always looked up and said that if they ever reached those heights then everything would be solved. And now I was being told to jump off?

And anyway, if I had eventually reached this point, and it was not an easy journey, there was no way that I was going to climb all the way back down again. If Rhea had said that the three of us had reached the stage where we can do it then she must have known better than us what we were capable of. I took another look down into the bottomless depths. The worst that could happen was that I should die on the way down! I eventually decided that I was going to jump! So I jumped and waited to hit a rock or reach the ground and smash into 1,000s of tiny pieces. The sensation of plummeting like that was really unpleasant and I wanted it to come to an end. "I can feel that I've reached the ground!" Yet it wasn't the ground but rather water that I had fallen into. I carried on going down. I eventually came to the seabed and continued to sink into the sand but not so far. As I sank into the sand something opened up and I came into a very bright light and I wasn't only received by it but it melted me into itself and ended me.

When I woke the next morning and opened my eyes, I could still feel the infinite light in my whole being that I had experienced in my dream.

On another occasion, I had a similar experience but I was fully conscious with my eyes wide open. I felt a little strange in the evening and started to shiver. I thought I might have caught a chill and so I went to bed earlier than usual. When in bed, I thought that I might have a fever. I had more than a fever, the temperature of my whole body began to rocket to a dangerously high level. I lay in bed and felt myself becoming hotter and hotter. It felt as if someone kept throwing logs into a wood-burning stove. I had never had the feeling before of my temperature rising by the minute. The strange thing was that I didn't feel at all ill. I thought that I should get out of bed and look for a thermometer but I didn't seem to feel strong enough somehow. I must have had a temperature of 39 degrees Celsius by this stage and my body was on fire. I had only ever had a temperature this high once before but then I was seriously ill. I had been completely fine in the evening but my temperature had started to climb from the moment that I got into bed. I couldn't understand what was going on! But what happened next surpassed everything. My toes started to shake and then my feet. The shaking passed up my legs and into my thighs. The movement was totally rhythmical and it reminded me of waves in the sea. The rest of my body was soon to follow and now I was pulsing all over with an unknown force and there was nothing that I could do to stop it. My body seemed to move out of my control. It knew something that I didn't know. My temperature continued to rise and the rhythmic movement of my body from the tips of my toes to the top of my head grew faster and faster like I was a giant snake or a dolphin swimming at full speed. 1,000s and 1,000s of spasms passed through my body. When my temperature reached a certain level and my writhing reached a certain frequency, it was as if I had been struck by lightning and everything burst. I felt an enormous explosion but to the very tips of my hair and even in my fingernails. If I had to compare it to an orgasm then I would say the orgasm was a thimble and this was an ocean. Every cell in my body seemed to burst open with a sense of joy that was virtually unbearable and I flew out of my body and into, straight into, everlasting gloriousness. I could feel infinity where there is no duality only oneness, acceptance and love. I flew into and dissolved into the place I had always longed to be and I was no more. I no longer existed. I could have been in this state for hours when a decidedly less enjoyable thing happened: my body pulled me back. I couldn't do anything to stop this happening either. There was some law, some knowledge, that my body and my spirit knew but I didn't. Returning to my body, I still lay with my eyes open and I experienced my return with full consciousness as I had experienced my leaving.

My body had always known this thing that I had just experienced. I somehow remembered it and I knew that I knew of this. I searched for it but didn't know how I would find it. My body had let me into the greatest secret: the bliss of ecstasy. Completely consciously, alone and with no outside help from anyone or anything!

I also described this experience to my pupils. I told them that if I had experienced this, and it was in me, then it must also be in them and that their being must know this somewhere.

I didn't let everyone take part in the summer camp the following year. I wanted to protect myself and the others from unnecessary distractions. Only those were able to come whom I knew from my group sessions. I also set a very high standard. The aim of our camp was set in the title: "Through our hearts with the power of Heaven and Earth."

31

Something Has
Come to an End

This time we set out to familiarize ourselves with the power of the chakras at the camp. The aim was to feel the energy of the chakras through our hearts and to transmit them. I divided the seven energy centres over the seven days. In order to increase the pressure, we didn't practise the chakras one after the other but always from the opposite direction. We started with the highest which is a heavenly, spiritual energy and makes it possible for us to be incarnated onto the Earth that we might be born. The next was the first chakra which is the root chakra. Here, we looked at our openness to our life and our task on Earth. There were very few in the group who had a completely clear YES. If there isn't a strong, stable root, what will our body—the trunk of the tree—take nourishment from to allow the branches, leaves and flowers to grow?

And so we went up and down and down and up, from one day to the next and from one chakra to the next. The inner tension and the pressure grew and grew. But this could also be sensed in the energy of the group. I knew that when we reached the seventh chakra on the seventh day (that magical number 7!) then the energy would come bursting out that had been lying hidden in some for two years. This was negative energy like jealousy, discontent, envy, anger and revenge. I let the energy mount in the knowledge that it would eventually expel the alien and the impure. I also knew that those in the group who were really intent on working on themselves, and were not distracted by others watching them and possibly criticizing them, would be able to achieve great steps forward.

The spirits of the sky also lent a hand. They brought rain on the seventh day. I woke at 4.30 am and the rain was pouring down. This made it impossible to hold the morning meditation and the yoga class out in the open. We had been outside everyday so far and so we had never gone to the trouble of looking for another place in the building where most people were staying. There was plenty of space but we had to take all the furniture out and mop the floor in the big hall. So I went to all the rooms before the 5 am wake-up call and I told the first sleeping person that I came across that, although the rain was pouring down outside, anyone who wanted to could come out could do so and we would find a solution. I went out and I started to meditate in the area covered by the roof to the building. I was curious to see who would wake up of their own accord and so give themselves and the others the chance to join in the morning meditation and yoga session. At 5 am there was only me and another guy outside whom I had chatted to in some detail on the first day. He came from Germany and had been with us the year before as well. He had brought his son with him then but this time he came alone. He had become very close to one of the participants from Budapest and it was in this camp that their relationship deepened. The woman who reciprocated his feelings was the one who had run the afternoon yoga sessions this year and the year before. And now she was the one who was late and nearly missed all the exercises. In fact, she and the man in question hardly took part at all. I talked to them and said that if their new relationship was more important, they would be much better off leaving the camp. I said that I thought that they would have more than enough time to get to know one another better when the camp was over. Here they had the chance to learn more about themselves and about each other and this would surely help their relationship in the long run. Our "little chat" led to the woman taking offence and refusing to run the afternoon sessions. Her boyfriend, on the other hand, took my advice very seriously and, despite the way that his girlfriend was behaving, took part in all the programmes throughout the day. His girlfriend forbade him from carrying out exercises with anyone other than her. We could describe this as a private matter between the two of them despite the fact that she worked with the groups. But now that the work of the whole group was hindered, it pointed to her immaturity and egoism. Unfortunately, as we did exercises in a pair, I had to find someone else from the group to work with.

The exercise was forceful and energetic which meant that I had to watch all of the couples very closely. I went over to the woman who sat grumpily at the edge of the clearing and asked her to reconsider her position on all of this. I said that I would like her to come back to the group and practise not with her friend but with someone else. She still wasn't willing to take part. It was as if she was petrified at the thought of what her boyfriend was doing and what he might feel when working with someone else. She just sat and watched the group so I asked her to rather go back to her room because we really didn't need anyone sitting and watching us. She ran off crying and didn't show her face again all day.

The following morning, the German guy showed that he wanted to take part as he had sat outside before me under the porch for the early meditation. After a short time, the VOICE spoke again: **"Do you see how seriously they take the opportunity of the help that your work and that of the group gives them? They don't see, and they are playing with the situation. Neither they nor the situation has matured. They are just like children. All they want to do all day is to play in the sand. Then when they have to do something of their own free will, they run away and forget to take the step. It is a waste of your knowledge and time. Your work is done here for now. Go home and start writing your book!"**

I was sad to hear what the VOICE had to say; I had sensed and known this myself for weeks and months ever since I had started working regularly in Hungary. I did have very talented and some less talented pupils who put all their energy and will into their work. They were the ones to open up and blossom during this time. All the others just seemed to think that it was a good laugh to take part when so many people were talking about such things and it was even seen as being trendy.

When the VOICE stopped speaking, tears began to run down my face and down my dress. The heavens had been crying along with me since the early hours of the morning. In time, the rest of the people at the camp got up and about ten of them sat down to quietly meditate as they saw that I and the German guy had already completed our exercises. The others just slept on or made coffee to help them wake up. Breakfast came after the yoga. After the meditation, I told everyone that yoga would be after breakfast today as we needed to carry all the chairs and the tables from the main hall and we needed to mop the floor so that we could work in there.

I went up to the first floor and most of them followed me up. There was a German woman who had come for the first time this year. She knew of me from the work that I had been doing in Germany and she came along to learn more about herself through my work. She did this with the most incredible will and determination. I had only known her for a couple of months ever since she had been to a reflexology class that I had held. She had awoken immediately and wanted to know absolutely everything. She had been working up until then as an accountant in a large firm. Now, as I sit writing this, she has been running her own practise for six years. She came to the reflexology classes and repeated several of them and then went on to study natural healing methods at a school in Germany that put its students through very strict exams.

The hall really was packed with furniture but we still had two days to go and there was no other room big enough in the building which meant that we were left with no other choice than to empty it. The heavens continued to shed tear after tear.

Four or five people helped and I got stuck in too so that we would be ready in time for breakfast. We didn't see anything of the other 15 on the course. The odd face popped through the door to see if the room was ready yet, and when they saw that there was still a lot left to do they went back to have another cup of coffee! I was sadly silent and observed how this "day of the heart" was forming.

By the time we went to breakfast, we had unpacked the lot and only had the mopping to do. We only had the restaurant for an hour as there were other courses being held and other visitors staying in the wooden chalets. Two or three went off after breakfast to look for a mop and bucket to clean the floor in the hall. The staff still hadn't arrived at the guesthouse and so we were left to sort everything out ourselves. We used the hall as we were renting that whole part of the house. We had been outside for the rest of the week but it just happened to be that we were all pushed in together on this important day. The "day of the heart" slowly started to show its strength that we had been working on and building ourselves up to for nearly six days.

By the time that everyone had breakfast and changed for the yoga, the hard-working team had managed to mop the whole of the hall. The floor was still wet as we hadn't managed to find a dry cloth. People started to slowly turn up with their yoga mats. A couple even put theirs' down on the wet floor and sat down. Then two women appeared and announced: "But it's still wet, we simply can't work here!" This was despite the fact that several members of the group had now come back from their rooms with their own towels to dry the floor for themselves and for the whole group.

"We most definitely can work here!" I answered, seeing that the two of them were preparing to leave. "In fact, I am going to move the yoga to the afternoon and we are going to hold a plenary."

We normally did this after the morning break at exactly 10 am. It was then that we used to discuss anything and everything. I had asked everyone on the very first day not to discuss things or behind people's backs of behind closed doors but out in the open where we could all take part. I told them all to take these sessions seriously and be brave enough to express their opinions. It was an opportunity for a person to voice any problem that he or she might have and get input back from 30 or 40 people. There were one or two fallings out, and this time gave us all the chance to sort our problems out. There were several complaints about me and sometimes people would be unhappy about certain activities that had been held. I didn't generally express my opinion about anything and I let the group deal with the problem. The same had happened on the previous course when I had sent a man and his son home and when I had asked a woman whether she was sure that she wanted to stay there with us. The camp had been spilt into two factions on both of these occasions. In the case of the woman, she herself decided that she wasn't willing to remain in such a community where everything was set and pre-decided on her behalf. She had a particular problem with punctuality and that all participants had to take part in all the exercises and so on. She couldn't and she wouldn't accept this and that is why she decided that the place really wasn't for her. When the man and his son got sent home, I could see that people weren't able to fully appreciate the seriousness of the situation. I still wouldn't have been willing to take responsibility for them staying if every single member of the group had voted for them to remain. No one else was willing but then again, no one was aware of the risk that was being faced. They had no idea how serious it was to "sympathize" with what was being talked about.

The "day of the heart" plenary began. I could have cut the atmosphere and the energy in the room with a knife. The whole group was about to reach boiling point. The emotions rushed into one another within seconds and the energetic pressure of the last six days started to have its effect.

Those who had moved furniture and cleaned held the others responsible who had preferred to sleep and drink coffee rather than pitching in. They responded by saying that if they didn't willingly help then it was better that they didn't help at all.

"Then I am going to take it from here," I announced. "Who would have done it exactly? You? Then we really would have been waiting till bedtime!"

I had hit the nail on the head with the two women I had brought back from the door. They felt that my remarks were voiced directly at them.

"Especially if you treat us," they meant the two of them, "like someone talking to swine with pearls cast before them that they are supposed to swallow whole without knowing their value!"

They had summed up the situation in one. These happened to be two of the most sensitive people there but they weren't really so willing to work by themselves. They were full of anger and resentment because of their past and they didn't want to feel this way or they weren't able to let the feeling go. It somehow filled them and they were frightened that if they let it go, they would be empty and they would have nothing to take its place. I had spent a lot of time with them together and individually. I had established a very good relationship with one of them and we had often dined out and gone on trips to the theatre together. I really hoped that they would both be able to take the steps needed and that they would be able to deal with the tasks which they had been presented with. But unfortunately it didn't turn out quite like that. They announced that they had no intention of staying a single moment longer. Despite the fact that it was a plenary, no one said a single word either to support or criticize them. Everyone seemed to sense that their problems were largely related to themselves. The two women, seeing that no one was about to make a move, started to pack up their things.

I was the one to break the silence.

"I'm very sorry that you're really going to go. You really are faced with an enormous challenge and it is something that only you can do if you want to win through. Neither I nor the group can help you with this one but we are here for you whatever your decision turns out to be. I suggest that you both go out to the bathroom and take a good look in the mirror. And I want to ask that person who is making such a fuss here and is so full of anger and resentment, what is upsetting her so? Perhaps if you are able to identify with this individual, she will be willing to return here and to work on herself. If you leave now, you should know that this personality will leave but if you are able to return, another changed personality will ask for the group's help.

They left the room but they didn't return. However, the group itself was transformed. What these two women couldn't do could be done by the other members of the group. They all put everything forward for this day and were willing to do everything needed to move on.

It was a joy to behold. They were like warriors who had committed themselves to doing whatever it took to achieve victory. They were willing to change themselves, conquer their negative emotions and fears. I led my little group to victory with hope in my heart. Many became ecstatic during the course of the day and some even had visions. There were a few who were able to establish contact with their spirit leaders and others who contacted angelic beings.

The surprising and fascinating thing was the experience of one young man. This was also connected with me.

I had known him for about six months, through a friend who had taken part in the previous camp, and now he was here again. But he only stayed for the first couple of days as he had to leave because he said he had "pressing commitments". He was an actor and a dubbing job had come up that he wasn't able to move. He had so wanted to take part in this "heart camp" but fate had decided otherwise and his place was taken by his friend. He had been the previous year with his old companion with whom he had lived for years in a deep and very close relationship.

I had only known about the change in his relationship for about six months. He had invited me along with several other members of the group to a theatrical production where he was playing the lead role. He had reserved great seats for us all. I had never seen him act on stage before despite the fact that I had known him for about a year and a half. While we were waiting for the curtain to come up, I sensed an eye watching me from behind. I looked behind me to the left and saw a pair of dark eyes staring at me from about three rows back. I didn't recognize the face but I did know those eyes! Then the curtain went up and the play began and I was left with no time to think anymore about the eyes and where I might have known them from.

I stood chatting to my friends in the interval before running to the dressing rooms to congratulate my actor friend. We had all arranged to meet later on in a local restaurant and he gave me a knowing smile saying that he had a surprise for me that he would bring along to the meal.

It was a complete surprise. He stepped through the door of the restaurant with the selfsame young man whose eyes I had seen in the theatre. As chance would have it, the owner of the eyes happened to be my friend's new great love and he sat in the chair next to mine. Now he was close, I had an image form in my mind of where I knew him from in the first place.

He had been a terrifying priest from the Inquisition. I saw him in a hooded robe with those great, dark eyes of his that had radiated pitilessness and hate. He had wanted to destroy everything that was bad and that was heathen. This was all supposedly in God's name and with the help of faith. I couldn't swallow a morsel of my meal. He seemed to be watching me the whole time. What was it that he sensed? Why had he been watching me in the theatre? Did he remember something or was there someone who I reminded him of?

We got to know one another and each asked questions about the other. He knew a lot about me and about my work. He, on the other hand, had come as a total surprise to me. Now I wanted to know from him whether he was involved in spiritual matters.

"No, this is all new to me!" he answered. "It was my boyfriend who asked me to get involved and I have tried to meditate but only the once."

His face suddenly altered and I could see either fright or stubbornness in his expression.

"And how did it go?" I asked and I was mainly interested in finding out why his face had changed in the way that it had.

"It was terrible and I never tried again!"

He said it in such a way as to communicate: I don't want to talk to you or to anybody else about this and I want to forget about it forever!

I accepted this. His face was saying just the same. He had opened a door, seen something that had scared him and had decided never to go back there again and he had locked the door firmly shut.

The thing that I noticed was that I could read his every thought. Perhaps I had known him for a long time and that was why I could sense what he was feeling.

We ate while we chatted and joined in the conversation that the others were having but the robed monk kept reappearing in my mind.

We found ourselves standing next to one another at the end of the party when everyone was leaving for home.

"Strange, but I feel as if I know your eyes from somewhere! There has been a robed monk around you all evening!" I told him. Terror filled his face and his eyes seemed to virtually burn into mine: "Terrible! Can you see it as well? The robed monk is the exact reason that I daren't sit down and meditate again! The first time I tried it and my boyfriend showed me how to relax my mind and my body, he suddenly stood in front of me with horrible, hate-filled eyes.

"Yes, that's exactly how he appeared to me." But I didn't dare tell him that those were the eyes that had been looking at me in the theatre.

Then he seemed to want to make friends with me and to be close to me. We had a shared secret. For now, only the two of us knew and had seen the robed monk. He hoped that, by getting to know me, he would be able to find out more and possibly even free himself from this spirit being.

And that is what happened. He really wanted it to happen and he did all that he could to make it happen. I already had much more information but I didn't want to burden him with this and I wanted him to wrestle with his dark past that was following him.

He met the robed monk on "the day of the heart" and so did I. I was watching the group to see what was happening during the meditation. The guy started to suffer terribly. He went into a trance and I knew that the other one was now showing him his past lives. I saw it too and I experienced it along with him.

I was a woman whom they had locked in a cell and they continuously tortured. My crime was that I heard a voice and I had dared to tell other people. This had reached the ears of the Inquisition. They had dragged me off and they were using all the tools at their disposal to make me swear an oath of allegiance to Satan and to admit that I was working for him and that he was the owner of the voice.

I protested at the beginning: "What you say is impossible! I only ever hear the voice during prayer or reflection. When it speaks everything becomes light and I no longer feel my daily burden, my infinite poverty and just happiness and love. I have never said anything other than this must be what heaven is like if ever I finish this sad life on Earth." They claimed this was exactly how the devil manifested himself: promising everything beautiful and joyous. As I admitted that I had received all of this, it was taken as proof that I had surrendered to the prince of darkness. They tortured me with every tool they had at their disposal. I no longer resisted and I could now feel no pain. All I had to do was to close my eyes and I could see that I was soon going to be arriving home. The monk really despised me. He secretly hated me because I had faith. Now the past opened up before me and I saw his eyes as they kept constant watch through the keyhole in the cell door. I closed my eyes and I didn't open them again in that life.

On hearing of my death, the monk was infuriated because he had lost something and they even violated my dead body. I saw all of this before I finally left.

The boy was experiencing all of this now and he was really suffering. He recognized the tortured woman in the cell as being me. The "film" finished for me but it continued with another part for him. He was sitting in the theatre in the audience. The curtain rose and I was sitting on a throne surrounded by a crowd of happy people. I beckoned from the stage for him to come and join me. He protested at first and said he really had no business up there on the stage with all those happy "actors". The others urged him to join them and my constant reassurance eventually saw him come and join us. To his astonishment, his other, old self appeared from behind the curtain from the other side. He accused this individual of never leaving him alone and constantly disturbing his peace.

I joined the conversation from the throne: "Have you asked him why he follows you everywhere?"

"No!" he replied.

"Well, ask now then!" I suggested.

The hooded being fell crying at the feet of the other and asked: "Why won't you forgive me?"

My friend yelled back with hate and indignation: "Because I can never forgive you for what you did!"

I joined in again: "Are you really sure of that? Look around on the stage! All these people are your old victims and they have all forgiven you. But now a part of your today is still not able to accept what your old self did and you are the one who is not willing to forgive!"

He looked at me in disbelief and he could sense that what I was saying was all true.

"What about forgiving yourself, here, today along with the rest of us?"

"I really don't know if I'm capable of doing such a thing, though I would like to!"

A new individual appeared between the two of them. It was his higher consciousness and it said: "And if I were to help you?"

"I would like to try!" And now he was in tears but we heard the words he spoke to the robed monk: "I have been unable to forgive you so far, to forgive ourselves."

The image blurred and the three beings became one who went through an initiation. The words and the melting together of the three beings opened a door which I, as an old tortured victim, opened for him. He was able to enter the place for a short while which I had seen in that life and the reason that he tortured me was because he also wanted to go there.

He was now in light and love and he wept with joy as he told us all this in the group and we all cried along with him.

The whole group wept. Something had come to an end. An opportunity had been presented that it was possible to achieve if a person put everything they had into it. The others were crying because they hadn't dared or hadn't been able to do the same and now the chance had passed.

The next day was the last day. Everybody joined in with all their joy and all their sadness and we celebrated the whole day long. Based on their requests, we repeated all the best-loved yoga and meditation exercises and we ate lunch at a good restaurant nearby rather than in the guesthouse. Then we went to the playground and bathed and generally enjoyed each other's company.

The group decorated the hall in the evening and I wasn't allowed to see it until it was all finished. Everyone received a gift from someone but they didn't know from whom. They drew them in a raffle. I also received something from all those who had attended.

I cried and we all cried with emotion and the pain of having to say goodbye as I had explained that morning what the VOICE had said to me when the seven of us had sat outside under the porch for the morning meditation.

The other camp also came to an end. I received very pleasant news of the young man a little later. He had grown rather close to a lovable woman on virtually the last day. She lived alone with her son. They soon grew inseparable and they realized that they had a great need for one another. They married and they had a son who would be his father's teacher for the rest of his life.

The short-lived homosexual relationship had been a very important period in his life. Not only because this had meant that he had been able to meet me and to come along to the camp, but because he had lived as a religious priest in many of his former lives and only ever with men. His past as the robed monk, however, had closed his heart. His enlightenment had brought healing. He then went on to find a welcoming and loving individual and he became a happy and proud father and husband.

I hoped and I went on to hope that maybe another miracle would happen! Grace from the heavens?! Despite my bad experiences, I really did want to give more to all those who had given so much of themselves.

The words of the VOICE echoed in my ears: **"They have not fully matured and the situation is not yet here!"**

My money was starting to dwindle in the bank but I still had another six months to go! So I kept on hoping.

I carried on visiting every month and teaching and taking groups. I was invited to other towns and this is how I ended up in Sopron where my father organized things with his friends from the Reiki Society. But I also made it as far as Debrecen and several other smaller towns. For some reason, the "House of Light" or the "Light Centre" just didn't seem to be getting off the ground.

A lawyer friend prepared the legal paperwork for the "Light Centre" as a charitable foundation. The main thing that was missing was premises to be able to heal, teach and help people. This would require money. That was what I was waiting for, and despite many promises, the money just wasn't coming forward.

By the end of the year I was forced to realize that there was really nothing left to do but up sticks and—as the VOICE had said—return home and invest all my energy into the writing of my book.

My friends and pupils threw a small party for me before I was due to leave at Christmas. Masses of people came along to the last meditation session and only those stayed behind who had been through so much with me over the previous two years, and they were the members of the small group and those who had attended the camps.

The phone rang and someone picked it up and they beckoned for me to come because they didn't understand what was being said on the other end of the line.

It was a German friend who had called me in Budapest after not being able to get hold of me back home in Zurich. He hadn't known that I was in Budapest and all the people from the camp were with me.

"I was really desperate to get hold of you. I have had a really important dream. A light-being appeared in my dream and very seriously said: 'Do you no longer recall why you had to go to Hungary and take part in that camp? You went to meet Dorothea and to donate your money to the "Light Centre!" That was your task! Why have you forgotten this?'"

I didn't know whether I was dreaming or whether what I was hearing was real. Hope had arrived at last, just as I had hoped. He went on to say: "You know that Yesudian and Elisabeth Haich were both my teachers too and I really would have liked to follow in their footsteps. You are the one who wanted to take their spirit back to Hungary once more and that's what you told us at the camps. I have had enough of success and making money. I am going to sell my businesses and my property and I am going to help you establish the 'Light Centre' in Hungary."

This all sounded quite unbelievable but every word was true! A miracle had arrived at last! I had been helped again!

The group were delighted and the farewell party turned into a massive celebration. The following day, I extended my rent on the flat by three months and agreed to give three courses in the country. But what happened after that really was inexplicable. Our German friend, and I can finally write her name down: Gottheil, didn't call again for the whole three months. The folks from the camp told me that his new Hungarian girlfriend had gone out to join him in Germany and they had spent their first Christmas and New Year together in Israel. He hadn't been in touch and I had taken a loan from the bank. I couldn't wait any longer. I threw the few things that I had into the back of my car and I left Budapest. I had become ill during the three courses that I had taken on and I was running a fever by the end of the third one. So, I finally left Budapest.

I didn't hear any more of Gottheil for another six years. He had promised something to the light-being in his dream but he had promised the very same to the lot of us in Budapest. He really should have contacted me. I knew that he kept in touch with others from the camp but I really didn't want to disturb him. He was the one who should have known what he had promised and why he hadn't eventually kept his word.

Well, that's what I thought!

He phoned this year to say that he wanted to talk. True enough, he had also phoned three years before and said exactly the same thing and we had set a date when I was to have a little free time. He had planned to come to Zurich to discuss a few things with me. He didn't arrive at the agreed time but nor did he get in touch to say that he wasn't coming. He didn't phone afterwards either to offer an explanation.

I was intrigued to hear that he wanted to talk to me again. I said that I had been waiting for a good three years and he promised to come and see me this time. He seemed surprised and said that he didn't remember anything about any meeting. He managed to make it this time and he travelled several 100 kilometres to chat with me for no more than a couple of hours. By the time he arrived, he remembered that he really had planned to come and see me three years before but he couldn't seem to recall why he hadn't come in the end. He had even less idea as to why he should have forgotten.

He told me that he felt as if he was waking from a long sleep. I just listened to what he had to say because I was curious why he had finally come all this way after six years. He said that he had nearly sold all of his businesses and now he was trying to get rid of the last property and that he wanted to invest his money in something new and something spiritual. I gently reminded him of the dream that he had told me about six years before when he had called me in Budapest. The whole group had heard him when he had told me what he had promised me and also what he had promised the light-being.

He stared at me with great wide eyes. "That's so odd! I had forgotten all about it but now you tell me, I can recall the whole dream. But how or why did I forget all about it? I used to be quite proud of my memory and now it turns out that I forgot something really as vital as this!"

He also talked about the fact that he had been talking to a group over the last couple of months who wanted to build a "Light Centre" and he had promised them that he would provide the financial capital.

I just sat and listened. Just who was it who had made him forget his dream and his promise about the *Hungarian* "Light Centre"?

The thing reached a peak when he named the German town where the centre was to be built. I had finished working there the previous week after ten years, so that I would be able to dedicate all my time to writing my book. Then Gottheil asked me if I would be interested in teaching in this centre.

"I really can't answer that now. The most important thing for me at the minute is to finish my book. I really can't say what will happen after that! I can sense something, some decisive change, approaching. My book will be a turning point and not only for me. They have always directed me from above and it would seem that they now want something new for me. I can sense it but I haven't yet received the message. The only thing that is important at the minute is to finish my book or rather OUR BOOK."

32

Keeping
My Promise

Yes, I think that I have done and I do all that I have promised. But whom had I promised and where? What cause has my life served so far and become the contents of my book?

I didn't put this question to myself: it was my 13-year-old daughter, Toncsi. My ex-husband had moved out about a year before and I was trying to create a new household with my girls despite all the painful memories.

I was clearing up in the kitchen after lunch and my daughter Toncsi was standing next to me. I could sense that she wanted to ask or say something. It wasn't really like her to help me in the kitchen without being asked. "Tell me Mummy, what's your goal? What is it that you really want to achieve?"

I didn't know what it was that she really meant and I thought for a minute to work out what it was she was actually asking. She continued: "We all feel so much better now that Papa has gone. He wants to build his career. Finally, Claudia and I aren't stuck between two points of view. You have chosen a spiritual path. But what does that really mean? Where will it lead you and what do you want to do with it?" she asked again.

"Good question!" I answered. "I can't give you an exact answer to your question now. What I have realized so far is that something is missing from my life and that it should include something else. It didn't make me happy to be just a housewife and a mother and so

I have started to look around to see what it was that was missing. I would have liked to travel down this road together with Papa but he chose another route as you know. But I have never put your question to myself before."

My daughter had to go back to school and I was left alone at home with her question in my head. I wanted to know the answer to what she had asked immediately. I lay down under the pergola in the garden, on the grass, and I asked this very important question: "I want to know why I do what I do and what my aim is with all this." The question must have been very timely because the film soon started to roll and the answer appeared.

I saw the preparation for my present life and my current incarnation. I was living in a higher place and I had a role there as a teacher and a leader. I was entrusted to look after a large family, though not in the earthly sense. I could see myself and I appeared to be very excited. I had just come back from an important discussion and meeting with eminent leaders as well as even higher scholars, holy beings and angels. Their knowledge and level of advancement was demonstrated by the strength and magnitude of their light. I told my family the reason for my great excitement: "I am to return to the Earth once more!" Everyone was amazed.

"But you don't need to go back down there again!"

"No, but I can go down if I want to. The leaders have just told me that a very important era is about to begin on the Earth. The opportunity for development is vast but so is the risk of loss. They asked who was willing to take part and help out. I volunteered and I am happy to be able to take part in such important work. I can hardly wait to leave!"

My family was saddened by the news of this unexpected turn of events in our lives. They spoke for a while and then approached me.

"We have decided that we are all going to go with you to help you and to help everyone else!"

I was happy at what I heard but they had warned us all about the possible dangers of what we might face. I was proud of my family for doing what I had taught them to do.

"All for One and One for all!"

We all started to prepare as none of us knew when we would have to leave. I went to a spring that bubbled out of the hillside. I drank from the waters and there were also those who wanted to take water away in bottles that would later provide us with replenishment and protection.

I selected from my books. I would have liked to have taken them all with me. I was getting happier and more and more excited. The possibility that the higher beings had described to me had completely electrified me. I wrote down on a piece of paper my most important thoughts: what it was that I would do and have to do and solve.

I could hardly pick all my books up and I slipped the piece of paper into one of my books when I was standing on the starting line. Those travelling to Earth were lowered in individual cabins. I would liken them to cable cars that run up the sides of a mountain. These "cabins" were also lowered on cables but here the cables were invisible, although they still acted as a link between the two worlds. The little cabins stood waiting to leave along with me and my little family full of hope and curiosity. Who would arrive where and what life was awaiting them? How were we going to recognize one another? Was everyone in the family really going to be capable of solving the problem and return back home?

We all knew that it was a really big challenge and so was the danger. Despite this we were still all full of the joy of the work that we would have to do and the help that we would provide. We would be helping those below, finding and supporting each other and hopefully achieving the aim that we had been sent down for. We would do our absolute best.

I was getting more and more excited. "When can we go? When will I eventually be able to go?" I held my books and my knowledge close to me. There was an empty cabin standing open right in front of me. I stepped in and out of it. I knew that the time only came to eventually depart when the driver of the little cabin arrived. But the drivers (guardian angels and guardian spirits) were nowhere to be seen. They were also preparing, receiving final information, protection and energy just like we were. They were to invisibly accompany us and to watch and protect our steps. They wouldn't be able to get involved in our work but they would run to our aid if we asked them to. The higher beings would help us as well but they would not be coming with us. We would have to contact them if we required help or further directions of any kind.

The being is closed into the cabin which is about to be sent down to the Earth and their protector accompanies them on their journey, though on the outside of the cabin. The cabin itself was invisible but could be seen on a different energy level.

I kept on walking in and out of my cabin because I knew it was mine as I was the leader of my little group and so I was to leave first.

My excitement caused an unbelievable reaction. The process started all on its own without permission ever arriving. The energy radiating from my excitement was strong enough to close the door of the cabin tight. My guardian spirit ran over in panic when he saw what was going on.

"Your excitement has set the whole thing going before its time!" he shouted. "I can't go down any earlier because I'm not allowed. I will leave as soon as I can when the time and permission arrive. This will be the time that you should have left. You have got yourself into a lot of danger as you are going to be on your own for a while. You must remember that I may arrive late but I will be coming after you! The other thing is that you shouldn't be frightened by what happens on the way down as you are going to forget everything!"

I only picked up the last messages that he sent on my way down to the Earth because my cabin was now headed down with no protection.

"Well, I've done well! No guardian and no leader! It is just as well that I prepared so thoroughly!" I thought. Even still, the thought that I was going to be on my own for a while did disturb me. But that's what happened. I had started something going with my own impatience and now I had left before my time.

My cabin started to accelerate and I could feel the pressure building all the time. It started to really pick up incredible speed and passed through a long dark tunnel where a power appeared that was something like a wind. I was thrown to the side of the cabin to the point that I nearly fell out. I was horrified when the wind blew the golden papers from my hand on which I had written my notes.

"Terrible—and now this!" And all of a sudden, I had arrived on Earth and I realized that I had forgotten everything. When all the papers blew out of my hands in the tunnel, I was suddenly terrified that I would forget the job that I had to do. "Me here?" I thought. "Now I've gone and made my life really difficult. I have forgotten virtually everything." All I knew was that I had come from somewhere and that I had a job to do and I could hear echoes of "be careful, you will be without a leader for a while and the most important thing is not to be afraid!" But I couldn't remember where I had come from, who my leader was or what job it was that I had to do. And I couldn't even read my books that I still huddled to my breast.

I knew that I had an enormous problem facing me. First of all, I had to cast my mind back and try to recall my job and my goal. I knew that I had lost my notes in the long dark tunnel. My first thought was that I would have to go back. And now I looked around for the first time to see where it was that I had arrived. It was similar to a place that I somehow knew. It seemed so familiar. There was much less light here and everything had been flooded in light there. These are my last fragments of memory.

I was surrounded by beautiful scenery and rolling countryside. I saw a long line of people and I set off towards them. I saw that the people were stepping out of their cabins and all joining the long line. I tried to look and see what they were waiting for. When I got closer I could see that they were getting into new little cabins and these cabins were being lifted up to a higher place on a cable that I could now see. I watched to see what was going on.

So the beings were coming down from this high hill only to join a queue to be lifted back to the high hill. "So why did they come down in the first place? There's no point to this at all! I am definitely not going to do that!" I knew that I had come down with a mission and I had written it down, but all had been lost when I had bashed against the wall in the dark tunnel because I had been so frightened. I knew that I must get back to the tunnel because I couldn't remember anything without my papers! I could see that both the cables disappeared into the same tunnel. I knew that I had to go over there and see what exactly it was that had frightened me so much and caused me to forget everything. I set off towards the hill on foot. I reached a little house on my way. I thought that I might as well go in and see if I could find any further information. There was no one else there except for me and all the rooms were empty. There were photos on the wall in the last room. "I know these people! These are my husband and my little daughters!" Something started to clear in my mind. I knew that I had written that had to meet up with the members of my old family. It would seem that I was going to marry one of them which would mean that the other two members of the family could then be born. I was happy as I started to remember! I could see a picture on the wall of someone whom I didn't appear to know. It was a picture of a woman who wasn't a member of my family. "But what is her picture doing next to the one of my husband?" I knew. I remembered that she was the one who would one day take my place next to my husband.

I had hardly completed my thought when everything, including the house itself, disappeared. Then all I could see was a path leading up the side of the hill. I spent a lot more energy on the last part of the journey because now something had begun. My memory had started to return. There was another house with its doors and windows wide open. There was a woman inside who looked a lot like me and the whole room, even the windowsill, was full of valuable things. (What people consider to be valuable things.) There was a lot of gold and precious stones as well as very intricate jewellery. I could also see that there were thieves circling around the house. There was a particularly suspicious man among them who approached the woman with a broad smile on his face. I could see that his real face was covered by a mask. I couldn't see who he really was. I could see that the woman was me and that she couldn't see that the man was wearing a mask from where she was standing in the room. I couldn't warn her. Then my two daughters arrived as adults. They walked into the room and warned the woman about the danger of the man (who had now disappeared). They took the valuables off the windowsill and closed the windows. "Well, that ended well," I thought. Then everything disappeared again. I could see my two adult daughters again and this time they were helping by the cabins. There was some kind of transfer taking place and they were the leaders. It seemed that some cabins had arrived that had lost their strength on their journey and they were helping but I couldn't see how this was happening exactly. I was certain, however, that my daughters were adults. They had given me advice and had warned me of my blind faith, of danger and my over openness. Great! This is what had been written! I was to raise them until they would be able to offer me advice. Then they wouldn't need me any longer. I could see that they were now working to help spirits on their way home.

Then I realized that this place, where my daughters were hard at work with the passengers in the more comfortable cabins, must be some kind of gravitational point. I couldn't go any further either. My breathing became very strained and my body started to get heavier. "I can't go on!" I sighed.

"Yes, you cannot go on from here as a person with your usual human being," I heard the answer.

But who could have answered? I looked around. I couldn't see anyone nearby. "That must be my leader! It must be my spiritual leader! He has arrived!" I could remember that he had set off late, or been held back for some reason. Then I remembered that he would come as soon as he could and that I would be on my own for a while. Yes, this had something to do with the job I was to do. "I have to do everything without remembering a thing and being separated from my spiritual leader!" Now I started to remember and to recognize my leader and to ask him to help me. And so I asked: "How am I going to continue from here?"

"You know! You should remember this! But first look behind you!" he said. There was a massive crowd and 100s of people were following me up the hill.

"Now I remember! I remember this part as well! To find a new way, to lead by example and then they will follow."

"Yes, that's right!" said my leader. *"And now try to recall how you can move higher if it won't work as a human."*

He asked a good question because now I knew the answer: "I have to change into a bird and I will fly as a spirit with all the other spirit beings."

"That's it!" said my leader, overjoyed, *"and now take a look back!"*

Suddenly, the crowd behind me had all altered into birds.

I knew that this was written down as well! "Free the spirits in people and fly on the spiritual path."

I was now flying at the front and I knew that I had come to be a leader. I knew that if I did it, if I dare do it, then my followers would do the same. "Now I remember everything!" I thought as I flew. We glistened in the sky. The enormous flock of birds soared with outstretched wings and flew higher and higher. I suddenly started to feel heaviness again and so did the others. "We can't go on flying like this."

"We just can't fly on!" I said to my leader.

"No, you can't fly any further than this!" my leader agreed.

"Then what should I do?" I asked. I was starting to feel rather frightened as I could see the flock hardly moving in the air behind me.

"You remember!" I heard my leader say.

"THAT'S IT. That's IT! That was the goal!" It all came back to me now: "Remember where you came from, where you belong and you have already arrived home. In fact, when you truly remember you will KNOW that you never left in the first place. Only a little part of you went to learn something and to do a job. But my SELF was always THERE in the true HOME."

Now I could clearly remember my task, what I had taken on and what my mission was. I wanted to remind people of this who had faith and who had started to remember for themselves. I wanted to show them the way home so they could also reach home themselves.

As I sit writing my book, so many things are starting to spring to mind. In 1989 the VOICE told me that Hungary would be free and that people would long for the spiritual life. **"Then you will return home and give back to your roots what you still owe."**

"Can roots be above, and if so, what of my promise? I am on my way with my group! I will do all that I can for my roots on Earth, for my mother, my father, my homeland."

And here is a vision that I saw several times after 1989. Have I also managed to solve this? Light advertisements of Liberation Square! The "House of Light", "The Light Centre". It was all in the name of Yesudian and Haich and a continuation of their work.

The first thing is that I should never have worked for the Spiritual Investigators as that window looked out on a side street and not on Liberation Square. So I started to teach independently in the spirit of Yesudian and Haich. I was the one who promoted Elisabeth Haich's book, "Initiation", published in Hungary after the change in regime and I recommended it to András Novák, the leader of Sweetwater Publishing, and secured the agreement of the author. I was also able to take part in great honour and recognition in terms of Yesudian.

I came across important information while the book was being published. The publisher provided me with several copies of the work after it was published as thanks for my recommendation and help. I planned to give my parents a copy, have one for myself and give one to Auntie Erzsi.

My father read the book and the next time we met he said: "We used to know the Haich family really well. You could say that they owe their lives to your grandfather!"

"What? What are you saying? What did my grandfather ever have to do with the Haich family?" I asked, now very curious indeed.

My father told me that my grandfather used to work on the railways as an engine driver. Back then the Sopron railway was owned by the Sopron-Ebenfurt Corporation. Mr Haich was not only the director of this company but also an important shareholder. Mr Haich was Erzsébet's father. When the Soviet Republic was declared in Sopron, my grandfather was made director of the railways. He saw it as a great honour and he was a strict but just man. He had learned a lot during his time as the leader of a Hussar brigade during the Great War when he had spent a long time out of the country. He had told my father a lot about these times when he was a child. He was proud of his battle history in Dalmatia.

The short period of the Soviet Republic saw the poor oust the rich from their homes and from their land and they took everything for themselves. It wasn't wise to try to resist them in any way. The Haich family were also chased from their home and put before the Soviet Railway Court. My grandfather made a speech in their defence.

"Mr Haich cannot be held responsible for being born a wealthy man but the fact that his is a just and good man has done a lot. While I hold responsibility here, no good man shall be harmed. Go back to your home as you have always treated the workers well."

A couple of months later everything had changed: now it was my grandfather who stood before the court. This time Mr Haich spoke in his defence. He said virtually the same as my grandfather had said of him: "Mr Farkas cannot be blamed for having been born a poor man. However, he can be held responsible for being a good worker as well as an honest and just man." Then Mr Haich added: "He came to our defence when emotions were running high. I would like to express my gratitude and respect to him and invite him and his whole family to join us at our summer home on Lake Balaton."

It was something of a fairy tale for a director to take a holiday with an engine driver but that's what happened!

My poor grandfather was a victim of his work and the coal dust and steam went to his lungs. When I was a little child I can remember him lying in bed all day long and I must have been two or three years old when he died.

A year after the second camp and after my second trip to India, a friend came to stay with me in Zurich from Budapest. We met and, as I knew she loved Chinese food, I invited her to a Chinese meal although I hadn't been to the restaurant for what must have been at least ten years. We could only get a seat at a table for four. We weren't too bothered and we hoped that it wouldn't bother the other people too much who were sharing the table. We started to chat in Hungarian when someone came over and politely asked, in Hungarian, if they could join us at our table? I looked up and saw Mr Yesudian and his wife standing in front of me. We hadn't even noticed the other couple leave the table. They sat down and I introduced my friend to the hero of my youth whom I had only known from books at the time that I had married in Switzerland. When I was in St Gallen, I had been able to attend his classes but only on a couple of occasions. We were poor students back then and I couldn't really afford the luxury.

The next time I attended was when we moved to Zurich but still I didn't manage to go so often because of everything that was going on with my family and my work. This meant that I usually practised my yoga exercises on my own and studied at the same time.

I was also keen to hear Elisabeth Haich's talks on the Upanishads and the Bhagawad Gita, and I felt these deep in my soul. Then the VOICE came in 1989 and I grew much closer to Yesudian and Elisabeth Haich and that is when she asked me to call her Auntie Erzsi.

They both gave me their blessing when I first started to teach in Hungary. Unfortunately, I was never able to attend his yoga summer school in Ponte Tresa. I have only been there twice since then. Once was when I was on a fast a year before the first camp in Hungary. That is where I met Michael. I was intrigued by this boy even before his arrival. The new leaders of the Yesudian camp in Ponte Tresa didn't have a good word to say about him. When he arrived I understood what they had said and especially how one of the leaders felt. Michael, who must have been around 23, was as pure as an angel and as proud as a knight. His yoga positions were just as good as the yoga teacher who had bought the school. His friend, who always had a cigarette in his hand and had a very dark aura, really cursed this rare example of purity. The poor guy could see the incredible difference between the two of them and I was instantly on Michael's side. Now I knew that he was also a member of my old family.

I asked Michael whether he would like to come and help me in the preparations for my first camp in Hungary. He happily said "yes", and added that his parents had filled him with the love of Yesudian and Haich. He had been taking part in the camp in Ponte Tresa since he had been two years of age. His parents had stopped coming (they had long since divorced) but he had continued to attend with his grandmother or on his own. But he hadn't attended the camp for several years ever since Elisabeth Haich had died and Mr Yesudian had stopped teaching. He brought his father along to my camp in Hungary along with his best friend from France.

Now I told Mr Yesudian who had attended the camp in Hungary. And he was happy to hear that old friends of his had attended a camp that was run very much in his spirit.

The second time I had gone to Ponte Tresa, it had been with this very same girlfriend from Budapest, although the school was no longer running as the yoga teacher who had bought the place had been very ill and eventually died. This was the first time that my friend had been to see me in Zurich and she was struggling with a great deal of problems.

I offered to work with her and to take her to Ponte Tresa, where I could still feel Yesudian's spiritual strength. I was teaching in Budapest by that time and there was about a month to go before the first Hungarian camp. I wanted to collect strength myself before this great challenge.

My friend had a vision in the night to warn her that her life was in danger. We slept in a hotel because it was very late by the time we left the "holy" site of the Yesudian-Haich camp. We were just settling the bill the next morning when I saw that the place was called the "Hotel Svizzera" and it was in "via Ungharese". So it was "Hungarian Street" in the "Hotel Switzerland". I could not have imagined being given greater help from my old spiritual friend and role model, Selva Raja Yesudian. And so I left to open my first camp and after I had finished I came back here to Switzerland.

Yesudian also left another great gift behind for me. His manager called me after the chance meeting in the restaurant. He asked me to go and see him as he wanted to relay a request that Yesudian had of me. He had asked his agent to hand over the Hungarian representation of his whole spiritual legacy to me (his books). He would have liked to have completed his final book and to have it published in Hungary. His sudden death put an end to all of this.

His agent later refused to recognize me as his representative despite the fact that it was he, himself, who had handed the papers to me based on Yesudian's personal request.

Maybe my friends above, my leaders and those members of my family who have returned home already know why it was only possible to do this much for the "Liberation Square Centre of Light" in Hungary.

33

Swansong

It has been a joy to see my father or simply to hear his voice over the telephone in recent years. He was in a good mood and he loved living.

The only thing that gave him a problem was his fluctuating blood pressure. It was very dangerous as a sudden drop would result in him collapsing in a faint. This gave me a problem because he lived alone in the house and he might fall and bang his head or break a bone again and there was no one to come to his aid.

We were able to solve this problem with time. There was a nurse at the hospital who was keen to supplement her wage and so now she stopped by my father's house every day in her way to work as well as agreeing to clean and wash for him once a week.

My father used to meet his best friend at lunchtimes along with his friend's wife. They had reservations at a local restaurant where they often had lunch together. As fate would have it, his friend died suddenly and his wife was left a widow and completely alone. So now the two of them carried on lunching together and then they had a good idea.

The widow had been terribly affected by the death of her husband and so she happily said yes when my father suggested that they should spend their afternoons together.

The lunchtime programme soon changed. The lady stopped by at the restaurant and brought home the meal that they had paid for and they enjoyed a pleasant lunch together in my father's house.

Then my father would take a nap after his lunch and awake to find that everything had been tidied away in the kitchen and there was some treat prepared for him to enjoy with his coffee.

I was really pleased to hear of these new developments in my father's life. The loss of his friend had caused another break in his life but now he had the man's wife as support and something to live for. And now he wasn't alone for one single day.

I happily prepared to go and visit him in Sopron in August 2000. I went to Budapest for a few days and planned on spending a couple of days with him on my way back. He was looking forward to it as much as me.

The VOICE spoke a little while before my departure: **"Prepare yourself for the fact that your father is about to die!"**

"It's impossible, he is enjoying himself so much and he's happy again at last!"

"He will suddenly become ill and have to go into hospital. He may come out again for a short while but he will not live to see his next birthday."

My father was 79 years old and I was pleased that I was going to able to surprise him with something on his 80th birthday.

I had organized everything for him on his 75th birthday. I invited his closest friends and their wives to the restaurant that he liked so much.

I arrived on his birthday and said that we should go somewhere to celebrate. He was delighted by the fact that I had come all the way from Zurich just for his birthday. But the joy on his face was indescribable when we opened the door to the restaurant and he was greeted with a chorus of "happy birthday" sung by his friends and a toast in his honour. And now he was going to leave? I found it hard even to imagine.

When I arrived at Sopron on the train, I was greeted by my father's dear "lady companion", which is how he always referred to her.

"Your father had to be taken into hospital yesterday but he hopes that they will let him out in a day," she said.

"But what happened so suddenly? There was nothing at all wrong with him only the day before yesterday!"

"We don't know and the doctor doesn't seem to understand it either. His legs became so swollen that we called the doctor and he had him taken into hospital. He had hoped to be back at home by the time that you arrived."

I listened sadly. "So it had started after all!" I thought.

He welcomed us with laughter and a little embarrassment when we arrived at the hospital because he had wanted to greet me with hugs at home and in good health. He tried to comfort me when he saw my saddened expression.

"Go to Budapest for a couple of days and I'll be dancing a jig when you get back!" he joked. But he couldn't cheer me up.

The doctors assured us that he should be back on his feet in a just a few days as the medicine they had nowadays really was terrific!

My father really believed in doctors and medicine. I left him to his faith and hoped that it might even help him a little.

I dealt with a load of things in Budapest and he really was back at home when I went back down to Sopron but there was virtually no change with his swollen legs. The doctor raised his dose. I didn't say a thing but I would have much rather lowered it…

He did get up for meals but he spent the whole day in bed and was happiest to sleep.

I talked a lot with his friend's widow but I didn't tell her all that I knew. She had hopes just like me.

"It's just that he got sick so suddenly and the swelling in his legs can be handled with medicine. He has been taking a water tablet once a week," she went on, "but the doctor has now prescribed several a day just to start everything moving."

I was worried about his heart but it really wasn't my area and I didn't want to interfere. I looked at my father as he nodded and I knew that he would never be the same again. I felt sorry for the poor woman who was going to have such an enormous amount of work to do! She volunteered to sleep over at my father's house for as long as he was ill just in case he needed something. I was really very grateful for her help.

When I got back to Zurich, I soon fell back into my weekly routine of work and teaching. I couldn't stay with him and it seemed too late to help him.

It was my birthday on 22 August and I meditated for a long time and I thought of my father with a lot of love that night. I gave him back the seed that had helped me to be alive on the Earth today. I felt that he would be able use the creational energy that was in such a seed and that he would finish things.

I prepared myself to let him go and to say goodbye. I needed strength and help that I would be able to let everything go that was related to him in a way that I wanted to.

I travelled to the Island of Patmos in the autumn break at the beginning of October to ask for strength and help in the cave of the Prophet John.

In the meantime, my father had gone back into hospital. He had grown a lot weaker and even the lady who had been looking after him now needed to be looked after. She had been with my father 24 hours a day without a single day off. In my thoughts, I prepared my father for what was to happen and I called several times a day to ask after him.

The doctors also agreed that there was nothing left to do. Ten days later the phone rang and they asked me to go because they didn't know how the final period would last. They said that it could be a couple of weeks but it could just as easily be a couple of days.

I was back in Sopron in a couple of days. My father had altered beyond all recognition in just a couple of months. He was just skin and bones but his eyes shone when he saw me walk into the room.

They were playing a Hungarian folk song on the radio and my father started to sing virtually drunk with happiness and he clapped his hands together. We were all touched by the moment.

"We haven't seen him like this in all the time that he's been here in the hospital." They were amazed. "We knew that he had really been looking forward to seeing his daughter and that when you arrived he was sure to find strength and go home."

I smiled and my father nodded a "sure enough".

The people on the ward told me how he got up every night to leave for home but his legs wouldn't hold him. This meant that these two freshly-operated men had to somehow get him back into his bed. "How sympathetic people can be if they are dealing with similar problems themselves," I thought.

My father didn't really want to eat anymore but he allowed me to spoon feed him a little soup to keep me happy. He was constantly trying to catch my eye to see whether or not I was satisfied.

How things had changed! He had become the child and now it was he who wanted to see if people were satisfied and mainly that they should love him.

I also spoke to the doctor. He told me that my father had been waiting for me to arrive and he was still very hopeful of making a recovery. They didn't tell him anything different and left him to hope.

I took freshly squeezed orange juice when I went back in to see him that night and he drank it through a straw, though he still couldn't eat. I asked the nurse not to force him to eat if he didn't want to.

He didn't want to eat a thing the next morning so they put him on a drip. I looked at his eyes. He had changed so much in just one day. His eyes were no longer those of a young child but those of a newborn. They were large, startled and curious: "What is happening to me? Where am I and where am I going? Will they accept me? Will they look after me and nurture me?"

He was on his way to another place and he was full of fear and worry. I suddenly saw my own eyes as a newborn in him and my whole life flashed before my eyes. I felt and I saw everything that had happened with the two of us: I saw everything from the moment that he and my mother had set off to have me aborted and felt the pain in my head and my little heart, in my soul during the seventh month. Then came all the sadness and disappointment that I suffered because of his behaviour. I felt my defencelessness and exposure, the hostility of his second wife and all the lies and falseness that I had been forced to go through then.

The images flashed in front of me and the emotions of the memory passed through my body in waves.

Suddenly, the film came to an end and everything disappeared with it. There were no longer any old pictures; no longer any old memories. There was an emptiness that was the sign of a new beginning.

It was as if my father had sensed what had been happening inside me and his eyes seemed startled and questioning. "This is the startled look of a newborn again or perhaps just before birth takes place," I pondered.

I whispered very softly in his ear: "Papa, everything has gone, somehow everything has disappeared! There is nothing left to forgive or let go. There's nothing here at all!"

His eyes softened: "Then I can leave in peace?" he asked.

I whispered everything into his ear that I knew about behaviour before and during death. I asked him to give himself over and to let everything go. That he should trust and have total faith and that I would be there to accompany him on his way. I told him I would be with him for a further three days as death set in and that I would give him strength. (How happy I was now that I had accompanied the dying before!)

He opened his eyes wide and looked at me with no more question in his expression. Wonder, amazement and total trust radiated from his eyes. There wasn't the faintest sign of fear. (Thank God, he had understood, believed and accepted everything that I had said.)

I asked him whether he had understood everything and whether he had any more questions. I asked him to close his eyes and I would care for his body and his aura.

I cleaned everything, replenished it and closed it. He lay with his eyes closed while I prayed for him and asked for help from his and my leaders and angels to see that everything happened as best it possibly could.

He kept his eyes closed after I left. His eyes were still closed the following morning and so I went to look for the head doctor. I told her that my father was now on his way to let go of the weight of life and I asked her to take him off the drip and not to give him any injections of medicine. I asked that they keep an eye on his heartbeat but not to move him. If his heart had finished its job, I asked them to leave him in peace for 72 hours.

Now the doctor asked me a question: "Why? Then he'll be dead."

Then I told her that someone who was "dead on the outside" still had a great deal of work to do. He has to shed his physical shroud and discover his delicate inner-body with which he was going to leave the Earth on his journey to the other dimension.

The woman listened attentively. Then she said that they would have liked to perform an autopsy on him to try and work out why he had been taken ill so suddenly.

I asked them not to do that either.

"We completely understand what you are saying," she replied. Then she thought for a moment before she spoke again: "It is going to be quite tough to find a place where he won't be disturbed for three days. If it isn't a problem, we could place him a refrigerated area. We could explain it away by saying that he was being stored before being taken away to be cremated."

I was happy that she was so helpful and I thanked her from the bottom of my heart for her kind cooperation.

"I should thank you!" she corrected. "I have learnt things from you that I had never even heard before. Something tells me that everything you have said is very true! My father is also very ill and I am very happy to have learnt what I have because I will be able to use it with him."

We were both very grateful to one another.

I organized everything in Sopron and my father's helper dealt with everything that was left to do. I drove back to Switzerland and tried to get all my work finished off there because I was soon to come back with my daughters for my father's—their grandfather's—funeral.

My father lay motionless with his eyes closed for a further two days just as he had closed his eyes after I had told him those secrets. The smile remained on his face to the end just as it had when I had last seen him.

The doctor managed to organize the three days peace and quiet that I had asked for. After 72 hours, they took my father's empty body away that had carried his spirit for nearly 80 years and cremated it.

He died on the 22 October. It was exactly two months after my birthday when I had given him back the gift of birth.

At the funeral, I stood with my daughters next to the family grave where my father's parents and his second wife were resting. I was very proud of my father just as he had been of me in the last few years of his life!

Papa, we won, despite everything and despite everyone!

The story that had such a sad beginning now ended like a fairy tale; with victory. I was soon able to sell the house that my father had transferred to my name while he had still been alive. It was only then, after having waited for so long, that, with the help of this money, I was able to take a two-month holiday and fulfil my final promise and write my book—our book—to finally be able to place it in your hands first in Hungarian. Since that is the language of the country where I was born into this life of mine.

Epilogue

My spiritual leader asked to be able to dictate this conclusion. He is also a Voice. But now I would like to speak about the various other voices. Where I wrote the word "Voice", spiritual beings were always talking and not the spirits of people who have died but rather the spirits of high master teachers. My earthly teacher, Franz Lichtenecker, also relays these spirits. When he does this, he switches off completely and when he is in a complete trance, these higher leaders talk, educate and teach us through him.

They started to teach me the very same things at first in dreams and this went on for years. I always knew in the morning that they had taught me and that I had learned something but I was unable to remember what it was. They slowly raised the curtain that veiled my consciousness despite my constant struggle to stop this happening. I wanted to be just like all the others who didn't want to see and didn't want to know. In fact, they don't know anything at all. I wanted to be just like them and I wanted them to love me, accept me and I wanted to be one of them. They didn't do this. They rejected, excluded and hated me.

My leader has just interrupted: *"This is exactly what I wanted to achieve with you: that you shouldn't care less whether they love you or hate you. You have to do your job whatever people feel about you.*

But just take a look back, even in just this life, and see how changeable people have been and especially their emotions. There were those who loved you, admired you and wanted to place you on a pedestal; on

a throne. Over time, they started to do the opposite and they even start-
ed to hate you. They wanted you to give everything over to them that
you have and especially your knowledge. They literally wanted to take
it all away! As this wasn't possible and they were able to do nothing
to help their own learning, they wanted you to disappear from their
sight and from around them. That is why they did everything in their
power to make this happen. Often the teacher is killed at times like
this and often along with his or her closest student. This process can
be seen with many students of religion in history.

Those who started off hating began to love and respect as time
passed. They did all that they could at the beginning to prove that you
are not right. They did a great deal of work and the opposite of what
they thought was proven to be true and they became your followers
and true believers. They are good workers at the price of their own
suffering. They worked for it and so they achieved it and they de-
served it."

My leader has fallen silent and so I can continue. I hear my leader's
voice from within like an inner teaching. It comes and then grows
quiet. It explains again and again until I finally understand.

The second, the great VOICE, is different. He is the leader of my
leaders. He is the greatest. He is the one who broke into my life in
1981, some 22 years ago. He is the one who fought for my life before I was even born and alarmed my mother. He does not teach, he
does not explain, he does not repeat. He announces. Whether I like
it or not, whether I can accept it or not—this doesn't affect him. He
knows everything and he moves everything. He is the one who announced the impossible thing about the Eastern Block back in 1989
that neither I nor Elisabeth Haich nor Yesudian was able to believe
let alone imagine.

Everything that he has told me has happened and all despite
the fact that sometimes I was unable to do as he asked, as I thought
that it was impossible at the time. This was out of my consideration
for my surroundings at the time: my husband, my children, my parents and my friends. I would much rather suffer than to see them

suffer. This is why my spiritual leaders forgave my resistance and they solved the problems instead of me.

One of my spiritual leaders is a very kind and considerate teacher of mine. He always teaches me with stories. He knows that if he uses animals as examples, I am much more likely to accept what it is that I have to change.

I was taking a walk just the other day and he asked that I write the following in my book (in our book). He asked me to stop teaching like an elephant teaching mice.

"What do you mean exactly?" I asked.

"The mice live happily in the mouse hole. They pop their heads out now and again and see the elephant and stare in awe at the elephant and think that they would like to be big and strong just like the elephant. They ask the elephant to teach them how it was that he became an elephant. They tell him that he can come into the mouse hole and tell all the mice because all of them really want to know. The elephant makes himself very small so that he can fulfil their wish, enter the mouse hole and teach the mice. He has just started to speak when his spiritual energy explodes the mouse nest. They run around in a rage and reprimand him: "You have ruined our mouse hole and now where are we going to hide when the cat comes along?" The elephant tells them that it was they who asked him to teach them how a mouse becomes an elephant. And an elephant isn't afraid of a cat! They all run away and don't listen to him as they are all busy looking for another mouse hole.

Do you see? You should wait for those who have already become elephants and they will allow themselves to be led."

I chuckled as I walked. How right he was! An example comes to mind now that my leader told me via my teacher, Lichtenecker, right back at the beginning of my "awakening". There a horse was the simile: *"They keep different horses in different stables. There are stables that have very expensive racehorses. Here perhaps I should use the term "magic steed" but I know that you would object. You are a racehorse in a stable like this. These horses are worth a fantastic amount of money. It is possible to win a lot of money with these horses but it took a massive amount of energy to bring this strength and ambition out of these horses that had once run wild and free. You are such a racehorse to us as you are to your other companions. It has also taken a lot of work for us to turn you into what you are now and so that you can gallop. You put an awful lot of energy into this as well. We let you go in the direction of the finishing post so that you can gallop off and win for us and for everyone. You run and gallop to show everything you know and make good all the hopes that are attached to you. You see a horse pulling a plough as you make your way along one day. You stop because you feel sorry for it. I could also use the example of a mule pulling a terribly heavy load and you would react in the same way. You go over to help it. People look at you and wonder what kind of horse you actually are. You are not like them at all! You stopped of your own volition and sympathy and you harness yourself up in front of the plough or the heavy cart. You can't move it either. They laugh at you and think that you are behaving like an ox. You stand ashamed and now you are quite exhausted. You always needed a lot of time to recharge your batteries and for us to set you going again. Don't do this anymore!"*

I have done this time after time because I felt pain at seeing the heavy load that others carry!

He also comforted me with a beautiful story when I went through the pain of the divorce from my husband. Two months after his girlfriend introduced herself in my dream, all four of us went away on a last family holiday to Sicily. We stayed in Taormina which had been a dream of mine from childhood.

The place was beautiful and just as it had been when I had first seen it in a painting at the National Gallery—*"The ruins of the old Greek temple at Taormina"* by Csontváry. But even this failed to cheer me up. I went out onto the terrace and sadly lay and sunbathed. I was on the verge of tears and my dear leader "showed a film" to comfort me.

In the film—just as in his teachings—there were animals and this time they were birds. There were two groups. One group flew high in the sky while the other scratched around on the ground looking for edible seeds. The eyes of two of the birds met: one from the upper and one from the lower group. You could see from this that each wanted to learn about the life of the other. One of the birds swooped down from the sky and joined its companion on the ground where the ground bird began to tell the sky bird all about where to find the best seeds. Then two more little birds appeared next to them and now they taught and raised these birds together. When they were happy pecking away with all the others, the "bird from above" suddenly spoke: "Now the time has come for me to teach you how to fly!"

"Yes, yes, in a while!" replied the ground bird. The bird that had swooped down tried again a little later and the ground bird pointed to all the new shiny seeds on the ground: "First, you have got to learn all about these completely new seeds because they are sure to be especially delicious," it said.

"I have been wanting to talk to you about these seeds for ages. It seems to me that they are scattered further and further apart and we have to travel greater distances to find them. And I don't like these new seeds at all. I have started to feel very heavy ever since we started to eat these seeds. I don't even feel like flying anymore and it doesn't seem so important to me now," the other one objected.

"No, you are getting it all wrong. You haven't realized that they aren't throwing these beautiful shiny seeds in front of all of us. We can consider ourselves to be very fortunate birds: we are the chosen ones," said the ground bird.

"I don't believe that. I can feel that they are doing me no good. I'm not going to eat anymore of them and I would like to ask you to do the same."

"Well, I think that they are delicious and I feel honoured to be a chosen bird. You can do just exactly what you want but don't keep bothering me with your fears," it concluded.

The bird from above became very sad. Could it be possible that its companion was no longer interested in flying? But it continued to practise its flying exercises from a little hill nearby. Its wings started to grow heavy and so it did exercises to be able to teach its companion. It was sad because it practised more often and for longer but now it practised alone.

One day, a flock of birds flew over the little hill. Our little bird felt homesick for the sky and was drawn by its emotions and flew with the help of its little wings. It took one last look down at its companion and all the others pecking away on the ground.

"It is so sad that there are birds that even want to forget that they have got wings and that they once were able to fly!"

Still when I thought back to my task in this incarnation, which is to lead the others home as a spiritual bird, my leader reminded me of my mistake: *"You fly at the front because you know the goal and you can remember where to fly back to. It's just like the birds that have a homing instinct. They choose the strongest one that knows the way home. You are flying happily home when it suddenly occurs to you to check whether everyone is able to follow you and fly with you. The thought will become unbearable in the end and you will fly back to the ones lagging behind to strengthen them and encourage them to keep going, but then what will happen to the ones who had been flying right behind you? They will have lost their leader. They will lose direction and either get lost or someone else will take over the lead who doesn't necessarily have the ability. Everything will have changed by the time that you fly back to the front. You will have wasted masses of energy and exhausted yourself in the process. If you are still able to take over the lead at the front, your group will now be slower which will lead to more and more of them becoming too tired and dropping out of the group.*

It isn't your responsibility and job to keep running to the back all the time like a sheepdog and bark at the flock to stop any of them from lagging behind or falling by the wayside. You have become a leader bird. This is your job! Those who fall away or lag behind are victims of their own fate!"

I hoped that I managed to understand this. Arjuna suddenly springs to mind. He was a heroic Indian prince who had trouble accepting that he had to fight against his false half-brothers and his blind father. They did all they could to rid him of everything and finally they accused him of raising an army in a foreign land—where he had been living in exile for many years, expelled from his own part of the country—in order to attack his father and brothers and remove their land, wealth and throne. His treacherous brothers had ransacked his land and they feared that everything would be found out and so that is why they wanted to annihilate their brother in battle. In the meantime, Arjuna's people had only managed to survive the difficult years in the belief that one day their king would return and they would once again be able to live in peace and truth.

Arjuna couldn't decide. That is when Krishna arrived and offered his help to the prince. He asked him what it was that he would like: whether he would lead his army to battle or whether Krishna himself should drive Arjuna's battle chariot. Arjuna chose the latter as he, himself, was incapable of fighting against his own blood. Krishna warned him: "You were born a prince! This is not only your fate but also your task! You need to lead your people with truth and peace. Your bothers are evil and your father is blind but your people have faith in you and are waiting for you to liberate them from the rule of evil. The result of the battle has already been decided and you cannot change that, whatever you may do. But it is your karma and only YOUR karma to take responsibility and to lead your people to victory.

Finally, I would like to close my book with a message from the VOICE which he shared with me before an appearance on television in Budapest. A young woman asked for my help to solve a certain problem. She continually repeated that she had inherited her obesity and thinning hair from her father, her fear from her mother and all her bad qualities had been inherited from someone or other. I attempted to give her the example that I often gave as advice to those taking part in my course. We do not inherit illness and bad qualities from our family, only a tendency. However, if we allow them to develop then they may well turn into full-blown illness. Then I was interrupted by the VOICE who said the following. I will give him the last word in my book:

If you believe that your birth father is your true father,
    then you will be just like him.
If you believe that your birth mother is your true mother,
    then you will be just like her.
If you believe the people that you live among are truly your people,
    then you will have to live their fate.
But if you know who your true father is,
    then you too will reach his greatness.
If you know who your true mother is,
    then you too will radiate her beauty.
And if you know which is your true people
    then, with their help, you will save yourself,
    your birth father and mother and the people that
    have adopted you.

Thanks and Thanksgiving

My book "Én nem csak feleség és anya voltam ..." was self-published in Hungary with 2,500 copies. Its success was like a small bomb and it soon sold out. My friends quickly advised a translation in English – one of the world languages. When the translation was finally finished, I was involved in other vital projects.

This book awoke like "Sleeping Beauty" on 22 August 2017! Enjoying the sunshine on my birthday, I took a long walk and found a small sign by a house entrance. A friendly lady opened the door, asking me politely what I wanted. It was the publisher Anne Rüffer. I told her the story of my book, while she listened and then said: "Send me the manuscript and I will review it." She soon contacted me and said that she would support my book publication. She also had a recommendation for a translator from England. I thought I was dreaming!

Suzanne Kirkbright refreshed my 13-year-old, outdated translation. Suzanne certainly achieved a "masterpiece", and I express my warmest gratitude! At the publishing house Saskia Noll instantly won my trust. Saskia carefully prepared the layout, and she was there for all my questions and to give advice. Special thanks to Saskia for your wonderful achievement!

The book will soon go to print; I would like to give a blessing beforehand. Just like mothers once blessed their sons when they left home to explore the wide world and seek their fortune.

"May God make a level path for my book."

With thanks and in gratitude, *Dorothea*